Library of
Davidson College

Approaches to Greater Flexibility of Exchange Rates
The Bürgenstock Papers

APPROACHES TO GREATER FLEXIBILITY OF EXCHANGE RATES

The Bürgenstock Papers

ARRANGED BY

C. Fred Bergsten

George N. Halm

Fritz Machlup

Robert V. Roosa

EDITED BY

George N. Halm

PRINCETON UNIVERSITY PRESS
PRINCETON, NEW JERSEY
1970

Copyright © 1970 by Princeton University Press
All rights reserved
L.C. Card: 78-111633
I.S.B.N.: 0-691-04196-2

This book has been composed in Linotype Times Roman
Printed in the United States of America
by Vail-Ballou Press, Inc., Binghamton, New York

Preface

IN THE summer of 1968 we recognized the urgent need that new steps be undertaken to enhance the possibility of a study of greater flexibility of foreign-exchange rates by the world's monetary authorities. We felt that two new approaches were in order: an intensive study of the various proposals for limited flexibility; and a confrontation between academic economists and practitioners from the banking and business world.

Under a grant extended by the Ford Foundation to Princeton University, two international conferences were planned to bring together practitioners and economists in about equal numbers to discuss the possible advantages or disadvantages of an international adjustment process aided by greater, but still limited flexibility of foreign-exchange rates. There was also an about even division between Americans and residents of other countries.

The first conference met from January 29 to 31, 1969 at Oyster Bay, New York, with 38 persons attending from eight countries. Its primary objective was to identify the major technical and policy issues that are raised by various proposals for greater exchange-rate flexibility. A paper, "Toward Limited Exchange-Rate Flexibility" by George N. Halm, was distributed to the prospective participants of the Oyster Bay Conference. It is reprinted as the first essay in the present volume.

The discussions at Oyster Bay led to the formulation of two alternative lists: "Possible Topics for Further Discussion," by Robert V. Roosa and Milton Friedman, respectively; and a "Proposed Outline for Conference Papers," by C. Fred Bergsten. These lists are reproduced as the second paper.

Most of the participants of the Oyster Bay Conference promised to write papers that were to serve as basis for deliberations at the second conference to be held from June 22 to 28, 1969 at Bürgenstock near Lucerne, Switzerland. The 38 participants, 32 of whom had also been at Oyster Bay, came from ten different countries.

The papers collected in this volume are, in part, these original contributions. Some were altered after the Bürgenstock discussions and several papers were written only after the second conference.

The Bürgenstock Papers were unsolicited in the sense that the authors were free to choose their subjects, a fact that accounts for the somewhat uneven coverage of the listed topics as well as for some overlapping. Nevertheless, the papers fall rather naturally into six major sections: (I) introductory statements; (II and III) essays for and against greater flexibility; (IV) practical proposals and suggestions for the implementation of greater flexibility; (V) papers on the effects of greater flexibility on

PREFACE

the forward-exchange market; and (VI) papers on the impact of limited flexibility on different countries and groups of countries. A final section (VII) contains papers that, although they would not fit readily into one of the first six sections, are decidedly relevant to the issues being discussed.

The participants of the Oyster Bay and Bürgenstock Conferences wanted to come to a better understanding of the problems that the introduction of greater, but still limited, flexibility of foreign-exchange rates would solve or create; they did not aim at a consensus. Everyone understood from the beginning that no unanimously endorsed reform proposal could emerge from a discussion of exchange-rate flexibility by such heterogeneous groups as those brought together at Oyster Bay and Bürgenstock. Most practitioners were known to be skeptical of certain proposals for greater flexibility that were supported by a large and growing number of academic economists. Furthermore, the recommendations for a wider "band," a "crawling peg," or a combination of the two, concern intricate technical matters and have, as compromise proposals, less appeal than the more straightforward opposites of permanently fixed parities or freely floating exchange rates.

A convergence of views had not been expected under these circumstances. Indeed, it was not anticipated that the participants in the two conferences would agree, even in principle, on the desirability of some form of greater exchange-rate flexibility, however modestly conceived or implemented. It came as a surprise, therefore, when the answers to a questionnaire showed that a large majority of the participants of the Bürgenstock Conference favored a move toward greater flexibility of exchange rates.

This informal poll was taken near the end of the conference. The participants were asked what changes, if any, they would like to see in the present exchange-rate system. Even though the poll was taken before the devaluation of the French franc and the revaluation of the German mark, the questions allowed the respondents to assume that there had been a prior realignment of existing parities. It was further agreed that advocates of fully flexible rates could vote in favor of limited flexibility if they felt that the former was politically unrealistic at the present time.

Of the 34 participants who replied, only three favored making no change in the present system. Six favored a modest widening of the band by amounts ranging up to ±2½ per cent; these were all practitioners—officials of banking or business firms. Eighteen participants voted for versions of a band-and-crawl system with a width of the band up to ±3 per cent, and a maximum rate of annual parity changes up to 2½ per cent. Within this group, which was evenly split between practitioners and academics, there were different views as to whether the gliding-parity arrangements should be automatic, presumptive, or discretionary.

PREFACE

The seven remaining respondents—all academics—favored even more flexibility in one form or another, and generally expressed a personal preference for freely floating rates (as did one or two of the previous group).

A press release of June 30, 1969, announcing the publication of *The Bürgenstock Papers,* expressed the opinion of the majority as follows:

> A group of 38 experts in international finance has just completed a week of meetings at Bürgenstock, near Lucerne in Switzerland. Twenty officials of banking and business firms and eighteen academic economists from ten different countries have been reviewing proposals for increasing flexibility in exchange rates. Various methods by which countries could adjust the parities of their currencies in terms of the U.S. dollar were considered, as well as possibilities for widening the range of permissible fluctuation in the market rates of these currencies.
>
> The group did not include any officials of governments or central banks. Since all members participated as individuals, a list indicating only names and nationalities is attached. No detailed statement of recommendations is planned. The group anticipates that various papers by its members will be published later in the year, following revisions to be made by the authors in the light of the past week's discussion. In advance of the publication of these papers, the group has authorized release of the following summary of conclusions:
>
> After reviewing the recent experience of the international monetary system, the participants recognized that structural changes in international supply and demand and in capital movements, as well as divergent rates of economic growth, differences in economic objectives and policies, and varying trends in prices and costs among nations would from time to time call for changes in the exchange rates of particular currencies. There was a consensus that such changes when appropriate should take place sooner, and, thus, generally be smaller and more frequent, than during the past two decades. Following their analysis of all of the current proposals for change, some participants pointed toward a need for greater readiness by countries to adjust the established parities of their currencies within the existing framework. A majority favored both widening the range (or "band") within which exchange rates may respond to market forces, and permitting a more continuous and gradual adjustment of parities. They stressed that such innovations should be so framed as to facilitate continued international economic cooperation, while leaving individual countries or groups of countries free to adapt their own approach to their own individual circumstances.
>
> Throughout, the participants had in mind the need for improve-

PREFACE

ments that would facilitate balance-of-payments adjustment in ways consistent with the domestic objectives of governments and the elimination of many restrictions on trade, current payments, and capital movements.

The Bürgenstock Conference has shown that it is not true that all practitioners favor the present system of fixed but adjustable parities. On the contrary, the first attempt toward an exchange of views between practitioners and academic economists led to the discovery of much common ground in their criticism of the present arrangements and their desire to improve the adjustment mechanism.

However, the participants were not unanimous in these conclusions and those who thought that greater flexibility of exchange rates was desirable were still far from agreeing in detail on the nature and the degree of such flexibility.

The Bürgenstock Papers represent the first concerted effort to find the best approach to greater albeit limited flexibility of foreign-exchange rates. The papers that reject greater flexibility serve as counterweight to the much larger number of essays that propose some form of flexibility for a variety of reasons.

GEORGE N. HALM

Contents

Preface, GEORGE N. HALM   V

PART I. INTRODUCTION   1

1. Toward Limited Flexibility of Exchange Rates, GEORGE N. HALM   3
2. Two Lists of Topics for Further Study and a Proposed Outline for Conference Papers, ROBERT V. ROOSA, MILTON FRIEDMAN, C. FRED BERGSTEN   27
3. On Terms, Concepts, Theories, and Strategies in the Discussion of Greater Flexibility of Exchange Rates, FRITZ MACHLUP   31
4. Currency Parities in the Second Decade of Convertibility, ROBERT V. ROOSA   49
5. Comments on Mr. Roosa's Paper, GEORGE N. HALM   57
6. The United States and Greater Flexibility of Exchange Rates, C. FRED BERGSTEN   61
7. Decision-Making on Exchange Rates, STEPHEN N. MARRIS   77

PART II. THE CASE FOR GREATER FLEXIBILITY OF EXCHANGE RATES   89

8. The Case for Flexible Exchange Rates, 1969, HARRY G. JOHNSON   91
9. Comments on Mr. Johnson's Paper, GEORGE N. HALM   112
10. The International Monetary System: Some Recent Developments and Discussions, GOTTFRIED HABERLER   115
11. Fixed Exchange Rates and the Market Mechanism, GEORGE N. HALM   125
12. The Adjustment Process, Its Asymmetry, and Possible Consequences, MARIUS W. HOLTROP   129
13. Entrepreneurial Risk under Flexible Exchange Rates, HERBERT GIERSCH   145
14. The Wider Band and Foreign Direct Investment, DAVID L. GROVE   151
15. The Business View of Proposals for International Monetary Reform, JOHN H. WATTS   167

PART III. THE CASE AGAINST FLEXIBLE EXCHANGE RATES   177

16. The Outlook for the Present World Monetary System, PETER M. OPPENHEIMER   179
17. Comments on Mr. Oppenheimer's Paper: A More Optimistic View, THOMAS D. WILLETT   186

CONTENTS

18. Could the Crises of the Last Few Years Have Been Avoided by Flexible Exchange Rates?, MAX IKLÉ   187
19. Notes for the Bürgenstock Conference, ANTONIO MOSCONI   199
20. Why I Am Not in Favor of Greater Flexibility of Exchange Rates, GIULIANO PELLI   203
21. Greater Flexibility of Exchange Rates: Effects on Commodities, Capital, and Money Markets, EMIL KUSTER   209
22. Selected Case Studies Relating to Foreign-Exchange Problems in International Trade and Money Markets, EMIL KUSTER   211
23. Comments on Mr. Kuster's Papers, RICHARD N. COOPER   216

PART IV. PRACTICAL PROPOSALS AND SUGGESTIONS FOR IMPLEMENTATION   219

24. The International Monetary Game: Objectives and Rules, LAWRENCE B. KRAUSE   223
25. When and How Should Parities be Changed?, ROBERT V. ROOSA   233
26. A "Realistic" Note on Threefold Limited Flexibility of Exchange Rates, WILLIAM FELLNER   237
27. Asymmetrical Widening of the Bands Around Parity, GEORGE H. CHITTENDEN   245
28. Sliding Parities: A Proposal for Presumptive Rules, RICHARD N. COOPER   251
29. The Fixed-Reserve Standard: A Proposal to "Reverse" Bretton Woods, DONALD B. MARSH   261
30. Rules for a Sliding Parity: A Proposal, THOMAS D. WILLETT   271
31. Some Implications of Flexible Exchange Rates, Including Effects on Forward Markets and Transitional Problems, C. M. VLIERDEN   275
32. A Technical Note on the Width of the Band Required to Accommodate Parity Changes of Particular Size, HARRY G. JOHNSON   280
33. Short-term Capital Movements and the Interest-Rate Constraint Under Systems of Limited Flexibility of Exchange Rates, THOMAS D. WILLETT   283

PART V. EXCHANGE-RATE FLEXIBILITY AND THE FORWARD MARKET   295

34. The Forward-Exchange Market: Misunderstandings Between Practitioners and Economists, FRITZ MACHLUP   297
35. Forward-Currency "Costs": A Zero Sum Game?, JOHN H. WATTS   307
36. Comments on Mr. Watts's Paper, FRITZ MACHLUP   309

37. Exchange Risks and Forward Coverage in Different Monetary Systems, EGON SOHMEN   311
38. The Effect on the Forward-Exchange Market of More Flexible Rates, W. F. J. BATT   317
39. Comments on Mr. Batt's Paper, FRITZ MACHLUP   320
40. Flexible Exchange Rates and Forward Markets, EDWIN A. REICHERS AND HAROLD VAN B. CLEVELAND   323

PART VI. POTENTIAL IMPACT OF EXCHANGE-RATE FLEXIBILITY ON DIFFERENT COUNTRIES OR GROUPS OF COUNTRIES   332

41. Canada's Experience with a Floating Exchange Rate, 1950–1962, DONALD B. MARSH   337
42. A Floating German Mark: An Essay in Speculative Economics, HERBERT GIERSCH AND WOLFGANG KASPER   345
43. Japan's Twenty-Year Experience with a Fixed Rate for the Yen, TADASHI IINO   357
44. The Problem of Floating Exchange Rates from the Swiss Viewpoint, MAX IKLÉ   365
45. Balance-of-Payments and Exchange-Rate Problems in Sweden, Denmark, and Finland, ERIK LUNDBERG AND ÅKE LUNDGREN   371
46. European Integration and Greater Flexibility of Exchange Rates, WOLFGANG KASPER   385
47. Comments on Mr. Kasper's Paper: Requiem for European Integration, ANTONIO MOSCONI   388
48. Comments on the Papers by Messrs. Mosconi and Kasper: Red Herrings, Carts, and Horses, STEPHEN N. MARRIS   392
49. The Agricultural Regulations of the European Economic Community as an Obstacle to the Introduction of Greater Flexibility of Exchange Rates, FRIEDRICH A. LUTZ   401
50. The Concept of Optimum Currency Areas and the Choice Between Fixed and Flexible Exchange Rates, THOMAS D. WILLETT AND EDWARD TOWER   407

PART VII. MISCELLANY   416

51. Import Border Taxes and Export-Tax Refunds Versus Exchange-Rate Changes, GOTTFRIED HABERLER   417
52. Government and the Corporation: A Fallacious Analogy, HARRY G. JOHNSON   425

Contributors   427

Index   429

Approaches to Greater Flexibility of Exchange Rates
The Bürgenstock Papers

Part I. Introduction

THE SERIES of introductory papers begins with George N. Halm's essay "Toward Limited Flexibility of Exchange Rates," written for the Oyster Bay Conference. It tries to establish the urgent need for a thorough examination of the possible advantages or disadvantages of more-flexible exchange rates. The paper is followed by "Two Lists of Topics for Further Study and a Proposed Outline for Conference Papers," formulated by Robert V. Roosa, Milton Friedman, and C. Fred Bergsten, that emerged from the discussions at Oyster Bay.

Fritz Machlup's exercise "On Terms, Concepts, Theories, and Strategies in the Discussion of Greater Flexibility of Exchange Rates" undertakes in its semantic part "to do the most necessary cleaning-up job preparatory for a discussion in which the participants will not want to waste time by misunderstanding one another as they use words in ambiguous ways."

Robert V. Roosa's paper "Currency Parities in the Second Decade of Convertibility" attempts to prove that limited flexibility of exchange rates is not merely a second-best compromise, but actually the best way of systematizing changes of exchange rates once they have become unavoidable.

C. Fred Bergsten's essay "The United States and Greater Flexibility of Exchange Rates" discusses the effects of more limited flexibility on the United States as key-currency country, and points out that the United States would gain from the elimination of the present devaluation-revaluation asymmetry.

Stephen Marris' paper "Decision-Making on Exchange Rates" is based on his Princeton Essay "The Bürgenstock Communiqué: A Critical Examination of the Case for Limited Exchange-Rate Flexibility." Marris argues that under a system of limited flexibility "it should become normal for a country's exchange-rate policy to be examined regularly in the same way as its fiscal, monetary, and other policies are already scrutinized in such international organizations as the IMF, the OECD, the BIS and the institutions of the EEC." Against the background of the present adjustable-peg system with its serious obstacles to rational decision-making, Marris favors a system of limited flexibility because of the opportunities it provides for better decision-making on the national and international level.

· 1 ·

Toward Limited Flexibility of Exchange Rates

GEORGE N. HALM

Introduction

IN ITS 1964 report on the balance of payments,[1] the Joint Economic Committee of the United States Congress recommended that "the United States, in consultation with other countries, should give consideration to broadening the limits of permissible exchange rate variations," and in its March 1965 *Report* it urged once more a study of this idea: "Broadening the limits of exchange rate variations could discourage short-term capital outflows through free market forces, on which we should continue to place our main reliance; permit greater freedom for monetary policy to promote domestic objectives; discourage speculation against currencies by increasing the risk; and to some extent promote equilibrating adjustment in the trade balance. . . ."[2]

Noting again, in August 1965, that it was unaware that any exploration of the advantages and disadvantages of widening the limits of exchange-rate variation had occurred since it had first recommended such study, the Joint Economic Committee expressed the opinion that "to ignore promising proposals for improvement would appear to us a luxury which the free world can ill afford. We do not insist that broader limits for exchange rate variations be adopted, for we have not fully explored their implications nor weighed any possible disadvantages against the benefits we recognize. But we do insist that the expertise of the administration be brought to bear on the idea and that it receive the serious consideration which it merits."[3]

There is no published evidence to the effect that the administration has heeded the urgent appeal of the Joint Economic Committee, which was equally disregarded by other governments, the International Monetary Fund, and the Group of Ten.

Today, three years later, the situation is still unchanged. In September 1968, the Joint Economic Committee repeated its recommendation of a wider band "in view of the persistent international deficits on the part of

---

Previously published as Princeton Essay in International Finance No. 73, March 1969.

[1] Joint Economic Committee, *Report on the United States Balance of Payments* (Washington: U.S. Government Printing Office, 1964), p. 18.

[2] Joint Economic Committee, *Joint Economic Report*, March 17, 1965 (Washington: U.S. Government Printing Office, 1965), p. 15.

[3] Joint Economic Committee, *Guidelines for Improving the International Monetary System* (Washington: U.S. Government Printing Office, 1965), p. 20.

the United States, the widespread imposition of autarchic restrictions on trade and capital flows in response to reserve losses, and an incipient rise in protectionist sentiment both in this country and the rest of the world." [4] The International Monetary Fund and the Group of Ten, however, continue to insist, at least publicly, that the present system of fixed, though not unalterably fixed, parities has worked well. Nevertheless, it is obvious that the present arrangements have not been working smoothly. They have led to repeated crises of confidence, to political tensions between Europe and the United States, and even to the introduction of quantitative controls that contradict our professed desire for increased freedom in international economic transactions. These difficulties have not been exclusively caused by exogenous forces; they are to a large extent the result of major defects inherent in a system that tries to join together incompatible elements.

One such defect concerns the use of dollar balances as the main source of additional international liquidity reserves. A constant growth of foreign-held dollar balances implies a continuous external deficit of the United States and, considering the gold convertibility of official foreign dollar balances, a deterioration of the United States' net reserve position. The present handling of the liquidity problem, therefore, decreases confidence in the system. The forthcoming creation of Special Drawing Rights may eventually end this dilemma. But the SDR scheme is to come into operation only after a drastic reduction in the deficit of the United States—a dangerous policy that, if adopted, would make the situation worse before it became better. Reforms of the international monetary system must pay careful attention to the problems of transition from old to new arrangements.

Another basic weakness of the present international monetary system comes from the fact that the system is based on fixed, though not unalterably fixed, exchange rates, together with free convertibility of the major currencies into one another—and of dollars into gold—at fixed parities. In spite of all assurances to the contrary, this so-called adjustable-peg system has shown itself to be a poor compromise between fixed and flexible exchange rates. The reason is obvious. A combination of fixed exchange rates, currency convertibility, and imperfect harmonization of the national economic policies of the member countries cannot work well. As soon as national economic policies diverge—as when, for example, different rates of inflation prevail—fixed exchange rates become disaligned rates, even if they had originally been correct or "equilibrium" rates. Disaligned rates give wrong signals to international trade, international capital flows, and domestic production in the various countries. External and internal tensions will then lead to growing insistence

[4] Joint Economic Committee, *Next Steps in International Monetary Reform* (Washington: U.S. Government Printing Office, 1968), p. 6.

that these "fundamental disequilibria" be corrected through devaluations of deficit and upvaluations of surplus currencies; and these discrete peg adjustments, once they have become unavoidable, will cause severe shocks in the market economies in which wrong price signals have been permitted to lead to misallocations.

In failing to solve the adjustment problem, the adjustable-peg system intensifies the weaknesses of the reserve-currency system. A deficit country with an overvalued currency can maintain convertibility only so long as it possesses a sufficient supply of foreign exchange; and a financial crisis caused by peg adjustments leads to an additional emergency demand for liquidity reserves. This explains the present overemphasis on the liquidity problem. The dilemma becomes critical when doubts in the maintenance of the dollar-gold parity lead to attempts to eliminate the external deficit of the United States before a new system has been firmly established. The new system should not only provide for international liquidity reserves independent of a continued deficit of the United States, it should reduce the demand for liquidity reserves through a better adjustment mechanism.

We ought to find out whether greater exchange-rate flexibility can provide the presently lacking adjustment mechanism and, if so, how greater exchange-rate flexibility can be built into the international monetary system.

The Case for Fixed Exchange Rates

Considering the obvious shortcomings of today's international monetary system, it is, at first, surprising that fixed exchange rates meet with the almost unanimous approval of bankers, businessmen, and government officials. If it concerned other prices of strategic importance (such as wages or interest rates), these same persons would oppose a policy of administrative price fixing as inconsistent with the basic principles of a market economy. They know that price fixing tends to lead to quantitative restrictions and eventually to bureaucratic administration of the economy from the center. Why, then, should exchange rates be an exception from this rule?

The main argument is that fixed exchange rates provide a firm and reliable basis for international trade and international financial transactions. If, however, fixed exchange rates can only be maintained by influencing demand and supply conditions on the foreign-exchange market through substantial changes in domestic economic policies or even through quantitative restrictions, the cost of a fixed-rate system can exceed its benefits.

As far as quantitative restrictions are concerned, the case for fixed exchange rates is difficult to uphold. In introducing exchange controls, we abandon the principles of the market economy. If we want currency convertibility and multilateral trade, we cannot argue for fixed exchange rates once they are sustainable only via quantitative restrictions.

Whether and to what extent monetary and fiscal policies ought to be employed to maintain currency convertibility at fixed exchange rates is an open question. The answer will depend on such circumstances as the relative importance of foreign to domestic transactions, the existing price elasticities, and the relative emphasis on domestic or external balance. Where downward price and wage inflexibilities prevail, the maintenance of fixed exchange rates may imply undesirable results in terms of employment and growth. The cost of maintaining convertibility at fixed exchange rates may then exceed the benefits, and it can no longer be taken for granted that fixed rates are better than flexible rates. The fact that the U.S. Government found it advisable to introduce quantitative restrictions in lieu of monetary measures shows that the costs of contractionist policies were considered too high.

The following remarks on arguments for fixed exchange rates are incomplete; they merely try to show that the prevalent wholesale rejection of arguments for exchange-rate flexibility is not justified, particularly when we keep in mind that the present system of international payments permits discrete peg adjustments in the case of fundamental disequilibrium.

The strong attachment of central bankers to fixed exchange rates is easy to understand. Only when the monetary authorities are duty-bound to convert the national currency freely into other currencies at fixed parities, will these authorities be induced to harmonize, as best they can, their national monetary policies with those of the other members of the international payments system. We are told that only the fear of running out of liquidity reserves will assure the necessary monetary discipline and the harmonization of national credit policies. Having received the mandate to defend the exchange value of the national currency and to maintain its free convertibility, the central banker is upheld in his political struggle inside the government (for example, against inflationary deficit spending) and outside (for example, against pressure groups with monopolistic market influence who press for "permissive" money creation).

While much can be said for this argument, it is not correct to assume that discipline is exclusively fostered by the fear of losing liquidity reserves and of endangering convertibility. Maintenance of convertibility can no longer be used as an argument in the defense of fixed exchange rates once exchange controls have been introduced and full convertibility has thereby been abandoned. Furthermore, the size of the liquidity reserves is not the only gauge by which the central bank can judge the international position of the currency. "After all, exchange rate movements are very clear and loud warning signals. They are much more noticeable by the public than are reserve movements. It seems reasonable to expect that, in deficit countries of major importance as well as in surplus countries, clearer signals would gradually *increase* rather than reduce effective pressure toward responsible behavior." [5]

The argument that fixed exchange rates foster monetary discipline rests on the assumption of *limited* reserves. However, some advocates of fixed exchange rates want to soften the impact of an external imbalance on domestic policies through the supply of *very large* liquidity reserves. This, for example, is the attitude of Sir Roy Harrod, who considers fixed exchange rates advisable because a depreciation of the national currency would imply increasing import prices and interfere with an "incomes policy" that tries to keep wages and prices in line by moral suasion rather than by the use of monetary instruments. But, if an incomes policy is to be substituted for monetary and fiscal measures, we have to doubt the ability of the country to maintain a given fixed exchange rate in the long run. Peg adjustments will then become unavoidable and may prove more damaging than flexible exchange rates to the success of an incomes policy.

Most of the reasoning in favor of fixed exchange rates can be applied only to permanently fixed rates. In the adjustable-peg system the monetary authority can count on the International Monetary Fund's permission to alter the gold parity of the national currency in the case of "fundamental" disequilibrium. Once parity adjustments are permissible, most of the arguments for fixed exchange rates collapse: the long-run transactions no longer rest on the safe foundation of a stable international value of the currency unit; monetary and fiscal policies are no longer forced to defend international liquidity reserves through inconvenient domestic policies; and harmonization of national credit policies can no longer be counted on, with the result that needed adjustments are brought about belatedly and abruptly through devaluations and upvaluations. Emphasis in recent years on liquidity rather than adjustment indicates the increasing erosion of the very discipline and harmonization on which the advocates of fixed exchange rates try to rest their case.

The Case for Freely Flexible Exchange Rates

Consistent application of the principles of a market economy argues for exchange rates that would be free to adjust automatically to changing conditions of demand and supply in the foreign-exchange market. Automatic exchange-rate variations would bring about external equilibrium by changing directly and instantly the prices of all commodities in

---

[5] William Fellner, "On Limited Exchange-Rate Flexibility," Chapter 5 of *Maintaining and Restoring Balance in International Payments,* edited by William Fellner, Fritz Machlup, and Robert Triffin (Princeton, N.J.: Princeton University Press, 1966), p. 122.

terms of other countries' monetary units. In a system with fixed exchange rates, on the other hand, balance-of-payments adjustments are the result of a long-delayed, roundabout, and painful process through alterations of aggregate spending that exert deflationary and inflationary pressures, often with undesirable consequences for the national economies.

It is easy to ridicule a system with freely fluctuating exchange rates by exaggerating the claims of the advocates of greater flexibility. It can be doubted that the latter really expect that exchange-rate variations would "automatically offset the impact of disparate national policies upon the international pattern of prices and costs . . . without any interference with each country's freedom to pursue whatever internal monetary and credit policy is chosen." [6] Overstatements like these prevent serious discussion. A system with freely fluctuating exchange rates could not work satisfactorily in a country with endemic inflation, but neither could other payments systems with free convertibility be successful under similar conditions. The very mention of exchange-rate flexibility seems somehow to convey the idea that one would have to expect either self-aggravating depreciations or extremely wide fluctuations or, finally, an irresistible urge to practice competitive exchange depreciation. It is evidently taken for granted that to stray from the virtuous path of exchange-rate rigidity would mean the end of both national monetary discipline and international cooperation.

This view is overly pessimistic. Easing constraints on domestic economic policies may, on the contrary, improve the internal equilibrium of an economy, with beneficial results for the other members of the international payments system. How widely the exchange rates fluctuate will depend on the degree of international economic harmonization that can be achieved under the realistic assumption that each member of the system tries to reach high employment and income levels. The exchange-rate variations needed for the achievement of both external and internal equilibrium may be modest. A system with flexible exchange rates does not postpone the adjustment process and is likely, therefore, to avoid the development of discrepancies that, under a system of fixed exchange rates, may eventually lead to adjustments of parities or the introduction of quantitative restrictions.

Nor does a system of exchange-rate flexibility have to apply equally to all members of the international payments system. Where blocs of countries manage a high degree of internal harmonization, intra-bloc rates need not fluctuate at all, while between blocs exchange-rate variations may serve as an elastic link.

That countries in a system with flexible rates would pay no attention

---

[6] Robert Triffin, *Gold and the Dollar Crisis* (New Haven, Conn.: Yale University Press, 1960), p. 82.

INTRODUCTION

whatever to their external balances is as unlikely as complete neglect of the national employment situation under fixed exchange rates; nor would floating rates be an invitation to competitive exchange depreciation. Indeed, why should central bankers who have made an excellent record of international monetary cooperation be expected to use beggar-my-neighbor policies as soon as rigid parities are abolished? Why should multilateral surveillance be incapable of solving problems of international monetary cooperation under exchange-rate flexibility? We should remember, furthermore, that the present system of adjustable pegs, with its undervaluation of pegged surplus currencies, comes closer in effect to competitive exchange depreciation than a system that would permit market forces to operate.

However, notwithstanding these arguments in favor of flexible exchange rates, most practitioners and some academic economists strongly believe that complete freedom for exchange-rate variations would mean the end of monetary discipline, that exchange rates would fluctuate wildly, and that, far from producing external equilibrium, the system would be injurious to international trade relations and capital flows. Whether right or wrong, these beliefs are too firmly ingrained to permit serious practical consideration of a system of *unlimited* exchange-rate flexibility.

The Band Proposal

Rejection of both the present system of adjustable pegs and the system of unlimited exchange-rate fluctuations leaves us with some form of *limited* exchange-rate variations as a compromise between rigidity and flexibility. According to the oldest and best-known version of limited flexibility, the so-called band proposal, exchange rates are to be allowed to fluctuate within a wider range or "band" than the very narrow margins around par values that are permitted under Article IV of the Fund Agreement.

The idea of widening the margins between the so-called gold points under the gold standard system is very old. Robert Torrens, for example, opposed David Ricardo's plan to substitute gold bullion for gold coin with the argument that coin was "a less eligible article for export," permitted wider margins between the gold points and, thereby, greater freedom for domestic monetary policy.[7] This, we notice, happened in 1819, when prices and wages were still flexible downward and national-income and employment policies were virtually unknown.

Today's monetary authorities, though opposed even to moderately flexible rates of exchange, are not unwilling to make use of small exchange-rate variations permitted by the Fund. Robert V. Roosa, for ex-

---

[7] Jacob Viner, *Studies in the Theory of International Trade* (New York: Harper and Brothers Publishers, 1937), pp. 206–207.

ample, points out that "within the relatively narrow band which is . . . permitted under the rules of the International Monetary Fund, there must be room for market prices to demonstrate the basic strength or weakness of any currency." He also argues, convincingly, that "we want and need the sensitive signals of changes in fundamental forces that are reflected in price fluctuations in free markets." However, while Roosa reasons here implicitly for exchange-rate flexibility, he, nevertheless, expresses the fear that public authorities would come under pressure to manipulate the rates and that this could lead "to competitive devaluation, and on to trade and exchange restrictions." Free exchange markets, therefore, could "degenerate into disorderly chaos if they do not have some fixed point of reference." Since the widened band retains this fixed point of reference, Roosa admitted more recently that "the wider band might some day be of some use." [8]

The band proposal suggests three fixed points of reference by permitting exchange-rate variations around fixed par values and within predetermined support points. Assuming that a monetary authority maintains a given dollar parity and uses the dollar as "intervention currency," it will supply dollars without limit when the upper support point is reached, thus preventing a depreciation of its own currency unit; similarly, it will stand ready to buy dollars in unlimited amounts at the lower support point to prevent a further appreciation of its own currency unit. The rate of exchange is both fixed and free: attached to the parity as reference point, and free to rise and fall between the support points.

Whether this compromise between rigidity and flexibility favors discipline or freedom will depend on the width of the band, in conjunction with the supply of international liquidity reserves. Relatively small reserves combined with a relatively wide band can have about the same effect as a combination of larger reserves with a narrow band. It would not be correct to say, therefore, that a widening of the band will lower monetary discipline or that exchange-rate rigidity can be relied upon to compel the adoption of policies leading to adjustment. Adjustment and liquidity are to a large extent substitutes. We must remember, though, that extended use of reserves is preferable to fast real adjustment only in the case of temporary and reversible imbalances of international payments; that more deepseated imbalances must be eliminated; and that

[8] The four quotations are from different sources. The first two are from the articles "The Beginning of a New Policy" and "Banking and the Balance of Payments," both reprinted in Joint Economic Committee, *Factors Affecting the United States Balance of Payments* (Washington: U.S. Government Printing Office, 1962), pp. 328 and 339. The third is from Roosa's book *Monetary Reform for the World Economy* (New York and Evanston: Harper and Row, 1965), p. 27. The fourth is from Milton Friedman and Robert V. Roosa, *The Balance of Payments: Free versus Fixed Exchange Rates* (Washington: American Enterprise Institute, 1967), p. 35.

INTRODUCTION

more flexible exchange rates may be preferable to rigid rates in bringing about both external and internal balance.

The practical success of the widened band will depend on whether or not the permitted exchange-rate variations can perform their market functions while maintaining confidence in the stability of the situation. Only practical experience will tell. It may prove desirable to widen the band gradually as the parties engaging in foreign-exchange transactions gain confidence in the new mechanism. On the other hand, too timid an approach might prevent foreign-exchange variations of the size needed to produce equilibrium, particularly if the new system were not started on the basis of true equilibrium rates for convertible currencies. A general realignment of the member countries' parities might greatly help the transition from the present system to one with a wider band.

How the Widened Band Works

The present system of the adjustable peg achieves a pseudoflexibility by permitting large discrete revaluations. The system, in fact, is rigid and brittle. The widened band, on the other hand, would combine smooth adjustments through continuous exchange-rate variations with guaranteed limits to these fluctuations at the support points. The latter would be guideposts, clear signals for the monetary authority to support the adjustment process through domestic monetary policies. But these "interferences" with domestic economic policies would be rare because external adjustment would no longer be delayed as under the adjustable-peg system.

Adjustment of the trade balance through exchange-rate variations would still take time, but its start would be immediate and automatic instead of being postponed for years. Exchange depreciation inside the band will lead to increasing exports and decreasing imports, though, of course, not without a time lag. The exchange rate, therefore, may first tend to depreciate below the long-run equilibrium point for the new market conditions. As Erik Lundberg [9] and James E. Meade [10] have pointed out, this temporary excess depreciation will induce private speculation to move funds from the surplus into the deficit currency in expectation of a rebound when real adjustment has taken place. The short-run flow of private speculative capital will help finance the temporary deficit and thereby prevent an overreaction in the process of trade adjustment when no serious fundamental disequilibrium is involved.

The mechanism of trade adjustment through varying exchange rates

[9] Erik Lundberg, "The Dilemma of Exchange-Rate Policy," in *Skandinaviska Banken Quarterly Review*, Vol. 35 (October 1954).
[10] James E. Meade, "The Future of International Payments," reprinted in Joint Economic Committee, *Factors Affecting the United States Balance of Payments* (Washington: U.S. Government Printing Office, 1962), p. 246.

needs no elaboration, and postwar experiences suggest that a band of a total width of 10 per cent would in most cases have sufficed to maintain external equilibrium without parity changes or excessive supplies of international liquidity reserves, since the process of adjustment would have been set in motion without delay.

The additional risk in foreign transactions could be taken care of by the forward exchange market. The cost of hedging cannot be a serious consideration in a competitive market economy. This cost, in any case, is less serious than the private and social costs of delays in the adjustment process under a fixed-rate system.

There is no reason to expect that exchange-rate variations within a band of 5 per cent on each side of parity would lead to competitive exchange depreciation or exchange restrictions. On the contrary, it is the present fixed-rate system which, by permitting long periods of over- and undervaluation of currencies, has led to unfair advantages and the introduction of restrictive policies.

Band Proposal and Capital Movements

The advocates of fixed exchange rates take it for granted that exchange-rate flexibility would be detrimental to desirable international capital movements. They are wrong, at least with regard to short-term movements. The introduction of a widened band would favor equilibrating capital flows and discourage disequilibrating speculation, whereas a system of abrupt adjustments of parities will always be exposed to speculative disturbances.

To understand the connection between exchange-rate variations and short-term capital movements we must first distinguish between non-dilemma and dilemma cases.

Let us assume that a country has reached its state of full employment through the application of expansionist monetary and fiscal policies that have raised prices and made the country less competitive at fixed exchange rates. Full employment has exerted an upward pressure on wages, and a high level of economic activity and national income has stimulated imports further, that is, over and above the increased propensity to import owing to relatively more attractive foreign prices. The full-employment country, therefore, will have acquired a deficit in its balance of payments. For similar but opposite reasons, an underemployed and depressed economy can be assumed to have attained a surplus in its balance of payments.

The combination of internal contraction with external surplus, and internal expansion with external deficit, fits classical assumptions as well as Keynesian theory, for it can be expected that successful employment policies will create external deficits through their price and income effects. The difference between the classical and Keynesian models consists in the emphasis on price effects in the former and income effects in the latter and on different emphases in objectives. The classical model gives priority to external, the Keynesian to internal, balance.

The case in which the deficit country enjoys full employment and the surplus country suffers from unemployment is regarded as a nondilemma case, because economic policies aiming at external and internal balance need not conflict. The deficit country with full employment can be expected to have high interest rates because of its high level of economic activity, and it may raise these rates in an attempt to combat domestic inflation and to attract short-term foreign funds to eliminate the deficit. The surplus country, by contrast, tries to stimulate economic activity through low interest rates, thereby encouraging an outflow of short-term capital that, owing to the country's surplus position, would create no problems.

In a system with fixed exchange rates, the changing differential in interest rates between deficit and surplus countries is expected to help adjust national price levels and the trade balance, while the induced international flow of short-term capital helps finance the deficit until the adjustment is completed. Even under the old gold standard (that is, before 1914) the interest-rate differentials were supported by the small exchange-rate variations between the gold points. The exchange rate of deficit country D would depreciate temporarily and make it more attractive for speculators in surplus country S to purchase D-currency, enjoy temporarily the higher interest rate in D, and repurchase S-currency after equilibrium has been achieved and D-currency has returned to parity.

A widening of the band would strengthen these equilibrating short-term capital movements. The capital flows induced by exchange-rate variations alone might even be strong enough to provide the needed foreign funds to finance the temporary external imbalance and give the monetary authorities the opportunity of handling interest-rate changes with greater consideration of the requirements of internal equilibrium. If the central banks were permitted and inclined to intervene inside the band, they could determine the relative dosage of exchange-rate and interest-rate variations.

Now we must turn to the dilemma cases. A dilemma case exists when the means to achieve internal balance conflict with those needed to attain or maintain external balance. This time the deficit countries suffer from underemployment, while the surplus countries enjoy a high level of economic activity. The co-existence of unemployment and payments deficit may be due to monopolistic pressures forcing prices up even in the face of unemployed resources and inadequate aggregate demand. Another cause for the appearance of a serious dilemma between external and internal balance may be the attempt by a country to make extraordinarily large payments abroad. Such payments may be connected with military aid, economic aid, sudden repayments of foreign loans, the unfreezing of frozen balances belonging to foreigners, reparations, or any other sudden shifts of substantial amounts of capital. This so-called transfer problem is an extreme case of the difficulty that arises when we try to allow international capital movements in economies in which total expenditures, prices, and incomes are inflexible. No international payments system can effect transfers in huge amounts and maintain internal balance for the paying country. The widened band would be no exception to this rule.

What private short-term capital movements can be expected in dilemma cases? The answer depends on the international payments system. We assume, first, a system with fixed, but not unalterably fixed, exchange rates and, second, a system with limited exchange-rate flexibility under a widened band.

When deficit country D carries on domestic employment policies by lowering interest rates while surplus country S, at full employment, raises interest rates to keep inflation in check, and both countries maintain a fixed parity between their currency units, private capital will flow from D to S and thereby increase external imbalance for both. This capital flow is clearly disequilibrating. As deficits and surpluses grow, redoubled efforts in S to stop inflation and in D to increase employment will only lead to further rounds of surpluses and deficits. Something will have to give eventually. Either the internal problem can be solved without worsening the external imbalance or the peg will have to be adjusted —unless exchange controls are introduced.

The first alternative would be the most attractive if it were possible to divorce monetary policies cleanly from fiscal policies or if the credit market could be divided into watertight compartments. In the latter case, the short-term rates of interest could be used to guide international short-term funds in the right direction, while internal adjustment would be left to the long-term rate. Similarly, monetary policy could serve the purpose of external adjustment, while internal equilibrium could be the responsibility of fiscal policy. For example, a surplus country with full employment, suffering from price inflation, would raise taxes rather than interest rates. So far, however, there is no evidence that we shall be able to separate monetary policies cleanly from fiscal policies or to compartmentalize the credit market effectively.

That it is impossible to compartmentalize the credit market effectively was emphasized by Keynes when he pointed out that credit is undifferentiated and, like water, "will remorselessly seek its own level over the whole field unless the parts of the field are rendered uncompromisingly watertight,—which in the case of credit is scarcely possible." [11] Recent

---

[11] John Maynard Keynes, *A Treatise on Money*, Vol. 2 (New York: Harcourt, Brace and Company, 1930), p. 319.

INTRODUCTION

experiences with the surtax in the United States have made it clear how far removed we still are from a substitution of fiscal for monetary policies for the achievement of both external and internal balance.

It has already been pointed out that peg adjustments and exchange restrictions are undesirable. How successful, then, would a widening of the band for permissible exchange-rate variations in dilemma cases be? Would increased exchange-rate flexibility help restrain the disequilibrating capital flow that is certain to be generated under fixed exchange rates?

As in the case of fixed exchange rates, the interest rate would be low in deficit country D, to increase employment, and high in surplus country S, to stop inflation. The interest differential, therefore, would still tend to guide the international flow of private short-term capital in the wrong direction. But in a system with exchange-rate flexibility exchange-rate variations would tend to counterbalance the interest-rate differential. The exchange rate of S-currency would appreciate, the rate of D-currency would depreciate and these changes in exchange rates would reduce, compensate, or overcompensate the profit to be derived from the interest differential. Disequilibrating capital flows from low-interest country D to high-interest country S would be reduced, stopped, or even reversed by the exchange-rate differential that grows with each additional capital transfer. In other words, market forces would take care of the situation.

When the "Flexible" Rate Gets Stuck

Other things remaining equal, the need for international liquidity reserves depends on the success or failure of the adjustment process. In the theoretical case of unlimited exchange-rate flexibility (and no intervention whatever on the part of the monetary authorities in the foreign-exchange market) no international liquidity reserves would be needed. Exchange-rate variations would keep demand and supply continuously in balance. In a system with fixed rates, free convertibility, and poor harmonization of national monetary policies, the demand for international liquidity reserves could be insatiable, particularly in countries with endemic inflation. The case of the widened band lies in between. The need for liquidity reserves may well be substantially smaller than under the adjustable-peg system. First, because the adjustment process would be promoted by the variations of the exchange rates and, second, because private capital movements would be induced to help finance deficits while the external imbalance lasts. If exchange-rate variations could be kept safely within the band, a small emergency reserve would suffice.

Of course, the band system can fail just as any other system of international payments can if adjustments by means of exchange-rate variations and by means of monetary measures are not strong enough to counterbalance the disequilibrating forces of diverging national economic pol-

15

icies. But it is not likely that the exchange rates will get stuck permanently at the support points if the system is established on the basis of near-equilibrium rates, if the right width is chosen for the band, and if a reasonable degree of international monetary coordination prevails.

As for the expected length of the adjustment period, it must be remembered that, while the process gets instantly started, the results will not be instantaneous. Before we know how long the adjustment process will take, we cannot regard the clinging of the exchange rates to the support points and the use of international liquidity reserves to maintain convertibility at these points as indications of failure. However, since it is the very essence of the band proposal that excessive delays in the adjustment process are avoided, permanent maintenance of the exchange rates at the support points is not good enough. The system might then be said to have reverted to the present adjustable-peg arrangement.

The Gliding Parity

Before we try to answer the question of what to do when the exchange rates continue to press against the support points of a widened band, it is necessary to investigate other arrangements for the achievement of limited exchange-rate flexibility, which go under such names as "sliding parity," "gliding parity," or "crawling peg." Such proposals have been made by James E. Meade, John H. Williamson, J. Carter Murphy, E. Ray Canterbery, and William Fellner.[12] Fellner's essay contains a statement by 27 economists advocating a wider band and a gliding parity.

These proposals have the common idea that very small and frequent parity changes ought to be substituted for the present system of discrete and, accordingly, large adjustments of the peg. While "gliding parity" and "widened band" are logically distinct systems, most advocates of limited exchange-rate flexibility favor a combination of the two approaches in the form of a "movable band."

Two main advantages are claimed for a gliding parity: first, that exchange-rate adjustment will in each case be very small (for instance,

---

[12] James E. Meade, "The International Monetary Mechanism," in *The Three Banks Review*, No. 63 (September 1964) and "Exchange Rate Flexibility," in *The Three Banks Review*, No. 70 (June 1966); John H. Williamson, *The Crawling Peg*, Essays in International Finance No. 50 (Princeton, N.J.: International Finance Section, 1965); J. Carter Murphy, "Moderated Exchange Rate Variability," in *The National Banking Review*, Vol. 3, No. 2 (December 1965) and "Moderated Exchange Rate Variability: Reply," in *The National Banking Review*, Vol. 4, No. 1 (September 1966); E. Ray Canterbery, *Economics on a New Frontier* (Belmont, Calif.: Wadsworth Publishing Company, 1968), pp. 212–216; William Fellner, "On Limited Exchange-Rate Flexibility," in *Maintaining and Restoring Balance in International Payments*, edited by William Fellner, Fritz Machlup, and Robert Triffin (Princeton, N.J.: Princeton University Press, 1966), pp. 111–122.

only ⅙ of 1 per cent in any one month) so that dangerous disequilibrating capital movements will be reduced to manageable proportions; and, second, that frequent but small adjustments would under specified conditions of disequilibrium be permitted to continue beyond predetermined limits so that the gliding parity could correct for disparities in national monetary policies that cannot be harmonized within the widened band.

Proposals for small but frequent adjustments of parities must answer such questions as: (1) How frequently are the parities to be changed and what are the limits for each individual adjustment? (2) Under what conditions are the member countries of the system to change their parities? (3) Are these changes to be automatic or discretionary? (4) Are they to be unilateral or subject to approval by the International Monetary Fund? (5) Is the gliding parity designed to eliminate fundamental disequilibria which have been permitted to develop or is it to prevent such developments through prompt parity changes? (6) How can disequilibrating speculation, the bane of the adjustable-peg system, be avoided?

The proposal for a gliding parity could be interpreted as an attempt to improve the system of parity changes that was to be the mainstay of the international adjustment mechanism of the *Keynes Plan* of 1943.[13] Keynes proposed that the value of the currencies of the members of a Clearing Union should be fixed, but not unalterably, in terms of an international unit called bancor; that there should be an orderly and agreed method of determining the relative exchange values of national currency units; and that the system have an international stabilizing mechanism. This mechanism was to rest predominantly on relatively frequent parity changes. If a member's deficit balance with the Union exceeded a quarter of its quota on the average of at least two years, the member would be entitled to reduce the value of its currency in terms of bancor, provided that such reduction did not exceed 5 per cent, without the consent of the Governing Board of the Union. Since it would take some time to reach this deficit level, Keynes' order of magnitude comes close to that of the new suggestions (for instance, 2 per cent per annum, according to Meade and Williamson). The difference lies in the fact that the more recent plans for a gliding parity divide parity adjustments into small and, accordingly, frequent installments.

Keynes proposed further that a member who reached a debit balance with the Union equal to one-half of his quota could be requested to devalue and to control outward capital movements. A member whose credit balance exceeded one-half of his quota on the average of at least one year should discuss with the Governing Board "the appreciation of its local currency in terms of bancor, or, alternatively, the encourage-

[13] *Proposals by British Experts for an International Clearing Union* (April 1943), Part II, Section 8.

ment of an increase in money rates of earnings." The Keynes Plan "aimed at putting some of the responsibility for adjustment on the creditor country as well as the debtor." Considering that a surplus country's obligation to accept bancor checks would have been limited not by its own quota but by the aggregate deficits of its potential debtors, the Keynes Plan stressed upvaluation more than devaluation.

Keynes was aware that the proposed adjustment mechanism through parity changes—directly geared, as the latter were, to deficit and surplus balances with the Union—would have created a climate of disequilibrating capital movements and could not have succeeded without the control of speculative short-term capital movements, "both inward and outward." He never explained how these controls could have been administered in an international payments system that aimed to support multilateralism through currency convertibility.

The new gliding-parity proposals try to eliminate disequilibrating capital movements without the imposition of exchange controls. The individual parity adjustments would be so small that speculation could be kept in check by differentials in national short-term rates of interest. However, difficulties might arise, once again, in the so-called dilemma cases where a country whose currency is to be devalued does not want to raise the interest rate because of its unsatisfactory employment situation, and a surplus country, under inflationary pressure, is reluctant to lower its interest rate to compensate for an upvaluation of its currency.

Proponents of a gliding parity argue for frequent but small and strictly limited parity adjustments. They fear that a freely floating rate could lead to self-aggravating speculation and also that a system with freely fluctuating rates lacks the political virtue of "acceptability." The proposed schemes differ in detail, but all make it clear that the momentarily given rate can change by no more than a very small amount within a specified period.

In James E. Meade's proposal, the present IMF rules would be revised in the following way: "Basic adjustments to meet a fundamental disequilibrium would be hedged around with even more safeguards and would be made even more exceptional than at present. The allowance of an initial 10 per cent adjustment would be abolished; but in its place member countries would be permitted to alter the par value of their currencies by not more than $\frac{1}{6}$ per cent in any one month; moreover, they would undertake to depreciate their currencies by $\frac{1}{6}$ per cent in any one month if, but only if, they were faced with a continuing balance-of-payments deficit and to appreciate by this amount if, but only if, they were faced with a continuing surplus in their balance of payments. This system might perhaps be called that of the *Sliding Parity*. For if the right to change the parity were exercised every month, the exchange value of the currency would be changed continuously at 2 per cent per annum." [14]

Similarly, John H. Williamson suggests that the members of the International Monetary Fund undertake that any changes in par values needed to correct a fundamental disequilibrium "would be carried out gradually, at a maximum rate of $\frac{1}{26}$ of 1 per cent per week, rather than in a sudden discrete jump." [15]

Both Meade and Williamson recognize that an incentive will exist to transfer funds from a currency undergoing devaluation to a currency undergoing upvaluation, and both suggest that this tendency may have to be neutralized by interest-rate differentials. We have already seen that in a dilemma situation the creation of an artificial interest-rate differential is undesirable from the standpoint of reaching or maintaining domestic economic equilibrium. Meade, therefore, hopes that the national authorities can "rely on budgetary policies and—insofar as they can be determined independently of short-term rates—upon long-term rates, for the control of domestic economic expansion." [16] However, the use of artificially created interest-rate differentials tends to reduce or eliminate one of the advantages of exchange-rate flexibility: far from being partially freed from attention to the country's balance-of-payments position, national monetary and fiscal policies would often be constrained by the necessity to prevent disequilibrating capital transfers.

To eliminate this potential difficulty, J. Carter Murphy suggests that the parities be permitted to change daily, the parity being calculated as the moving average of the closing market prices on the 307 previous business days. Since the daily market price would be strictly limited to a band of a total width of only 3 per cent, Murphy believes that the maximum parity changes "should be such as to make speculation a relatively unremunerative activity." He assumes, however, that both countries are able "to avoid policies which create continuous uni-directional disturbances to exchange markets." [17]

We have already seen that Meade proposes that even small parity changes should take place only if the member countries are faced with a continuing deficit or surplus in their payments balances. This definition implies that a disequilibrium develops quite visibly and that it is then worked off in small but frequent installments. The same situation is even more clearly indicated by Williamson's assumption that a fundamental disequilibrium exists, that the parity is slowly adjusted to the proper level, and that the authorities will even announce by which total amount the parity will have to be changed over the next few years.

The Meade-Williamson proposals would leave little doubt as to the

[14] Op. cit., 1966, p. 22. [15] Op. cit., p. 2. [16] Op. cit., 1966, p. 23.
[17] Op. cit., 1965, p. 102.

coming development of certain parities, while Murphy's calculation of the daily rates would not only make the development of the parities obvious, but might even produce wrong rates for present conditions, owing to his formula's exclusive emphasis on past conditions.

If unidirectional deviations of national economic policies cannot be avoided and shifting parities are used, the problem of disequilibrating speculation could perhaps best be solved by a system that makes it impossible for the private speculator to gauge accurately the speed, extent, and, perhaps, even the direction of coming parity changes. For this purpose a somewhat ambiguous adjustment formula would have to be used.

E. Ray Canterbery suggests a method to determine a basic disequilibrium that would be less likely to inform would-be speculators about coming parity changes. A monetary-reserve-base coefficient would express weekly reserve losses as shares of a given base-reserve value. The formula could be altered from time to time and would be secret.

It will prove difficult to construct a formula for measuring imbalances that are equivalent to small permitted parity changes. Such a formula for the fine-tuning of parities will be so hard to find that it seems more likely that the gliding parity is not meant to maintain international balance continuously, as a floating rate would, but rather to work off gradually larger, and therefore more obvious, disequilibria in small and frequent installments of parity changes.

The Movable Band

Most advocates of a gliding parity want to combine it with the widened band for permissible exchange-rate variations. This combination can be recommended, unless we fear that the simultaneous use of band and gliding parity would seriously weaken the firm guidance for national monetary policy that we hope to gain from *fixed* support points.

Both proposals rest on the same arguments against the present system of fixed, but not unalterably fixed, exchange rates. It makes sense to combine the gliding parity with the widened band when we assume that unidirectional deviations of national monetary policies will exceed the adjustment capabilities of a widened band. For the same reason it makes good sense to consider the widened band as the first step on the road to greater flexibility of exchange rates and the gliding parity as the second step.

The proposal for a movable band contains part of the answer to the question of what should be done when the exchange rates press for too long against the support points of a widened band. In this state of international payments disequilibrium the following measures might be considered:

(1) Redoubled efforts to push the parities back inside the band through application of domestic monetary policies.

(2) Encouragement of equilibrating private capital movements.

(3) Arrangements for larger official international liquidity reserves to be able to correct international imbalance "without resorting to measures destructive of national and international prosperity." [18]

(4) Insistence that all equilibrating policies be symmetrical, that is, that the surplus countries bear their proper share of any adjustment burden.

(5) Adjustment of parities in very small steps, both up and down, to compensate for shifts in the purchasing-power parities of the members, which exceed the compensatory effects of exchange-rate variations inside the band.

(6) Arrangements for these parity shifts by the International Monetary Fund with the fullest cooperation of the members, whether in deficit or surplus, so that disequilibrating movements of capital can be avoided and the fear of competitive exchange depreciation assuaged.

(7) Harmonization of domestic monetary policies so that the remaining divergencies do not exceed the combined adjustment powers of the widened band and the gliding parity.

Movable Band and Reserve Currency

A widened or even a movable band could be introduced with greater ease if all members of the international payments system were essentially equal as to importance and position in the system. The International Monetary Fund was not designed for the use of reserve currencies and the Keynes Plan excluded explicitly such use of national currencies apart from working balances. In the present system, however, foreign-held dollar (and sterling) balances are indispensable, and growing dollar balances raise a confidence problem resulting from the deterioration of the net-reserve position of the United States. Furthermore, while other countries are able to change their parities in the case of a fundamental disequilibrium, the reserve-currency position of the dollar rules out a dollar devaluation for fear of a run on gold and precipitation of a world-wide liquidity crisis.

This situation seems to argue for the maintenance of fixed exchange rates rather than for a change-over to flexibility, at least until the present system has been liquidated or rendered innocuous. Notwithstanding the forthcoming creation of Special Drawing Rights, we must, therefore, answer the question how a wider band or even a gliding parity could be introduced today. How can confidence in the dollar be maintained if the dollar is permitted to fluctuate more widely in terms of other currencies?

The other members of the system maintain their parities by using the dollar not only as common denominator but also as intervention currency. Their monetary authorities sell dollars to avoid a depreciation of

[18] International Monetary Fund, Articles of Agreement, Art. I–v.

the national currency (or an appreciation of the dollar) and buy dollars to prevent an appreciation of the national currency (or a depreciation of the dollar). Today they intervene at support points that deviate from the official dollar parity by less than 1 per cent, while under the widened band they would intervene when the margin has reached, for example, 5 per cent. Assuming that, at any particular moment, country A supports the value of its currency at the lowest support point and country B its currency at the highest support point, they would each differ in opposite directions by 5 per cent from the dollar parity, but differ from one another by 10 per cent. We note, furthermore, that with a complete reversal of the balance-of-payments position of A and B, a change of about 20 per cent would occur in their respective positions.

This doubled width of the band can be shown by the following example. Under assumed par values of 1 U.S. dollar = 5 French francs = 4 Deutsche marks and permissible exchange-rate variations of 5 per cent up and down:

    lowest rate of Fr.fr.: $1 = Fr.fr. 5.25
    highest rate of Fr.fr.: $1 = Fr.fr. 4.75
    lowest rate of D.M.: $1 = D.M. 4.20
    highest rate of D.M.: $1 = D.M. 3.80

When the French franc is at its lower and the Deutsche mark at its higher limit, Fr.fr. 5.25 = D.M. 3.80, or D.M. 1 = Fr.fr. 1.38. When the French franc rises to its upper limit and the Deutsche mark falls to its lower limit, Fr.fr. 4.75 = D.M. 4.20, or D.M. 1 = Fr.fr. 1.13. The total variation of the French franc between $1.38 and $1.13 is $0.25, or 18.1 per cent of $1.38 and 22.1 per cent of $1.13.

But what is true for currencies A and B would not be true for the dollar with which foreign monetary authorities carry out their interventions and to which they peg their currencies. Playing the role of international money as means of exchange (transaction and intervention currency) and unit of account (common denominator), the dollar finds itself internationally in a special position. When currencies A and B are in extreme and opposite positions, they are 10 per cent apart, while the dollar as common denominator can differ from any other currency by not more than 5 per cent or one-half of the width of the band. As long as the dollar is used as intervention currency it can never fluctuate except via permitted fluctuations of other currencies.

The widened band, therefore, would not quite eliminate the element of asymmetry that is connected with the role of the dollar as intervention currency. Today all Fund members except the United States enjoy the potential use of the safety value of peg adjustments in the case of fundamental disequilibrium; and under a widened band the adjustment possibilities via exchange-rate variations for the United States would only be one-half of those of other members of the Fund. Should the United States nevertheless welcome a widened band?

An affirmative answer would have to consider that the present situation of the United States also implies certain advantages. The role of the dollar as reserve currency also means that all surplus countries stand ready to buy dollars in unlimited amounts when an oversupply of dollars must be taken off the market to prevent an appreciation of the surplus currencies. This means automatic financing of deficits of payments of the United States through automatic accumulation of official foreign dollar balances. If the band for permissible exchange-rate variations is widened while the dollar is still used as reserve currency, the effect on the United States will be in the nature of a compromise. The regular advantage of the widened band, that is, its beneficial adjustment effects on trade and capital flows, would be limited to one-half of the potential maximum effect for other countries; but to the extent that surplus countries would have to buy dollars at the margin, they would still finance a remaining deficit of the United States. A quasi-automatic supply of liquidity for the reserve-currency country compensates for the more limited elbow-room for exchange-rate adjustments.

Technical difficulties could arise if the band were widened while the gold value of the dollar remained relatively fixed as at present. The dollar could depreciate and appreciate in terms of other currencies by as much as 5 per cent, but in terms of gold by only 1 per cent. Accordingly, it would seem that central bankers would prefer gold to the dollar as the safer reserve asset or that, in the case of an expected dollar depreciation, they would move into gold and, in the case of a dollar appreciation, into dollars. However, we ought to be able to assume that considerations other than mere security or profitability will prevail.

The following arguments attempt to show that the maintenance of gold convertibility of the dollar at the present rate need not prevent the introduction of a wider band or even the adoption of a gliding parity.

(1) The present gold policy under which the London gold market is no longer supplied out of official gold holdings would have to become a permanent feature of the international payments system.

(2) A well-functioning system of exchange-rate flexibility within a widened band would leave the average value of private and official dollar balances unchanged as the balance-of-payments positions of the member countries tend to reverse themselves again and again, owing to the adjustments brought about by exchange-rate variations and by remedial monetary policies. Thus there would normally be no reason for central bankers to change dollars into gold.

(3) Other things remaining equal, dollar balances are more attractive

than gold. The interest earned on these dollar balances will more than compensate for the losses from modest and temporary dollar depreciations.

(4) Should it be necessary to move the band, the proposed limit of 2 per cent per annum would still be within the range in which losses in gold value can be compensated by earnings of interest. The interest rate to be paid on official dollar balances could be adjusted correspondingly. The criticism that the credit market cannot be compartmentalized would not apply because the arrangement would be limited to transactions with central banks.

(5) In view of a possible movement of the band extending over years (at 2 per cent per annum) without reversing itself, a gold-value guarantee of official dollar balances could be considered.

Questions for Discussion

The introduction of a system of limited exchange-rate flexibility requires the thorough discussion of many questions. Vague fears must be dispelled, transition difficulties overcome, and choices made between several versions of limited flexibility. The cost of experimenting can be reduced if the whole problem is viewed from several angles before practical work begins.

THE LACKING ADJUSTMENT MECHANISM

If the present system has been working adequately, why the repeated international monetary crises, the disalignment of exchange rates, and the introduction of exchange restrictions? Whatever the reasons, can we hope to eliminate the causes of external imbalance while maintaining rigid exchange rates? How long can we shore up the present system by *ad hoc* arrangements? Would the introduction of Special Drawing Rights eliminate the major weakness of the present system—the absence of a functioning adjustment mechanism?

FIXED EXCHANGE RATES

Why should we be justified in violating the basic principles of the market economy in the foreign-exchange market? Why should this important market not perform the function of equilibrating demand and supply? Why should it be immune to the known dangers of price control? Can fixed exchange rates have their claimed disciplinary effect on national monetary policy (1) if full employment is the primary concern of national economic policy, (2) if international liquidity reserves are very large, (3) if the financing of balance-of-payments deficits is guaranteed for the country whose money serves as intervention currency, (4) if the parities can be changed in the case of "fundamental" disequilibrium? If monetary discipline cannot be relied upon, can the desired results be achieved by an incomes policy?

FREELY FLUCTUATING EXCHANGE RATES

If price signals are needed in the foreign-exchange market, are the margins now permitted sufficient? Precisely, why should freely fluctuating exchange rates lead to (1) wide price variations, (2) self-aggravating speculation, (3) destruction of monetary discipline, (4) competitive exchange depreciation? How do reserve losses and exchange-rate variations compare as signals on which to orient responsible monetary behavior? Why must it be taken for granted that international monetary cooperation will cease to operate as soon as exchange rates are permitted to fluctuate?

THE BAND PROPOSAL

Could a wider band for permissible exchange-rate variations combine the discipline of a fixed parity with sufficient flexibility inside the band? Would the argument for a widened band still hold if the parity were permitted to glide? How much would the band have to be widened to provide an adjustment mechanism for international trade? Would a band of a total width of 10 per cent have avoided the imbalances of the last ten years? Would the width of the band needed for trade adjustment be compatible with confidence in the system of international payments? Assuming that exchange rates have become disaligned under the present system, would the introduction of a wider band have to be preceded by a general realignment of parities or should the width of the band be so generous that existing deviations of parities can be absorbed without exhausting the newly permitted flexibility? Would it be desirable to begin with a modest widening of the band, for example, a doubling of the range now permitted, and then to continue to broaden the band as experience and confidence are gained? Would private speculation tend to be equilibrating or disequilibrating? How effective and how expensive would hedging operations be? Must we assume that private and social costs connected with greater exchange-rate flexibility will be greater than those of the present system? Should exchange-rate variations between fixed support points be completely free or should the monetary authorities be permitted to intervene even before the support points have been reached? How could surplus countries be induced to let their currencies appreciate?

THE GLIDING PARITY

Should parity adjustments be permitted under carefully defined circumstances, provided that these adjustments are very small and frequent? Under which conditions should these adjustments be permitted? Should they be quasi-automatic or depend on permission by the International Monetary Fund? Can an adjustment formula be found precise enough to permit measurements whose exactness matches the smallness of the permitted changes, or are these small and frequent changes meant only to give the quality of gradualness to contemplated large parity adjustments? How can disequilibrating speculation be avoided in a gliding-parity system? Can speculative capital flows be prevented by artificial interest-rate differentials? Are these differentials compatible with the desired freedom for domestic monetary policy? Can domestic economic policy rely exclusively on fiscal instruments so that the monetary instruments are available for the achievement of external balance? Should the monetary authorities intervene so as to make the direction and degree of parity changes less obvious? Could a gliding-parity formula be precise enough to serve international monetary cooperation, yet vague enough to prevent anticipation of parity changes by private speculators?

THE MOVABLE BAND

Should widened band and gliding parity be combined in a movable band? Would a movable band seriously weaken the guidance of monetary policy that is to be gained from fixed support points? Should the widened band be considered a first step toward limited exchange-rate flexibility and the gliding parity be introduced, as a second step, when the exchange rates get stuck at the support points? How can surplus countries be induced to let their parities glide upward when the formula demands?

WIDENED BAND, GLIDING PARITY, AND THE DOLLAR

How can widened bands, gliding parities, or both be introduced into the present international payments system? How would the dollar in its role as reserve, transaction, and intervention currency be affected? Could a widened or a movable band be introduced while gold convertibility of the dollar at $35 an ounce of gold is maintained? Assuming that the dollar as intervention and reserve currency cannot move as much and as freely as other currencies, could the United States be satisfied with one-half the width of the band that is enjoyed by other countries? Would the automatic borrowing rights enjoyed by the United States compensate for this restriction? Would the introduction of a widened or a movable band reduce or increase the need for international liquidity reserves? What changes in the Articles of Agreement of the International Monetary Fund would be implied?

· 2 ·

Two Lists of Topics for Further Study and a Proposed Outline for Conference Papers

Possible Topics for Future Study

ALTERNATIVE A by Robert V. Roosa

(1) The essential elements of the existing exchange-rate system and its shortcomings.
(2) The operational design of the wider band and crawling peg proposals and the problems of transition.
(3) The impact of the proposed exchange-rate arrangements on balance-of-payments adjustment—including trade and capital flows, domestic economic performance, and international coordination.
(4) The functions of forward markets and speculation in the performance of alternative exchange-rate systems.
(5) Special problems relating to the role of the U.S. dollar, its link to gold, and the International Monetary Fund.

ALTERNATIVE B by Milton Friedman

Given a band of $\pm X$ per cent, and a sliding parity of Y per cent per year,
(1) What should be the value of X?
(2) What should be the value of Y?
(3) How should changes in parity be determined?
(4) In what terms should parity be defined—gold, or the dollar, or what?
(5) What provisions should be established for official intervention within the band?
(6) How should the transition to the new from the existing arrangements be accomplished?

Proposed Outline for Conference Papers by C. Fred Bergsten

Each topic should include:
    A. consideration of each of the three basic alternatives—a band of ± 5 per cent, a sliding parity of a maximum 2 per cent per year, and a combination of these two;
    B. a comparison between each and the present international monetary system.
  I. Impact on the Balance-of-Payments Adjustment Process
    A. Is the additional adjustment achieved (if any) in dilemma cases

greater than the improper adjustment that may occur in non-dilemma cases?
   B. Is the effectiveness of the proposed small changes in exchange rates proportionate to large changes?
   C. Would they tend to equalize the impact of adjustment as between surplus and deficit countries?
   D. How do they compare with alternative adjustment devices that represent effective exchange-rate changes on specific accounts in the balance of payments (for example, border tax adjustments, interest equalization tax, taxes on foreign travel)?
   E. Would short-term capital movements offset "real economic effects"? Would they be stabilizing or destabilizing?
   F. Would they help or hinder the implementation of needed large or small changes in parities?
II. Effect on International Economic and Foreign Policies
   A. Impact on the relationship between policy instruments and targets.
   B. Would domestic economic policy, especially monetary policy, become freer or more constrained?
   C. On the objectives of balance-of-payments structure, as well as overall payments positions.
III. How Many Exchange Rates Should or Would Actually Fluctuate?
   A. Would the dollar?
   B. Would the European currencies fluctuate internally or together externally?
   C. More generally, would currency areas develop?
IV. Effect on the Role of the Dollar
   A. Would there be any change in its role as a transactions and intervention currency?
   B. Would there need to be a change in United States gold policy?
   C. If so, would there need to be a change in its role as a reserve currency?
   D. Should the United States receive some compensation in return for the minimization of potential adjustment caused by the roles of the dollar?
V. Effect on the Forward Exchange Market
   A. How much additional forward cover would be required?
   B. Would it be forthcoming? How? Would new institutions be required?
   C. What would be its cost?
   D. How would these results affect the volume of:
      1. trade

2. capital investment
3. liquid flows including the Eurodollar market.
VI. The Effect on International Cooperation
   A. Would the need for such cooperation change?
   B. Would the incentives for such cooperation change? (The answers to III should be considered.)
VII. Impact on the Need and Desire for International Liquidity
VIII. Transitional Questions
   A. Are discrete parity realignments a necessary precondition?
   B. Should the band be widened or the parity be allowed to slide by small steps?
   C. How will the decisions on Special Drawing Rights be affected? (Consider the answer to VII.)
IX. Rules of the Game
   A. Should a sliding parity be automatic or discretionary?
   B. Should the adoption of a sliding parity be coupled with the abolition of permission for large exchange-rate changes?
   C. Should intervention be permitted? If so, how should it be regulated?
X. Case Studies
XI. The Marsh Proposal (Fixed Reserves with Fixed or Flexible Exchange Rates)
XII. Comparison With Freely Flexible Exchange Rates
XIII. The Outlook for the Present Monetary System

• 3 •

On Terms, Concepts, Theories, and Strategies in the Discussion of Greater Flexibility of Exchange Rates

FRITZ MACHLUP

I AM KNOWN, or even perhaps notorious, for my fondness of semantic exercises. Some of my friends will probably wince at reading this lead sentence and will mutter under their breath, "There he goes again!" Fear not! I shall not unravel 57 varieties of meaning of flexibility, 15 of band, 14 of crawl, and 13 of peg. I shall try to do only the most necessary cleaning-up job preparatory for a discussion in which the participants will not want to waste time by misunderstanding one another as they use words in ambiguous ways.

Not that I shall attempt to dictate to anyone in which of the possible meanings he should use an ambiguous term. There should be freedom of speech, even freedom of vague and ambiguous speech. Still, it may help if we know where some of the semantic traps are hidden; for we can then be on guard and, if we *want* to be understood, we can steer clear of the most likely confusions.

Besides these objectives, my comments are intended to serve still other purposes. In some instances I shall propose distinctions that seem helpful in getting a sharper focus on the issues before us. Finally, I shall warn against the exaggerated claims that partisans sometimes make for the faultless working of a recommended system, new or old. The question is not of perfection but only of comparative troublesomeness.

PEGS AND PARITIES

Since a great deal will be said in our papers about pegs and parities, we ought to decide whether we understand these words to mean the same thing or different things.

Since John Williamson spoke about crawling pegs where James Meade spoke about sliding parities, one would be justified in regarding the two terms as synonymous. Yet, there are many currencies (more than 20) for which no par value (parity) has been established but whose exchange value in terms of the dollar has been "pegged" by the respective monetary authorities; and there are other currencies (about 15) for which the par value agreed with the International Monetary Fund has been disregarded, yet the dollar exchange rate has been "pegged" (though the peg was changed from time to time). Thus, we

This paper was published in *Banca Nazionale del Lavoro Quarterly Review*, No. 92 (March 1970).

had better accept the fact that in many situations the peg is not a parity and the parity is not the peg.

If we use the word peg to denote the intervention rate, that is, the exchange rate at which the monetary authorities of a country intervene in the market in order to keep the currency from falling or rising in the foreign-exchange market, then we should really speak of two pegs: a selling price and a buying price of the dollar. Where the band between the maximum selling price and the minimum buying price is narrow—say, 2 per cent, as stipulated in the Fund Agreement—it would perhaps be excessive pedantry to speak of the "two pegs" around the parity. But if the band is widened, it may be quite practical to speak of the two extreme official intervention rates as a pair of pegs.

We cannot legislate about the "correct" use of these words. In most instances we shall not be greatly mistaken if we understand pegs to be parities or close to parities, and parities to be maintained by means of pegs. But we ought to be on guard for exceptional situations in which pegs and parities are not the same. In what follows here I shall go slow on the word "peg" and speak mostly of parities. But I want it to be understood that these need not be par values agreed with the Fund, but may be average intervention rates fixed for longer or shorter periods.

For a certain class of countries a very particular system of adjusting the exchange rate has developed. In countries in which the rate of price inflation has been so fast that long delays in exchange-rate alignment would lead to intolerable misallocations of productive resources, frequent readjustments of exchange rates are strongly indicated. Some of these countries have no fixed parities (or have disregarded what was once announced as the "par value" of their currencies). They may, however, have official exchange rates, pegged temporarily and changed periodically, perhaps as often as once or twice a month. Such a change cannot be described as a glide (or crawl), because it is too big to qualify for these descriptions. On the other hand, the designation "jumping peg" is also out of place, since "jump" has the connotation of a sudden abrupt change after a long delay. Borrowing from the vocabulary employed to characterize the rate of price increase as creeping, trotting, and galloping price inflations, some commentators speak of the "trotting peg" as descriptive of the system that provides for fast movements of the official exchange rate for currencies in a process of trotting inflation.

The trotting peg will not concern us much in a discussion that is chiefly designed to deal with the currencies of countries with only creeping price inflations. These countries usually have valid official par values of their currencies and for these countries the choice is between jumping or gliding parities.

ALTERNATIVE EXCHANGE-RATE SYSTEMS

It will be helpful to have terminological consistency in talking about alternative exchange-rate systems. I propose that we distinguish systems with *unchangeable* parities, *abruptly adjustable* parities, *gradually adjustable* parities, and *no* parities. The phrase "fixed parities" ought to be avoided, because it covers both unchangeable and adjustable parities, and is, therefore, ambiguous. Alternative designations would be "jumping parities" for abruptly (or discretely) adjustable parities, and "gliding parities" for gradually adjustable ones. The category of no parities includes freely flexible (floating) exchange rates, but it includes also exchange rates influenced by unsystematic official interventions in the exchange market and by restrictions on certain types of transactions, so that the absence of official parities is not equivalent to "free flexibility."

Perhaps a comment on unchangeable parities is in order. Parities are unchangeable only under gold-coin standards where gold coins comprise a substantial part of the monetary circulation. Under the gold-bullion standard, where gold does not circulate as currency, but is bought and sold only by the monetary authorities, the official price of gold can be changed, and parities are no longer unchangeable. To be sure, there can be systems that prescribe, by means of unchangeable legal requirements, fixed ratios between the supply of money and the official gold holdings (with an unchangeable price of gold). Such orthodox gold-standard systems would be compatible with unchangeable exchange rates, but could endure only if the people in the countries concerned were willing to forget about stable rates of employment, economic growth, and several other national objectives. It is a waste of time to discuss this theoretical possibility. Whether we like it or not, it is not in the cards. This reduces the choices to three: jumping, gliding, or no parities.

RATE OF CRAWL AND WIDTH OF BAND

When is a change a *jump* and when is it a *glide?* Or, in more formal language, what is a *discrete* adjustment of the parity and what is a *gradual* one?

There is no historical precedent to guide our terminological decision. Economic theory suggests that we call changes in foreign-exchange rates *gradual* if the effects that confident expectations of such changes would have upon the foreign-exchange market could be offset by relatively modest differentials between the interest rates prevailing in the countries concerned. I propose to use 3 per cent per year and 1 per cent at a time as the watershed, and to call adjustments of exchange rates that exceed these limits discrete or abrupt. In a stricter sense, adjustment of a parity can be called gradual only if the upper limit of the rate of change is a

33

small fraction of 1 per cent per week or month. The most widely cited plan for a gliding parity proposes as an upper limit for adjustments $\frac{1}{26}$ of 1 per cent per week (which, if continued in the same direction, would accumulate to a little over 2 per cent a year). A recent variant would set the upper limit at $\frac{1}{10}$ of 1 per cent for any half-month (which could cumulate to a maximum change of about 2½ per cent per year).

Discrete changes in the parities of major currencies, under the Bretton Woods rules, have varied from the 5 per cent upvaluations of the German mark and the Dutch guilder in 1961 to the 38.7 per cent devaluation of the French franc in 1949. Most of the parity jumps came as weekend gambols, usually after months of persistent rumors, private speculations, and official disavowals.

Both with discrete and with gradual adjustments of the parity, the exchange rates may be allowed to deviate from parity to some extent. The band of permissible or permitted fluctuations may be wide or narrow. These adjectives call for specification. Since the Fund Agreement permits fluctuations of up to 1 per cent on either side of parity, that is, a band of 2 per cent of parity vis-a-vis the dollar, one might speak of a "wider" band whenever its total width exceeds 2 per cent. Since Switzerland, however, permits—on paper, though usually not in practice—fluctuations within a band of 3 per cent, it is more convenient to take this as the starting point for any "widening" of the band. A wider band will mean, therefore, one with a total width of more than 3 per cent. Most discussions of a wider band visualize spreads of 4, 5, 6, 8, or 10 per cent.

To define the band in terms of total width rather than in such phrases as "X per cent either side of parity" is preferable, because it would be possible to have asymmetrical distances from parity. Some monetary authorities may wish to allow the price of the dollar in their own exchange market to fall by 4 per cent, but to rise by only 2 per cent from parity. This would still be a band 6 per cent wide, but the parity would not be in its center.

On what kind of considerations would one favor a band with the parity off center, that is, a band with asymmetrical distances of the edges from the parity? Evidently such an arrangement would appeal only to a monetary authority that regards deviations of the exchange rate of its currency from parity more likely to be in one direction than in the other. German economic experts, for example, would probably not think that the market rates of the German mark will fall below parity so often and stay there for so long a time as they may rise and stay above parity. If then, because of comparative rates of demand inflation at home and abroad, the pressure of the free market is expected to be far more consistently in the direction of a strong posture of the German mark, there is sense in providing more leeway for the market value of the mark to rise than to fall.

If the differences in the rates of demand inflation persist for several years, a band around parity, however wide and however asymmetrical, would not provide flexibility for very long. The exchange rate of the German mark would reach the upper edge of the band and stay there, forcing the German monetary authorities to accept "imported inflation." The only escape would be a crawl, or glide, of the parity. With the differences in inflation rates always in the same direction, the glide would be in one direction only: upward.

The idea of a gliding parity has little appeal to bank and treasury officials in countries with consistently higher-than-average rates of inflation. They fear the downward glide of the parity might accelerate the price inflation and create a lasting inflationary bias in the policies of business and organized labor. If the system of the gliding parity is more readily acceptable in countries with strong aversion to price inflation than in countries unable to avoid higher speeds of creeping inflation, the one-way crawl may have better chances of realization than two-way variability of the parity. See the papers by William Fellner (Part IV) and Herbert Giersch (Part II).

If the parities of various currencies are expressed in terms of the dollar, a band of X per cent for fluctuations of the dollar-exchange rate of any currency implies that the exchange rates between any two other currencies can fluctuate by $2X$ per cent. If, for example, at some date the French franc were at the upper edge of the band vis-a-vis the dollar, and the Italian lira at the lower edge, and subsequently the franc were to fall to the lower edge and the lira to rise to the upper edge, each, therefore, moving across the entire band, the cross-rate between franc and lira would have changed by a percentage twice the width of the band for dollar-rate fluctuations. This large spread in permissible cross-rates makes some practitioners shudder when they hear proposals to widen the band for the dollar-rate to 10 per cent: it would mean 20 per cent for the exchange rates between any two currencies for which the 10 per cent band vis-a-vis the dollar is used.

GREATER FLEXIBILITY

"Greater" in the expression "greater flexibility" is intended to mean "more than exists at present," but "less than unlimited" flexibility. If variations of exchange rates are to be limited, this implies the need for interventions by the monetary authorities through buying or selling the chosen "intervention currency," usually the dollar, whenever its price threatens to rise above or fall below the chosen limits. These limits would be set by the upper and lower edges of the band around the parity or by the maximum allowable adjustment of the parity, or both. Some monetary authorities believe that it is expedient, or even necessary, for them to intervene in the exchange market even well within the limits.

Other authorities disagree, and both sides claim that their views (theories) are firmly based on practical experience. Without attempting here to argue one or the other side of the controversial question, I want to explain an expression used by economists: they speak of "managed flexibility" if the monetary authorities intervene in the market by buying or selling foreign exchange before the edges of the band or the limit to an allowed change of parity are reached.

A compromise regarding the scope of market interventions has been proposed in the form of a band within a band. The inner band, say, 3 per cent of parity, would be entirely unmanaged, a range for free-market forces to operate, without any official sales or purchases; the two surrounding rims or border-bands, each, say, $1\frac{1}{2}$ per cent wide, would be the ranges in which the monetary authorities could play in the market in order to meet their obligation to keep the market "orderly" (or to satisfy their feeling of importance, as the free-marketeers would put it). This would represent managed flexibility around a core of unmanaged flexibility.

Changes in parity would always be managed in the sense that only market interventions would assure that the change is of a particular magnitude, not more and not less. In a system that combines a wider band with a crawl of the parity, the move of the parity may be within the band around the previous parity, so that it would be possible for the actual exchange rate to remain unchanged despite the official adjustment of the parity. In such a case the authorities would not have to intervene at all, unless they wanted to for some reason, real or apparent. In any case, an adjustment of the parity, however small, would move the band of *permissible* exchange-rate fluctuations, even if the *actual* exchange rate, being well inside the band, were unchanged.

I have said that greater flexibility still meant limited flexibility and, therefore, implied a scope for official interventions in the exchange market through buying or selling foreign currency. The limits to the exchange-rate variations thus far discussed would be set by the width of the band, by the maximum crawl-rate of the parity, or both of these. A very different system of greater flexibility would not limit the variations of exchange rates but would, instead, limit the authority of monetary authorities to prevent variations of exchange rates through interventions in the market. This limitation of official buying or selling in the foreign-exchange market could take the form of setting limits to the changes in the monetary reserves held by the authorities. If the authorities have intervened by selling foreign currency and have thus prevented an excess demand for foreign exchange from reducing the exchange value of the domestic currency, their net reserves would have declined. A limit to the extent of permissible depletion of reserves would stop further official sales of foreign exchange. If the authorities have intervened by purchasing foreign currency and have thus prevented an excess supply of foreign exchange from raising the exchange value of the domestic currency, net reserves would have increased. A limit to the extent of permissible accumulation of reserves would stop further official purchases of foreign exchange.

A system of this sort was used for several years in Canada, and successfully so, according to the testimony of the most qualified analysts. The limits to permissible changes in official reserves were set by the monetary authorities themselves, not by any international agreement. With appropriate institutional provisions this kind of "limited invariability" of exchange rates might well work on an international scale. The papers by Donald B. Marsh (Parts IV and VI) are dedicated to the description of the *modus operandi* and to the advocacy of such a scheme. Robert Triffin has elsewhere given qualified endorsement to the idea of limiting official intervention in this fashion. The basic idea is relatively simple: since continuing large accumulations or decumulations of foreign reserves are indications of misaligned exchange rates (fundamental disequilibrium), countries should be committed to stop these accumulations or decumulations; as they stop intervening in the exchange market, exchange rates will be allowed to adjust themselves to the market forces. The scheme is properly regarded as one of "greater flexibility of exchange rates" in that it prevents the authorities from keeping exchange rates rigidly disaligned for too long a time.

TYPES OF GLIDING-PARITY SYSTEMS

Before our two conferences I used to distinguish two types of gliding-parity systems: one with discretionary adjustments, the other with formula-determined adjustments. The discussions at Bürgenstock and especially the paper by Professor Richard Cooper (Part IV) taught me that clearer exposition required four sets of distinctions: the changes in parities could be

(1) either prophylactic or therapeutic,
(2) either discretionary or formula-determined,
(3) either equilibrating or disequilibrating, and, finally,
(4) spontaneous, presumptive without sanctions for nonconformance, presumptive with sanctions for nonconformance, or mandatory.

A change in parity, or rather a sequence of small and continuous changes in parity, is prophylactic if it is intended to prevent imbalances of payments from arising or from worsening; it is therapeutic if it is designed to remove or reduce existing imbalances. When the German Council of Economic Experts proposed a few years ago that the German mark be upvalued by 2 per cent a year, this glide of the parity was meant to be prophylactic. For, as the Germans were planning to limit the rate of their price inflation to 2 per cent a year, but expected most of their important trading partners to inflate by at least 4 per cent a year, an unchanged exchange rate would produce a payments surplus with a consequent expansion of effective demand resulting in a higher rate of domestic price inflation than had been planned—a so-called "adjustment inflation." The proposal was not accepted and the German mark became badly undervalued. The upvaluation in October 1969 was primarily therapeutic.

A change in parity is discretionary if the decision is made on the basis of an *ad hoc* judgment by the authorities and not on the basis of a rule or formula adopted in advance. (A prophylactic change is always discretionary in that it involves a judgment of future developments, not a reliance on recorded data of the past. A therapeutic change may be discretionary or formula-determined.) A formula-determined change in parity is guided by a set of rules that tell which statistical data should be taken into account to indicate when, in what direction, and by how much the parity should be changed. The indicators most widely discussed for this purpose are the spot rates in the foreign-exchange market recorded during the preceding period (six months or more), the movements of forward-exchange rates, changes in net foreign reserves, changes in the basic balance of payments, and the trend in the current account. There are many strong reasons why formulas confined to these data may at certain times lead to very wrong results. More studies of past performance and of hypothetical cues given by various alternative formulas (rules of thumb) will probably improve the instruments of navigation in these still insufficiently explored waters. My hunch is that exchange-rate variations within a wider band will be better indicators than variations within the narrow band permitted in the past; they must be combined, of course, with data on official interventions, which may have concealed the effects of free-market forces, and possibly also with data on presumably temporary (or even reversible) movements of private capital funds.

The third set of distinctions, between equilibrating and disequilibrating changes of parity, may apply either to intentions or to actual effects. Some intentionally equilibrating changes may turn out to be disequilibrating in their actual effects. This can happen even in formula-determined adjustments, where the data used as indicators are unreliable, incomplete, or ill-chosen. It is easy to imagine a situation in which the adopted formula dictates a change in the wrong direction or to a wrong extent, or indeed a change when none is "indicated" in the actual circumstances. Unintentional disequilibration can, of course, occur also through discretionary changes in parity, where the insight or judgment of the authorities is faulty. All therapeutic changes are intended to be equilibrating; they attempt an adjustment of an existing disequilibrium. Prophylactic changes are likewise intended to be equilibrating, not with reference to an existing, but rather to an incipient disequilibrium, that is, to one that would emerge if the parity were not adjusted to an ongoing change in relative incomes and prices. Parity changes that are disequilibrating by intention could conceivably be the result of pressures by export industries and industries competing with imports. These changes would be in the nature of competitive devaluations, designed to create a payments surplus, to accumulate foreign reserves, to increase domestic employment, or to "export unemployment." Operational criteria for the distinction may be found in the balance sheets of the banking system, especially the central bank. A downward adjustment of the parity may be intended to adjust for a past or ongoing expansion of the portfolio of domestic assets acquired by the banks and, thus, to stop or avoid the resulting loss of foreign assets; on the other hand, it may be intended to produce an increase in foreign assets. In the former case, the change is equilibrating, an adjustment to an overexpansion of domestic credit; in the latter case, the change is disequilibrating, designed to engineer an expansion of domestic liquidity and effective demand by means of a more active foreign balance (more exports, fewer imports).

The fourth set of distinctions refers to the voluntary or involuntary character of parity adjustments, all of the intentionally equilibrating kind. (A formula-determined change may still be entirely voluntary if it is neither imposed nor strongly urged by foreign or international bodies.) We may distinguish four degrees of outside influence, ranging from 0 to 100 per cent. The parity adjustment is spontaneous if no foreign influence has been exerted in its favor. The adjustment is presumptive—this is Cooper's term—if, on the basis of previous agreements or understandings, this move can be expected as the appropriate reaction to the performance of certain indices and indicators. The presumption may be backed only by moral force, the adjustment being "the right thing to do," or it may be backed by certain sanctions imposed by other countries or international agencies in order to make nonconformance more unpleasant. Finally, the adjustment may be mandatory, perhaps not only in the sense that the country in question is firmly committed to it under international rules, but also that other countries or an international agency have ways and means to enforce the move, for example, by interventions in the foreign-exchange markets.[1]

---

[1] The international reserve pool (settlements account or conversion account) that I proposed elsewhere was to be empowered to adjust the exchange rates of currencies according to continuous and large accumulations or decumulations of the deposits that the countries in question hold in the pool. See Fritz Machlup, *Remaking the International Monetary System* (Baltimore, Md.: Johns Hopkins Press, 1968), pp. 117–118.

GREATER FLEXIBILITY OF EXCHANGE RATES

FLEXIBLE, STABLE, INVARIANT

Flexibility is often confused with instability. This is understandable since, if flexibility is the opposite of inflexibility or rigidity, it means that it permits variations, and wide variations represent instability. Two illegitimate steps are contained here: one, from permissible potential variations to actually occurring variations; the other, from variations to wide variations. Moreover, two ideas are missing: one, the distinction between variations around a point—oscillations—and trend-like variations in one direction, and, secondly, the indispensable reference to the time period involved—changes from day to day, year to year, or over several years.

Civil engineers know the difference between rigidity and flexibility of materials for use in the construction of high buildings exposed to winds of variable strength, and they must provide flexibility in order to avoid the eventual collapse of the structure. While such analogies may contribute to the comprehension of word meanings, they do not settle the question whether flexible or rigid exchange rates will be more stable in the long run. And this, after all, is one of the questions before us.

History tells us little about the relationship between flexibility and instability of exchange rates. Of course, many countries had very unstable exchange rates in periods when they had flexible rates, but in these periods fixed rates would not have worked at all. History provides examples of very stable flexible rates, and many examples of very unstable rates fixed and refixed over time. Certainly, in the long run, fixed rates need not be stable, and flexible rates need not be unstable. Confusion between flexibility and instability must not be tolerated.

This prohibition does not rule out speculation about the effects of greater flexibility in exchange rates upon the psychology, determination, and diplomacy of central bankers. Some hold that heavy losses of foreign reserves under inflexible exchange rates serve as effective warning signals to monetary authorities hard pressed by spendthrift governments and investment-minded businessmen, and that these signals are indispensable for monetary discipline. Others, however, hold that depreciations of the currency in the foreign-exchange market serve as even better warning signals, coming on sooner (if rates are flexible) and more conspicuously. Unfortunately, neither reading the record of the past nor analyzing views and attitudes expressed at present will solve the argument about the future comparative effectiveness of the two kinds of warning signals in inducing greater discipline in monetary and fiscal policy. The question, nevertheless, remains meaningful and relevant, even if we cannot answer it now.

A purely semantic question regarding flexibility can and should be cleared up here. Since a foreign-exchange rate necessarily involves two

INTRODUCTION

currencies, and since the fixing and pegging of a rate may be the concern of only one of the two countries involved while the other country perhaps does not care whether the rate is held invariant or not, it is logically permissible to say that the exchange rate is fixed from one country's point of view, but flexible from the other country's point of view. This other country, as, for example, the United States, neither intervenes nor holds the rate-pegging country to its interventions in the exchange market; the exchange rate could, therefore, vary as far as the United States is concerned. Not doing anything to keep the rate from varying, the United States may regard the rate as flexible even if it is in fact inflexible as a result of the pegging operations of the fixed-rate country.

This subjective interpretation of flexibility has probably more often confused than elucidated the issue. It is simpler to regard an exchange rate as flexible only if neither of the two countries in question undertakes to keep it invariant within narrow limits. Since the dollar is the most widely used intervention currency, one should understand, of course, that the decisions about greater flexibility are up to the countries other than the United States. It should also be understood that a system of greater flexibility does not imply universal flexibility; it means merely that countries are not discouraged from opting for greater flexibility of their dollar exchange rates. Perhaps only a few countries would find it advantageous to do so. Too many participants in the worldwide discussion of the issue seem to assume that a system of greater flexibility would *compel* their own countries to give up the exchange practices to which they have become accustomed. This is neither implied nor presumed. Countries would be free to fix or flex their exchange rates as they pleased.

OVERVALUATION, UNDERVALUATION

The reason why some countries may prefer greater flexibility of the exchange rate of their currency is the realization that a rate fixed at one time at an equilibrium level is unlikely to remain an equilibrium rate very long. All sorts of things happen to transform a correct exchange rate into an incorrect one, at which the balance of payments is chronically in surplus or in deficit, unless adjustment is engineered through inflating or deflating effective demand.

An exchange rate at which a country's basic balance of payments is chronically in surplus may be said to undervalue its currency; an exchange rate at which its basic balance of payments is chronically in deficit may be said to overvalue its currency. Undervaluation is most quickly corrected by means of upvaluation, overvaluation by means of devaluation; but an abrupt change of parity is unlikely to hit upon the correct rate. Moreover, since upvaluations and devaluations involve difficult political decisions, they are usually deferred for too long a time,

41

causing the basic disalignment and imbalance to worsen. Gliding adjustments of the parity are supposed to be easier, causing fewer political difficulties and smaller economic shocks, but this is not my concern at this juncture. The question to which I seek an answer is whether there are any clear criteria of undervaluation and overvaluation, apart from payments surpluses and deficits.

Let us immediately reject as useless the merely impressionistic contentions of so-called experts who give us their own intuitive judgments of the relative values of currencies. Next we must reject the naive valuations by tourists based on their experiences in shopping, dining, and lodging abroad and at home; the price comparisons of tourists are badly biased and have, in any case, very limited relevance for the balances of payments of large countries. Next in line for rejection are the price-index comparisons by economists who have misunderstood the purchasing-power-parity theory; they have not learned, or have forgotten, that the relative prices of internationally traded goods reflect the actual exchange rates, however disaligned, and that the relative prices of consumer goods, the cost of living, do not reflect the relative competitiveness of the countries' industries in foreign trade. Even very special indices, such as wholesale prices of domestic products, labor cost per unit of output, or unit cost of export articles, may tell little about changes in relative competitiveness. Indeed, even if all the price indices of all the countries in question had remained unchanged or had increased by an equal proportion, this would say nothing about the competitiveness of the industries that are most important in the trade of the nations.

The search for criteria is perhaps hopeless, since the concept of competitiveness is not adequate for our purpose as long as it is silent on the attainable sales volumes. At particular prices and exchange rates, a country may be able to "push out" a certain quantum of exports and "pull in" a certain quantum of imports, but its net export surplus may or may not be sufficient to finance the country's capital outflows and unilateral payments. A country's currency may at the same time be regarded as "undervalued," if the country needs no more than an even balance of trade, and "overvalued," if the country needs a surplus sufficiently large to meet payments due on its foreign debts or to finance its direct investments abroad. Any change in net financial transfers (capital balance and balance of unilateral payments) changes the equilibrium value of the currency and, therefore, transform a "correct" valuation into an over- or undervaluation.

Several respected theorists in international economics object to this formulation. They prefer to develop definitions under which over- and undervaluation of a country's currency, and under- and overcompetitiveness of its industry, are independent of the financial transfers made and received (or payable and receivable). If there is no agreement on the meanings of these terms, it may be best to forego their use. As a matter of fact, some of us tried hard in our discussions to avoid using any of the ambiguous expressions, but we did not always succeed. Questions came up: "Is the pound sterling still (or again) overvalued?", "Can the overvaluation of the French franc be remedied, at a tolerable social cost, through adjustment of effective demand?", "Would gradual upvaluations of the German mark suffice to take care of its present undervaluation?". In these and similar questions, the blacklisted expressions popped up and proved irrepressible. (The discussions took place before the franc and the mark were re-aligned.)

Believers in the definitiveness of the verdicts of the free market can point to rather simple criteria: Whenever the supply of foreign currencies is such that a country's monetary authorities have to buy them in order to prevent their prices from falling, these prices evidently overvalue the foreign currencies, for, at the given exchange rates, private demand is not sufficient to take all that is offered in the market. Whenever the demand for foreign currencies is such that a country's monetary authorities have to sell out of their foreign reserves in order to prevent their prices from rising, these prices evidently undervalue the foreign currencies, for, at the given exchange rates, supply from private sources is not sufficient to satisfy the private demand.

The verdict "disequilibrium" on the evidence that the monetary authorities have to buy or sell foreign currencies in order to keep the rates from falling or rising, and, thus, on the ground of official reserves increasing or decreasing, suggests the kind of evidence that would support a verdict of "equilibrium." The suggestion, however, is wrong. If the exchange rates stay at the announced level while the monetary authorities neither buy nor sell in the foreign-exchange market and their reserves, therefore, remain unchanged, this is not sufficient evidence that the exchange rates are equilibrium rates. For there are several auxiliary techniques that can be used to hide excess supply or excess demand in the market, for example, corrective measures that are taken in the hope that adjustment of effective demand as well as adjustment of exchange rates can be avoided. These corrective measures are ordinarily regarded as only temporary or stop-gap measures, either because they could not be continued very long, or because their continuance would be deemed undesirable. Examples are special intergovernmental transactions and arrangements among central banks; tax incentives or disincentives affecting private capital movements; regulations requiring discrimination in interest rates payable on foreign and domestic accounts; swap agreements (repurchase agreements) between central banks and commercial banks, shifting foreign currencies from official to private holdings and back; various other devices to attract or repel the inflow of funds, or to encourage or discourage outflows; restrictions or prohibitions of capital exports; restrictions and controls of imports of goods and services.

In resorting to measures of this sort, a government implicitly recognizes that the official exchange rate overvalues or undervalues its currency. For several years I have characterized some of the restrictive measures taken by the United States as "concealed partial devaluations" of the dollar. German government officials have spoken of the border-tax arrangements enacted at the end of 1968 as *Ersatzaufwertung* (substitute upvaluation) of the German mark. Still, the spot rates in the foreign-exchange market remain unchanged and accretions or losses of foreign reserves are avoided or reduced below the volume that would correspond to the extent of the overvaluation or undervaluation.

If then the recorded changes in official foreign reserves do not—as long as corrective measures, restrictions, and controls are employed to affect supply and demand in the foreign-exchange market—fully reflect existing over- or undervaluations of the currency in question, what statistical adjustments can be made to get a more reliable picture of the situation?

For a country with an undervalued currency one begins, of course, with the reported increase in official net reserves (minus any new allocations of unearned reserves such as Special Drawing Rights), but has to add the following items: any increase in liquid foreign balances held by commercial banks under swap arrangements with the central bank; all special intergovernmental transactions that made use of official reserves (such as prepayments of foreign loans); outflows of private capital induced by special incentives and inflows averted by special disincentives; imports of goods and services induced by special tax or tariff abatements and exports prevented by special tax levies. (The last items can only be estimated, but such estimates should periodically be furnished by the governments appraising the assumed effectiveness of their balance-of-payments measures.)

For a country with an overvalued currency, one has to add to the decrease in official net reserves any new allocations of unearned reserves; any decrease in liquid foreign balances held by commercial banks under swap arrangements with the central bank; all special intergovernmental transactions that augmented official reserves; private capital inflows induced by special incentives and outflows averted by special disincentives; outflows of capital prevented by prohibitions and controls; exports of goods and services induced by special tax incentives or other forms of subsidies, and imports prevented by special taxes, tariff increases or surcharges, quota restrictions, or foreign-exchange controls. (Again, several of these items would be estimates, but a requirement for governments to furnish estimates of the effectiveness of their balance-of-payments measures would be very wholesome: if the estimates were low, the restrictive measures would obviously not be justified; if they were high, however, the degree of overvaluation of the currency would be made a matter of record and the fundamental disequilibrium calling for exchange-rate adjustment would become manifest.)

This is still not all. If one recognizes that the balance of payments can be affected by temporary (or even reversible) changes, one will attempt to separate ephemeral items from recurring ones and adjust the balance of official sales and purchases of foreign exchange by the net balance of presumably nonrecurring transactions. The verdict of over- or undervaluation of particular currencies will then depend on the experts' judgments as to which items and what amounts can be expected to continue and, thus, to make up the long-run supply and demand in the foreign-exchange market. Of course, such judgments have to be supported by reasoned argument.

The comments on the problem of sizing up the over- or undervaluation of a currency should be relevant for considerations of any kind of exchange-rate adjustment, discrete or gliding, discretionary or formula-determined. However, if so much estimating, guessing, and judging goes into some of the variables employed, the distinction between discretion and formula becomes rather questionable.

THE DILEMMA OF ADVOCACY: HARD-SELL OR MODESTY

The advocates of greater flexibility of exchange rates are faced with a dilemma. If they want to "sell" their plans, they must present them with enthusiasm and describe in glowing terms how well they would work; at the same time they may have to make compromises and be satisfied with stripped-down versions of greater flexibility so little different from the inflexible system of today that they cannot achieve what is promised. On the other hand, if the advocates refrain from making exaggerated claims, if they promise neither perfection nor solution of all pressing problems and, moreover, if they insist on sufficient flexibility to have it contribute decisively to real adjustment in cases of hitherto chronic deficits and surpluses in the balances of payments, then they may not be able to win acceptance for their plans.

Believers in price flexibility thus have a difficult choice to make. Either they encourage the adoption of an insufficiently flexible system, which will consequently disappoint their clients and compromise the theory of flexible exchange rates, or, if they are unwilling to make exaggerated claims for their system and to make concessions, they will be unable to get their ideas across. It takes no courage to choose the second alternative: the uncompromising and, therefore, unsuccessful advocate will always be able to take pride in his fidelity to principles; he will not be blamed for having promised more than could have been delivered; and he can at every new crisis tell the world how short-sighted the authorities had been in rejecting his advice. To choose the first alternative is to take several calculated risks, for only with a good deal of luck will the system with less inflexible, but still insufficiently flexible, exchange rates avert some of the crises that would have occurred under the system of "fixed" (abruptly adjustable) rates; regarding any crisis that is averted, it will be impossible to prove that there would have been a crisis had exchange rates been even less flexible; and regarding any crisis that is not averted, it will be impossible to convince the critics that the crisis is the consequence of too little flexibility and not of too much.

Assume, to illustrate the point, that the men in charge of international monetary arrangements are willing to accept a band of a total width of 4 per cent with no glide of parity. What are the chances for such a system of "greater flexibility" to work? Since the effects of such small variations in exchange rates upon the flow of goods and services (real adjustment) are probably not very large and only some effects upon capital flows (financial correctives) can be expected, the slightly widened band would be only a minor improvement. It would be ineffective in preventing progressive disalignments that result from a consistent divergence in the rates of price inflation in different countries. Thus, while a few difficulties arising from minor disturbances might be mitigated or avoided, the problem of fundamental disequilibrium unadjusted for many years would remain. When the inevitable crisis of confidence arrived, some "authorities" would no doubt blame the crisis on the departure from the good old system of the narrow band.

Is this risk worth taking? The advantages of a band only slightly widened are probably too small relative to the risk of having the "experiment" wrongly interpreted. What degree of flexibility should the believer in greater flexibility regard as the minimum acceptable? To decide how flexible he ought to be in accepting a compromise, he might consider the relative probabilities of disequilibrating changes to be large or small, continuing or reversible, reinforced or offset by policy measures.

It must be taken for granted that there will always be disequilibrating changes. To mention the most likely ones, there will be discrepancies between national rates of demand inflation as well as price inflation;[2] there will also be different rates of growth, with different income elasticities of demand for imports and with different biases toward import-competing, export-oriented, and foreign-trade-indifferent industries; in addition, there will be shifts in demand, in labor supply, and several other things affecting the flow of goods and services at given exchange rates; and, last not least, there will be changes in the international flow of capi-

---

[2] I stress the distinction because demand inflation may be much more effective in causing deficits in the balance of payments than price inflation, which in fact is mitigated by the deterioration of the balance of trade. In open economies prices need not rise as the excess demand spills over into other countries.

tal. All these changes can be countered by monetary and fiscal policies adjusting aggregate demand. However, adjustment through absolute deflation of effective demand in deficit countries is practically impossible for social and political reasons, and adjustment through price inflation in surplus countries is not very popular either. The question is now whether in most instances the effects of the disequilibrating changes can be effectively countered by alterations in exchange rates within the range of flexibility afforded by the band or crawl conceded by the monetary authorities. If the bulk of the rate adjustments that would be required by the disequilibrating changes can with ease be accommodated by the compromise arrangement, the system will work almost as well as if it allowed even greater flexibility. If, however, most of the required rate adjustments would be too big to be accommodated by the permitted flexibility, there will be troubles similar to those arising at inflexible (abruptly adjustable) rates. The troubles under more flexible rates may be just a little less severe, because of the greater risk for speculators and the modicum of adjustment achieved in the more elastic fringes of the current account.

The relative importance of wider band or gliding parity depends on which type of disequilibrating change will be dominating. If we believe that discrepancies in the rates of demand inflation will be the most persistent causes of imbalance and that the inequality in the tempo of inflation will be consistent—say, that there will be consistently less inflation in Germany than in France—then a gliding parity would be more important than a much wider band. If we believe, on the other hand, the disequilibrating changes will take turns in pushing particular economies first one way and then another, a wide band would be the thing to have.

Judging from the experience of the past few years, one may say that a realist should vote for a glide of parity with a wider band, that is, a gliding widened band. And, to be more specific, he should vote for a glide of about $1/26$ of 1 per cent a week, which would add up to some 2 per cent a year, and for a band of a total width of no less than 5 per cent of parity. In explaining his vote, he should make clear that even this degree of flexibility cannot take care of all eventualities. Revolutionary wage boosts, ratified by a policy of demand expansion, cannot be fully countered by exchange-rate variations within the voted limits, unless they are followed by a wage stop at home and demand expansions abroad. Likewise, it may not be possible by means of exchange-rate adjustments of the specified extent to equilibrate the foreign-exchange markets in the case of sudden large shifts in international capital movements.

· 4 ·

Currency Parities in the Second Decade of Convertibility

ROBERT V. ROOSA

As THE international monetary system enters the second decade of convertibility, new questions arise. In the earlier stages of the Bretton Woods system, as country after country moved toward resumption of the unrestricted use of its currency for making current account payments, the overriding question was where to establish the parity for each currency. Today, the questions are when and how those established parities should be charged.

That transition should come as no surprise. The dynamic changes around the world that have flourished in the monetary environment of the past decade have necessarily brought a scattering out among nations —in the pace and composition of their production, as well as in the pattern of their prices and the potentials of their productivity. In time, since all countries have not advanced in unison on all fronts, the exchange-rate relationships that were about right at the beginning will eventually no longer fit.

Initially, and quite understandably, there was a bias throughout the first decade of convertibility toward holding the established exchange rates. This was the way to provide a settled framework, within which the markets of each advancing nation could evolve a viable pattern of payments to and from the changing world outside. And indeed, there is much to be said for that kind of settled framework at any given point in time. But, with the passage of time, revisions must in some way be brought about. It was originally helpful, in edging toward orderly payments relationships after the resumption of convertibility, to encourage a presumption that exchange rates, once established, should be held. It may now be equally helpful, as convertibility moves into its next phase, to encourage a presumption that revaluations or devaluations should, from time to time, occur.

The position of the United States in all of this is still unique. Because most other currencies establish their own parities in terms of the dollar as the center currency, this country's exchange rate will inescapably be the composite result of the rates set by those other countries in terms of dollars. But for those countries and for the International Monetary Fund, as the fountainhead of the system, and, indeed, for the United

Substantial parts of this paper appeared in the *Nihon Keizai Shimbun* (Tokyo), June 14–15, 1969.

States, as a very interested bystander, the issue is how best to accomplish necessary exchange-rate changes. Certainly the ineptitude that often characterizes, and the aura of self-sacrifice or of defeat that customarily surrounds, a revaluation or devaluation today cannot continue if a system of established (though changeable) parities is to survive.

To be sure, agreeing upon the criteria for determining where a rate should be presents an even greater challenge than agreeing upon how a change to a new rate should be brought about. Approximations through a computation of "purchasing power parity," for example, are becoming less and less relevant in determining an appropriate rate, partly because an increasing proportion of the total payments of most countries consists of movements of capital, and a shrinking proportion consists of flows of goods. The challenge of defining criteria for locating the suitable rate will not be considered in these comments, however. The questions of how and when to change parities present a sufficiently formidable undertaking for the present.

Can Exchange Rate Determination Be Left to the Market?

One introductory point does have to be made: that the question of changing exchange-rate parities cannot be sidestepped by airily leaving all of that to the market, through reliance upon a system of full and free flexibility for all rates. Such an approach implies an unworldly detachment on the part of governments, and monetary authorities, from forces they are most reluctant to leave out of control. Having set the boundaries, governments can, to be sure, let the day-to-day determination of actual trading rates be determined by the market; indeed, market pressures upward or downward on the current rate can be a useful indication of further actions to be taken, domestically or internationally, by any country. But to leave the entire process of exchange-rate determination to the forces of the market would seem to suffer from the same kind of circularity that made the old "needs of trade" doctrine a mischievous guide to the determination of the money supply within nations.

Perhaps that doctrine deserves a brief digression, for it was regarded, off and on for more than a century, as the answer not only to the obvious need for some control over the creation of money within each country, but also to the obvious desirability of keeping that control out of the hands of fallible men. Its proponents thought there was a fortuitous organic relationship between the borrowing "needs of trade" and the appropriate supply of money, a relationship that could make the creation of money dependent upon natural causes, with the total money supply determined by the aggregate flow of goods through the processes of production and distribution. In actual practice, this neat pattern never appeared; no naturally determined, stable internal exchange rate between money and goods has ever been found. Ultimately the world had

INTRODUCTION

to accept Walter Bagehot's dictum that "money does not manage itself," and then set about finding satisfactory ways to determine the money supply independently, accounting, of course, for the flows of goods as one important factor in the considerations.

Whatever the pitfalls of managed money, they were found to be fewer than the hazards of relying upon the market to perform for the economy as a totality the kind of role that a market may quite rightly be expected to fulfill for the individual parts of the economy. That is, market processes that are reliably capable of allocating flows among sectors of the economy, once the approximate magnitude of the total supply of money has been determined, cannot also be relied upon to determine what that supply of money itself should be. Disagreement continues, of course, over whether the money supply of any country should be varied at the discretion of the central bank or in accordance with an objective formula. And market processes do play a role in working out the final calibration of the actual money supply at any given moment, within the framework established by the independent action of the central bank. There is no longer any disagreement, however, that reliance on the needs of trade, the "forces of the market," to set the appropriate level of the money supply will inevitably create a vicious circle of disruptive cumulative force, alternately generating inflation and deflation.

An analogous temptation to rely upon a natural market process has, however, dominated much of the academic writing on foreign exchange rates. Yet to many practitioners this effort seems to suffer from the same kind of problem of circularity that appeared in earlier efforts to transpose market processes from the parts to the whole, domestically.

There is no doubt that when a nation's money supply is varied according to changes in the aggregate volume of credit required for the array of separate transactions included in its flow of production and trade, the result is unacceptable fluctuations in the general level of prices, leading to disruptive reactions upon the underlying transactions themselves. Yet may it not be equally likely that, when the external price (exchange rate) of a nation's currency is varied according to the total flow of transactions across its borders, the result may similarly be an unacceptable variation in the supply of funds available for external payments, leading to disruptive reactions upon the underlying transactions crossing its borders? Surely the exchange rate must stand still long enough to help determine an orderly and sustainable pattern of flows, instead of having to respond to every random fluctuation in the aggregate of flows—not only on trade but also on capital account—that happens to be taking place.

An independently determined quantity of money plays a part in stimulating or limiting the aggregate of domestic activity in order to achieve viable balance between money flows and real flows within a domestic

51

economy; an independently determined exchange rate should, it would seem, have a similar role in stimulating or limiting inpayments or outpayments to help achieve a viable balance between the aggregate of everything flowing out and everything flowing in, for a dynamic economy in a dynamic world. Yet at any point in time, the money supply and the exchange rate should be given, so that the significant adjustment will occur in real activity. Adjustment can hardly be expected, in any simple or unique way, to run in the opposite direction, that is, from activity to the money supply or from activity to the exchange rate. Indeed, the same logic that calls for independent determination of a nation's money supply would seem to call for independent determination of its exchange rate. At best, both might be determined as joint products of a common independent approach.

Without pursuing this digression further, perhaps enough has been said to justify a presumption, at least, that exchange rate parities, and the band for market fluctuations around those parities, will have to be established through some kind of man-made procedures. This presumption should also imply that there is merit in trying to achieve agreement among nations, implicitly or explicitly, on the most suitable methods for bringing about a change in parities. For a change will be needed, in a dynamic world, whenever sustained experience has shown that viability in any country's economic relations with the outside world is not being attained by changes in activity alone, that is that a country's foreign exchange reserves are either persistently rising or persistently falling, by substantial amounts.

The Implications of Recent Rigidity

The dilemma of how and when to change led to widespread disruption in the exchange markets and payments flows before the British devaluation, and some others related to it, in November 1967. The same dilemma was at work in November 1968, when a debacle of confrontation occurred at Bonn among governments, and between two officials of one government, concerning the possibility of a change in parity for the German mark and the French franc. And that dilemma was revived once again, in May 1969, with reference mainly to those same two currencies. By successive approximation, if not by any higher art, some observers thought they had discerned at that time a roughly appropriate pattern of change, centering on an upward revaluation of the German mark, close to the parity of the Dutch guilder, with the French franc adjusting downward to perhaps two-thirds of that higher German mark parity.

In the aftermath of General de Gaulle's resignation on May 6, 1969, an almost universal hope for prompt assertion of positive new leadership

INTRODUCTION

within the Common Market turned many eyes toward Germany. By upvaluing an exchange parity that was distorting payments flows from inside and outside the Common Market, Germany could signal its grasp of the responsibilities and opportunities of the need for constructive leadership. No such reassurance was provided, however; indeed, quite the contrary occurred. A domestic, political Donnybrook produced, on May 14, the remarkable *immer und ewig* commitment to make the existing German mark parity remain "always and eternal." Yet within the seven preceding business days, following public remarks by one German Minister intimating the possibility of change, some $4–$5 billion reportedly had flowed into Germany's relatively sterile reserves, bringing them virtually equal for a time to the reserves of the United States, whose dollar supports so much of the entire world's monetary transactions.

Near the end of September, as national elections approached, and the two leading political parties contested over the exchange rate parity, market uncertainty became even greater, and funds abundantly flowed into Germany. After severely limiting official foreign exchange trading on the two business days before the election, the German authorities decided, with the acquiescence of the International Monetary Fund, to reopen markets on the next business day after the election on new terms. While reserving the option to intervene at any time, the Bundesbank formally but temporarily ceased to offer German marks at the established margin over parity.

As of this writing (October 1969), the new government has not been installed, but the German mark has edged upward under the hovering guidance of the Bundesbank to roughly 7 per cent over the old parity. For several days, funds have been moving out of Germany on a substantial scale, anticipating the eventual re-establishment of a stated parity at around this level, once a new government becomes operational near the end of October.

Although this specific experiment probably is not the important precedent for greater rate flexibility that many observers have suggested, the long ordeal preceding action nonetheless has provided a further graphic example of the kind of strains that develop, as they did before the earlier French devaluation, when a political stalemate thwarts an economically necessary adjustment of exchange rates.

It is at least partly with the objective of dissolving political stalemates of this kind in the future that such proposals as those for a wider band, or a moving peg, or a crawling band have been advanced with increasing interest over recent months. They strike at the heart of the recent dilemma, namely, the inability of many governments to make timely changes in exchange rates, up or down, as a matter-of-fact recognition of fundamentally changed conditions in their external economic relations.

GREATER FLEXIBILITY OF EXCHANGE RATES

Current Proposals for Lessening Rigidity

The "wider band" proposal, if accepted by the Fund membership, would permit exchange rates in the trading market to move up or down by perhaps 2 per cent on either side of parity, or possibly as much as 5 per cent on either side. The "moving peg" proposal would provide for regular revision of each exchange rate (as against the U.S. dollar) by some specified percentage, possibly 1 or 2, each year in accordance with an agreed formula. The "crawling band" proposal, more felicitously called the "dynamic peg," would combine both of the others, by providing that each currency parity be revised upward or downward as a moving average of the actual rates that have occurred within the wider band.

The prerequisites for the satisfactory operation of any or all of these three new approaches would seem to be general agreement and general adherence by most Article VIII (convertible currency) members of the IMF. If leading countries should still reserve the right to make larger changes on their own initiative, then, inescapably, many of the same doubts and the same dilemmas that have harassed the foreign-exchange markets of the world over recent months would continue. But perhaps not all; for particularly because the two currencies that were most seriously out of alignment were readjusted in August and October 1969, the way may be eased for use of one or another of these proposed approaches to make possible a more gradual adaptation to new distorting influences in the future as they begin to occur. An agreed approach contemplating sudden, and possibly more frequent, changes in parities might in itself moderate the prevailing rigidity in governmental attitudes toward either revaluation or devaluation, an end well worth achieving if the cost is not too high.

What of the costs? Having learned much from the Oyster Bay–Bürgenstock meetings, I now think, in connection with the wider band, that the costs may be great but perhaps not prohibitive, particularly if the band were to be asymmetrical. That is, the band might be higher above parity than below (perhaps 3 per cent above and 1 per cent below), reflecting the difference in the resistance experienced by governments in facing appreciation, as against depreciation, of exchange rates. The moving peg taken alone, however, might simply introduce a new kind of rigidity, with the form of that rigidity depending on the formula chosen.

The crawling band—although it seems by far the best among the variants of rate adjustment, since it would merely reflect what had happened, or been allowed to happen, in practice on average within the wider bands—would also involve a risk of stimulating even greater unrest over parity changes. For a run might be precipitated out of any currency whenever movement within the allowable scope of current variation projected a plausibly predictable pattern of future decline in the parity. Conversely, and perhaps even more disruptively, a projection of appreciation might cause a run into a particular currency, not merely for reasons of financial "speculation" (that aspect has been overdrawn in much recent comment) but because of the prudent desire on the part of all businesses to minimize costs.

Forward markets could, as they do now, blunt some of the impact of a run for some currencies. But the cost to many individual enterprises of their side of a forward hedge, that is, the discount at which they could sell the future foreign currency proceeds of exports, for example, to acquire their own currency, would, as the quotations soar during a run, become almost prohibitive. At the least, the risks of a serious distortion of trade patterns, if not an actual diminution of potential trade, would seem to be considerably greater than they are today.

Some element of this kind of cumulative overreaction will be present under any arrangements, of course, whenever change in a parity begins to appear likely. Yet changes must, as already indicated, be made, and, hopefully, they will be made more often and by smaller amounts. It is clearly worthwhile to study intensively, from all sides, these various proposals for systematizing change. When such studies have been completed by men experienced in market operations, as well as by academic observers—a process toward which the Oyster Bay–Bürgenstock meetings should contribute materially—the financial officials of various countries and the International Monetary Fund, and ultimately the governments concerned, will have to make some critical decisions, choosing either among these new approaches or for a refurbishing of the existing *ad hoc* approach.

Despite all that has been done to cushion or contain temporary flows of funds among nations, and despite the major contribution toward strengthening the world's reserves that is soon to be provided by the Special Drawing Rights in the International Monetary Fund, something must also be added to the procedures for bringing about needed changes in exchange rates. As the first objective of any new arrangements or understandings, change, when it is justified by persisting shifts in economic relationships, must be made more respectable, less dramatic, and thus politically more tolerable. To be sure, there is nothing in the design of the present system, including all the Articles and Regulations of the International Monetary Fund, to prevent any desirable changes in the parities themselves from being made now, *ad hoc,* from time to time. What is lacking is the readiness and will on the part of governments. Central banks, as might be expected of experts closely involved, are generally quite ready for change, and alert to the need.

It is the intransigence of governments to take the action the present system calls for that gives rise to the agitation for new techniques.

Though none are without costs and shortcomings, the widespread discussion of them will serve a useful purpose if it impels the members of the IMF to face the need for a choice. For, in my view, if the system is not to suffer incessantly from massive and disruptive currency runs and reserve shifts, into some currencies at times, out of some currencies at others, the governments of the leading countries must soon choose among one or more of the new approaches, including the alternative that is often passed over in the desire to find something more strikingly new: that of making *ad hoc* changes more readily, within an agreed framework of consultation.

My own judgment is that the approach likely to come closest to realizing the purposes common to the band and peg proposals—that of assuring limited flexibility within a politically tolerable framework—will also be the one that involves the least abrasive adaptation of present central banking practices and arrangements, including the IMF provisions themselves. To illustrate that judgment, I have prepared a brief paper for Part IV of this volume. While recognizing that the responsibility for needed action will have to rest on sovereign governments, acting within the form and spirit of the IMF Articles to which they all subscribe, I think there can also be a place for the main conclusions that seemed to me to derive from the Bürgenstock meetings:

> that the sense of opprobrium that has been associated with parity changes in the past should be dispelled;
>
> that an atmosphere should be created in which smaller, more frequent, parity changes would be considered the norm;
>
> that central banks should not have to defend, nor should international firms have to speculate upon, parities that each knows will have to be changed in time by a sizeable amount;
>
> that the present bias toward excessive devaluation and inadequate revaluation of currencies should be moderated; and
>
> that drastic upheavals should, if at all possible, be avoided in the intricate network of markets, contracts, understandings, and confidence that form the basis for flourishing international trade, investment, and production.

• 5 •

Comments on Mr. Roosa's Paper

GEORGE N. HALM

MR. ROOSA's rejection of "full and free flexibility" of foreign-exchange rates rests on an interesting new argument. A floating rate of exchange suffers, according to Mr. Roosa, "from the same kind of circularity that made the old 'needs-of-trade' doctrine a mischievous guide to the determination of the money supply within nations."

I confess that I cannot see any similarity between the defunct commercial-loan theory and the argument for floating exchange rates, short of the claim in both cases that a given problem would be solved automatically.

The "needs-of-trade" theory said that the discounting of prime commercial paper would automatically adjust the supply of money to the volume of trade and thereby maintain stable commodity prices. The most important error in this theory was, of course, that the demand for credit is not independent of the rate of interest and that, if the discount rate has the power to influence the amount of borrowing, the supply of money could not be the passive and neutral product of the volume of trade.

The "needs-of-trade" theory was intimately connected with the gold-flow mechanism. The discount rate was more or less automatically determined by the international flow of gold. This fact ruined the notion that the supply of money was automatically following the needs of trade. However, central bankers were furnished with a convenient device for setting "correct" discount rates without being forced to think about domestic monetary policy. Had they not enjoyed the benefit of the gold-flow mechanism, the whole fiction of the "needs-of-trade" would have instantly collapsed.

The correctness of this interpretation is born out by Governor Strong's statement: [1]

> Until we get back to the automatic flow of gold which affects bank reserves and brings into play the automatic reactions from loss of reserves, I do not believe we are going to have all the satisfaction from the Federal Reserve System that we will have after that time comes.... I have great confidence that when the time comes to conduct these things as they were in former years, a lot of the need

[1] Quoted by J. M. Keynes, *A Treatise on Money* (New York: Harcourt, Brace & Co., 1930), Vol. 2, p. 305.

for the type of management which has to be applied in the present situation will be eliminated. We won't have to depend so much on judgment, and we can rely more upon the play of natural forces and their reaction on prices.

Mr. Roosa is correct, of course, when he rejects the "needs-of-trade" theory and concludes that the market cannot be relied upon to decide what the supply of money should be and that, therefore, money will always have to be managed money. However, it is strange that Mr. Roosa concludes from this statement that the advocates of floating exchange rates are also wrong when they want to let market forces determine the exchange rates. He argues as follows. Just as wrong manipulation of the domestic money supply leads to fluctuations of price levels, so will fluctuations of exchange rates lead to unacceptable variations in the supply of funds available for external payments. "Surely the exchange rates must stand still long enough to help determine an orderly and sustainable pattern of flows, instead of having to respond to every random fluctuation in the aggregate of flows—not only on trade but also on capital account—that happens to be taking place."

This statement seems to rule out any widening of the band or any parity change since both trade and capital flows originate every day. There is never a notch where the knife of parity change could cut without hurting somebody. I also wonder why the foreign-exchange market should be so different from other markets, where prices, too, are exposed to all kinds of influences without fluctuating erratically. The whole concept of our market economy would become ludicrous if this conception of price behavior would have to be applied generally.

Mr. Roosa compares "an independently determined quantity of money" and its beneficial effects on the national economy with "an independently determined exchange rate," which would play a similarly beneficial role internationally; and he comes to the conclusion that "the same logic that calls for independent determination of a nation's money supply would seem to call for independent determination of its exchange rate" and that "at best, both might be determined as joint products of a common independent approach."

Mr. Roosa compares items that cannot be compared. The national supply of money is an item that must be managed somehow because the "needs-of-trade" theory is wrong; the exchange rate is a price and the presumption is that, as a price, it should not be fixed. This is particularly true when we are realistic and assume that the money supply in different nations is not the result of a common approach. If there is inadequate coordination of national monetary policies, and the exchange rates are independently fixed and thereby prevented from adjusting themselves to diverging national price trends, we are exposed to all the difficulties we have experienced since the reintroduction of currency convertibility.

If we insist on fixing the exchange rates and maintaining currency convertibility, then it makes sense to subject the domestic money supply to external influences as the "needs-of-trade" theorists were unwittingly willing to do. Today, however, this is politically out of the question and likely to end in quantitative restrictions.

· 6 ·

The United States and Greater Flexibility of Exchange Rates

C. FRED BERGSTEN

THE United States is by far the most important single country in the international monetary system, and the dollar is the key currency of the system. It is difficult to imagine any significant change in the system that is unacceptable to the United States. Any proposals for change, such as those for increasing the flexibility of exchange rates, must, thus, be tested for their effect on the United States alone, as well as for their broader effects on the system as a whole.

This paper will attempt to assess those effects. It will avoid repeating the general analyses of greater flexibility of exchange rates developed elsewhere in this volume, except where necessary to clarify a particular point regarding the United States and the role of the dollar. It will refer throughout to "greater flexibility of exchange rates" without citing specific schemes, lumping together the crawling peg and the wider band except where explicitly differentiating between them.

Two major considerations are often cited as militating against any possible interest in greater flexibility on the part of the United States.

The first relates to adjustment and runs as follows. Removal of the present presumption against exchange-rate changes would generate greater movements of exchange rates. This would produce more depreciation than appreciation because of the greater pressures on deficit than on surplus countries, because of the general reluctance of countries to lose reserves or risk deterioration of their competitive positions, and because it would lead to a relaxation of the "discipline" of fixed rates. These exchange-rate movements would take place against the dollar, because of its role as the pivot currency of the system. The dollar would, thus, become increasingly overvalued and the competitive position of the United States would steadily deteriorate.

The second relates to confidence and liquidity. The dollar is now widely held as a reserve currency and an intervention currency by foreign monetary authorities, and as a transactions currency by private foreigners. One important reason for its attractiveness is the widespread

---

The research underlying this paper was carried out while the author was a Visiting Fellow at the Council on Foreign Relations, for whose support he expresses deep gratitude. The views expressed herein are wholly personal and in no way represent the official views of the Government of the United States.

perception of the stability of its price in terms of other currencies. (Its price stability in terms of gold is also important for some monetary authorities.) Increasing flexibility of exchange rates would destroy this stability and, hence, jeopardize both future increases in foreign dollar holdings and the huge volume of outstanding dollar assets. Introduction of such flexibility could, thus, preempt an important source of financing for any future balance of payments deficits of the United States and generate immediate demands for conversion of outstanding dollars into American reserve assets, neither of which would appeal to the United States.

There are several immediate answers to these propositions. In terms of stability alone, the dollar—as the pivot currency—would be able to fluctuate only half as much vis-a-vis any single currency as would any other currency. It would remain as stable as gold and SDRs because both would retain a fixed relationship to the dollar under the probable techniques for implementing greater flexibility described below. And "discipline" would probably decline more in other countries than in the United States, in view of the relatively small effect of the American international financial position on its overall economy, so that the depreciation of other currencies might simply offset their increased rates of inflation and leave the dollar, even more clearly than today, as the leading candidate for stability over the long run.

More importantly, the two considerations cited contradict each other. If American adjustment is prejudiced by depreciations against the dollar greater than would be called for by relative price changes, the resulting appreciation of the dollar with regard to a weighted average of all other foreign currencies could only result from foreign willingness, or even desire, to increase their dollar holdings. In turn, this appreciation—or even a widespread perception that such appreciation was likely—would increase the attractiveness of the dollar as a financial asset. It would, thus, enhance the likelihood that dollar accruals by foreign nations would provide financing for any American payments deficits prompted by the appreciation of the dollar.

Conversely, any actual or expected net depreciation of the dollar beyond what would be called for by relative price changes—which might stem from foreign distaste for dollars and, in turn, discourage foreign holdings—would, of course, contribute to an improved competitive position for the United States and, hence, would probably lead to an improvement in its balance of payments. The United States would, thus, need less balance-of-payments financing and, particularly if pushed into surplus, could readily liquidate outstanding dollar holdings.

The United States would, thus, benefit from either the adjustment or the confidence-liquidity effects of greater exchange-rate flexibility. The more it would benefit from one, however, the less it would benefit from the other. And the United States would certainly prefer greater adjustment to further financing, in view of their relative effects on the long-term stability of the system. One basic issue throughout this paper will be the net effect on the United States of the trade-off between the two.

The Interests of the United States

The United States has interests both broad and narrow in the international monetary system.

Because of its broad objectives in economic and foreign policy, the United States has a major stake in the maintenance of an effective monetary system. This means a system that minimizes the impediments to international transactions. More specifically, it means a system in which countries are assured of sufficient liquidity to finance imbalances of payments while adjusting any underlying imbalances through policies consistent with their other legitimate national objectives.

Effective adjustment must, of course, be predicated on effective domestic economic policies. However, these policies may not be implemented soon enough to restore equilibrium by themselves. And adjustment must also be possible in those "dilemma" cases where policies required to regain external equilibrium run counter to those needed to meet domestic objectives. Selective controls over international transactions, which have been used increasingly in recent years, are almost always ineffective in restoring equilibrium and—after their inevitable proliferation—must give way eventually to other measures in any event. In addition, they can cause serious problems for economic and foreign policy and will do so increasingly if reliance upon them continues to grow. The broadest interest of the United States in the monetary system would, thus, be served by an improvement in the use of exchange rates to help accomplish effective adjustment.

The narrow interest of the United States is difficult to distinguish from this broader interest. Improvement in the system as a whole means less risk to foreign holders of dollars and to those who rely heavily on the Eurodollar market to meet ongoing business needs, as well as to the United States. This has been dramatically demonstrated since March 1968 by the effect of the two-tier gold system, adopted essentially for reasons of system-wide confidence, in reducing the potential threats to the dollar.

In addition, it is as much for international as for national reasons that the United States must be able to adjust any disequilibrium in its own payments position both gradually and by means consistent with its domestic objectives. Elimination of an American deficit through rapid domestic deflation would generate repercussions of recession throughout the world, as well as create unacceptable social, economic, and political problems at home. Elimination of an American surplus through rapid domestic inflation could set off a global wave of price rises. And the

United States can use the policy-mix approach only to a limited extent, because it would trigger a sharp escalation of interest rates throughout the world, and because increased interest rates in the United States worsen the American balance of payments, by sharply increasing payments by the United States to foreign holders of dollars, as well as help it by attracting capital inflows (if rate increases in the United States are not fully offset by increases in foreign interest rates).

Most uses of restrictions by the United States are likely to be ineffective in achieving adjustment, simply postponing the need for more definitive action and, therefore, increasing the magnitude of the steps needed later. An improvement in the exchange-rate mechanism might, thus, help adjust any disequilibrium between the United States and the rest of the world if it provided for an earlier and, hence, more gradual attack on the problem. Such an improvement could bring broader benefits as well, since restrictive action by the United States for payment reasons encourages additional controls and protectionist sentiment in the United States and elsewhere in the world.

The Options for Greater Flexibility

These general conclusions must be tested against the specific manner in which limited flexibility would operate in practice. Theoretically, there are six possibilities.

(1) The dollar could remain convertible into gold at $35 per ounce with all other currencies free to fluctuate more freely in terms of the dollar. This makes eminent economic sense, since only $N-1$ currencies can possibly fluctuate consistently in a world of N currencies (or currency areas). It would represent the smallest change from the present system, in which discrete parity changes and the limited flexibility that exists within the present margins take place in terms of the dollar, and would, thus, be the most likely to win widespread acceptance. The following analysis will focus on this option.

(2) All other currencies could be free to fluctuate more freely in terms of the dollar with the United States no longer converting dollars into gold on demand at $35 per ounce. This would mean adoption by the United States of "current account convertibility" as defined in the Articles of Agreement of the International Monetary Fund.[1] The United States would then intervene in the exchange markets, if necessary, with foreign exchange obtained through sales of its reserve assets or borrowings. This approach would appear as more of a change from the present system than would Option 1, although in practice it would not be very

[1] It could also mean abandonment by the United States of *any* convertibility obligation. However, this would probably not produce a system of limited exchange-rate flexibility, at least not of the negotiated type being discussed in this volume.

different. It would, however, probably introduce the additional complication of requiring negotiation of a Reserve Settlement Account, into which monetary authorities could deposit their dollars and perhaps other reserve assets in exchange for SDRs or some other international asset, to cushion the political implications of the abandonment of gold convertibility.

(3) A currency other than the dollar could become the pivot of the system, with all other currencies, including the dollar, free to fluctuate more freely with respect to it. This is not a practical option at present because no other currency is a plausible candidate for the center role. On a more limited scale, however, one or several currencies might become key currencies for a certain geographical region and, thus, move toward sharing the dollar's international roles.

(4) All currencies, including the dollar, could be free to fluctuate more freely in terms of gold with market intervention carried out in gold. (Gold could also become simply the numeraire of the system with intervention continuing in dollars and the two-tier system continued. In practice, however, this is virtually the same as Option 2.) This would require reintegration of the official and private markets for gold through abandonment of the two-tier system, including legalization of private gold holdings in the United States and elsewhere. It would greatly enhance the role of gold and reverse the highly desirable evolutionary trend away from reliance on gold for monetary purposes.

Implementation of this approach would almost certainly require a massive initial increase in the price of gold, to enable present holders of dollars to acquire enough gold to use for intervention purposes without completely draining the reserves of the United States and other large holders. In addition, such a return to reliance on gold—buttressed by the relative stability that gold might then be perceived to enjoy relative to the dollar—would increase the desire of monetary authorities to hold their reserves predominantly in that form, and would make them unwilling to accept reductions in their holdings to make intervention balances available to others.

Such an increase in the price of gold is overwhelmingly objectionable on both economic and political grounds. In addition, under this option the value of world reserves would be subject to sizable fluctuation, as the price of gold and of any national currencies held in reserves fluctuated relative to each other, thus injecting a new element of instability into the system. This approach will not be considered further.

(5) All currencies, including the dollar, could be free to fluctuate more freely in terms of Special Drawing Rights with market intervention in SDRs. (Like gold, SDRs could become the numeraire with intervention continuing in dollars. This too would mainly change the cosmetics of the system.) This approach is only a theoretical possibility at present,

since SDRs can be held only by monetary authorities. Any extension of its use to include the private sector would have to avoid replicating the problems caused by the dual character of gold prior to March 1968. It will not be considered further in this paper.

(6) The concept of market intervention could be abandoned altogether, replaced by frequent clearing of balances among central banks. This would be akin to the mechanism that actually operated among the members of the European Payments Union. Under it, central banks could accumulate all other currencies with an assurance that any net balances would be converted periodically. Thus, there would be no need for an intervention currency. Applied on a global scale, this approach would be extremely cumbersome, and will not be considered further.

Greater Flexibility and the Dollar

How then would a pattern of greater flexibility of exchange rates be likely to operate in the near future?

It must first be noted that only a few currencies would in practice probably wish to crawl or fluctuate within a wider band. Most countries would probably continue to peg their exchange rates within the narrow (or no) band to the major country to which their economies were closely related.[2]

For example, a de facto dollar area—which might include such major countries as Japan and Canada—could emerge. Such an area already exists in practice, but would become more apparent if countries continued to peg to the dollar rather than exercise their new option of letting their exchange rates flex.

The logic of the European Community suggests that it would seek to retain fixed exchange rates among its member states. This would require a major stride forward in their economic integration, or a willingness for large-scale financing among the members, or both. It might also require some technical innovations that might lead to use of one of their currencies as per Option 3. (At a later stage of EC integration, of course, they might adopt a common currency that could play such a role.) On the other hand, each member could continue to intervene with dollars, but at an intervention level designed for the Community as a whole.

If the United Kingdom were to remain outside the EC, the sterling area might live on with exchange rates of its members fixed internally

[2] This means that any negotiated system would probably have to permit such continued pegging. It would also, however, have to assure that enough currencies actually fluctuated to avoid aborting the basic objectives of the adoption of greater flexibility. One reconciliation would be to make greater flexibility optional for all countries but with prior understandings, at least among the members of the Group of Ten, as to which rates would actually fluctuate in practice.

and sterling fluctuating more freely relative to the dollar. Its membership might shrink, however, with several countries moving into the dollar area instead.

If Japan decided to flex relative to the dollar, a yen area in the Far East could develop along similar lines. "Member countries" would probably accomplish this by continuing to intervene with dollars, but at intervention points in line with those of the yen.

In fact, it is precisely between these broad areas that improved techniques of adjustment are needed to deal with the disequilibria that may have existed in the postwar period. The United States and the sterling area have been in persistent deficit, often simultaneous with underutilization of domestic resources. The EC has been in persistent surplus, and Japan may now be achieving such a position, often simultaneous with excessive levels of demand pressure. (Of course, some or all of these imbalances may not have represented disequilibria, reflecting as they did the conscious policy decisions of a great number of countries.) The following analysis assumes that only a few major exchange rates would actually move more freely, although most of the analysis could be applied to the broader case as well.

However many currencies were actually to fluctuate more freely, the dollar would almost certainly remain the pivot of the system. Monetary authorities in each of the fluctuating countries would define their currencies in terms of the dollar and intervene in the exchange markets in dollars, as they do at present. This would have several implications for the United States.

First, the United States would remain largely passive with regard to market intervention.

Second, there would be no commonly regarded "exchange rate of the dollar." Such a rate could be determined only implicitly, by calculating a weighted average of all other exchange rates. Rates of all other currencies (or key currencies of currency areas) would be commonly defined as their price in terms of dollars.

Third, the dollar could fluctuate vis-a-vis any single currency only half as much as could any other currency. Assuming flexibility as in Option 1, there would continue to be no fluctuation in the gold-dollar or SDR-dollar prices. The dollar, gold, and SDR would all be equally stable.

Fourth, passiveness on the part of the United States would obviate the international coordination problems that could be caused if the monetary authorities of the key currency country and the monetary authorities of other countries had different ideas about the proper exchange rates between their currencies.

It is striking that all of these features also exist in the present system, indicating how little in practice would be the changes due to limited flexibility. They would probably become more obvious, however, under a system where some other currencies were in fact fluctuating more freely.

Effects on Adjustment

A passive intervention policy would certainly not mean that the United States would be indifferent to the exchange-rate movements that occurred in a world of greater flexibility. The reasons were stated at the outset of this paper: the United States could get either more adjustment or more financing, and would prefer more adjustment. And the greater opportunity for exchange-rate changes could produce a tendency toward depreciation of other currencies relative to the dollar, which would steadily impair the competitive position of the United States.

The United States could not get much worse off in this regard, however. Under the present system, there is a quadruple bias against the dollar, against which all exchange-rate changes take place:

payments pressures prompt or force devaluations, but seldom prompt or force revaluations;

revaluations tend to be smaller than necessary since countries are even less susceptible to fears of a need for additional revaluation than to pressures to move upward in the first place;

devaluations tend to be larger than necessary to prevent speculation on further devaluation, although this effect may be offset for major countries by their desire to avoid triggering responsive devaluations by others;

any single devaluation generates pressures on other countries to devalue, both because of legitimate fears over loss of competitive position (exacerbated by the tendency for the initial devaluations to be excessive) and because devaluation is easier to justify politically if done in response to a like movement by another country.

Under the present system, American payments deficits have, to a significant extent, been caused by these biases toward devaluation against the dollar. In the 1950s, the American balance of payments suffered from the excessive and widespread devaluations of 1949 (coupled with the maintenance of controls elsewhere). In the early 1960s, it suffered from the excessive French devaluations of the late 1950s, the inadequate German (and perhaps Dutch) revaluation in 1961, and the failure of other surplus countries (such as Italy and Austria) to revalue at all. All four aspects of the bias against the dollar thus played an important role in the development and perpetuation of the deficits of the United States.

The United States has, thus, had to maintain a much better record of price stability than virtually all other countries just to avoid losing its international competitive position. The United States did hold its share of world export markets during its period of amazing price stability in the early 1960s, which was however probably maintained at some cost in terms of domestic unemployment. But this analysis suggests why at least this indicator of the competitive position of the United States did not improve, even during a period when sharp increases in outflows of capital obviously provided some direct boost to exports.[3]

Each of the four biases should be removed or at least mitigated if greater flexibility of exchange rates were to work in practice as outlined in theory:

It would be based on rules or presumptions under which a surplus country would have the same responsibility to permit appreciation of its currency as a deficit country would have to permit depreciation of its currency.

The same rules or presumptions would assure that the amount of the appreciation was sufficient to remove the disequilibrium.

The system should reduce the amount of currency depreciations.[4] First, it would make an earlier start on the removal of disequilibrium and would, therefore, normally reduce the extent of the adjustment needed. Second, and more important from the standpoint of the dollar, the rules should provide countries with a high degree of confidence that depreciation could continue until a new equilibrium rate was reached and, therefore, reduce the need to overshoot the mark. This effect would be re-emphasized by the knowledge that depreciation could begin again if necessitated by the onset of a new disequilibrium.

It should reduce the "follow-the-leader" tendency to devalue, because any rate could begin to move as soon as disequilibrium became apparent. This is partly because greater flexibility would to some extent de-dramatize and de-politicize changes in rates.

In terms of adjustment, the United States would, thus, benefit to some degree simply from the reduction in the amounts of depreciation of

[3] This analysis also suggests why most foreign monetary authorities were willing to accumulate dollars to finance a large part of the American deficit during this period. The dollar accumulations provided an umbrella for their own rapid growth and the elimination of their restrictions on international transactions in two ways: they provided a rapid increase in international liquidity and they enabled the rest of the world, on balance, to avoid adjustment, thereby improving its competitive position against the largest factor in the world economy—the United States itself.

[4] There is a contrary view that greater flexibility would induce wage increases and, hence, increase the amount of depreciations. The point is certainly arguable, but it is also arguable that relatively small and frequent rate changes will be more easily absorbed by labor, since they would become more routine, and be less shocking, than large discrete parity shifts.

other currencies and perhaps in the number of such depreciations. This suggests that the United States should prefer a symmetrical system of greater flexibility to an asymmetrical system that permitted only upside flexibility. The great benefit for the United States, however, would come from the elimination—or any reduction—of the revaluation-devaluation asymmetry of the present system and the shift in the moral burden of responsibility to adjust that would accompany it.

The Effects on Dollar Balances

It seems clear that private holdings of dollars would continue to rise with the need to finance international transactions under a system of greater flexibility. But a major question concerning the interest of the United States in such a system is whether it would lead monetary authorities to seek to disgorge their present dollar holdings, or avoid dollar accumulations in the future, or both of these.

We can identify a number of reasons why monetary authorities hold dollars in their reserves. (These reasons differ among countries due to different weightings of economic and political objectives and different degrees of economic ties with the United States.) Most basic are the opportunity for interest earnings and convenience of holding an asset widely useable without a need for conversion. Monetary authorities will take advantage of these opportunities, however, only if they are confident that convertibility, particularly into other national currencies, but also into other reserve assets widely used in the system, will be preserved with little risk of capital loss.[5]

The outlook for American balance-of-payments performance is critical to whether such confidence can be maintained, both for its current effect and because of its impact on the ratio of American liquid assets to external liabilities. Rates of domestic price increase and overall economic growth are in turn central to the outlook for payments equilibrium. Other important factors that lead to foreign official dollar holdings are the overall political and economic role played in the world by the United States; gross capital outflows from the United States; the continued presence of adequate financial markets; relative aloofness of the American economy, and, hence, the dollar, from external disturbances; and avoidance of controls on the use of the currency.

The basic criterion had two components: continued convertibility and little risk of capital loss. For countries that continued to peg their currencies to the dollar, there would of course be little change from the pres-

---

[5] They may also be interested in stability per se rather than risk of loss. I have noted earlier, however, that under Option 1 there would be no change from the present equality of stability of the dollar and its two chief reserve asset rivals, gold and SDRs. Under Option 2, some might perceive gold or SDRs to be more stable, although others might react oppositely.

ent situation. The better adjustment of any American disequilibrium, which should derive from greater flexibility, should better assure all countries about the continued convertibility of the dollar and reduce even further the possibility of a change in the price of gold, the only financial reason why monetary authorities may have been uneasy over their holdings of dollars. And by helping the United States to adjust, greater flexibility would eliminate the need for the present controls over some international transactions by the United States and the possibility of tighter controls in the future—improving still further the attractiveness of the dollar.

On the other hand, the value of the dollar in terms of a weighted average of other currencies would depreciate, relative to the same price in the present system, if this adjustment conclusion is correct. This decline would be very slow, however, under any of the variants of greater flexibility now being considered, and would not of itself, probably, have much negative effect on holders of dollars. In absolute terms, of course, such a weighted average value of the dollar could be appreciating. Despite recent problems, the United States has a better long-term record of price stability than any other country, and few would bet against the dollar over the long haul. And the relatively closed nature of the American economy makes the dollar more susceptible to appreciation because policy in the United States is less likely than policy in most countries to be motivated by concern about the balance of payments and by overt mercantilism.

The major problem would come if one or two of the fluctuating currencies exhibited a strong bias toward appreciation relative to the dollar. (The mark and the yen might represent such cases.) Two questions must then be asked: Would any of these other currencies meet the requirements for key currency status sufficiently to draw balances away from the dollar? Could the United States or the appreciating country avoid such shifts through interest rate policy?

Sterling seems to be the only other currency that meets the wide range of requirements for key currency status, and long-term trends suggest that sterling is unlikely to appreciate steadily against the dollar. Germany's financial capabilities are improving rapidly, but its exposed geographic position and absence of a world political role—which is one major reason why its authorities continue to be completely negative about assuming any key currency role—make it doubtful that the mark could take much business away from the dollar. A promising possibility would seem to be some linkage between the UK's financial capabilities and still-global interests and the Continent's economic weight and potential political power, but there appears to be little movement toward such a merger even in the context of possible British entry to the Common Market.

The Swiss authorities are even more adamantly opposed to key currency role for their franc, and they are quite right in view of the smallness of their economy and its extreme sensitivity to external transactions. Finally, although Japan shares a certain economic resemblance to Germany, it is much less far along the road both financially and politically.

We have already noted that the opportunity for yield is an important factor that induces foreign monetary authorities to hold dollars. Any anticipated depreciation of the dollar, even in terms of a single other currency, could thus be offset by increasing that yield. And Willett shows (in Paper No. 33) that (1) any interest rate constraint in the crawling-peg system is likely to be less than under the present system and (2) that the constraint is not very great in absolute terms once the initial stock adjustment, which could, however, be quite prolonged, has taken place. He also notes that any net constraint that remains due to the crawling peg could be reduced further by a greater widening of the band.

It would thus appear feasible for the United States to use interest-rate policy to induce increased dollar holdings or to deter movements out of the dollar if it wanted to do so to help meet its international financial objectives. Given the assumptions that there could be no more than one or two other currencies that could attract shifts from the dollar, however, it would probably be far more efficient from the standpoint of the system as a whole if those other countries were to adapt their interest-rate policies to the need to prevent destabilizing shifts. This is because of the impact of American interest rates on all other countries, given the weight of the United States in the world economy, and because of the relatively closed nature of the American economy and, hence, the disproportionate effects on its domestic economy (and on the world economy) of the required change in interest rates. Such policies could, therefore, properly be made part of the amended rules of the game.

Political Considerations

Finally, what of the politics of a system in which other currencies moved more freely around the dollar, enhancing the appearance of the dollar as the lodestar of the system and its bastion of stability?

First, I have already noted that the system in practice would not differ very much from the present system. Second, only a few currencies could in practice be expected to fluctuate more freely. All other countries would retain their present fixity (to the dollar or some other currency) just as the dollar would retain its fixity (to gold). Third, the continued tie of the dollar to gold would continue to exercise its present degree of discipline on the United States, while all other countries would gain an additional degree of flexibility in their adjustment policies.

INTRODUCTION

Most important, however, is the fact that the present system brings little real pressure to bear on the United States. The major surplus country, Germany, agreed publicly in 1967 not to buy gold from the United States. Some others follow a similar policy in practice, and there is a widespread perception that the United States, if confronted with demands for large gold conversions, would suspend the gold convertibility of the dollar rather than suffer further large losses of reserves.

If this is true, other countries have to add to their dollar reserves or initiate adjustment on their own when the United States is in official settlements deficit. They could, therefore, only gain from acquiring an additional policy instrument to fend off unwanted dollars in a more efficient way than the present mechanism for changing exchange rates. At the same time, the United States would benefit from the increased responsibility of other countries to permit adjustment and their increased moral obligation to hold dollars if they did not.

In addition, greater flexibility of exchange rates would "bottle up" inflation or deflation to a greater extent within its country of origin. This would reduce the possibility that Europe would have to "import inflation" from the United States or that the United States could "export unemployment" to the rest of the world.

There is one other probable political gain to other countries vis-a-vis the United States in such a system. Given the relatively small impact of foreign transactions on the economy of the United States, it is highly doubtful that the United States will ever permit balance-of-payments developments or foreign authorities to exercise overriding influence over its domestic policy. However, the exchange rate of the dollar has a relatively small impact on the American economy. American authorities should, thus, be prepared to accept much greater foreign influences over the exchange rate than over its domestic policy. Any system that increased the influence of exchange rates in the adjustment process should enhance the influence of foreign developments and foreign authorities.

If the political appearance of a fixed dollar in a world with several major currencies fluctuating around it were unacceptable, despite all these factors, one remedy would be to move to Option 2. The United States might accept a change in its obligations under the (revised) Articles of Agreement of the IMF by pledging to intervene in the exchange markets to defend the exchange rate of the dollar—within the wider band, or by regulating the rate of the crawl. This would mean that the United States would no longer pledge to convert foreign official dollars into gold at a fixed price (and vice versa), but would, rather, accept the same obligation now accepted by all other IMF members. Because the elimination of gold convertibility might cause unease among some monetary authorities—both those who now hold dollars and those who now hold gold—such a step would probably have to be accompanied by the creation of a Reserve Settlement Account, which would permit conversion into SDRs (or some other international asset) of any present reserve assets no longer wanted under these conditions.

In practice, such a system would require little, if any, intervention by the United States. As long as the dollar retained its intervention currency role, other countries would *ipso facto* maintain the dollar within its limitations as they carried out their own obligations under the Articles of Agreement. (In fact, intervention by the United States would create a redundancy problem unless any such intervention was limited to the time when exchange markets abroad were closed because of time differentials.) The system would thus operate in a manner virtually identical to Option 1.

The main difference would be the substitution of a dollar legally subject to the same rules as all other countries for the present system of gold-dollar convertibility. As a result, there would no longer be any foreign pressure on the United States by direct conversion of dollars into gold or threats thereof. There would seem to be less occasion for any such pressure, in any event, if my conclusion is correct that greater flexibility would improve the likelihood of adjustment to any payments disequilibrium between the United States and the rest of the world. If it were deemed necessary to create a Reserve Settlement Account to smooth the transition to this system and to determine the future relationship among the various reserve assets, that would be another difference —and one that would certainly complicate and slow the adoption of greater flexibility.

Conclusion

The foregoing analysis suggests that there are no overriding reasons why the United States should oppose greater flexibility of exchange rates. The arguments so far advanced against an American interest in such a system do not stand up to analysis. In fact, any of the technically feasible approaches to such an evolutionary change would appear to offer some advantage to the United States—both in terms of its broad interest in an effective international monetary system and its narrower interest in its own international financial position.

The interest of the United States would be maximized if the rules or presumptions that governed any increase in flexibility were to eliminate or even reduce the present "quadruple bias" against the dollar, which makes adjustment extremely difficult for the United States. If other countries were unwilling to commit themselves irrevocably to upside fluctuations when market forces suggested them, however, the United States could still expect to gain adjustment benefits from the changes in the rules affecting currency depreciations. It would, thus, benefit more from a symmetrical system of greater flexibility than from an asymmetrical system that permitted only upside flexibility, although it could of course expect significant benefit from the asymmetrical system alone.

If others were unwilling to commit themselves to upside fluctuations, of course, the dollar would face even less risk of confidence problems and both the foreign countries and the United States would want to keep open the option of foreign accumulations of dollar inflows as at present. If a confidence problem were perceived to exist under any of the greater flexibility variants, it could be handled by introducing appropriate rules for interest-rate policies by countries whose parities were expected to crawl steadily upward, by American interest-rate policy, or by a sufficient widening of the band.

The United States should, thus, have in mind some particular proposals that would maximize its advantage if included in the rules or presumptions of any new system of greater exchange-rate flexibility. Acceptance of these proposals would make it most clear that the adoption of such a system would be in the interest of the United States.

Fortunately, these changes would also seem to be in the interest of the other major countries. They would gain an additional policy instrument for use in adjusting their own payments positions, although they might prefer less firm rules on upside rate changes in order to preserve their present option of accumulating dollars rather than adjusting. They would gain even more than would the United States from the improvement in the overall system, in view of their greater reliance on international transactions. They could lose little of substance vis-a-vis the United States, since they do not now bring substantial pressure on it to adjust. The various approaches discussed in this volume should, therefore, be suitable for serious international discussion.

· 7 ·

Decision-Making on Exchange Rates

STEPHEN N. MARRIS

Now that the pound sterling and the French franc have been devalued, the German mark revalued, and the price of gold is back to $35 an ounce, it is tempting to sit back and say what had to happen has happened. It was unpleasant while it lasted, but things will be all right from now on. This view will appeal to those who feel that our recent difficulties have not been due so much to the present exchange-rate system, as to a series of bad decisions by politicians with insufficient economic understanding and political courage. In their view, salutary lessons should have been learned by both governments and international organizations, and from now on all that is needed is a determined effort to make better use of the institutional arrangements set out in the Articles of Agreement of the IMF.

The purpose of this paper is to take a look at the obstacles to rational decision-making on exchange rates, which seem to be *inherent* in the present "large-change-or-not-at-all" system, and the arguments of those who believe that these can be overcome only by changing the rules so that governments will feel freer to make smaller and more frequent parity changes. The emphasis is placed on decision-making at the governmental and international level because exchange rates are, par excellence, an emanation of national sovereignty; thus, many (though by no means all) of the most important issues lie in this area.[1]

The recent, key exchange-rate changes have been of the order of 10–15 per cent. This is certainly much smaller than the convulsions of the interwar period, but, for a medium-sized economy with a large external sector, they are still, in economic terms, very large. An overnight change of 10–15 per cent in the price of all transactions accounting for as much as one-quarter of GNP will have, in time, a major impact on both the level and distribution of income in the country concerned. At the time of sterling devaluation it was estimated that the stimulus to exports and the restraining effect on imports would, other things being

---

I am deeply indebted to the Brookings Institution, Washington, D.C., for the opportunity to write this paper while on leave of absence from the Organization for Economic Co-operation and Development in Paris. The views expressed are my own, and in no way purport to represent those of the OECD, or of the staff members, officers, or trustees of the Brookings Institution.

[1] I have attempted a more comprehensive review of the subject in "The Bürgenstock Communiqué: A Critical Examination of the Case for Limited Exchange-Rate Flexibility," Princeton Essays in International Finance No. 80, 1970.

equal, increase total demand by an amount rising to the equivalent of 3 per cent of GNP over a period of eighteen months to two years. Similarly, if the devaluation proved successful, that is, if it was not nullified by subsequent price-wage interactions, there would be a shift from personal income to profits equivalent to up to 2 per cent of national income, with significant changes in the distribution of profits and of rates of return on capital between different firms, industries, and sectors of the economy.

Governments are bound to hesitate before taking a step with such far-reaching consequences. Unless the economy happens to be in recession (devaluation case) or over-heating (revaluation case), the parity change will require a radical alteration in demand-management policies. Simply at the technical level this is likely to pose severe problems. Domestic demand has considerable momentum of its own, and attempts to alter its direction suddenly meet great resistance. In fact, it could be held that, at least in devaluation cases, it is just not possible to turn domestic policy around rapidly enough to parry the effects of a 10–15 per cent parity change, so that the benefits expected from the change will inevitably be seriously eroded by subsequent domestic price developments.

Political considerations give even stronger grounds for hesitation. The restrictive measures needed in a devaluing country will be extremely unpopular. In both devaluing and revaluing countries, there will be strenuous objections to the effects on the distribution of income. And, in a world in which nationalistic sentiments still run very deep, these resentments will be compounded by strong feelings that devaluation is a blow to national prestige, or that revaluation involves "giving in to the deficit countries."

Politicians would normally want to make widespread consultations before taking such a major step, but, because of the pressing need for secrecy, this may not be possible. At levels of government below the top, devaluation (or revaluation) may become a forbidden subject, and policy advice may become distorted through excessive emphasis on all methods of adjustment other than exchange-rate changes. Finally, if a decision is put off too long and a crisis develops, short-term considerations—the amount of the central bank's forward commitments, fear of a public outcry about "letting the speculators get away with it," etc.—may lead to a virtual paralysis in the decision-making process.

In view of all this, one is more inclined to sympathize with those responsible for exchange-rate policy in national governments, rather than criticize them. Good reasons for putting off a large parity change abound. There may be too much domestic overheating, or, in revaluation cases, a temporary weakness in domestic demand. The government may feel it has too small a parliamentary majority to take such a major step; a decision may have to be put off because of impending elections. There may be doubts about how many other countries might follow suit, and about the future course of world trade and of prices in other important countries. The list could be a very long one.

Under the present rules the exchange rate is assumed to be innocent until it is proved beyond doubt to be guilty. The authorities are, therefore, expected to wait stoically, while the evidence accumulates, until a change is needed of a size that is bound to cause a major economic and political upheaval. It is clear that, other things being equal, their task would be much easier if it were possible to devise a system under which they could make smaller and more timely changes. The changes in demand-management policies required would be smaller and could be better graduated. There would be less outcry from interest groups unfavorably affected. There would be less need for secrecy. Exchange-rate changes would no longer be headline news. The general strategy of the exchange rate policy to be followed would still be a matter for decision at the highest level, but the tactics and timing could be left to the monetary and fiscal authorities.

There is another aspect of the present system that has perhaps not received the attention it deserves, namely, the obstacles that it puts in the way of rational decision-making at the international level. Any country with a currency of international importance considering a parity change will want to know how its partners are likely to react; indeed, it cannot make a sound decision without this knowledge. But the need for secrecy must severely limit the scope for proper international consultation. It is hard for an outsider to judge how serious this has been in the recent past, but the available evidence suggests that, as far as major parity changes are concerned, we are still not very far from the jungle where the rule is to shoot first and ask questions afterwards.

It would be wrong, of course, to underestimate the importance of the spectacular growth of international economic consultation over the last twenty years. Mutual understanding of each others' problems has increased enormously, and, slowly but surely, more effective means are being evolved to bring collective pressure to bear on countries to follow policies consistent with the general interest. But what about exchange rates? When a major currency is concerned, the fact that any change is likely to be of the order of 10–15 per cent is bound to make people hesitate, just as it does within the domestic decision-making machinery.

Even though it seems clear that a country should devalue, other countries will hesitate to take the lead in pressing for a change. They know it will weaken their own trading position somewhat, and will cause a major disturbance in international money and financial markets. They also know that devaluation involves heavy political costs for the government concerned, and they are highly conscious that they might find themselves in the same uncomfortable position at some later date. There may be less hesitation in urging revaluation, but again political costs are involved, and other countries with strong currencies may hold back from fear that they might be forced to follow suit. International organizations can afford to be more disinterested. But they also may hesitate to press their case too far, because they do not want to be accused of unsettling the exchange markets, and because, looking at their own longer-run interests, they are worried about nationalistic resentment in the country concerned against being told what to do by foreign bureaucrats. Thus, even when it is obvious to outside observers that a country is, to use the euphemism, in "fundamental disequilibrium," it is still a big step from being prepared to *agree* to parity change to positively *urging* it.

Despite the lessons that have been learned over the last few years, these inhibitions are unlikely to disappear because they are inherent in a system that regards exchange-rate changes as a last resort. Too much attention will be devoted to other methods of adjustment, and when, eventually, a change in the parity can no longer be put off, there will be too little time for proper discussion and analysis of the effects on the country concerned and on other countries.

Clearly, the situation would be quite different under a system of limited flexibility. With small parity changes there would be little risk of chain reaction, and the poker-game features of the present system should largely disappear. More or less continuous consultation on the general line of the exchange-rate policies being followed should be possible. There would no longer be the need for agonizing over-the-weekend decisions. Devaluing countries would know that, if necessary, they could make further changes in the same direction without great drama; revaluing countries would know that it would be relatively easy to reverse their decision if this proved necessary.

It should become normal for a country's exchange-rate policy to be examined regularly in the same way as its fiscal, monetary, and other policies are already closely scrutinized in such international organizations as the IMF, the OECD, the BIS, and the institutions of the EEC. And, with so much less at stake, it should be much easier to bring collective pressure to bear. Willingness to give conditional credit to deficit countries, which already involves detailed multilateral examination of other aspects of a country's policies, would come to require a consensus that its exchange-rate policy was appropriate, and, in cases of doubt, creditors might insist that some use should be made of the provisions for small parity changes. It is less easy to bring pressure to bear on surplus countries, but it would probably be wrong to underestimate the powers of objective analysis and moral suasion. With small changes domestic political pressures should be greatly reduced, and it would be much eas-

INTRODUCTION

ier for other countries and international bodies to bring the issues out into the open.

The obstacles to rational decision-making on exchange rates under the present rules need to be emphasized because they provide the essential background to the search for better alternatives. It could still be, of course, that like democracy, we have invented the worst possible system, except for all the others. This, however, remains to be demonstrated. The rest of this paper concentrates on how decision-making might evolve under a system of limited flexibility, under which governments would be encouraged to make parity changes of only, say, 1 per cent or less at any one time. Attention is focused on two diametrically opposed criticisms: that in practice governments would find it no easier to make small changes than large ones; or, on the contrary, that it would be too easy and, hence, lead to abuse.

The original proposals for a "crawling peg" came from academic economists, and typically involved an *automatic* link between parity changes and the behavior of market rates over some past period. This always seemed unrealistic, as being unacceptable to governments, cumbersome, and likely to produce perverse results in practice. Attention has now switched to schemes in which the initiative for parity changes would remain with national authorities, perhaps with some general rules or other devices designed to ensure that the system operates as intended. Critics suggest, however, that so long as the initiative lies with governments the same difficulties may arise as with the present system. The authorities will find themselves under constant scrutiny by the market. Once they make a parity change, however small, there will be expectations of further changes in the same direction, setting off powerful speculative forces. After a time, it is held, they will find that it was in fact easier to make large once-and-for-all changes.

It has been suggested that this danger could be avoided by combining the crawling peg with a somewhat wider band within which market rates would be allowed to fluctuate around the official parity. With a carefully designed system of this kind it is held that the authorities would find that they were able to make small parity changes in the knowledge that these need not necessarily have any immediate effect on the exchange rate in the market. Suppose that under the new rules the authorities were permitted to make parity changes of up to, but not exceeding 1 per cent in any period of six months, and to allow market rates to diverge by up to ±2 per cent from the par value.[2] A country is experiencing domestic overheating and in the market its currency falls to between 1 and 2 per cent below parity. The authorities take action to restrain domestic

---

[2] The parity options would not be cumulative, that is, if they had not been used they could not be carried forward.

81

demand, but reviewing the situation, they conclude that some permanent damage has been done to the country's competitive position and decide to lower the parity by 1 per cent. The rate already prevailing in the market would still, however, be well within the new upper intervention point, so that this action need not in itself have any effect on market rates.

Of course, the market may well interpret the parity change as signalling the likelihood of further steps in the same direction still to come. But under a discretionary system the authorities would be free to intervene in the spot or forward markets to prevent any immediate further decline in the spot rate, and thus keep the market guessing as to their own expectations concerning the future trend of the market rate and the parity. There is a close parallel here with discount-rate changes. According to the circumstances and their own operational experience, the authorities may decide either to lead the market or to follow it. So long as they have this choice, most of the drama surrounding parity changes should disappear; they would not overnight make a lot of people richer or poorer. Exchange-rate movements would be, in part, a function of what was happening in the exchange markets, but would, over time, depend on how the authorities interpreted signals coming from the market, and what policies—including exchange-rate policy—they decided to adopt to meet the situation.

Because of the desirability of minimizing the immediate disturbance caused by parity changes in the exchange markets, some writers have proposed that they should be made in a series of extremely small steps at very short intervals, $2/52$nd per cent at weekly intervals, for example. It is true that the smaller the parity change at any one time, the less should be the direct impact on the exchange rate in the market; but at the same time the greater will be expectations of further changes in the same direction. It is suggested, however, that the speculative flows that these expectations would generate could be stemmed fairly easily by maintaining offsetting, covered forward-interest differentials in line with the expected future movement of the exchange rate. Indeed, it is sometimes proposed that the authorities should announce in advance their intention to gradually raise or lower the parity over some given period, or until further notice.

This idea is intellectually interesting in that it carries the idea of getting away from the present large and unpredictable parity changes to its logical extreme, but, to many, it may smack too much of "fine tuning." An alternative is to see whether it would be possible to get around the problem of expectations concerning further parity changes by devising a system in which the authorities had enough room to maneuvre in the exchange markets to be able to make in one step parity changes of a size sufficient to be regarded as a significant contribution to the necessary ad-

INTRODUCTION

justment. This is the idea behind the proposed rules mentioned above, under which changes of up to 1 per cent could be made in any six months. Taking an economy starting from a position of reasonable external equilibrium, it is argued that a parity change of 1 per cent should in time have a significant effect on external balance; enough, that is, to offset anything that, in the normal course of events, is ever likely to happen to a country's basic competitive position in the course of six months. If this is correct, it would follow that the market should be prepared to regard a 1 per cent parity change as an adequate adjustment for the time being, until the appearance of new evidence to the contrary.

This solution represents a compromise between the two extremes. Parity changes would still be made in distinct discrete steps over a time interval that allowed time for a new assessment of how the situation was evolving and, if necessary, for consultation with partner countries and international organizations. But they would be small enough to be undramatic and without great impact on the exchange and money markets. This sounds attractive. Whether it would work depends on a number of factors.

(1) The authorities would have to be prepared to use their parity options without waiting for all the evidence to come in. If they hung on until the market became convinced that a change of significantly more than 1 per cent was needed, speculative crises could build up that might be even more difficult to handle than those under the present system. Many may feel, however, that it is quite impossible to know with any certainty that a parity change of 1 per cent (or even 5 per cent) is needed in any given situation. The rejoinder is that the same is true for other major policy instruments, such as fiscal and monetary policy. Because of the lags and unknowns, the authorities can never have more than a rough idea about the precise timing and magnitude of changes in taxes and monetary variables required to meet a given situation. What they, in fact, do is take a view about the direction in which they should be moving, modify policies accordingly, and then stand ready to make further changes in either direction as the situation develops. Under a new set of rules this is exactly how they could, and should, behave with regard to exchange rates.

(2) Parity changes large enough to be regarded as a significant contribution to longer-run adjustment could be only relatively neutral with respect to the going exchange rate if they were, nevertheless, no bigger, and preferably smaller, than the short-run fluctuations up and down in the exchange that the authorities were prepared to tolerate, or, to put it the other way around, that the market had become accustomed to see quite often reversed without

triggering off parity changes. This sounds contradictory, but may not be so in practice. From the authorities' point of view, the objection to permitting much in the way of short-term fluctuation is the danger that a downward movement becomes self-perpetuating, that is, import prices rise setting off a price-wage spiral causing permanent damage to the country's competitive position. This danger is greater the smaller the country, and the larger its foreign sector. Experience shows, however, that how traders respond to exchange-rate changes depends a great deal on whether they think they are likely to be permanent or not. Up to some point, short-term fluctuations would probably not get passed on into domestic price levels. Given this, it is suggested that the authorities would find that they could permit a sufficient amount of fluctuation in market rates within the band to give them the desired freedom of action with regard to discrete parity changes.

Many government officials find these arguments unconvincing, and are especially worried about the problems of managing a depreciating currency under a system of limited flexibility. Others suspect that they may be unduly influenced by experience gained during the crises inevitably generated by the present system. If the exchange rate is taken down from its pedestal and stripped of its nationalistic trappings, is it really so different from other major policy variables? True, it has significant price effects, demand effects, income-distribution and wealth effects, but so do they. With suitable institutional arrangements, managing a depreciating currency should not be so very different from managing a declining government bond market. It might be uncomfortable, but would the problems be insuperable so long as the government's overall economic policy was consistent with national solvency?

This leads to the more fundamental criticism that with greater flexibility the authorities would feel *too* free to change the exchange rate. It is held that the obstacles to devaluation are a necessary barrier against the strong inflationary forces in the world, and that without them governments would be too often tempted to devalue when what was needed was to restrain domestic demand. One rather obvious rejoinder is that if obstacles to devaluation have been a barrier to inflation, resistance to revaluation has in some cases resulted in more inflation than there would otherwise have been. Moreover, it can be argued that even if there is less inflation in periods where, under the present system, a country is putting up a prolonged struggle to avoid a large devaluation, there may not necessarily be less inflation in the country *on average,* if in the end a large devaluation proves inevitable, with all the inflationary problems this involves, compared with a scenario in which the situation had been

INTRODUCTION

met by a series of smaller exchange-rate changes accompanied by smaller shifts in demand management policies.

Turning to the decision-making process itself, it is argued that the danger of overhasty resort to devaluation can easily be exaggerated. First, it is suggested that with *limited* flexibility the immediate relief to the balance of payments that could be obtained by using the parity option allowed under the rules would be small relative to the cost to the balance of payments of failure to bring domestic overheating under control. Experience seems to indicate that over the first six to twelve months following a devaluation, the gains in foreign currency tend to be negligible or negative because of the deterioration in the terms of trade, and that in the second year they are unlikely to exceed 1–2 per cent of the volume of transactions for each 1 per cent reduction of the exchange rate. Against this, a degree of domestic overheating sufficient to endanger the price level quickly leads to a widening gap between the growth of imports and exports, which can easily reach as much as 10 percentage points after twelve to eighteen months. Over a period of one or two years, therefore, small parity changes would be only a very partial and inadequate substitute for demand restraint, so that external discipline should not be significantly reduced.

More generally it is suggested that limited flexibility should make it easier to follow well conceived demand-management policies. A responsible government, faced with domestic overheating, may prefer not to see an immediate fall in its exchange rate, since this will push up import prices and increase the need for restrictive action. A more sensible course may be to take the necessary restrictive action, and then, if, when demand pressures have eased, some permanent damage seems to have been done to the balance of payments, to use a small devaluation as an early step in a reflationary program.

A second line of argument concerns volatile capital movements. Under the present system there is a rather strong tendency for a deterioration in a country's external current balance caused by domestic overheating to be covered by large capital inflows. (The recent experience of the United States provides a good example.) By cushioning the loss of reserves, this has been an important factor easing the external pressure on the authorities to take prompt action to deal with the domestic situation. But with more flexibility there would be stronger expectations of (small) parity changes in the relatively near future. This might inhibit compensating capital movements and, hence, put more pressure on the authorities. (By the same token it might make domestic monetary restraint more effective because it would be less easily undermined by inflows of interest-sensitive funds.) It is not very clear how important this factor would be in practice with a system of limited flexibility. To some extent, however, it seems likely that there would be a tendency for pressure to build up more quickly than at present on the official reserves of countries with a generally poor record for keeping inflation under control.

A much broader argument is that persistent currency depreciation should provide as strong an incentive to keep inflation under control as reserve losses and foreign borrowing, if not stronger. This is often disputed by those with experience of operating the present system. In their view, fixed rates have provided a bulwark against political irresponsibility. Policy advisers have been able to go to the government and insist that restrictive action be taken because otherwise reserves and credit facilities will run out. To them it seems obvious that with greater flexibility, lowering the parity would seem the easy way out.

In the first instance, and in an unchanged political setting this may well be true. But it is argued that if one is concerned with a *persistent* tendency to devalue rather than restrain demand, then allowance must be made for the likelihood that the political setting will change. Under the present system the exchange rate, for obvious reasons, can never be the subject of constructive political debate; at best it leads to mutual recrimination after the event. If the drama were removed, exchange-rate policy would become subject to exactly the same comment and criticism as monetary and fiscal policy. In a country that continuously devalued, the government would soon find itself under attack from the opposition. Devaluation has price-raising effects, and rightly or wrongly is regarded by public opinion as a blow to national prestige. Unlike reserve losses, it cannot be concealed from the public, nor can its consequences be put off into the future as with foreign borrowing.

Perhaps in reality the "stickiness" of exchange rates has not been such an effective constraint as it may have seemed, particularly for major countries. Foreign borrowing may be a relatively easy option for a major country because of reluctance on the part of its creditors to envisage a large devaluation. Resort to controls may often be an even easier option, in political terms, since the real costs are generally either obscured or put onto other countries. Thus, it can be argued, the external consequences of inflation should be both more obvious, and easier to bring home to public opinion, if they showed up sooner as a persistent decline in the external value of the currency, rather than reserve losses, controls, large scale foreign borrowing, and, eventually, a large devaluation (which, with luck, can be blamed on someone else).

The basic theme underlying most of these arguments is that, in a world of nation-states, good economic management depends not so much on rules written into international agreements, as on the political will and technical competence of national governments. Ultimately, the only real defense against inflation, and against controls and a return to

INTRODUCTION

protectionism, is the verdict of public opinion expressed through democratic political processes after informed debate of all the relevant issues, including the exchange rate. If this is accepted, it follows that the most —and the best—that can be done is to devise a system that enables exchange rates to be brought within the scope of normal decision-making processes. It is claimed that this should be possible at the national level with a carefully designed system of limited flexibility. At the international level such a system should also make it easier to get on with the slow but essential task of working out common attitudes, and building up institutional arrangements under which increasingly effective pressure can be brought on national governments to follow policies consistent with the best interests of the international economy as a whole.[3]

It is, of course, tempting to go on and suggest that, although one must rely essentially on national decision-making processes, it would nevertheless be a good idea to have some rules or other devices to safeguard the system from abuse. There can be no objection to proposals along these lines in principle, but it is important to realize that in practice they may involve a basic contradiction. If a system of limited flexibility is to yield the advantages claimed for it, the first and over-riding rule must be that *large* parity changes should be avoided. Countries must conduct their affairs in such a way that parity changes larger than those permitted under the rules will never, under normal circumstances, be needed. Proposals for additional rules must, therefore, be scrutinized carefully to see that they would not limit countries' freedom of action to the point where this became impossible.

There are several proposals for rules that would permit only small *upward* adjustment of parities in terms of the U.S. dollar, or would in other ways put pressure on countries to revalue while making it difficult to devalue. For a given amount of adjustment needed in the cross-rate between the currencies of a surplus and a deficit country, these proposals would call for twice as much action by the surplus country as would be needed under a "symmetrical" system. One could try to devise rules to bring strong pressure to bear on surplus countries to revalue, but this is not easy. Before long, therefore, the system might seize up; deficit countries would find themselves getting into a situation where a comparatively large devaluation was necessary, and one would be back to the well known difficulties of the present system.

There would, therefore, seem to be a strong a priori case for keeping the rules permitting small parity changes as simple and unrestrictive as possible, and looking for other ways to deal more directly with the various dangers envisaged in different quarters. If, for example, the main concern is about failure to control inflation in deficit countries, this

---

[3] For a discussion of the case for and against greater exchange-rate flexibility within the EEC, see Part VI, papers 46, 47, and 48.

might best be met by arrangements under which a country that persistently exercised its devaluation options would, after a time, have to obtain the approval of the IMF before making any further parity changes. Or again, if the object of the proposal is primarily to ward off the danger that the system might develop a generalized devaluation bias vis-a-vis the U.S. dollar, one should ask whether there may not be other ways of dealing more directly with this problem.

Another line of approach is to suggest that what are needed are rules or other devices under which national authorities would be more or less obliged to respond promptly to signals coming from the market. As already noted, this idea is likely to appear particularly attractive to academic economists. Again, although there can be no objection in principle, there may be serious doubts as to whether, in practice, the market can be relied upon to give the right signals. If it cannot, one is forced back to the conclusion that any new system will have to rely primarily not on ingenious rules, but simply on the opportunities it provides for better decision-making at the national and international level.

Part II. The Case for Greater Flexibility of Exchange Rates

IN HIS essay, "The Case for Flexible Exchange Rates, 1969," Harry G. Johnson argues for floating exchange rates, because they would permit countries to use their economic policies primarily for domestic objectives and to remove quantitative restrictions on international trade and capital movements. However, he is willing to experiment with limited exchange-rate flexibility.

Gottfried Haberler's paper, "The International Monetary System: Some Recent Developments and Discussions," points to the drift to *ad hoc* creation of international liquidity and to quantitative restrictions, criticizes the view that fixed parities would be better because they would permit inflation to spread, and argues, as do Johnson and Grove, that exchange-rate variations are a clearer signal for monetary policy than changes in reserves.

George N. Halm tries to show in his note, "Fixed Exchange Rates and the Market Mechanism," that the fixing of parities, like the fixing of other market prices, does not fit the basic character of the Western market economies and forces governments into such policies as *ad hoc* creation of liquidity, discrete and large-peg adjustments, incomes policies, and exchange controls, which tend to be detrimental to the normal working of a market economy.

In his paper "The Adjustment Process, Its Asymmetry, and Possible Consequences," Marius W. Holtrop finds that the main shortcoming of the present system is the great asymmetry in the adjustment process between surplus and deficit countries. He considers freely flexible exchange rates impracticable, but sympathizes with a movable-parity system that need not be viewed as a departure from Bretton Woods. Movable parities would give surplus and deficit countries the option of combining changing parities with less inflationary or deflationary behavior.

Herbert Giersch's paper, "Entrepreneurial Risk under Flexible Exchange Rates," argues for a system in which exchange-rate variations neutralize unpredictable changes in economic policies. Present overvaluations and undervaluations distort the competitive game. Giersch rejects the widely held view that small countries should integrate their policies with those of their bigger neighbors by means of exchange-rate pegging.

In his contribution, "The Wider Band and Foreign Direct Investment," David L. Grove challenges the view that greater freedom for exchange rates to move would create major uncertainties and curtail private investment abroad. Within a wider band "speculators would be set against speculators, instead of all speculators ganging up against the central bank."

"The Business View of Proposals for International Monetary Reform" is the topic of John H. Watts's paper, in which he points out that exchange-rate fluctuations are not likely to jeopardize overall corporate earnings of the multinational firm. The specialized commodity trader, however, may find that the cost of protection against exchange risks can exceed profit margins. On the whole, businessmen are increasingly realizing that the nuisance or even loss involved in exchange-rate variations pales beside the prospect of an acceleration of restrictions on trade and investment.

· 8 ·

The Case for Flexible Exchange Rates, 1969

HARRY G. JOHNSON

Introduction

BY "FLEXIBLE exchange rates" is meant rates of foreign exchange that are determined daily in the markets for foreign exchange by the forces of demand and supply, without restrictions on the extent to which rates can move imposed by governmental policy. Flexible exchange rates are, thus, to be distinguished from the present system (the International Monetary Fund system) of international monetary organization, under which countries commit themselves to maintain the foreign values of their currencies within a narrow margin of a fixed par value by acting as residual buyers or sellers of currency in the foreign exchange market, subject to the possibility of effecting a change in the par value itself in case of "fundamental disequilibrium"; this system is frequently described as the "adjustable peg" system. Flexible exchange rates should also be distinguished from a spectral system frequently conjured up by opponents of rate flexibility: wildly fluctuating or "unstable" exchange rates. The freedom of rates to move in response to market forces does not imply that they will in fact move significantly or erratically; they will do so only if the underlying forces governing demand and supply are themselves erratic, and in that case any international monetary system would be in serious difficulty. Flexible exchange rates do not necessarily imply that the national monetary authorities must refrain from any intervention in the exchange markets; whether they should intervene or not depends on whether the authorities are likely to be more, or less, intelligent and efficient speculators than the private speculators in foreign exchange, a matter on which empirical judgment is frequently inseparable from fundamental political attitudes.

The fundamental argument for flexible exchange rates is that they would allow countries autonomy with respect to their use of monetary,

---

The title acknowledges the indebtedness of all serious writers on this subject to Milton Friedman's modern, classic essay, "The Case for Flexible Exchange Rates," written in 1950 and published in 1953 (M. Friedman, *Essays in Positive Economics* (Chicago: University of Chicago Press, 1953), pp. 157–203, abridged in R. E. Caves and H. G. Johnson (eds.), *Readings in International Economics* (Homewood, Illinois: Richard D. Irwin, for the American Economic Association, 1968), chap. 25, pp. 413–37). This paper was first published in Harry G. Johnson and John E. Nash, *UK and Floating Exchanges* (London: The Institute of Economic Affairs, 1969).

fiscal, and other policy instruments, consistent with the maintenance of whatever degree of freedom in international transactions they chose to allow their citizens, by automatically ensuring the preservation of external equilibrium. Since, in the absence of balance-of-payments reasons for interfering in international trade and payments, and given autonomy of domestic policy, there is an overwhelmingly strong case for the maximum possible freedom of international transactions to permit exploitation of the economies of international specialization and division of labor, the argument for flexible exchange rates can be put more strongly still: flexible exchange rates are essential to the preservation of national autonomy and independence consistent with efficient organization and development of the world economy.

The case for flexible exchange rates on these grounds has been understood and propounded by economists since the work of Keynes and others on the monetary disturbances that followed World War I. Yet that case is consistently ridiculed, if not dismissed out of hand, by "practical" men concerned with international monetary affairs; and there is a strong revealed preference for the fixed-exchange-rate system. For this, one might suggest two reasons: first, successful men of affairs are successful because they understand and can work with the intricacies of the prevalent fixed-rate system, but being "practical," they find it almost impossible to conceive how a hypothetical alternative system would, or even could, work in practice; second, the fixed-exchange-rate system gives considerable prestige and, more important, political power over national governments to the central bankers entrusted with managing the system, power that they naturally credit themselves with exercising more "responsibly" than the politicians would do, and that they naturally resist surrendering. Consequently, public interest in and discussion of flexible exchange rates generally appears only when the fixed-rate system is obviously under serious strain, and the capacity of the central bankers and other responsible officials to avoid a crisis is losing credibility.

The present period has this character, from two points of view. On the one hand, from the point of view of the international economy, the long-sustained sterling crisis that culminated in the devaluation of November 1967, the speculative doubts about the dollar that culminated in the gold crisis of March 1968, and the franc-mark crisis that was left unresolved by the Bonn meeting of November 1968 and still hangs over the system, have all emphasized a serious defect of the present international monetary system. This is the lack of an adequate adjustment mechanism, that is, a mechanism for adjusting international imbalances of payments toward equilibrium sufficiently rapidly as not to put intolerable strains on the willingness of the central banks to supplement existing international reserves with additional credits, while not requiring countries to deflate or inflate their economies beyond politically tolerable limits. The obviously available mechanism is greater automatic flexibility of exchange rates (as distinct from adjustments of the "pegs"). Consequently, there has been a rapidly growing interest in techniques for achieving greater automatic flexibility, while retaining the form and assumed advantages of a fixed rate system. The chief contenders in this connection are the "band" proposal, under which the permitted range of exchange rate variation around parity would be widened from the present 1 per cent or less to, say, 5 per cent each way, and the so-called "crawling peg" proposal, under which the parity for any day would be determined by an average of past rates established in the market. The actual rate each day could diverge from the parity within the present band or a widened band, and the parity would, thus, crawl in the direction in which a fully flexible rate would move more rapidly.

Either of these proposals, if adopted, would constitute a move toward a flexible rate system for the world economy as a whole. On the other hand, from the point of view of the British economy alone, there has been growing interest in the possibility of a floating rate for the pound. This interest has been prompted by the shock of devaluation, doubts about whether the devaluation was sufficient or may need to be repeated, resentment of the increasing subordination of domestic policy to international requirements since 1964, and general discontent with the policies into which the commitment to maintain a fixed exchange rate has driven successive governments: "stop-go," higher average unemployment policies, incomes policy, and a host of other domestic and international interventions.

From both the international and the purely domestic point of view, therefore, it is apposite to reexamine the case for flexible exchange rates. That is the purpose of this essay. Because of space limitations, the argument will be conducted at a general level of principle, with minimum attention to technical details and complexities. It is convenient to begin with the case for fixed exchange rates; this case has to be constructed, since little reasoned defense of it has been produced beyond the fact that it exists and functions after a fashion, and the contention that any change would be for the worse. Consideration of the case for fixed rates leads into the contrary case for flexible rates. Certain common objections to flexible rates are then discussed. Finally, some comments are offered on the specific questions mentioned above, of providing for greater rate flexibility in the framework of the IMF system and of floating the pound by itself.

The Case for Fixed Exchange Rates

A reasoned case for fixed international rates of exchange must run from analogy with the case for a common national currency, since the effect of fixing the rate at which one currency can be converted into another is, subject to qualifications to be discussed later, to establish the equivalent of a single currency for those countries of the world economy adhering to fixed exchange rates. The advantages of a single currency within a nation's frontiers are, broadly, that it simplifies the profit-maximizing computations of producers and traders, facilitates competition among producers located in different parts of the country, and promotes the integration of the economy into a connected series of markets, these markets including both the markets for products and the markets for the factors of production (capital and labor). The argument for fixed exchange rates, by analogy, is that they will similarly encourage the integration of the national markets that compose the world economy into an international network of connected markets, with similarly beneficial effects on economic efficiency and growth. In other words, the case for fixed rates is part of a more general argument for national economic policies conducive to international economic integration.

The argument by analogy with the domestic economy, however, is seriously defective for several reasons. In the first place, in the domestic economy the factors of production as well as goods and services are free to move throughout the market area. In the international economy the movement of labor is certainly subject to serious barriers created by national immigration policies (and in some cases restraints on emigration as well), and the freedom of movement of capital is also restricted by barriers created by national laws. The freedom of movement of goods is also restricted by tariffs and other barriers to trade. It is true that there are artificial barriers of certain kinds to the movement of goods and factors internally to a national economy (apart from natural barriers created by distance and cultural differences) created sometimes by national policy, for example, regional development policies, and sometimes by the existence of state or provincial governments with protective policies of their own. But these are probably negligible by comparison with the barriers to the international mobility of goods and factors of production. The existence of these barriers means that the system of fixed exchange rates does not really establish the equivalent of a single international money, in the sense of a currency whose purchasing power and usefulness tends to equality throughout the market area. A more important point, to be discussed later, is that if the fixity of exchange rates is maintained, not by appropriate adjustments of the relative purchasing power of the various national currencies, but by variations in the national barriers to trade and payments, it is in contradiction with the basic argument for fixed rates as a means of attaining the advantages internationally that are provided domestically by a single currency.

In the second place, as is well known from the prevalence of regional development policies in the various countries, acceptance of a single currency and its implications is not necessarily beneficial to particular regions within a nation. The pressures of competition in the product and factor markets facilitated by the common currency frequently result instead in prolonged regional distress, in spite of the apparent full freedom of labor and capital to migrate to more remunerative locations. On the national scale, the solution usually applied, rightly or wrongly, is to relieve regional distress by transfers from the rest of the country, effected through the central government. On the international scale, the probability of regional (that is, national in this context) distress is substantially greater because of the barriers to mobility of both factors and goods mentioned previously; yet there is no international government, nor any effective substitute through international cooperation, to compensate and assist nations or regions of nations suffering through the effects of economic change occurring in the environment of a single currency. (It should be noted that existing arrangements for financing balance-of-payments deficits by credit from the surplus countries in no sense fulfill this function, since deficits and surpluses do not necessarily reflect, respectively, distress in the relevant sense, and its absence.)

Third, the beneficent effects of a single national currency on economic integration and growth depend on the maintenance of reasonable stability of its real value; the adjective "reasonable" is meant to allow for mild inflationary or deflationary trends of prices over time. Stability in turn is provided under contemporary institutional arrangements through centralization of control of the money supply and monetary conditions in the hands of the central bank, which is responsible for using its powers of control for this purpose. (Formerly, it was provided by the use of precious metals, the quantity of which normally changed very slowly.) The system of fixed rates of international exchange, in contrast to a single national money, provides no centralized control of the overall quantity of international money and international monetary conditions. Under the ideal old-fashioned gold-standard, in theory at least, overall international monetary control was exercised automatically by the available quantity of monetary gold and its rate of growth, neither of which could be readily influenced by national governments, operating on national money supplies through the obligation incumbent on each country to maintain a gold reserve adequate to guarantee the convertibility of its currency under all circumstances at the fixed exchange rate. That system has come to be regarded as barbarous, because it required domestic employment objectives to be subordinated to the requirements of international balance; and nations have come to insist on their right to use interventions in international trade and payments, and in the last resort to devalue their currencies, rather than proceed farther than they find politically tolerable with deflationary adjustment policies.

The result is that the automatic mechanisms of overall monetary control in the international system have been abandoned, without those mechanisms being replaced by a discretionary mechanism of international control comparable to the national central bank in the domestic economic system, to the dictates of which the national central banks, as providers of the currency of the "regions" of the international economy, are obliged to conform. Instead, what control remains is the outcome on the one hand of the jostling among surplus and deficit countries, each of which has appreciable discretion with respect to how far it will accept or evade pressures on its domestic policies mediated through pressures on its balance of payments, and, on the other hand, of the ability of the system as a system to free itself from the remnants of the constraint formerly exercised by gold as the ultimate international reserve, by using national currencies and various kinds of international credit arrangements as substitutes for gold in international reserves.

In consequence, the present international monetary system of fixed exchange rates fails to conform to the analogy with a single national currency in two important respects. Regions of the system are able to resist the integrative pressures of the single currency by varying the barriers to international transactions and, hence, the usefulness of the local variant of that currency, and, in the last resort, by changing the terms of conversion of the local variant into other variants; moreover, they have reason to do so in the absence of an international mechanism for compensating excessively distressed regions and a mechanism for providing centralized and responsible control of overall monetary conditions. Second, in contrast to a national monetary system, there is no responsible, centralized, institutional arrangement for monetary control of the system.

This latter point can be rephrased in terms of the commonly held belief that the fixed-rate system exercises "discipline" over the nations involved in it, and prevents them from pursuing "irresponsible" domestic policies. This belief might have been tenable with respect to the historical gold standard, under which nations were permanently committed to maintaining their exchange rates and had not yet developed the battery of interventions in trade and payments that are now commonly employed. It is a myth, however, when nations have the option of evading discipline by using interventions or devaluation. It becomes an even more pernicious myth when one recognizes that abiding by the discipline may entail hardships for the nation that the nation will not tolerate being applied to particular regions within itself, but will attempt to relieve by interregional transfer payments; and that the discipline is not discipline to conform to rational and internationally accepted principles of good behavior, but discipline to conform to the average of what other nations are seeking to get away with. Specifically, there might be something to be said for an international monetary system that disciplined individual nations into conducting their policies so as to achieve price stability and permit liberal international economic policies. But there is little to be said for a system that either obliges nations to accept whatever rate of world price inflation or deflation emerges from the policies of the other nations in the world economy, or obliges or permits them to employ whatever policies of intervention in international trade and payments are considered by themselves and their neighbors not to infringe the letter of the rules of international liberalism.

The defenders of the present fixed-rate system, if pressed, will generally accept these points but argue the need for a solution along two complementary lines: "harmonization" of national economic policies in accordance with the requirements of a single world currency system; and progressive evolution toward international control of the growth of international liquidity, combined with "surveillance" of national economic policies. The problem with both is that they demand a surrender of national sovereignty in domestic economic policy, which countries have shown themselves extremely reluctant to accept. The reasons for this have already been mentioned; the most important are that there is no international mechanism for compensating those who suffer from adhering to the rules of the single currency game, and that the nations differ sharply in their views on priorities among policy objectives, most notably in respect of the relative undesirability of unemployment on the one hand and price inflation on the other. The main argument for flexible exchange rates at the present time is that they would make this surrender of sovereignty unnecessary, while at the same time making unnecessary the progressive extension of interventions in international trade and payments that failure to resolve this issue necessarily entails.

The case for fixed exchange rates, while seriously defective as a defense of the present system of international monetary organization, does have one important implication for the case for flexible exchange rates. One is accustomed to thinking of national moneys in terms of the currencies of the major countries, which currencies derive their usefulness from the great diversity of goods, services, and assets available in the national economy, into which they can be directly converted. But in the contemporary world there are many small and relatively narrowly specialized countries, whose national currencies lack usefulness in this sense, but instead derive their usefulness from their rigid convertibility at a fixed price into the currency of some major country with which the small country trades extensively or on which it depends for capital for investment. For such countries, the advantages of rigid convertibility in giving the currency usefulness and facilitating international trade and investment outweigh the relatively small advantages that might be derived from exchange rate flexibility. (In a banana republic, for example, the currency will be more useful if it is stable in terms of command over foreign goods than if it is stable in terms of command over bananas; and exchange-rate flexibility would give little scope for autonomous domestic policy.) These countries, which probably constitute a substantial numerical majority of existing countries, would, therefore, probably choose, if given a free choice, to keep the value of their currency pegged to that of some major country or currency bloc. In other words, the case for flexible exchange rates is a case for flexibility of rates among the currencies of countries that are large enough to have a currency whose usefulness derives primarily from its domestic purchasing power, and for which significant autonomy of domestic policy is both possible and desired.

The Case for Flexible Exchange Rates

The case for flexible exchange rates derives fundamentally from the laws of demand and supply, in particular, from the principle that, left to itself, the competitive market will establish the price that equates quantity demanded with quantity supplied and, hence, clear the market. If the price rises temporarily above the competitive level, an excess of quantity supplied over quantity demanded will drive it back downward to the equilibrium level; conversely, if the price falls temporarily below the competitive level, an excess of quantity demanded over quantity supplied will force the price upward toward the equilibrium level. Application of this principle to governmental efforts to control or to support particular prices indicates that, unless the price happens to be fixed at the equilibrium level—in which case governmental intervention is superfluous—such efforts will predictably generate economic problems. If the price is fixed above the equilibrium level, the government will be faced with the necessity of absorbing a surplus of production over consumption. To solve this problem, eventually it will either have to reduce its support price, or devise ways either of limiting production (through quotas, taxes, and the like) or of increasing consumption (through propaganda, or distribution of surpluses on concessionary terms). If the price is fixed below the equilibrium level, the government will be faced with the necessity of meeting the excess of consumption over production out of its own stocks. Since these must be limited in extent, it must eventually either raise its control price, or devise ways either to limit consumption by rationing, or reduce the costs of production (for example, by subsidies to producers, or by investments in increasing productivity).

Exactly the same problems arise when the government chooses to fix the price of foreign exchange in terms of the national currency, and for one reason or another that price ceases to correspond to the equilibrium price. If that price is too high, that is, if the domestic currency is undervalued, a balance-of-payments surplus develops and the country is obliged to accumulate foreign exchange. If this accumulation is unwelcome, the government's alternatives are to restrict exports and encourage imports either by allowing or promoting domestic inflation, which in a sense subsidizes imports and taxes exports, or by imposing increased taxes or controls on exports and reducing taxes or controls on imports; or to appreciate its currency to the equilibrium level. If the price of foreign exchange is too low, the domestic currency being overvalued, a balance-of-payments deficit develops and the country is obliged to run down its stocks of foreign exchange and borrow from other countries. Since its ability to do this is necessarily limited, it ultimately has to choose among the following alternatives: imposing restrictions on imports or promoting exports (including imports and exports of assets, that is, control of international capital movements); deflating the economy to reduce the demand for imports and increase the supply of exports; deflating the economy to restrain wages and prices or attempting to control wages and prices directly, in order to make exports more and imports less profitable; and devaluing the currency.

In either event, a deliberate choice is necessary among alternatives that are all unpleasant for various reasons. Hence, the choice is likely to be deferred until the disequilibrium has reached crisis proportions; and decisions taken under crisis conditions are both unlikely to be carefully thought out, and likely to have seriously disruptive economic effects.

All of this would be unnecessary if, instead of taking a view on what the value of the currency in terms of foreign exchange should be, and being, therefore, obliged to defend this view by its policies or in the last resort surrender it, the government were to allow the price of foreign exchange to be determined by the interplay of demand and supply in the foreign exchange market. A freely flexible exchange rate would tend to remain constant so long as underlying economic conditions (including governmental policies) remained constant; random deviations from the equilibrium level would be limited by the activities of private speculators, who would step in to buy foreign exchange when its price fell (the currency appreciated in terms of currencies) and to sell it when its price rose (the currency depreciated in terms of foreign currencies). On the other hand, if economic changes or policy changes occurred that under a fixed exchange rate would produce a balance-of-payments surplus or deficit, and, ultimately, a need for policy changes, the flexible exchange rate would gradually either appreciate or depreciate as required to preserve equilibrium. The movement of the rate would be facilitated and smoothed by the actions of private speculators, on the basis of their reading of current and prospective economic and policy developments. If the government regarded the trend of the exchange rate as undesirable, it could take counteractive measures in the form of inflationary or deflationary policies. It would never be forced to take such measures by a balance-of-payments crisis and the pressure of foreign opinion, contrary to its own policy objectives. The balance-of-payments rationale for interventions in international trade and capital movements, and for such substitutes for exchange rate change as changes in border tax adjustments or the imposition of futile "incomes policy," would disappear. If the government had reason to believe that private speculators were not performing efficiently their function of stabilizing the exchange market and smoothing the movement of the rate over time, or that their speculations were based on faulty information or prediction, it could establish its own agency for speculation, in the form of an exchange stabilization fund. This possibility, however, raises the questions of whether an official agency risking the public's money is likely to be a smarter speculator than private individuals risking their own money, whether, if the assumed superiority of official speculation rests on access to inside information, it would not be preferable to publish the information for the benefit of the public rather than use it to make profits for the agency at the expense of unnecessarily ill-informed private citizens, and whether such an agency would in fact confine itself to stabilizing speculation or would try to enforce an official view of what the exchange rate should be, that is, whether the agency would not retrogress into *de facto* restoration of the adjustable peg system.

The adoption of flexible exchange rates would have the great advantage of freeing governments to use their instruments of domestic policy for the pursuit of domestic objectives, while, at the same time, removing the pressures to intervene in international trade and payments for balance-of-payments reasons. Both of these advantages are important in contemporary circumstances. On the one hand, a great rift exists between nations like the United Kingdom and the United States, which are anxious to maintain high levels of employment and are prepared to pay a price for it in terms of domestic inflation, and other nations, notably the West German Federal Republic, which are strongly averse to inflation. Under the present fixed-exchange-rate system, these nations are pitched against each other in a battle over the rate of inflation that is to prevail in the world economy, since the fixed-rate-system diffuses that rate of inflation to all the countries involved in it. Flexible rates would allow each country to pursue the mixture of unemployment and price trend objectives it prefers, consistent with international equilibrium, equilibrium being secured by appreciation of the currencies of "price stability" countries relative to the currencies of "full employment" countries. The maximum possible freedom of trade is not only desirable for the prosperity and growth of the major developed countries, but essential for the integration of the developing countries into the world economy and the promotion of efficient economic development of those countries. While the post-World War II period has been characterized by the progressive reduction of the conventional barriers to international trade and payments—tariffs and quotas, inconvertibility and exchange controls—the recurrent balance-of-payments and international monetary crises under the fixed-rate system have fostered the erection of barriers to international economic integration in new forms—aid-tying, preferential governmental procurement policies, controls on direct and portfolio international investment—that are in many ways more subtly damaging to efficiency and growth than the conventional barriers.

The removal of the balance-of-payments motive for restrictions on international trade and payments is an important positive contribution that the adoption of flexible exchange rates could make to the achievement of the liberal objective of an integrated international economy, which must be set against any additional barriers to international commerce and finance, in the form of increased uncertainty, that might follow from the adoption of flexible exchange rates. That such additional uncertainty would be so great as to reduce seriously the flows of international trade and investment is one of the objections to flexible rates to be discussed in the next section. At this point, it is sufficient to make the following observations. First, as pointed out in the preceding section, under a flexible-rate system most countries would probably peg their currencies to one or another major currency, so that much international trade and investment would in fact be conducted under fixed rate conditions, and uncertainty would attach only to changes in the exchange rates among a few major currencies or currency blocs (most probably, a U.S. dollar bloc, a European bloc, and sterling, though in the event sterling might be included in one of the other blocs). For the same reason—because few blocs would imply that their economic domains would be large and diversified—the exchange rates between the flexible currencies would be likely to change rather slowly and steadily. This would mean that traders and investors normally would be able to predict the domestic value of their foreign currency proceeds without much difficulty. But, secondly, traders would be able to hedge foreign receipts or payments through the forward exchange markets, if they wished to avoid uncertainty; if there were a demand for more extensive forward market and hedging facilities, than now exist, the competitive profit motive would bring them into existence. Third, for longer-range transactions, the economics of the situation would provide a substantial amount of automatic hedging, through the fact that long-run trends toward appreciation or depreciation of a currency are likely to be dominated by divergence of the trend of prices inside the currency area from the trend of prices elsewhere. For direct foreign investments, for example, any loss of value of foreign-currency earnings in terms of domestic currency, due to depreciation of the foreign currency, is likely to be roughly balanced by an increase in the amount of such earnings consequent on the relative inflation associated with the depreciation. Similarly, if a particular country is undergoing steady inflation and its currency is depreciating steadily in consequence, interest rates there are likely to rise sufficiently to compensate domestic investors for the inflation, and, hence, sufficiently to compensate foreign portfolio investors for their losses from the depreciation. Finally, it should be noted that the same sort of political and economic developments that would impose unexpected losses on traders and investors through depreciation under a flexible-exchange-rate system, would equally impose losses in the form of devaluation, or the imposition of restrictions on trade and capital movements, under the present fixed-rate system.

The Case Against Flexible Exchange Rates

The case against flexible exchange rates, like the case for fixed exchange rates, is rarely if ever stated in a reasoned fashion. Instead, it typically consists of a series of unfounded assertions and allegations that derive their plausibility from two fundamentally irrelevant facts. The first is that, in the modern European economic history with which most people are familiar, flexible exchange rates are associated either with the acute monetary disorders that followed World War I, or with the collapse of the international monetary system in the 1930s; instead of being credited with their capacity to function when the fixed-exchange-rate system could not, they are debited with the disorders of national economic policies that made the fixed-exchange-rate system unworkable or led to its collapse. The second, and more important at this historical distance from the disastrous experiences just mentioned, is that most people are accustomed to the fixed-exchange-rate system, and are prone to assume without thinking that a system of flexible rates would simply display in an exaggerated fashion the worst features of the present fixed-rate system, rather than remedy them.

The historical record is too large a topic to be discussed adequately in a brief essay. Suffice it to say that the interwar European experience was clouded by the strong belief, based on pre-World War I conditions, that fixed exchange rates at historical parity values constituted a natural order of things to which governments would seek eventually to return, and that scholarly interpretation of that experience leaned excessively and unjustifiably toward endorsement of the official view that any private speculation on the exchanges based on distrust of the ability of the authorities to hold an established parity under changing circumstances was necessarily "destabilizing" and antisocial. It should further be remarked that European interwar experience does not constitute the whole of the historical record, and that both previously (as in the case of the U.S. dollar from 1862 to 1879) and subsequently (as in the case of the Canadian dollar from 1950 to 1962) there have been cases of a major trading country maintaining a flexible exchange rate without any of the

THE CASE FOR GREATER FLEXIBILITY

disastrous consequences commonly forecast by the opponents of flexible rates.

The penchant for attributing to the flexible-rate system the problems of the fixed-rate system can be illustrated by a closer examination of some of the arguments commonly advanced against floating exchange rates, most of which allege either that flexible rates will seriously increase uncertainty in international transactions, or that they will foster inflation.

One of the common arguments under the heading of uncertainty is that flexible rates would be extremely unstable rates, jumping wildly about from day to day. This allegation ignores the crucial point that a rate that is free to move under the influence of changes in demand and supply is not forced to move erratically, but will instead move only in response to such changes in demand and supply—including changes induced by changes in governmental policies—and normally will move only slowly and fairly predictably. Abnormally rapid and erratic movements will occur only in response to sharp and unexpected changes in circumstances; such changes in a fixed-exchange-rate system would produce the same or more uncertainty-creating policy changes in the form of devaluation, deflation, or the imposition of new controls on trade and payments. The fallacy of this argument lies in its assumption that exchange-rate changes occur exogenously and without apparent economic reason, an assumption that reflects the mentality of the fixed-rate system, in which the exchange rate is held fixed by official intervention in the face of demand and supply pressures for change, and occasionally changed arbitrarily and at one stroke by governmental decisions whose timing and magnitude is a matter of severe uncertainty.

A related argument is that uncertainty about the domestic currency equivalent of foreign receipts or payments would seriously inhibit international transactions of all kinds. As argued in the preceding section, trends in exchange rates should normally be fairly slow and predictable, and their causes such as to provide more or less automatic compensation to traders and investors. Moreover, traders averse to uncertainty would be able to hedge their transactions through forward-exchange markets, which would, if necessary, develop in response to demand. It is commonly argued at present, by foreign-exchange dealers and others engaged in the foreign-exchange market, that hedging facilities would be completely inadequate or that the cost of forward cover would be prohibitive. Both arguments seek to deny the economic principle that a competitive system will tend to provide any goods or services demanded, at a price that yields no more than a fair profit. They derive, moreover, from the experience of recent crises under the fixed-rate system. When exchange rates are rigidly fixed by official intervention, businessmen normally do not consider the cost of forward cover worth their while, but when everyone expects the currency to be devalued, everyone seeks to hedge his risks by selling it forward, the normal balancing of forward demands and supplies ceases to prevail, the forward rate drops to a heavy discount, and the cost of forward cover becomes "prohibitive." Under a flexible-exchange-rate system, where the spot rate is also free to move, arbitrage between the spot and forward markets, as well as speculation, would ensure that the expectation of depreciation was reflected in depreciation of the spot as well as the forward rate, and, hence, tend to keep the cost of forward cover within reasonable bounds.

A further argument under the heading of uncertainty is that it will encourage "destabilizing speculation." The historical record provides no convincing, supporting evidence for this claim, unless "destabilizing speculation" is erroneously defined to include any speculation against an officially pegged exchange rate, regardless of how unrealistic that rate was under the prevailing circumstances. A counterconsideration is that speculators who engage in genuinely destabilizing speculation, that is, whose speculations move the exchange rate away from rather than toward its equilibrium level, will consistently lose money, because they will consistently be buying when the rate is "high" and selling when it is "low" by comparison with its equilibrium value; this consideration does not however exclude the possibility that clever professional speculators may be able to profit by leading amateur speculators into destabilizing speculation, buying near the trough and selling near the peak, the amateurs' losses being borne out of their (or their shareholders') regular income. A further counterconsideration is that under flexible rates speculation will itself move the spot rate, thus generating uncertainty in the minds of the speculators about the magnitude of prospective profits, which will depend on the relation between the spot rate and the expected future rate of exchange, neither of which will be fixed and independent of the magnitude of the speculators' transactions. By contrast, the adjustable peg system gives the speculator a "one-way option": in circumstances giving rise to speculation on a change in the rate, the rate can move only one way if it moves at all, and if it moves, it is certain to be changed by a significant amount—and possibly by more, the stronger is the speculation on a change. The fixed-exchange-rate system courts "destabilizing speculation," in the economically-incorrect sense of speculation against the permanence of the official parity, by providing this one-way option; in so doing it places the monetary authorities in the position of speculating on their own ability to maintain the parity. It is obviously fallacious to assume that private speculators would speculate in the same way and on the same scale under the flexible rate system, which offers them no such easy mark to speculate against.

The argument that the flexible exchange rate system would promote inflation comes in two major versions. The first is that under the flexible-rate system governments would no longer be subject to the "discipline" against inflationary policies exerted by the fixity of the exchange rate. This argument in large part reflects circular reasoning on the part of the fixed rate exponents: discipline against inflationary policies, if necessary for international reasons, is necessary only because rates are fixed, and domestic inflation both leads to balance-of-payments problems and imposes inflation on other countries. Neither consequence would follow under the flexible-exchange-rate system. Apart from its external repercussions, inflation may be regarded as undesirable for domestic reasons; but the fixed-rate system imposes, not the need to maintain domestic price stability, but the obligation to conform to the average world trend of prices, which may be either inflationary or deflationary rather than stable. Moreover, under the adjustable peg system actually existing, countries can evade the discipline against excessively rapid inflation by drawing down reserves and borrowing, by imposing restrictions on international trade and payments, and in the last resort by devaluing their currencies. The record since World War II speaks poorly for the anti-inflationary discipline of fixed exchange rates. The reason is that the signal to governments of the need for anti-inflationary discipline comes through a loss of exchange reserves, the implications of which are understood by only a few and can be disregarded or temporized with until a crisis descends; the crisis then justifies all sorts of policy expedients other than the domestic deflation that the logic of adjustment under the fixed-rate system demands. Under a flexible-rate system, the consequences of inflationary governmental policies would be much more readily apparent to the general population, in the form of a declining foreign value of the currency and an upward trend in domestic prices; proper policies to correct the situation, if it were desired to correct it, could be argued about in an atmosphere free from crisis.

The second argument, to the effect that a flexible exchange rate would be "inflationary," asserts that any random depreciation would, by raising the cost of living, provoke wage and price increases that would make the initially temporarily lower foreign value of the currency the new equilibrium exchange rate. This argument clearly derives from confusion of a flexible with a fixed exchange rate. It is under a fixed exchange rate that wages and prices are determined in the expectation of constancy of the domestic currency cost of foreign exchange, and that abrupt devaluations occur that are substantial enough in their effects on the prices of imports and of exportable goods to require compensatory revision of wage bargains and price-determination calculations. Under a flexible-rate system, exchange rate adjustments would occur gradually, and would be less likely to require drastic revisions of wage- and price-setting decisions, especially as any general trend of the exchange rate and prices would tend to be taken into account in the accompanying calculations of unions and employers. Apart from this, it is erroneous to assume that increases in the cost of living inevitably produce fully compensatory wage increases: while such increases in the cost of living will be advanced as part of the workers' case for higher wages, whether they will in fact result in compensatory or in less than compensatory actual wage increases will depend on the economic climate set by the government's fiscal and monetary policies. It is conceivable that a government pledged to maintain full employment would maintain an economic climate in which any money wage increase workers chose to press for would be sanctioned by sufficient inflation of monetary demand and the money supply to prevent it from resulting in an increase in unemployment. But in that case there would be no restraint on wage increases and, hence, on wage and price inflation, unless the government somehow had arrived at an understanding with the unions and employers that only wage increases compensatory of previous cost of living increases (or justified by increases in productivity) would be sanctioned by easier fiscal and monetary policy. That is an improbable situation, given the difficulties that governments have encountered with establishing and implementing an "incomes policy" under the fixed-rate system; it is under the fixed-rate system, not the flexible-rate system, that governments have a strong incentive to insist on relating increases in money incomes to increases in productivity, and, hence, are led, on grounds of equity, to make exceptions for increases in the cost of living. It should be noted in conclusion that one version of the argument under discussion, which reasons from the allegation of a persistent tendency to cost-push inflation to the prediction of a persistent tendency toward depreciation of the currency, must be fallacious: it is logically impossible for all currencies to be persistently depreciating against each other.

Contemporary Proposals for Greater Flexibility of Exchange Rates

INCREASED FLEXIBILITY IN THE IMF SYSTEM

The extreme difficulties encountered in recent years in achieving appropriate adjustments of the parity values of certain major currencies within the present "adjustable peg" system of fixed exchange rates, as exemplified particularly in the prolonged agony of sterling from 1964 to 1967 and the failure of the "Bonn crisis" of November 1968 to induce the German and French governments to accept the revaluations of the franc and the mark agreed on as necessary by the officials and experts concerned with the international monetary system, has generated serious interest, especially in the United States administration, in proposals for reforming the present IMF system so as to provide for more flexibility of exchange rates. It has been realized that under the present system, a devaluation has become a symbol of political defeat by, and a revaluation (appreciation) a symbol of political surrender to, other countries, both of which the government in power will resist to the last ditch; and that this political symbolism prevents adjustments of exchange rates that otherwise would or should be accepted as necessary to the proper functioning of the international monetary system. The aim, therefore, is to reduce or remove the political element in exchange-rate adjustment under the present system, by changing the system so as to allow the anonymous competitive foreign exchange market to make automatic adjustments of exchange rates within a limited range.

The two major proposals to this end are the "wider band" proposal and the "crawling peg" proposal. Under the "wider band" proposal, the present freedom of countries to allow the market value of their currencies to fluctuate within 1 per cent (in practice usually less) of their par values would be extended to permit variation within a much wider range (usually put at 5 per cent for argument's sake). Under the "crawling peg" proposal, daily fluctuations about the par value would be confined within the present or somewhat wider limits, but the parity itself would be determined by a moving average of the rates actually set in the market over some fixed period of the immediate past, and so would gradually adjust itself upward or downward over time to the market pressures of excess supply of or excess demand for the currency (pressures for depreciation or appreciation, rise or fall in the par value, respectively).

Both these proposals, while welcomed by advocates of the flexible-exchange-rate system, to the extent that they recognize the case for flexible rates and the virtues of market determination as contrasted with political determination of exchange rates, are subject to the criticism that they accept the principle of market determination of exchange rates only within politically predetermined limits, and, hence, abjure use of the prime virtue of the competitive market, its capacity to absorb and deal with unexpected economic developments. The criticism is that *either* economic developments will not be such as to make the equilibrium exchange rate fall outside the permitted range of variation, in which case the restriction on the permitted range of variation will prove unnecessary, *or* economic change will require more change in the exchange rate than the remaining restriction on exchange-rate variation will permit, in which case the problems of the present system will recur (though obviously less frequently). Specifically, sooner or later the exchange rate of a major country will reach the limit of permitted variation, and the speculation-generating possibility will arise that the par value of that currency will have to be changed by a finite and substantial percentage, as a result of lack of sufficient international reserves for the monetary authorities of the country concerned to defend the par value of the currency.

In this respect, there is a crucial difference between the "wider band" proposal and the "crawling peg" proposal. The wider band system would provide only a once-and-for-all increase in the degree of freedom of exchange rates to adjust to changing circumstances. A country that followed a more inflationary policy than other nations would find its exchange rate drifting toward the ceiling on its par value, and a country that followed a less inflationary policy than its neighbors would find its exchange rate sinking toward the floor under its par value. Once one or the other fixed limit was reached, the country would, to all intents and purposes, be back on a rigidly fixed exchange rate. The crawling peg proposal, however, would permit a country's policy, with respect to the relative rate of inflation it preferred, to diverge permanently from that of its neighbors, but only within the limits set by the permitted range of daily variation about the daily par value and the period of averaging of past actual exchange rates specified for the determination of the par value itself. For those persuaded of the case for flexible exchange rates, the crawling peg is, thus, definitely preferable. The only question is the empirical one of whether the permitted degree of exchange-rate flexibility would be adequate to eliminate the likelihood in practice of a situation in which an exchange rate was so far out of equilibrium as to make it impossible for the monetary authorities to finance the period of adjustment of the rate to equilibrium by use of their international reserves and international borrowing power. This is an extremely difficult empirical question, because it involves not only the likely magnitude of disequilibrating disturbances, in relation to the permitted degree of exchange rate adjustment, but also the effects of the knowledge by government of the availability of increased possibilities of exchange-rate flexibility on the speed of governmental policy response to disequilibrating developments, and the effects of the knowledge by private speculators that the effects on the exchange rate of current speculation will determine the range within which the exchange rate will be in the future, on the assumption that the crawling peg formula continues to hold.

Evaluation of how both the wider band and the crawling peg proposal should work in practice requires a great deal of empirical study, which has not yet been carried out on any adequate scale. In the meantime, those persuaded of the case for flexible exchange rates would probably be better advised to advocate experimentation with limited rate flexibility, in the hope that the results will dispel the fears of the supporters of the fixed-rate system, than to emphasize the dangers inherent in the residual fixity of exchange rates under either of the contemporary popular proposals for increasing the flexibility of rates under the existing fixed-rate systems.

A FLOATING POUND?

The argument of the preceding sections strongly suggests the advisability of a change in British exchange-rate policy from a fixed exchange rate to a market-determined, flexible exchange rate. The main arguments for this change are that a flexible exchange rate would free British economic policy from the apparent necessity to pursue otherwise irrational and difficult policy objectives for the sake of improving the balance of payments, and that it would release the country from the vicious circle of "stop-go" policies of control of aggregate demand.

A flexible-exchange rate is not, of course, a panacea; it simply provides an extra degree of freedom, by removing the balance-of-payments constraints on policy formation. In so doing, it does not and cannot remove the constraint on policy imposed by the limitation of total available national resources and the consequent necessity of choice among available alternatives; it simply brings this choice, rather than the external consequences of choices made, to the forefront of the policy debate.

The British economy is at present riddled with inefficiencies consequential on, and politically justified by, decisions based on the aim of improving the balance of payments. In this connection, one can cite, from many possible examples, the heavy protection of domestic agriculture, the protection of domestic fuel resources by the taxation of imported oil, the subsidization of manufacturing as against the service trades through the Selective Employment Tax, and various other subsidies to manufacturing effected through tax credits. One can also cite the politically arduous effort to implement an incomes policy, which amounts to an effort to avoid, by political pressure on individual wage- and price-setting decisions, the need for an adjustment that would be effected automatically by a flexible exchange rate. A flexible exchange rate would make an incomes policy unnecessary. It would also permit policy toward industry, agriculture, and the service trades to concentrate on the achievement of greater economic efficiency, without the biases imparted by the basically economically-irrelevant objectives of increasing exports or substituting for imports.

The adoption of flexible exchange rates would also make unnecessary, or at least less harmful, the disruptive cycle of "stop-go" aggregate demand policies, which has characterized British economic policy for many years. British governments are under a persistently strong incentive to try to break out of the limitations of available resources and relatively slow economic growth by policies of demand expansion. This incentive is reinforced, before elections, by the temptation to expand demand in order to win votes, in the knowledge that international reserves and international borrowing power can be drawn down to finance the purchase of votes without the electorate knowing that it is being bribed with its own money, that is, until after the election, when the successful party is obliged to clean up the mess so created by introducing deflationary policies, with political safety if it is a returned government, and with political embarrassment if it is an opposition party newly come to power. If the country were on a flexible exchange rate, the generation of the "political cycle" would be inhibited by the fact that the effort to buy votes by pre-election inflationary policies would soon be reflected in a depreciation of the exchange rate and a rise in the cost of living. Even if this were avoided by use of the government's control of the country's international reserves and borrowing powers to stabilize the exchange rate, a newly elected government of either complexion would not be faced with the absolute necessity of introducing deflationary economic policies to restore its international reserves. It could instead allow the exchange rate to depreciate while it made up its mind what to do. Apart from the question of winning elections, governments that believed in demand expansion as a means of promoting growth could pursue this policy *a outrance,* without being forced to reverse it by a balance-of-payments crisis, so long as they and the public were prepared to accept the consequential depreciation of the currency; governments that believed instead in other kinds of policies would have to argue for and defend them on their merits, without being able to pass them off as imposed on the country by the need to secure equilibrium in the balance of payments.

While these and other elements of the case for a floating pound have frequently been recognized and advocated, it has been much more common to argue that a flexible exchange rate for sterling is "impossible," either because the position of sterling as an international reserve currency precludes it, or because the International Monetary Fund would not permit it. But most of the arguments for the presumed international importance of a fixed international value of sterling have been rendered irrelevant by the deterioration of sterling's international position subsequent to the 1967 devaluation, and in particular by the Basle Facility and the sterling area agreements concluded in the autumn of 1968, which, by giving a dollar guarantee on most of the overseas sterling area holdings of sterling, have freed the British authorities to change the foreign exchange value of sterling without fear of recrimination from its official holders. Moreover, the relative decline in the international role of sterling, and in the relative importance of Britain in world trade, finance, and investments, characteristic of the post-World War II period, has made it both possible and necessary to think of Britain as a relatively small component of the international monetary system, more a country whose difficulties require special treatment than a lynch-pin of the system, the fixed value of whose currency must be supported by other countries in the interests of survival of the system as a whole.

Under the present circumstances, adoption of a floating exchange rate for the pound would constitute, not a definitive reversal of the essential nature of the IMF system of predominantly fixed exchange rates, but recognition of and accommodation to a situation in which the chronic weakness of the pound is a major source of tension within the established system. The International Monetary Fund is commonly depicted in Britain as an ignorantly dogmatic but politically powerful opponent of sensible changes that have the drawback of conflicting with the ideology written into its Charter. But there is no reason to believe that the Fund as the dispassionate administrator of an international monetary system established nearly a quarter of a century ago to serve the needs of the international economy, is insensitive to the tensions of the contemporary situation and blindly hostile to reforms that would permit the system as a whole to survive and function more effectively.

· 9 ·

Comments on Mr. Johnson's Paper

GEORGE N. HALM

HARRY G. JOHNSON argues that for those persuaded of the case for flexible rates, the crawling peg is definitely preferable to the wider band because the latter would provide only a once-and-for-all increase in the degree of freedom of exchange rates to adjust to changing circumstances. However, the question need not be which of the two instruments for greater flexibility we *prefer:* the band or the crawl. There is no need to choose. In all probability both band and crawl will be used and in this cooperation of band and crawl the band is more important than Johnson suggests.

In overemphasizing the crawl we underestimate the equilibrating power of the widened band. We should not be unduly impressed by the divergences of national monetary policies as they exist today. These divergences were in part produced, and certainly exaggerated, by overvaluations and undervaluations, as they are maintained under the adjustable-peg system. The postponement of adjustments has made things increasingly worse. We had, in fact, a system that led to *maladjustments.* The maintenance of wrong exchange rates pried the monetary policies of the member countries further apart by enhancing both inflationary and deflationary trends. Surplus countries with undervalued currencies exposed themselves to added inflationist pressure, while deficit countries, unwilling to interrupt national economic expansion for reasons of external balance, went deeper and deeper into deficit. These developments could not have happened to the degree to which they did occur had flexible rates within a widened band been permitted to help balance the external accounts. It is wrong, therefore, to base estimates on the needed degree of exchange-rate variations or parity changes on the experiences of the more recent past.

If we want to be pessimistic about the future divergences of national monetary policies and the integrating power of exchange-rate variations inside a widened band, we shall also have to ask whether even a crawl of not more than 2 per cent per year will be enough and whether a faster crawl could solve the problem of disequilibrating speculation, which will inevitably be connected with substantial parity changes.

Nothing argues against a combination of band and crawl. Both rest on the same criticism of the present system, and both will provide more flexibility. It makes sense to add the crawl to the widened band when we assume that unidirectional deviations of national monetary policies may eventually exceed the adjustment capabilities of the band. For the same reason, it makes sense to consider the widened band the first step on the road to greater flexibility and the gliding peg the second step.

Crawl and band support one another. The band may be able to aid the crawl. It can provide guidance for the practical operation of a gliding-peg system. For this operation it will be essential to gauge the degree of the existing external imbalance, which calls for the shifting of the parity. Variations of exchange rates within a widened band may offer the most reliable evidence. Furthermore, if the band is relatively wide in comparison with the permitted yearly crawl (say, 6 per cent against 2 per cent), the parity adjustments can take place, as it were, *inside* the band and, thus, become invisible. This point is important in view of the difficulties that may be caused by private speculation.

In deciding on the relative importance of band and crawl, we should not forget that the widened band permits market forces to operate while the crawling-peg arrangement deals with a difficult question of price-setting. If we interpret the trend toward limited-exchange-rate flexibility as a partial return to the operational procedures of a market economy, the band is more attractive than the crawl, and we may conclude that the crawl should not be stressed at the expense of the band.

· 10 ·

The International Monetary System: Some Recent Developments and Discussions

GOTTFRIED HABERLER

Recent Crises and How They Were Dealt With

SINCE 1967 the international monetary system has been buffeted in rapid succession by acute crises: the run on sterling and sterling devaluation in November 1967; speculation against the dollar and a huge deficit in the balance of payments of the United States in the last quarter of 1967 and the early months of 1968; the gold rush leading to the discontinuation of the gold pool and introduction of the two-tier gold market in the spring of 1968; the rebellion of students and workers in France in May and June 1968, which, overnight, transformed the French franc from one of the hardest currencies into one of the weakest currencies of the industrial countries; new pressure on the French franc and a huge inflow of funds into Germany, in autumn 1968 and again in 1969.

How did the world deal with these successive blows? Each time huge sums were raised to prop up the currencies under attack and, more important, the countries involved introduced more and more controls: the British controls were successively tightened; in January 1968 the Johnson Administration put a virtual embargo on capital exports to developed countries, tightened capital export restrictions all around, and proposed the imposition of a stiff tax on United States tourists, border taxes, and other restrictions. Fortunately, the tax on tourists was rejected by Congress and, later in the year, quite unexpectedly, the turmoil in Europe and high interest rates in the United States brought relief in the shape of a huge capital inflow. France introduced full-fledged exchange control, and, in November 1968, an agreement was reached by which the German mark underwent what the Germans now call an *Ersatz*-upvaluation and the French franc an *Ersatz*-devaluation by a manipulation of border taxes on imports and tax rebates on exports. (The German word *Ersatz* is preferable in this connection to the English "substitute," because it suggests the substitution of an inferior, inefficient measure for an honest, open change in the exchange rate.)

This paper is a slightly revised version of the Introduction to the second edition of Gottfried Haberler, *Money in the International Economy* (London: The Institute of Economic Affairs and Cambridge, Mass.: Harvard University Press, 1969). The points raised in the following paper (written in the spring of 1969) are further developed in the text of the pamphlet.

115

Thus, the trend toward liberalization of international trade and payments, which had started after the war and has served the world so well, has come to an end, despite the successful conclusion in 1968 of the Kennedy Round of tariff negotiations, which will significantly reduce the tariffs of the industrial countries over the next few years.

The fact that the French franc and sterling are still under pressure and the balance of payments of the United States is in a precarious position—a sharp deterioration of the trade balance in 1968 was overcompensated by unnatural and probably unsustainable capital imports—strongly suggests that the series of acute crises has not yet reached its end.

Is Anything Wrong with the Present System?

An increasing number of experts, mostly, but not only, academic economists, have come to believe that something is wrong with the system: specifically, that the balance-of-payments adjustment mechanism must be improved by making exchange rates more flexible. A widening of the band of permissible fluctuations of the rates around parity and a "crawling" or "sliding" peg are the measures that many experts favor.

However, most of the top officials responsible for monetary policy in the leading industrial countries still cling to the system of fixed rates. They insist that nothing is wrong with the Bretton Woods system; national policy mistakes and accidents, not defects of the international monetary system, are responsible for the series of crises.

It is true, of course, that the international monetary system is not responsible for the French upheaval and the consequent inflation; nor is it responsible for the fact that the Germans, the Dutch, and the Swiss somehow manage to maintain employment without much inflation while many others are not so successful; nor can it be blamed for the ineptitude of British monetary policy and the irresponsibility of the British trade unions; nor is it responsible for the war in Vietnam, the expenditure explosion caused by the so-called "Great Society" programs of the Johnson Administration, and the mistakes of monetary and fiscal policies in the United States, which have produced the inflation since 1965. It is also true that the present system could work if everybody behaved, if there was competition in the labor market, or at least no wage push.

It is equally clear, however, that under modern conditions, with full employment and rapid growth (differently interpreted in different countries) as the supreme objectives of economic policy, with different sensitivities to inflation in different countries, with different attitudes, power, aggressiveness, and senses of responsibility of labor unions in different countries, one has to expect divergent trends in different countries of wages, costs, and prices. Under these circumstances, one has to expect, furthermore, stubborn disequilibria and acute balance-of-payments crises to occur from time to time, and the international monetary system should be so constructed that imbalances can be adjusted without a progressive drift toward controls, and without creating intolerable unemployment and slack. The argument that nothing is wrong with the system because the trouble comes entirely from accidents, policy mistakes, and different policy trends in different countries, completely misses the point and is in fact entirely irrelevant.

Let me illustrate how the flexible system could have worked by reference to an extreme case, namely, that of the French franc: If the French franc and some other currencies, not necessarily all, had had a wider band, the franc, being a strong currency, would have been near the upper edge of the band before May 1968. In May it would have fallen precipitously to the lower edge, providing an automatic devaluation of the franc of 8 or 9 per cent, depending on the width of the band. This would have been much more effective than the *Ersatz*-devaluation through tax manipulations, and would have brought considerable relief by improving the current balance. With the system of the crawling peg, the parity of the franc would have slowly moved down, in case the drop of the rate inside the band proved insufficient to restore equilibrium.

Arguments For and Against Greater Flexibility

What are the substantive arguments against greater flexibility? It is said again and again that more flexibility would undermine confidence and lead to disturbingly large flows of speculative capital. This observation overlooks the fact that it is the present mechanism of the adjustable peg or jumping parity that makes the system a sitting duck for speculators.

This patent and well-known fact is also overlooked by those who argue that the Bretton Woods Charter permits adjustment of exchange rates in case of fundamental disequilibrium, and urge that more frequent use be made of that possibility. It is true that in practice the exchange-rate system has become much more rigid than the framers of the IMF Charter anticipated (except for highly inflationary, less developed countries, where maintaining nominally fixed rates for long periods would lead to intolerable consequences). The reason for the rigidification of the structure of rates, however, was precisely the knowledge that frequent, substantial changes in the rates, the system of the adjustable peg or jumping parity, is the most unsettling system of all; it is inferior in this respect to the old-fashioned gold standard, under which exchange rates are credibly fixed, and to a floating rate, which denies the speculator the one-way option offered to him by the adjustable peg. This was dramatically demonstrated by the German experience in 1969. Prior to the election of the German Bundestag on September 28, 1969, billions of dollars flowed into Germany. When the fixed rate of the mark was abolished on September 30, and the exchange rate was allowed to float, speculation immediately came to an end.

Another standard argument against flexible rates is that they will undermine monetary discipline and, thus, strengthen the propensity to inflate. The answer is that a falling exchange rate, under a regime of flexible rates, is a clearer signal to the monetary authorities than a shrinking international reserve that something is wrong; it should, therefore, be a stronger inducement to tighten money supply, unless resistance to inflation has been broken down altogether, as is unfortunately the case in many less developed countries. In these cases, a floating rate at least minimizes the damage by making the imposition of direct controls unnecessary; open inflation is far less damaging than repressed inflation.

A more subtle argument against flexible rates, now often heard, is that flexibility may have its merits in the so-called "dilemma cases," but is out of place in "nondilemma situations." The dilemma referred to is a conflict between the requirements of internal and external equilibrium. If a deficit country suffers from unemployment or a surplus country suffers from overheating (overfull employment and inflation), a dilemma or conflict exists because different policies are required for the restoration of internal equilibrium on the one hand and external equilibrium on the other. In these cases, it is said, a change in exchange rates offers a way out of the dilemma. (It is now fairly generally conceded that mixing monetary and fiscal policies, "operation mix," or manipulating short- and long-term interest rates, "operation twist," do not offer a solution to the dilemma.)

On the other hand, when a deficit country suffers from inflation or a surplus country suffers from unemployment and deflation, no dilemma or policy conflict exists. The United States at present can be said to be a nondilemma case, because inflation coexists with a very weak balance of payments. Such a country, it is said, should disinflate and not seek a change in the exchange rate. Disinflation would be good both for the balance of payments and for internal equilibrium; therefore no policy dilemma or conflict exists.

Similarly, a surplus country that has unemployment, Germany three years ago, for example, should pursue expansionary monetary and fiscal policies that would simultaneously reduce unemployment and the surplus in the balance of payments. Again, no policy conflict exists, and the exchange rate should be left unchanged; in such a case, the currency should not appreciate as it would under a regime of floating rates.

This reasoning, although superficially plausible, is subject to serious criticism. First, a nondilemma case can easily become a dilemma case. It is quite possible, or even probable, that the degree of disinflation required from the point of view of internal equilibrium would be insufficient to restore external equilibrium. If inflation has gone on for a while, its consequences become embedded in the country's wage-and-price structure and thus disinflation, stopping inflation, may not be enough to eliminate external imbalance; what would be required is that inflation be rolled back, in other words, deflation and unemployment: the dilemma has reappeared. For example, in 1966 Germany had a recession and was thus a "dilemma case"; in 1968 full employment was restored, prices had started to rise again, but the balance of payments surplus persisted: the dilemma had reappeared.

Second, exchange flexibility cannot be turned on and off with the changing pattern of external and internal equilibrium. A flexible rate either exists or it does not. The argument in question, therefore, has to fall back on recommending the use of the adjustable peg, rather than a floating rate, whenever a policy dilemma arises. The argument is therefore subject to the serious criticism of the adjustable-peg system. One should also observe in this connection that the diagnosis of concrete situations as dilemma or nondilemma cases will often be very difficult, and will give rise to endless and potentially serious disagreements and controversies between policymakers inside each country, as well as between experts of different countries. A regime of floating rates avoids this whole tangle of difficulties and radically reduces the danger of international frictions and controversies.

Third, suppose a country operates under the rules of a floating rate. Then dilemmas find their automatic solution whenever they appear. In the nondilemma case, if a country's policies are efficiently managed, the country would pursue, according to the case in question, anti-inflationary or expansionary monetary and fiscal policies to restore internal equilibrium, precluding the need for large changes in the exchange rate.

Realistically, however, we have to reckon with the possibility, or probability, that same countries' internal policies will not be what they should be; in other words, countries often neglect or delay restoration of internal equilibrium. Under the floating-rate system, external equilibrium is maintained in such cases even if internally disequilibrium (inflation or deflation) persists. An important implication of this is that no country can export its inflation or deflation (unemployment) to other countries; or looked at from the other side, no country need fear being infected by inflation or deflation from abroad.[1]

There is, however, another aspect to this insulation, which has recently turned into an argument for fixed rates and against flexible rates. Ed-

[1] This, of course, does not mean that under flexible exchange rates a country is immune to other, microeconomic influences from abroad. It may gain or lose important export markets, and individual firms or industries may experience favorable or unfavorable changes through foreign competition or policy measures. Moreover, such microeconomic impulses may give rise to macroeconomic repercussions.

ward M. Bernstein in a very important paper,[2] points out that, under a fixed rate, inflation originating in any one country spreads to the rest of the world, while, under the floating rate, it is "turned inward." Under the fixed rate, the inflation in the inflating country is alleviated because the supply of real resources is augmented by imports. The country can run an import surplus—if it has a sufficient international reserve—and its expenditures ("absorption") are greater than its domestic output. In other words, it lives "beyond its means" and it "exports inflation."

Similarly, a country suffering from recession gets relief from developing an export surplus, as Germany did on a huge scale in 1966 and 1967. In other words, it "exports deflation and unemployment." [3]

Under the floating rate, when the balance of payments is kept continuously in equilibrium, a country has to swallow the inflation or deflation it generates and cannot get relief by unloading part of the burden on others. It is not quite clear why this is an unmitigated disadvantage from the point of view of the world as a whole. It should also be kept in mind that this "advantage" of the fixed-rate system exists only so long as the international reserve lasts. When a country runs out of reserves (or exhausts its credit line) and props up the fixed exchange rate with controls, the rigid rate becomes an unadulterated evil.

Situations are conceivable in which the flow of reserves from the deficit country to the surplus country serves the interest of both: suppose the deficit country suffers from inflation and the surplus country from deflation; then inflation is damped down in the deficit country by "exporting" part of it and deflation is alleviated in the surplus country by the "importation" of a little inflation. This seems to be the case that Bernstein has in mind. In this case, under the floating-rate system, both countries will have to use internal monetary and fiscal policy a little more vigorously in order to achieve the same improvement in internal equilibrium that they would enjoy automatically under the fixed-rate system.

This situation can, however, hardly be regarded as the rule or even a

[2] "Flexible Exchange Rates and Balance of Payments Adjustment," December 11, 1968, not yet published, will appear in the Proceedings of the Claremont Conference, edited by Randall Hinshaw. The paper has had, however, considerable influence even before becoming available to the general public.

An essentially similar defense of the fixed-rate system was put forward in an important speech (at Chatham House, London, 1967) by Paolo Baffi, General Manager of the Banca d'Italia, "Western European Inflation and the Reserve Currencies," reprinted in *Banca Nazionale del Lavoro Quarterly Review*, Rome, March 1968. See also the criticism of Baffi's point in *U.S. Balance of Payments Policies and International Monetary Reform: A Critical Analysis* by Gottfried Haberler and Thomas Willett (Washington, D.C.: American Enterprise Institute, 1968), p. 70.

[3] These words need not carry any moral condemnation. Germany did not cash her dollars into gold and tried through long-term exports of capital to offset the huge surplus on current account, thus minimizing adverse effects abroad.

frequent occurrence. Moreover, it would be a strange coincidence if the same *magnitude* of external imbalance (deficit and surplus) would serve internal equilibrium in both countries alike, and nobody could tell beforehand in any concrete case whether this complete harmony of interest exists.

There is another implication of the preceding analysis that is worth pointing out because it has been generally overlooked. Since, under flexible rates, inflation and deflation are "turned inward," to use Bernstein's expression, while the fixed-rate system alleviates inflationary and deflationary pressures for any one country by partly deflecting them to other countries, we must conclude that flexible rates provide a stronger inducement than fixed rates for the monetary authorities to restore monetary equilibrium. This point strengthens the argument advanced earlier to the effect that from the point of view of checking inflationary, and deflationary, developments at the source the flexible-rate system is superior to the fixed-rate system, because a falling exchange rate is a clearer warning signal than a deteriorating reserve position.

Geographic Limits of Flexibility

In practice, exchange flexibility is not intended to mean, as it is often pictured in abstract discussions, that each and every currency in the world should fluctuate freely in terms of all others. Many small countries will prefer either to peg their currencies to that of some large country or to form blocs with fixed rates. Nobody would go to the extreme and recommend that large countries with unified currencies should be broken up into regions with fluctuating exchange rates.

The question may be asked why we hear so little of balance-of-payments difficulties between regions of the same country, while they are so common between countries. Many answers have been given: greater mobility of factors of production, labor, and capital; large automatic financing of imbalances through reshuffling of taxes and government expenditures; larger interregional reserves consisting of a common circulating maxim. In my opinion, the decisive circumstances are that monetary and fiscal policy are fully and automatically harmonized between regions while they often diverge between countries; that policy objectives, the weight given to full employment and growth, on the one hand, and to price stability, on the other, are the same as between regions, while they differ significantly between countries; and that the wage push (if it exists) is everywhere the same within a country because of the existence of nationwide trade unions.

All this does not exclude mild cyclical or even long-lasting conjunctural divergences between regions; there are, after all, cases of "depressed areas." But it sharply reduces the occurrence of serious balance-of-payments disequilibria and makes for speedy adjustment.

GREATER FLEXIBILITY OF EXCHANGE RATES

The Special Position of the Dollar

It has often been pointed out that the dollar occupies a very special position, because it is the most important reserve and transactions currency, and is overwhelmingly used in official interventions and more widely employed than any other in private transactions all over the world. One consequence is that it is virtually impossible for the United States to devalue the dollar unilaterally, if that should ever become desirable, or to adopt a floating rate. Suppose the United States tried to devalue the dollar by, say, 10 per cent. It would be perfectly legal because, unlike most other countries, the United States has not used up the right under the IMF Charter of changing the original parity of the dollar by up to 10 per cent without requiring permission from the Fund. It is to be expected, however, that most other countries would simply go along, and the net effect would be an appreciation of gold by 10 per cent in terms of most currencies of the world, which would neither check gold hoarding nor significantly increase international liquidity. Only a few hard currency countries on the continent might accept an appreciation of their currency vis-a-vis the dollar.

Similarly, the United States could not introduce a floating dollar unilaterally, even if it wanted to. How would it proceed? It could suspend gold convertibility of the dollar and declare that it would not try to stabilize the rate by intervention in the market.[4] But again, most countries would simply go along, and would continue to peg their currencies to the dollar. Probably only a handful of countries would choose to accept a floating dollar and let their currencies appreciate. True, all this might change if the United States pursued highly irresponsible inflationary, or deflationary, policies, but this has not yet happened. During the last three years, there has, indeed, been too much inflation both for internal comfort and external balance, but this does not alter the fact that over any somewhat longer period the purchasing power of the dollar has been better preserved than that of any other currency, including the German mark and the Swiss franc.

Unilateral inability to let the dollar float does not mean, however, that the United States can do nothing to promote the adoption of exchange flexibility, or that it is generally in a weak position. The United States has much influence in the IMF and should be able to rally a good deal of support if it decided to propose changes in the rules of the game. If a number of other countries adopted a floating rate system vis-a-vis the dollar, the dollar itself would enjoy the benefits of flexibility, even if the gold price in terms of dollars remained fixed at the present level. If no

---

[4] This would, of course, be suitably qualified to the effect that mild interventions for the purpose of ironing out very short-term fluctuations are not excluded, following the Canadian example of 1950–1960.

agreement on changes in the rules of the game could be reached and the balance of payments deteriorated, the United States could always suspend convertibility and leave to others the choice, either (a) to let their currencies float, to appreciate or depreciate, whatever the case may be, or (b) to go on pegging their currencies to the dollar and adding, if necessary, to their dollar holdings. Most countries would choose the latter course. It is sometimes said that the hard currency countries have a third option—to "retaliate" and impose controls—and that they most likely would do just that. Such a reaction on their part would, however, constitute not only a flagrant violation of the letter and the spirit of the IMF Charter, but would also be inconsistent and self-damaging for the countries that adopted the policy of controls. If a surplus country introduces controls it makes its surplus larger than before. Suspension of gold convertibility of the dollar would be a measure of last resort taken only if and when it appeared impossible to reach agreement on an improvement of the adjustment mechanism *and* a serious deterioration of the balance of payments of the United States developed. It follows that the alternative to suspension of convertibility would be a sharp tightening of controls, capital embargo, even on foreign capital, tourist taxes, border taxes, and similar measures. It would be wholly irrational for other countries to accept meekly harsh, inefficient, and wasteful controls, and react violently to the gentle and efficient adjustment mechanism of a floating rate or a change in the exchange rate.[5]

Irrational and inconsistent behavior can never be entirely excluded. Suppose some countries did react in that manner. What should the United States do? I would hope the United States would not reply in kind, for that would make things still worse. Since trade is a small fraction of American GNP, the United States can well afford to take it easy, and the offenders would soon discover that they are hurting themselves more than they hurt the United States. The upshot is that the United States need not and should not allow anybody to force it, for the purpose of defending the balance of payments, either to impose obnoxious and wasteful controls or to tolerate more unemployment than may be needed to check domestic inflation.

[5] It should be observed that the controls would hit not only the United States, but also the many other countries that would continue to peg their currencies to the dollar. That would make the irrational response by the hard currency countries much more obnoxious and difficult than if the United States alone were involved.

· 11 ·

Fixed Exchange Rates and the Market Mechanism

GEORGE N. HALM

"Good" economic policies must conform to the economic system in which they are applied. Price fixing, for instance, does not fit the logic of the market economy that relies on reactions to price changes. When prices are frozen, equilibrium between supply and demand must be maintained artificially by collective or governmental buying and selling operations and, eventually, by quantitative restrictions. Such controls often tend to multiply as if by chain reaction. Selective rationing, for instance, will have to include more and more articles because the purchasing power released by keeping prices artificially low and limiting demand shifts to other products. Their prices rise and tempt producers to leave the fields under price control. This increases the scarcities that led to the controls in the first place and forces the government to extend its controls. When the government fixes most prices, automatic adjustment of production to changes in demand or supply becomes impossible, and must be replaced by some form of central planning. Therefore, one of the basic rules of economic policy in market economies states that price controls should be used only in national emergencies.

The exchange rate enjoys the distinction of being the only price that is kept fixed even under normal conditions, with the nearly unanimous approval of government and private business. The explanation for this inconsistency is probably to be found in the fact that the exchange rate, as an expression of the international value of the currency unit, is made to share the quality of "price" stability of the domestic monetary unit, according to which "a dollar is always a dollar." Domestically, this monetary illusion does not prevent the functioning of the market economy, though it endangers it when inflation cannot be kept in check.

Internationally, the situation is different. With fixed exchange rates international transactions will not function normally unless all members of the international payments system follow roughly the same monetary and fiscal policies. If we can assume nearly perfect harmonization of these policies, no problem of international payments will arise, regardless of whether we use fixed or flexible exchange rates. But perfect harmonization of national policies cannot be achieved as long as different countries follow different Phillips curves.

Policies of monetary stabilization conflict with "the natural tendency of wages to rise beyond the limits set by the volume of money."[1] Stabilization has to make room for "permissive" money creation when unemployment threatens. When fixed exchange rates do not permit credit expansion, a choice must be made between international or domestic equilibrium.

It is true that a system with fixed parities gains some flexibility through the use of international liquidity reserves. One can even argue that the defense of liquidity reserves forces central bankers into "reasonable" monetary policies and achieves thereby the desired monetary "harmonization," which is the very basis of a system with fixed exchange rates. Fixed exchange rates, therefore, are credited with the maintenance of an otherwise unobtainable monetary discipline.

The fixing of exchange rates forces monetary authorities to change another strategic price, the rate of interest. To prevent the exchange rate of a deficit country from falling, the rate of interest is artificially increased, and monetary policies are constrained. Furthermore, there is a dangerous element of asymmetry in this process that supposedly harmonizes national monetary policies under the aegis of fixed exchange rates. A fixed exchange rate must be defended when it is an overvalued rate that leads to reserve losses. The opposite is not true. Undervalued rates lead to a competitive advantage, to a balance-of-payments surplus, and need not be corrected.

This asymmetry in the harmonization process may easily lead to a situation in which the fixed rates tend to be disaligned rates, with the surplus countries enjoying a permanent competitive advantage and the deficit countries suffering permanently from unwelcome restraints of their domestic policies. Price and cost rigidities have made it increasingly difficult for the monetary authorities of the deficit countries to maintain convertibility through credit restraints, while the surplus countries have done little to shoulder their share of the adjustment burden through expansionist policies, sometimes, of course, with the legitimate argument that further credit expansion would be too inflationary.

Despite these difficulties, fixed exchange rates were maintained while international payments crises were met with *ad hoc* arrangements for increased international liquidity. Only relatively rarely were "fundamental disequilibria" corrected by discrete parity changes. An asymmetrical adjustment process led to disaligned exchange rates, and impending parity changes led to disequilibrating speculation.

Repeated international monetary crises have shown that a system with fixed exchange rates cannot work well, particularly when countries with full employment must cure a balance-of-payments surplus by lowering their interest rates, and fight domestic inflation by raising them, while

[1] Lord Keynes, "The Objective of International Price Stability," *Economic Journal* (June–September, 1943), pp. 185–187.

deficit countries, on the other hand, try to cure the deficit with high interest rates and to stimulate investment and employment by a low rate.

To meet this dilemma situation, the following policies have been tried:

(1) Using monetary policies to achieve external balance and fiscal policies to achieve internal balance;

(2) Using an incomes policy, that is, a campaign of education and propaganda that brings home some basic economic facts to those concerned with wage and price fixing; [2]

(3) Creating more international liquidity;

(4) Discretely adjusting parities in "fundamental disequilibrium"; and

(5) Restricting the international flow of trade and capital by direct controls.

These policies have in common an inappropriateness to the character of the market economies in which they are applied.

The compartmentalization of monetary and fiscal policies cannot be carried to the point where these policies are applied at cross purposes. The fungibility of money excludes a policy that wants to combine high short-term rates of interest successfully with aggressive deficit spending. Similarly, the credit market cannot be separated into watertight compartments to attract foreign funds with high short-term rates, while low long-term rates are supposed to stimulate domestic investment.

Incomes policies are extremely difficult to apply sucessfully, particularly if they are to serve as a substitute for the strict monetary policies demanded by a combination of fixed exchange rates with convertibility in deficit countries. The advocates of an incomes policy are not able to furnish detailed guidelines for wage and price behavior in individual sectors of the economy. They have some general price and wage freeze in mind, probably combined with the threat that, without voluntary compliance, wage and price controls will have to be introduced.

Increased supply of international liquidity has probably done more than all other policies combined to prevent a breakdown of the present system of international payments. However, overemphasis on liquidity has diverted attention from a solution of the adjustment problem that is in conformity with the market economies of the member countries. *Ad hoc* supplies of international liquidity have permitted the *postponement* of exchange-rate corrections, and have harmed the market economies by exposing them to wrong price signals—the very opposite of a real adjustment process in a market system.

Discrete peg adjustments in the case of fundamental disequilibrium

[2] Roy Harrod, *Reforming the World's Money* (New York: St. Martin's Press, 1965), p. 38.

are belated corrections of disaligned rates. They are always preceded by disequilibrating speculation and have a shock-like impact. Devaluations and upvaluations are proof that the market mechanism had not been permitted to work.

Artificial restrictions of international transactions show that the international payments system in which these controls have to be used is not able to achieve its basic aim of free currency convertibility. The violation of the principles of the market economy becomes obvious. Clumsy administrative regulations try to do what the market could have done much better and with less cost.

The only system of international payments that is fully consistent with the basic character of the market economies is one with flexible exchange rates that entrusts the maintenance of external equilibrium to the price mechanism. Floating exchange rates are often rejected with the argument that they would tempt national monetary authorities into reckless behavior, though it should be remembered that changing exchange rates may be a more powerful disciplinarian than changing reserves, particularly since the inflation country could no longer count on being able to pass on part of the inflationary effects to other countries.

If freely floating exchange rates prove unacceptable, a system of limited exchange-rate flexibility should be considered on the grounds that it will make the optimum use of market forces in the foreign exchange market that current political attitudes permit.

Critics of a system with limited exchange rate flexibility often compare it with a nonexisting system of *permanently* fixed rates, or they argue as if fluctuating rates would add to already existing insecurities and risks under the adjustable-peg system. Both attitudes are wrong. The present system has many shortcomings that exchange-rate flexibility could eliminate. The pricing process would not be kept from working, peg adjustments would no longer guarantee profits from disequilibrating speculation, and the need for quantitative restrictions would disappear.

Recent discussions of the problem of international payments have shown little understanding of the essence of a modern market economy. Liquidity problems have monopolized our attention internationally while domestically we have argued in a pre-Keynesian manner as if it were still possible to expose monetary policies to the constraints that external disequilibrium imposes under a system of fixed exchange rates.

What we need is an international monetary policy that conforms to the working of the market mechanism, is supported by market forces, and does not interfere with those internal measures by which we have learned to maintain satisfactory employment levels.

· 12 ·

The Adjustment Process, Its Asymmetry, and Possible Consequences

MARIUS W. HOLTROP

Introductory Remarks

AS PREAMBLE to this discourse on balance-of-payments adjustment, I want to present my credentials. As president of the Nederlandsche Bank from 1946 to 1967, I have been responsible for monetary policy and, in an advisory capacity, have participated in the shaping of fiscal policy in the Netherlands during most of the post-World War II period. In the early 1950s, I set out in the Annual Reports of the Bank (particularly in the reports for the years 1950, 1951, and 1953) my philosophy about the relationship between internal monetary and fiscal policies and external equilibrium, and this philosophy has served as a basis for formulating policy standards. I have not materially changed my thinking on this problem since then. Meanwhile I have become perhaps a wiser, and I am sure a sadder man. As such I have learned that policies apparently explicable under favorable political circumstances in a relatively small, homogeneous country, with an exceptional high proportion of foreign trade, need not be so under less favorable circumstances, or in countries that are much larger and less homogeneous, and in which foreign trade plays only a minor role.

Recognition of the political and institutional impediments to the execution of certain policies should not debar us, however, from formulating what we believe to be desirable standards of policy. The fundamentals of the relationship between internal policies and external equilibrium are, in my opinion, identical for all countries, even though the magnitude of the parameters involved can be different. I do believe, therefore, that the experience of small countries has a general value and this justifies, I think, my talking to you on the basis of that experience.

In my twenty-one years in office, the Netherlands suffered four periods of balance-of-payments deficits. They were all caused by overexpenditure. The first and most serious one was that of the postwar reconstruction period. Overexpenditure under these circumstances seemed unavoidable. Yet, if it had not been for American aid under the Marshall Plan, the country would not have been able to restore equilibrium without a complete break in its progress toward reconstruction. We shall ever owe the United States a debt of gratitude for the aid then received.

This paper, presented to a seminar arranged by Model, Roland and Co., New York, on September 25, 1969, is a much elaborated version of the paper actually presented at Bürgenstock.

GREATER FLEXIBILITY OF EXCHANGE RATES

The other three periods of deficit occurred in 1951, 1956–1957, and 1966. In each case the deficit was, within a short time, overcome by applying what the authorities considered to be the appropriate monetary and fiscal policies. And if, in the years since 1964, the Dutch balance-of-payments position has appeared to be somewhat less solid than in the years before, this can easily be shown to coincide with the authorities' no longer living up to their own established rules of optimal monetary and fiscal behavior. I find in these hard facts a *prima facie* confirmation of the relevance of the philosophy underlying those rules.

Having thus sketched my experience and my prejudices, I shall now proceed.

The Nature and Measure of Balance-of-Payments Disequilibrium

Balance-of-payments adjustment is concerned with the policies aimed at the elimination of a disequilibrium in the external payments position.

TABLE 1

Balance of Payments	U.S.A.		West German Fed. Rep.	
Surpluses (+) and Deficits (−)	1968	Change in Regard to 1967	1968	Change in Regard to 1967
	in billions of U.S. dollars			
Balance on official reserve transactions	+1.64	+5.06	+1.69	+1.59
Balance on liquidity basis [a]	+0.09	+3.64	na	na
Balance on basic account [b]	−1.60	+1.54	+0.05	−1.61
Balance on nonmonetary transactions [c]	−2.64	+1.42	+1.25	−0.06
National liquidity balance [d]	−3.01	+1.58	+2.73	+1.43

Source: The figures have been calculated by the Nederlandsche Bank from official balance-of-payments statistics of the two countries concerned.

[a] Below-the-line item: changes in net foreign assets of monetary authorities and liquid foreign liabilities of the banking system.
[b] Below-the-line item: changes in short-term foreign assets and liabilities of residents, inclusive monetary authorities and banking system.
[c] Below-the-line item: changes in net foreign assets of monetary authorities and short-term foreign assets and liabilities of the banking system.
[d] Below-the-line item: changes in net foreign assets of monetary authorities and net foreign assets of the banking system.

As you know, there are many ways of defining the concept of equilibrium. We hear about deficits and surpluses "on official account," "on liquidity basis," and "on basic account," and we find that they may differ by billions of dollars (see Table 1). The essence of these differences lies in the choice of what transactions shall be considered to represent "below-the-line items." If we take as below-the-line only the increases or decreases in the net foreign assets of the monetary authorities, we have the notion of surplus or deficit "on official account." If we also consider as below-the-line all changes in the net foreign assets of the banking system, we have the notion of "national liquidity surplus or deficit." If we include only part of the changes in net foreign assets of the banking system, we have either the notion of balance "on liquidity basis," which is much used in the United States or the notion of balance "on nonmonetary transactions," which is much used by the OECD, depending upon what foreign assets or liabilities we do include.

My preference is to use the national liquidity balance. It expresses the changes in the volume of liquid assets held by the economy, as caused by the totality of foreign transactions. At the same time, it represents the gain or loss of net foreign assets by the monetary authorities and the banking system. It is immune to the shifts in foreign-asset composition in the accounts of either of these two, or to shifts in foreign assets between these two, shifts that can so easily be manipulated and that have no meaning whatsoever for the internal economy of a country.

The multitude of definitions of what constitutes equilibrium of payments raises the question what equilibrium nations should really strive for. One answer is that authorities will not be satisfied by less than maintaining their reserve position. If they are satisfied with that equilibrium, and if, also, the banking system does not want to increase its net foreign assets, this condition can be fulfilled by equilibrium on the national liquidity balance. If the latter is in deficit it means that the authorities, the banking system, or both must suffer a loss of net foreign assets. This is not a sustainable condition, not even for a reserve-currency country, though such a country can well afford to have its banking system run up short-term foreign liabilities while, at the same time, accumulating medium and long-term foreign assets.

I conclude, therefore, that equilibrium on the national liquidity balance is an essential condition for the long-term external equilibrium of any country. It also constitutes, as we shall see, a proper object of policies aimed at maintaining, or reestablishing, balance-of-payments equilibrium.

The Causes of Balance-of-Payments Surpluses and Deficits

The process of adjustment to balance-of-payments disequilibrium cannot be discussed intelligently without reference to the causes of surpluses and deficits. A state of disequilibrium can be caused by two sets of circumstances. First, by shifts in demand as between foreign and domestic goods and services, or foreign and domestic assets, due either to changes in the underlying preferences, or changes in their relative costs.

It is easy to find, in the postwar years, conspicuous examples of the influence of shifts of demand on world-payments conditions. In the area of consumer demand, I may mention the influence of the demand shift toward the small European car and of the development of massive tourism on the American payments deficit. Generally, one may think in this respect of any case where the elasticity of demand for a country's imports is different from the elasticity of demand for its exports. In the field of public demand, I may mention the consequences for external government expenditure of the increase in world-wide political and military responsibilities incurred by the United States. In the field of capital movements, one has to recognize that any opening up of new natural resources in underdeveloped areas will cause a flow of funds from richer to poorer countries that may well lead to payments deficits for the rich and surpluses for the poor countries. The vast opportunities for American industrial capital investment brought about by the creation of the European Common Market have similarly added to the American deficit and to the European surplus.

A second set of causes of payments disequilibrium is to be found in changes of aggregate global demand, resulting in proportionate changes in the demand for foreign goods and services, which are not compensated by parallel changes in foreign demand for domestic goods. Changes in aggregate demand that exceed or lag behind similar changes in other countries may be due to either differential rates of real growth, or differential rates of demand inflation, that is, growth of aggregate nominal demand that exceeds growth of real supply.

Examples of how differential rates of real growth, as such, tend to lead to deterioration in the balance of payments of the faster growing country are not so easy to quote because such differences in growth are often accompanied by other factors working in the opposite direction. The slowly growing country may, as an example, suffer from spells of demand- and cost-inflation, as has been the case in the United Kingdom. Or, in the fast-growing country, wage increases may lag behind increases in productivity, thus improving competitiveness in foreign markets. Let it suffice, therefore, to recognize that faster growth implies increased demand for imports without, by itself, leading to increased foreign demand for export goods.

That demand inflation must, by itself, necessarily lead to a deficit of payments is sufficiently clear to obviate examples. In the three Dutch payments crises mentioned earlier, there was never any doubt that it was internal demand inflation that had caused the deterioration in the balance-of-payments position and, further, that this demand inflation had been made possible by a rate of liquidity creation that exceeded the anticipated rate of real growth. Nor was there any doubt that the way to correct this situation was to put a stop to demand inflation by appropriate monetary and fiscal policies.

The Automatic, Self-Correcting Effects of Payments Surpluses and Deficits

Situations of surplus or deficit caused by shifts of demand or differences in rates of real growth have automatic, self-correcting, effects.

Under the fixed exchange-rate system, any payments surplus of an economy leads to the sale of foreign exchange to the banking system and, consequently, to an increase in the amount of money or other liquid claims on the banking system held by the public. If the surplus is earned on current account, such money represents income. This income will largely be spent and, in the process, will create new income. If the surplus is earned on long-term capital account, it will serve to finance investment, which again will generate new income. It is only when representing an accumulation of short-term capital that it is less sure whether it will, after some time-lag, be injected into the income stream or not. The process of generation of income started by the payments surplus will continue until a new equilibrium is established between the aggregate nominal income of the economy and its liquidity holdings.

This relationship between total nominal income and volume of liquidity, the latter consisting of money proper and other liquid claims on government and banking system, appears to be a rather stable one. In the United States it did not change over the last ten years by more than an average of ± 1.3 per cent over the year before, and by not more than minus 0.5 per cent cumulatively over the whole period.

How much of the generated increase of income will be nominal only and how much will be real depends on a variety of circumstances. If we assume that the internal monetary and fiscal policies of a surplus country were already successfully geared to achieving full employment and will in no way be changed because of the surplus, then the surplus cannot but lead to a rise in nominal income. This will affect the balance of payments in three ways. It will lead to an increased demand for foreign goods and services, the magnitude of which depends upon the marginal propensity to import. It will also mean an increase in wages that exceeds increases in productivity, which implies an increase in cost of production and prices, leading to a falling off of foreign demand for domestic goods. Finally, it will, at least initially, tend to bring down interest rates and raise asset values, thus creating incentives to reduce capital imports, increase capital exports, or both. Consequently, the balance of payments will tend to come back to equilibrium.

In the deficit country, reverse influences will make themselves felt. The deficit leads to a reduction in the volume of money or other liquid claims on the banking system held by the public. If the deficit is on current account, the outfall of demand will mean a loss of income. This will cause a reduction of expenditure, which will lead to further loss of income. If the deficit is suffered on capital account, it will, albeit with some time-lag, force a reduction of investment and thus generate a loss of income also. If we again assume that the internal policies are used to generate exactly enough liquidity to maintain full employment and are not going to be changed in reaction to the deficit, the deficit must lead to a situation of deficiency of aggregate demand. But this deficiency will not, as in the surplus case, lead to income changes only. On the contrary, it is to be expected that part of the brunt will fall on the volume of production, thus creating a situation of underemployment of resources. The downward stickiness of wages will prevent them from falling. At best, their upward trend will be stopped or slowed down. This will not prevent rather large reductions in entrepreneurial income, and will bring only small reductions in cost. As a consequence, the initial corrective influence on the payments deficit will come mainly from the reduction of imports and only to a minor extent from increased exports.

We must conclude, therefore, that though surplus and deficit, when not interfered with, constitute a self-correcting cybernetic system, this system is of an asymmetrical nature. It tends to lead to mainly nominal increases in income in surplus countries, meaning wage- and price-inflation, and to temporary real reductions of income in deficit countries, meaning underemployment of resources and retarded growth, but only partly a downward trend of unit cost of production.

The described tendencies are, moreover, reinforced by the secondary effects of surplus and deficit on the banking system. If payments surpluses and deficits are added to or taken out of official reserves, they increase or decrease the liquidity of the banking system and, thus, create an incentive to expansion or contraction of the active operations of this system. And if, as under the classical gold standard, even the central bank is supposed to gear its activities to the influx or efflux of gold, a tertiary multiplier is added, which will still further enhance the corrective forces loosened upon the economy by the impact of payments surplus or deficit.

If the deficit-surplus situation is not caused by shifts of demand but by a persistent excess of aggregate demand in the deficit country, one cannot say that the system is self-corrective. As long as the deficit country sustains its demand excess by internal liquidity creation, and as long as its reserves last, it will be able to export inflation to the surplus country without the resulting cost- and price-increases in that country leading to restoring balance. It is very important, therefore, for the surplus country to understand the cause of its surplus. Its policy reaction in the one case should be different from its reaction in the other.

Nature and Content of Balance-of-Payments Adjustment Policies

The strength of unhampered automatic adjustment forces is such that no modern government is willing to allow them to proceed unrestrained, since this would have unacceptable consequences for other policy aims. Modern government not only strives for balance-of-payments equilibrium, it also aims at full employment, maximum sustainable growth, and reasonable price stability. Surplus countries have appeared to be unwilling, or at least reluctant, to accept the inflationary consequences of surplus. They resent the inequity of price inflation; moreover, they fear that cost inflation may prejudice their competitiveness in case a perhaps-temporary surplus should disappear. Deficit countries, especially when still having large reserves, have proved unwilling to accept loss of production and employment as a price, even a temporary price, for speedily attaining payments equilibrium. The consequence has been that what we are used to refer to as adjustment policies are in fact policies that aim at preventing the automatic forces of adjustment to take their relentless course. At their best, such policies consist of partial compensation of the inflow or outflow of liquidity. Thus, they aim at allowing automatic adjustment to exert the beneficial part of its influence slowly, to wit, a favorable evolution of unit cost of production and of interest rates in deficit as against surplus countries while, at the same time, trying to prevent or temporize its unfavorable effects, to wit, price inflation on the one hand and underemployment of productive resources on the other. At their worst, such policies have prevented the automatic forces of adjustment to make themselves felt at all. At the same time administrative and fiscal restrictions on the free movement of goods and services and capital, as far as admissible or having qualified for exemption under the rules of the International Monetary Fund (IMF) and the General Agreement on Tariffs and Trade (GATT), have been substituted for automatism.

The extent to which automatic forces of adjustment have actually been suppressed cannot be better illustrated than by the course of internal liquidity creation in the past ten years in some of the outstanding deficit and surplus areas, namely, the United States and the United Kingdom, on the one hand, and the countries of the European Economic Community (EEC), particularly the West German Federal Republic, on the other.

According to the school of economic thinking to which I adhere, the maintenance of conditions of internal equilibrium demands that internal liquidity creation run parallel to potential real growth. Thus, aggregate demand will be sustained at a level that is neither excessive nor deficient, but suffices to absorb potential real supply under conditions of price stability. Should the liquidity quota of the economy, that is, the proportion between GNP and the volume of liquidity, show a tendency to trendlike change, monetary policy must take this into account, and liquidity creation will, generally, have to be adjusted. If liquidity creation is not kept within these bounds, an excess or deficiency of aggregate demand is bound to ensue, with all the consequences already described.

Policies designed to control the automatic forces of adjustment must, of course, not go so far as to nullify or even overcompensate for these effects. Yet, this is what we find to have happened rather generally in the case of deficit countries and, occasionally, in the case of surplus countries.

Table 2 presents, for a number of countries, figures on their internal liquidity creation, expressed as a percentage of the existing volume of liquidity and compared with their real growth, their price changes, the variations in their liquidity quota, and their national liquidity surpluses and deficits, the latter expressed as a percentage of the volume of liquidity. These figures show that, when comparing the two five-year periods 1959–1963 and 1964–1968, internal liquidity creation generally has shown a rising tendency. They further show that, when introducing the concept of "excess liquidity creation," meaning actual internal liquidity creation corrected for the trend of real growth and for the average changes of the liquidity quota, such excess liquidity creation was increasingly positive in the United States and the United Kingdom, while being rather moderate in the EEC countries jointly, and mostly negative in Germany. For the period 1964–1968, the figures show excess liquidity creation for the United States and the United Kingdom of 4.1 per cent and 6 per cent per year, respectively, for the EEC countries and Germany of only 1 per cent and 1.7 per cent, respectively.

Although, to contribute to reestablishing equilibrium, cost- and price-inflation should have been negative in the deficit countries it appears that in the United States prices, as measured by the GNP deflator, actually went up by almost 1½ per cent a year in the period 1959–1963 and by nearly 3 per cent a year in the period 1964–1968. In the United Kingdom, the percentages for the same periods were over 2 per cent and nearly 4 per cent a year, respectively. In the Common Market countries, where rising prices from the adjustment point of view have to be appreciated positively, average increases in the same periods were over 3½ per cent and over 3 per cent, in Germany over 3 per cent and nearly 3 per cent. The differences between deficit and surplus countries, even as far as being in a balancing direction, are, however, too small, especially in the last five-year period, to have any important impact on competitive conditions and, thus, on fundamental adjustment. As a matter of fact, in the last five years, labor cost per unit of product in industry went up in the United States by 11 per cent, in the United

TABLE 2

Yearly Averages	U.S.A. 1959–63	U.S.A. 1964–68	U.K. 1959–63	U.K. 1964–68	E.E.C. 1959–63	E.E.C. 1964–68	West German Fed. Rep. 1959–63	West German Fed. Rep. 1964–68	France 1959–63	France 1964–68	Netherlands 1959–63	Netherlands 1964–68
1. Internal liquidity creation (in % of vol. of liq. assets at end of previous year)	6.2	8.9	4.5	8.9	8.5	8.3	4.5	5.3	10.6	9.3	0.6	9.8
2. National liquidity surplus (in % of vol. of liq. assets at end of previous year)	−1.1	−0.7	−0.7	−3.1	3.7	1.7	4.7	3.7	4.9	0.1	5.3	0.2
2a of which surplus on current acc.	1.6	1.7	0.8	−0.7	4.1	3.2	8.9	8.1	3.5	0.2	5.6	−1.2
2b of which surplus on capital acc.	−2.7	−2.4	−1.5	−2.4	−0.4	−1.5	−4.2	−4.4	1.4	−0.1	−0.3	1.4
3. Average increase volume GNP (% increase during the year)	4.0	5.1	4.2	2.5	6.0	4.5	5.8	4.0	6.5	4.8	5.3	4.9
4. Average increase prices (GNP defl.) (% increase during the year)	1.4	2.8	2.3	3.8	3.7	3.2	3.1	2.8	4.6	3.5	3.3	5.5
5. Average increase liquidity quota [a] (% increase during the year)	−0.3	0.2	−2.6	−0.5	2.2	2.0	0.1	2.1	3.8	0.8	−2.7	−0.6
6. Excess liquidity creation (=1, minus average growth of 3 over the 10-year period and minus 5)	1.9	4.1	3.7	6.0	1.0	1.0	−0.5	−1.7	1.1	2.8	−1.8	5.3
7. Average liquidity quota [a] (as per end of year)	48.3	48.6	43.8	40.3	35.2	38.2	25.0	24.7	39.6	44.5	38.3	34.9
8. Average increase wage cost per unit of output (in industry, in local currency) (% increase year on year)	−0.5	2.2	1.5	3.6	na	na	3.8	1.6	5.8	4.1	2.8	3.9

Source: Figures on liquidity, GNP volume and prices are taken from data underlying the figures published in the table "Monetary survey of certain countries" in the Annual Report of De Nederlandsche Bank, 1968 and previous years; figures on wage cost per unit are obtained from the Central Planning Bureau, The Hague.

[a] Liquidity quota = liquid assets in % of GNP at current prices.

Kingdom, not including the effect of devaluation, by 19 per cent, and in Germany by 8 per cent. One can hardly be surprised that under these circumstances there was insufficient tendency for existing deficits and surpluses to disappear.

Causes of the Inadequacy of Adjustment Policies

The main reason why the authorities in deficit countries have pursued policies leading to such unsatisfactory results is, we must presume, that, rightly or wrongly, they were convinced that more restrictive policies would have brought about a deficiency of demand of such magnitude as to lead to an unacceptable rate of unemployment and loss of production.

Yet, other reasons may have played a role also. I mention:

(1) rejection of the idea that the volume of liquidity creation should be considered a significant criterion for measuring the efficacy of fiscal and monetary policies, a point of view that has certainly played a role in the United Kingdom;

(2) a mistaken confidence in the effectiveness of other policy instruments; and

(3) not to be excluded, insufficient political strength to be able to enforce more effective policies.

As far as the United States is concerned, it seems clear that in the early 1960s this country found itself in what is often referred to as "the dilemma case" of monetary policy, that is, the situation in which the demands of internal and external equilibrium were contradictory. The United States at that moment had to choose between aiming monetary and fiscal policies at full employment and maximum sustainable real growth, and attaining payments equilibrium. In the given circumstances internal considerations prevailed. Moreover, at that moment, payments equilibrium seemed to be moving closer and, as a matter of fact, was almost attained in 1964. One needs only to read the eloquent report of the Brookings Institution on the balance of payments of the United States in 1968, a prognostic report published in 1963, to appreciate the full force of the argument in favor of the chosen policy. Actually, this policy has proven successful in its impact on employment and growth of real GNP. What went amiss was that the chosen policy led to, or at least was accompanied by, a demand inflation stimulated by mounting government expenditure and financed by a measure of liquidity creation that far exceeded the possible rate of real growth. As a consequence, the balance of payments on current account could not but badly deteriorate, and so it did.

As to the surplus countries, they generally lived up to the prescription of the Brookings Institution report and allowed their economies to be inflated by their surpluses without putting up too much resistance. It is rare to find in the period 1964–1968 instances in which, in any year, the rate of internal liquidity creation in these countries did not exceed the real growth rate. Indeed, the only objection, within the framework of the fixed-parity system, one could possibly make against these countries' policies is that they did not stimulate cost- and price-inflation still further, so as to eliminate even more quickly their remaining surpluses.

As a matter of fact, some of them did. My own country, the Netherlands, for example, has, since 1963, hardly shown a surplus at all. It managed to reach this supposedly blessed state by indulging in a measure of liquidity creation, that is, what we call at home a measure of inflationary financing, as never attained before. This was accompanied over the years 1964–1968 by a quite satisfactory rate of real growth of almost 5 per cent a year, but also by an increase of wage cost per unit in industry of 4 per cent per year and an increase of prices, measured in terms of the gross national product deflator of $5\frac{1}{2}$ per cent per year. Under any normal conditions such a situation would have led to serious payments troubles.

It is, in my opinion, most regrettable that under present international economic conditions this is no longer so. Thus, the golden rules of sound economic behavior seem to have lost their compulsion without any new ones being offered in their stead. No longer does it seem necessary to believe that government expenditure, except for a limited fraction, should be paid for out of taxation or out of long-term borrowing; or that wages would not go up much more than productivity; or that an excess of inflationary financing leads to balance-of-payments deficit. Instead, it looks as if one has to accept inflation so as not be considered an international nuisance because of one's surplus. Yet, when at a certain moment inflationary forces get out of hand, one may suddenly find oneself in deep trouble, as France found itself last year.

Under the circumstances the adjustment process proper has lost any trace of symmetry. Deficit countries do not manage to bring down their unit cost of production and it is often argued that this would even be impossible because the acceptance of a certain demand deflation would tend to reduce output, thus raising, instead of reducing, unit cost.

Another argument is drawn from the discovery of the so-called "Phillips curve," that is, a curve showing the relationship between nominal wage increases and the rate of employment. This curve may show that a country when insisting on attaining a given low rate of unemployment may have to accept a rate of nominal wage increases that exceeds its sustainable rate of real growth. As a consequence it must accept a certain amount of price inflation and, in order to make things move, also a certain amount of excess liquidity creation.

When considerations of this nature determine the internal policies of major deficit countries, whose role in the framework of the international payments system is so important that the system cannot afford or does not wish to see them devalue their currency, it is clear that adjustment to payments disequilibrium cannot but come fully from the side of the surplus countries. These countries will have to inflate until their cost level has sufficiently gone up to allow equilibrium to be reestablished and, subsequently, may have to keep pace with a leading country with a very unfavorable Phillips curve. Should then, moreover, demand-shifts in favor of the surplus countries occur, there will be no other choice for them than to inflate still more. It is this situation that I call the ultimate asymmetry of the adjustment process.

Possible Alternatives to Adjustment by Inflation

It is understandable that under these circumstances renewed interest has appeared in the possibility to promote the adjustment process by introducing into the monetary system a greater measure of exchange-rate flexibility, particularly so in the direction of upvaluation.

I shall not discuss the pros and cons of a flexible rate system as such. I will simply state that I am not in favor of free flexibility. In my opinion it is inconceivable that the world could manage to live with freely flexible rates among over a hundred nations. Actually, a system of flexible rates would, I fear, result in the formation of a small number of antagonistic currency blocs and would lead to a breaking up of the world-wide cooperation in the field of trade and payments, which, even if one admits its deficiencies, still must be considered one of the great achievements of the postwar world. Yet, it would not seem impossible to borrow part of the techniques of exchange-rate flexibility in order to improve the existing fixed-rate system.

Ideally, a change in the exchange rate offers a perfect and immediate adjustment mechanism. It increases or decreases the cost of foreign goods and services for residents and at the same time decreases or increases the cost of domestic goods and services for nonresidents. Thus, it induces corrective shifts in demand without giving rise to any positive or negative impact on aggregate demand.

If a system of exchange-rate flexibility could be devised that in some way or another would allow for changes of parity, by the main surplus and deficit countries, of even as little as say 2 per cent a year, this might lead to almost a doubling of the best actual rates of adjustment experienced over any prolonged period of years in the past or, alternatively, to reducing to almost half the rate of price inflation many actual or potential surplus countries have been suffering of late.

Several suggestions to introduce a certain measure of flexibility into the existing system have been made in the course of the years. They are generally referred to as the "wider band" and the "crawling peg" proposals. They certainly have not yet been thought through sufficiently to be decided upon, but they definitely deserve our attention.

The wider band proposals suggest a widening of the 2 per cent band that the Articles of Agreement of the IMF allow the monetary authorities in regard to the control of the market rates of their currencies. The crawling peg proposals suggest the introduction of regular, small changes of the parities themselves, either on an automatic or on a discretionary basis. The expression "crawling peg" actually refers to a system of automatic adjustment with very small time intervals, possibly of even only one day. I shall hereafter use the expression "movable-parity systems" to refer to the totality of these proposals.

The proponents of a wider band often think in terms of margins of up to ± 5 per cent, instead of the ± 1 per cent of the IMF rules and the $\pm 3/4$ per cent to which the OECD countries have agreed to adhere. When considering that a margin of 5 per cent means a possible fluctuation of the actual rate of 10 per cent, and that this again means a possible fluctuation of 20 per cent between two currencies that reverse their position as strongest and weakest currency in the system, it is clear that much wider margins would bring into the system a great deal of uncertainty about the course of exchange rates, even in a relatively near future. This brings us very close to one of the disadvantages of the system of freely fluctuating rates. Moreover, the wider margin once being exhausted, the flexibility of the system in that one direction disappears and the system then falls back into the same characteristics as the present one.

For these reasons I do not see much merit in wider margins, unless they should be deemed a necessary complement of a properly working system of movable parities, which I do not think they are.

As to the movable-parity idea, I must say that my sympathy for it has, in the course of time, increased more and more. Small and possibly frequent changes of parity, made in agreement with the IMF, need not be viewed as a departure from the Bretton Woods system. This system definitely accepts the necessity of changes of parity in case of fundamental disequilibrium. Shifts of demand of a more permanent nature and of sufficient importance to bring a rate of exchange under sustained pressure do create situations of fundamental disequilibrium that must be corrected.

Experience has taught us, however, that the Bretton Woods system has been overoptimistic in expecting that the consequences of such demand shifts could be overcome by slow adjustment, brought about by following diverging monetary and fiscal policies in the deficit and surplus countries. It has been too confident also in the expectation that, in case of more fundamental disequilibrium, voluntary parity changes would offer a timely solution. As we know, parity changes among the major countries are usually made too late. This is so, partly, for economic reasons: governments are ever hopeful that their policies may be successful and that the tide will turn in time so that the upheaval of a change of parity can be avoided. Partly, however, the reasons are political: devaluation is usually considered to be a consequence of mistaken policies in the past, a judgment, incidentally, that may be grossly unfair when applied to deficits caused by shifts in demand. Revaluations are, usually, unpopular; this is because they always run counter to the short-term interests of producers, who generally constitute a well established pressure group. The result is that parity changes mostly occur after protracted periods of speculative expectations and in an atmosphere of financial crisis. The question is whether a way can be devised to make them more often, but in much smaller steps, so that the shock would be less severe and speculative involvement greatly reduced.

The systems of parity adjustment that have been suggested by a number of scholars are based on two different principles, namely, automatic adjustments and discretionary adjustments. They differ further mainly in respect to the admissible yearly magnitude and the admissible frequency of parity changes.

The automatic systems base the change of parity on the actual market quotations of a past period, for example a year, or on other objective criteria, such as the gain or loss of official reserves. The discretionary systems, on the other hand, would allow the authorities to decide on restricted parity changes, either to be declared in advance, for a given period ahead, or to be made from time to time and guided, but not forced, by the same rules as used for the automatic systems. The core of the system lies in the maximum admissible change per year. A figure of 2 per cent is rather generally suggested. On the one hand this would, when fully used, represent an appreciable contribution to adjustment. On the other hand, it would not force unacceptable interest differentials upon the money markets of the weak as against the strong currencies.

Space does not permit a detailed evaluation of these systems here. Suffice it to say that they are technically possible, that they could be applied within the existing framework of the rules of the Fund, and, what is important, that they could be optional.

As to the merits and demerits of automatic versus discretionary systems, it can be argued that an automatic system has the disadvantage of subjecting the determination of parity, which we are used to look upon as an attribute of sovereign power, to "blind market forces," albeit market forces that have been under control of the monetary authorities. I find no merit in the suggestion, sometimes made, that under an automatic system central banks should be denied the right of intervening in the market within the outer limits of the band. Automatism also has the drawback that changes of parity would be codetermined by the influence that short-term capital movements may have had on market rates in the past.

A great advantage of automatism, on the other hand, is that it would bring the possibly frequent, small parity changes outside the realm of political decision and, thus, also prevent attempts of pressure groups to influence such decisions.

Objections to the movable-parity idea will come from those who fear that far from strengthening the hands of those who seek to pursue responsible internal monetary, fiscal, and financial policies, this innovation might give further leeway to inflationary tendencies because of its providing a possibility of marrying continuous inflation with continuous slow depreciation of the currency.

The movable parity system should appeal, however, to all authorities who suffer from the dismal responsibility of having to acquiesce in a rate of cost- and price-inflation that they consider grossly inequitable, and that distorts business calculations, threatens the financing of public investment by destroying bond markets, and, at any moment, may get out of hand. I, for one, have wrestled with this responsibility, and I would certainly rejoice in seeing an innovation in the system that would bring to a potential surplus country the option between either combining a less inflationary behavior with a gradually rising parity, or sticking to a fixed parity, but then accepting on one's own responsibility the inflationary consequences of it.

Finally, a word about the role of the United States in such an innovated system. The U.S. dollar has become the almost universal intervention currency, used by other countries as the instrument to fulfill their obligation towards the Fund to maintain the par value of their currency within the prescribed limits. At the same time the United States fulfills this obligation by its declared willingness to freely buy and sell gold at $35 an ounce. Consequently, it is impossible for the United States to change its parity otherwise than by changing the gold price. If this official gold price were still linked to the free market price, it would at least be conceivable that the United States, too, could have small parity changes. Practically, however, there is no such possibility.

The suggested innovation would, therefore, not directly affect the United States. The dollar would remain, as it is now, the hub of the international payments system. Its central position would mean that if a maximum cumulative change of parity of 2 per cent per year were allowed, no currency in terms of the dollar could change its parity by more than 2 per cent a year. Other countries, however, might see the parity of some third country change in terms of their own currency by as much as 4 per cent a year, provided these two currencies would make the maximum move in terms of the dollar in opposite directions. This means that it is very desirable that the dollar should, indeed, be the most stable currency in the system in the sense of not being affected by either internal inflation or deflation, nor by demand shifts, for any deviation from this central position is by necessity transferred to the system as a whole, where no country can, in the long run, afford to do better or worse than the dollar by more than could be compensated for by these 2 percentage points a year.

I should like to conclude by expressing the hope that the dollar may soon approach this state of intrinsic stability. Even if this should happen soon, I think the suggested supplement to the Bretton Woods agreement would still deserve the most serious consideration. Every effort should be made to bring, either in this way or in some other way, more flexibility into the fixed-parity system. Its rigidity, which was never intended, is bringing us too many agonies.

· 13 ·

Entrepreneurial Risk under Flexible Exchange Rates

HERBERT GIERSCH

THE purpose of this note is to show that, under flexible exchange rates, entrepreneurial risk need not be greater than under a regime of rigidly fixed rates. Greater variations in exchange rates will not lead to greater variations of expected profits from activities involving foreign exchange transactions:

if the exchange rate varies such as to even out different trends in wage costs and price levels;

if the exchange rate varies such as to neutralize cyclical fluctuations of foreign demand;

if the exchange rate varies such as to make domestic monetary policy more effective, thus reducing the need for variations in interest rates.

We start by defining balance-of-payments equilibrium with particular regard to the international integration of markets: incoming payments and outgoing payments should be equal without:

restrictions on convertibility;

official interventions in the exchange market;

official transactions for balance-of-payments reasons;

other measures for balance-of-payments reasons involving discrimination between domestic and foreign producers or asset holders; and

perhaps also variations in exchange rates.[1]

Balance-of-payments equilibrium can, however, be brought about or maintained by changes in the rate of interest and subsequent private capital movements.

Balance-of-payments equilibrium in this sense:

offers individuals all opportunities connected with the international division of labor;

offers individuals full opportunities of exploiting international differences in capital yield;

excludes all official transactions designed to support an exchange

---

[1] Variations in exchange rates are only provisionally in the list on grounds to be mentioned later.

rate that, by being too low or too high, distorts the international division of labor and the international allocation of resources.

A constant exchange rate is provisionally included in the definition because of the widespread belief that variations in exchange rates place an additional risk on all activities involving foreign-exchange transactions.

This belief stems from the analogy with interregional trade and payments, where exchange rates are rigidly fixed "for eternity." Entrepreneurs believe that, in interregional trade, there is no government interference with private competition, so that the outcome of the game is likely to depend on the firms' relative efficiency. This belief is fairly correct, if one disregards discriminating measures of regional policy that may be introduced without notice. But for competition to be undistorted by government intervention, fixed parities are not a necessary condition.

What makes interregional competition under rigidly-fixed exchange rates so attractive are two conditions, which can also exist under flexible rates:

> an equality of interest levels that ensures that capital costs per unit of output are roughly the same for competing commodities produced with the same technique, disregarding transport costs to be included in the costs of capital goods;
> an equality of labor costs per unit of output, apart from differences in wage rates required for compensating higher transport costs in those locations where labor, by being immobile, accepts lower wages.

The second of these two conditions points to one major difference between interregional and international competition: if there are interregional differences in the Phillips curves, they must result in different employment levels and not in different labor costs. Where unit labor costs go up comparatively fast, firms are forced to dismiss workers, and where labor costs go up too slowly, firms offer more jobs than they can fill at the prevailing wage rate. With or without migration, the market mechanism ensures a parallel development of wage costs, and since capital movements ensure the equality of interest levels and capital costs among regions, the fixed rate of exchange that was an equilibrium rate originally, remains an equilibrium rate all the time. And all the time competitiveness is depending on performance rather than on differences in economic policy (including wage policy).

This certainty that governments cannot interfere with the competitive game in the interregional case is often contrasted with the sudden shifts in competitive strength arising from parity changes in international trade. But entrepreneurs can have the same confidence—that it is performance that matters—under a regime of flexible exchange rates:

if the exchange rate varies so as to even out international differences in cost and price trends arising from different Phillips curves or from different policies; and

if interest rates reflect international differences in the rates of inflation, so that real interest rates are about equal.

Both these conditions can be expected to rule in the medium run, if governments and central banks refrain from intervening in foreign exchange markets and from taking action designed to keep the exchange rate away from its equilibrium level. Assume that it has become evident:

that country F can maintain full employment only with an inflation of 4 per cent per annum; and

that country G is determined not to let the price level rise by more than 1 per cent per annum.

In these circumstances:

the F currency will depreciate in terms of the G currency by 3 per cent per annum; and

the interest level for all credits to be repaid in G currency will be 3 percentage points lower than the interest level for credits to be repaid in F currency.

There will be no distortion in trade and resources allocation between F and G, just as if both countries were members of a true common market and a single currency area. As long as both countries continue with their economic policy, the change in the exchange rate will be easily predictable. However, should economic policy in one or both countries change in an unpredictable way, the change in the rate of exchange will cease to be predictable; as an equilibrium rate it will, however, be a rate of exchange that neutralizes the impact of policy variations on the competitive game between the producers of F and G. The only risk that remains is the risk of bad internal monetary management.

To summarize: what matters if one talks about the risk in activities involving foreign exchange transactions is neither a fixed rate of exchange, nor a predictable rate of exchange, but a rate of exchange that neutralizes distortions arising from unpredictable changes in economic policy.

Can a flexible exchange rate, apart from evening out disparities in cost and price trends, equally neutralize international disparities in the business cycle? The answer, I believe, is yes. Assume a cyclical excess demand in F that is not matched by excess demand in G. The F currency then depreciates (additionally) in terms of G currency, as long as interest levels do not react. But in a framework of proper monetary policy, there is an interest mechanism to counteract this tendency for the F currency to depreciate. It works in a twofold way:

an inelastic credit system or a policy to tighter credit puts a brake on *F*'s boom by means of higher interest rates;

higher interest rates in *F* attract arbitrage capital from *G* so that the *F* currency depreciates less, and it may even appreciate.[2] *F*'s trade balance will show a tendency toward a deficit insofar as:

excess demand is not checked by higher interest rates;

the propensity to import is not reduced by higher import prices (due to the depreciation of the *F* currency);

higher imports are not balanced by additional exports (due to the depreciation of the *F* currency).

This deficit is financed by the arbitrage capital that is flowing into *F* as long as the investment boom in *F* calls for relatively high interest rates. From all this it follows that cyclical divergences give rise to variations in the rates of exchange, but that these variations are heavily damped if interest rates respond to cyclical divergences as well.

The same holds true the other way round: interest rates need not vary as much in response to cyclical disturbances if exchange rates are free to vary as well:

Assume that exchange rates are rigidly fixed and that monetary authorities are not permitted to control transactions and to intervene in the foreign exchange market. Any disturbance in *F* that pushes up investments and, thus, imports must then show its full effect on the interest rate so that the rate of exchange can remain constant in spite of a deficit in the trade balance.

Take the other extreme, which is perhaps even more unrealistic: if interest rates in *F* and *G* are rigidly fixed, it is the exchange rate that has to bear the full burden of the adjustment process: the *F* currency must depreciate until imports become sufficiently expensive compared with import substitutes and until sufficient resources are drawn into the export industries to maintain balance-of-payments equilibrium.

---

[2] To be exact, only spot and short-term forward rates appreciate. In the longer-term forward markets, a tendency to depreciate prevails, since arbitrageurs will want to sell immediately the additional *F* currency in forward markets. As Sohmen has shown, it is, however, the appreciation effect that is dominant. One reason is that foreign trade, which is transacted through spot and short-term forward markets, precedes the transactions that are hedged in forward markets. This shift in the timing is, above all, relevant with a view to cyclical fluctuations. The other reason is that, as has been shown above, spot and all forward rates will go up, as soon as the rise in interest rates starts to work on the internal economy by reducing demand, and, hence, cost and price rises. This general appreciation effect comes about the earlier and is the stronger, the more speculators anticipate the stabilization success of a rise in interest rates, and the more they try to profit through purchases of domestic currency. (See Egon Sohmen, "The Theory of Forward Exchange", Princeton Studies in International Finance No. 17, Princeton 1966, p. 33 ff.).

In between the two extremes there are many combinations, so that variations in interest rates are a substitute for variations in exchange rates and vice versa.

If there is a combination of interest-rate flexibility and exchange-rate flexibility that could be called optimum, it is unlikely to lie at the extremes. Why should a country have exchange-rate flexibility and fix the interest rate? And only the most ardent proponent of fixed exchange rates would be prepared to place the whole burden of balance-of-payments adjustment on interest rates, when governments create disturbances by trying to pursue their own economic policy. Entrepreneurs might be inclined to argue that their total risk could be minimized by official interventions in foreign exchange markets so that both interest rates and exchange rates would be more stable. Such a "socialization of risk," however, has the decisive drawback that then the exchange rate cannot be neutral. If the currency is not allowed to depreciate, it is the foreign competitors who are subsidized, and if the currency is prevented from appreciating, it is the domestic producers who get a premium. Any reductions in risk from unforeseen variations in exchange rates or interest rates are, thus, to be paid in terms of distortions in the competitive game.

In addition to risks resulting from variations in interest and exchange rates necessary for balance-of-payments equilibrium, there are risks from cyclical changes in demand. While large countries suffer from domestic cyclical problems and from their own policy errors, the small countries are likely to import the cycle from abroad. In spite of this, small countries are being frequently advised to "integrate" with their big neighbors by means of fixed exchange rates. The argument that this must be so because firms in small countries have such a big stake in exports, usually overlooks two points:

> First, a flexible exchange rate is a stabilizer with regard to fluctuations in external demand, just as a flexible price policy is the best strategy for a firm to stabilize employment, production, and sales.
>
> Second, and perhaps more important, a flexible exchange rate makes domestic monetary policy more effective. This implies that exchange-rate flexibility is a substitute for, say, tax rate flexibility or flexibility of public expenditures. While it has become an accepted doctrine in a number of countries that fiscal flexibility is a good thing for stabilizing the economy and reducing entrepreneurial risk, it is argued at the same time that exchange-rate flexibility, which would in effect help to stabilize the economy along "monetarist" lines, is a bad thing because it would increase entrepreneurial risk. Considering how inflexible fiscal flexibility actually is, it appears reasonable to presume that exchange rate flexibility is not merely a substitute but a superior instrument.

· 14 ·

The Wider Band and Foreign Direct Investment

DAVID L. GROVE

THE value of outstanding private foreign direct investments of the United States amounted to $59 billion at the end of 1967. The rate of growth was so great that this amount was nearly double that at the beginning of the decade. With such large sums involved, both businessmen and politicians, in considering proposals for a wider band for exchange rates, are bound to turn their attention to the question: "How would a wider band affect the foreign direct investment activities of American firms?" Their decision to endorse or oppose a wider band is likely to be significantly influenced by their assessment of the consequences not only for American trade, but for American direct investment as well. It is important, therefore, to explore what these consequences for direct investment are most likely to be, particularly because little has been written on this subject; this paper endeavors to make a start.

The prospect of greater freedom for exchange rates to move around established parities prompts many businessmen to point out that a new set of uncertainties would be introduced, that these uncertainties would be sufficiently large to constitute a major additional element of risk, and that, as a consequence, the flow of new investment abroad would be curtailed. These results, needless to say, they regard as being highly undesirable.

Behind this portrayal of the consequences of fluctuating exchange rates generally are the following notions:

(1) if exchange rates were free to fluctuate within a wider band, they would in fact jump around within the band very erratically;

(2) they would jump around a sharply declining trend, because there would be few balance-of-payments pressures on governments to eschew inflationary fiscal and monetary policies; and

(3) for direct investors, the prospects of exchange losses would outweigh the prospects of exchange rate gains; besides, direct investors for the most part do not wish to speculate on movements in exchange rates. As a consequence, the demand for forward cover would be so enormous that the supply would be inadequate, and the cost of such cover as would be available would be exceedingly high.

The assumptions and logic behind the position outlined above can be challenged on a number of counts.[1] Nevertheless, this does not mar the faithfulness of their portrayal of the views held by many American businessmen. More importantly, it is not the purpose of this paper to design an educational campaign to correct any fallacies that may be held in the business community. Rather, the purpose is to examine how direct investment abroad would fare under a wider band, in contrast with the present system. The assumption is made that, as direct investors acquired experience with a wider band, they would gradually adjust their actions to the realities of the new system's operations and, coincidentally, would discard any earlier misconceptions and unwarranted fears.

In order to compare the workings of a wider-band system with those of the present "fixed"-exchange-rate system, it will be helpful to trace through what the sequence of forces is, as imbalances develop under each type of system. After all, if each of these two systems were always to be in a position of equilibrium and were never nudged off this position, it should make little difference which system is adopted. In the real world, however, imbalances are always developing and interacting. The ultimate test of a system, therefore, is how efficiently it responds to imbalances. So this is the path of analysis we shall pursue in this paper.

Let us begin with the present system of "fixed" exchange rates. By "fixed," we mean exchange rates that are altered only after imbalances have been prolonged and massive. This is a fair description of how the system has been operating. That it *need* not be an *essential* characteristic of the system is another matter. But it *has* been a prevailing characteristic in the postwar period to date.

Case I—Fixed Exchange Rates and Overvaluation

Let us first examine the case in which the view is widely held that a given foreign currency has become overvalued with respect to the dollar. In such a situation, direct investment of the United States should be retarded, vis-a-vis the volume that would flow if the exchange rate were at a position of equilibrium. There are a number of reasons why one would expect this conclusion to be valid:

(1) If the country's currency is overvalued in relation to the dollar, American producers should be able to compete more cheaply in that market by exporting to it from the United States than by producing the goods through a subsidiary established in that country. (By "more cheaply," I mean, of course, cheaper than would be the case if the exchange rate were cut to its equilibrium value.) Moreover, production by a local subsidiary would be more vulnerable to competition from imports from other suppliers, a situation

---

[1] For example, with respect to the second notion enumerated, it is impossible for *all* exchange rates to have a declining trend.

that would tend to squeeze both profits and the scale of operations.
(2) The international cost situation would be less favorable for production through local subsidiaries in that country for export to third markets.[2]
(3) If a currency is regarded as being overvalued, the need for forward cover is greater, and the cost of cover is raised. This should serve as a deterrent to investment, though the higher cost, in and of itself, may be only marginally significant in many cases.
(4) A country with an overvalued currency is more likely to resort to controls on remittances of earnings and on other international transactions, and to economic nationalism, than is a country with no overvaluation problem. Exchange controls and economic nationalism are very serious deterrents to foreign direct investment.

A depreciating exchange rate without exchange controls is far less harmful to foreign investment than is overvaluation protected by controls. This is so because a country whose exchange rate would depreciate, in the absence of official intervention, usually is (or has been) marked by an accompanying inflation, which, in most circumstances, is the principal driving force behind the decline in the external value of the currency. The inflationary process, however, has an expansionary effect on the volume of business profits. As a general rule, the expansive effect on local currency profits will compensate for the adverse effects that downward adjustments of the exchange rate have on the dollar value of profits. What really hurts foreign investors is not timely devaluation, but, rather, devaluation avoided for a considerable period of time by controls on profit remittances, coupled with limitations on the forms of their interim investment. Then, when the devaluation finally does occur and the restrictions on remittances are eased, if this be the case, the investor finds that he has experienced a shrinkage in the dollar value of his accumulated blocked profits.[3] Moreover,

---

[2] It is assumed, in points (1) and (2) that the international cost-price relationships of the country would be better than those currently prevailing if the country moved to a new equilibrium exchange rate and enough time had elapsed for the price and income adjustments to have occurred. This should ordinarily be the case, although conceivably an example might be constructed in which there was *no* improvement in the commodity cost-price situation after the new equilibrium had been attained, but in which an improvement in the total capital accounts occurred sufficient to enable the country to acquire and maintain an acceptable level of international reserves, and thus be regarded as being "in balance."

[3] Whether he is worse off, *on balance,* will depend on the length of time, *before the imposition of controls,* during which he was able to purchase dollars for remittances at a price below the equilibrium rate. His windfall gain during any such period needs to be counterbalanced against any penalty suffered as a result of restrictions on remittances during the controls and as a result of the subsequent devaluation.

he has had to forego the use of these profits for the purposes intended at the earlier date when his desire to remit was blocked by controls, and, presumably, he had to rearrange his distribution of resources in a "second-best" sort of way that produced a smaller total net quantity of rewards.

Thus, any rational foreign investor, if given a choice between a country that devalues whenever its cost-price structure gets basically out of line and one that delays devaluation for as long as possible by exchange controls, will opt for the former.

Inasmuch as investors have learned from experience that controls on remittances of profits, and on the repatriation of capital as well, are fostered by a situation of overvaluation under the present system, their willingness to invest in countries with chronic balance-of-payments deficits is diminished.

A review of postwar experience discloses that controls over profit and capital transfers have been more common and more restrictive in the less developed countries than in the major industrial nations, although some forms of capital controls do exist in many of the latter. In both types of countries, however, overvaluation seems to be accompanied by an upsurge of economic nationalism, a factor that creates its own additional set of fears and risks for foreign investors.

(5) If a currency is overvalued, foreign investors have a strong incentive to remit as much of their earnings as possible at the "bargain" rate, as long as it lasts. These extra remittances may not be entirely offset by local currency borrowings, for a variety of reasons (credit problems, fear of general uncertainties, attitude of the foreign government toward such a substitution, for example). As a consequence, the rate of growth of foreign investors' investments is curbed.

(6) If a country is having a succession of balance-of-payments deficits, the risk of a devaluation is quite high, and, since countries seldom devalue by tiny amounts, the size of the risk is worthy of careful consideration in the formulation of a foreign company's investment plans in that country. If investments are made just before a devaluation, there are embarrassing explanations to be given to the board of directors about the choice of timing. Even if the two events do not follow so closely, a major devaluation may force a write-down of the dollar value of the investment on the books of the parent, if too short a period of time has elapsed for inflation in the country to have enhanced the local-currency value of the investment sufficiently to offset the effects of the subsequent devaluation, thereby making unnecessary any abnormal write-down in the dollar value of the investment on the parent company's books.

We conclude this section by noting that the present functioning of the international monetary system, under which currencies can become overvalued and remain so for a long time with the aid of controls and international credit, makes the risks to foreign investors very substantial and of sorts that are particularly difficult to assess: When will the devaluation eventually occur? How much will it be? What kinds of controls will be introduced in the meantime, how severe will they be, and what formulas will they employ? How strong will economic nationalism be and what forms will it take? As a consequence, a system that permits situations of overvaluation of currencies to build up and to persist for long periods is hardly a system favorable to foreign investment in the countries concerned. Yet, the present system has created such a situation in a number of countries.

Case II—Fixed Exchange Rates and Undervaluation

The present system not only permits some currencies to become, and long remain, overvalued, it, conversely, permits some currencies to become, and remain, undervalued. In this latter situation, foreign direct investment will be stimulated. There will be more foreign resources flowing to such countries, via foreign direct investment, than would occur if the exchange rate had been permitted to seek an equilibrium level throughout the period. The reasons parallel those given in the case of overvalued currencies, so they can be stated more briefly for the case of undervaluation:

(1) It will be cheaper ordinarily for prospective foreign investors to produce in the country with an undervalued currency than to export to that market, in relation to the comparative cost situation that would exist if the exchange rate were appropriate. Competition from imports in the local market will be less worrisome because imports will have to overcome the implicit tariff created by the undervaluation of the currency.

(2) The country generally will be a better place, in terms of costs, for foreign firms to produce for export to third markets. In effect, the central bank, by acting as a residual buyer of foreign currencies at a premium exchange rate, is subsidizing exports.

(3) Foreign investors have an opportunity of eventual capital gain should the parity of the currency be raised. Thus, there is no reason to delay investing in the country and there is some prospect of a possible profit. (Undervaluation is unlikely, in today's world, to be accompanied by a profit deflation, in terms of local currency, unlike the reverse situation of overvaluation and inflation.)

(4) Controls on repatriation of capital and earnings are nonexistent or minimal in countries with strong balance-of-payments posi-

tions, and the risk of such controls being introduced is small. Economic nationalism is less likely to become a major problem for many foreign investors (although it may still exist, or appear, with respect to certain types of activity).

(5) Foreign investors have a special incentive to retain earnings, and thus to build up their investments in the country.

Thus, countries with currencies widely regarded as being very cheap can be expected to attract more than the "appropriate" quantity of foreign direct investment, and the greater the anticipated unwillingness of the authorities to upvalue the currency, the greater will be the inducement to foreign investors.

CONSEQUENCES OF THE PRESENT SYSTEM

In short, the present system, which in practice has led to an accumulation of imbalances and to long delays in needed adjustments of exchange rates, has produced substantial risks and penalties for foreign direct investors in situations in which the receiving country's currency is either overvalued or likely to become so. Similarly, it has produced the prospect of substantial windfall gains in situations in which the receiving country's currency has become undervalued.

Whether the present system, which has demonstrated a strong tendency to drift into sticky imbalances, has resulted in a larger amount of total foreign direct investment worldwide than would have developed under a system having much more rapid corrections in exchange rates is an interesting question. However, it would seem reasonable to conjecture that if the countries that have accounted for the lion's share of the world's total foreign direct investment—the United States and the United Kingdom—happen to be countries whose currencies have for some years been *overvalued* with respect to the rest of the world (that is, the rest of the world's currencies, as a group, have been undervalued with respect to those countries), then one would expect that these dominant suppliers of direct investment have been investing more abroad than they would have under a balanced structure of exchange rates and that, as a result, the total worldwide volume of direct investment has been greater than it would have been under full equilibrium conditions. If the dollar and the pound sterling are overvalued (I think that a strong case can be made that they have been, relative to the rest of the world as a whole), then the present structure and system of exchange rates probably has inflated the worldwide volume of direct investment, given the capacity and traditions of the United States and the United Kingdom to invest abroad.[4] This conclusion certainly should hold true for the United

---

[4] One study estimates that, in the period 1957–1964, the United States supplied roughly 70 per cent of the world's direct investment private capital flow, and United Kingdom private direct investment abroad accounted for nearly 15 per

States; whether it also holds true for the United Kingdom and for the two nations combined depends upon whether British controls on foreign direct investment by their nationals have, in fact, been severe enough to reduce such investment to levels below those that would have prevailed without controls, if an equilibrium exchange rate had prevailed. At least some "feel" for this issue probably could be obtained by consulting informed opinion. So far as the U.S. is concerned, it is doubtful that its controls have yet had enough restrictive effect to neutralize the artificial stimulus to American direct investment abroad provided by the undervaluation of the currencies of the other industrial nations, taken as a group and excluding the United Kingdom, vis-a-vis the dollar.

Regardless of the tentative character of one's speculations about the worldwide volume of direct investment, there certainly has been misallocation, in the sense that the distribution of real resources via international direct investment has been different from what it would have been had relative national price levels and exchange rates been those that would have existed in the absence both of residual exchange transactions by the monetary authorities and of exchange restrictions.

The tendency for disequilibrium to develop and persist for long periods, and the resulting less-than-optimum international allocation of real resources, is the principal shortcoming of the present system. But, perhaps more importantly from the businessman's own viewpoint, the buildup of these disequilibria creates substantial risks and costs, both for international investment and for international trade. The main reason why this is so is that the timing, magnitude, and chain of consequences, of the adjustments that must inevitably at some point be made are bound to subject the business community to greater shocks, and ones that are harder to predict and guard against, than would be the case if adjustments in exchange rates were continuously responsive to changes in underlying demand and supply conditions. If the response were continuous, the adjustments would be gradual and small.[5] Over the long run, a world in which goods and capital can move relatively freely from where they can best be supplied to where they can be most productively employed requires, as a first condition, that the United States have a satisfactory balance-of-payments position; yet the present system apparently has made this requirement impossible to meet, in practice.

One reason why this requirement must be satisfied is that progress toward achieving and maintaining freer movement of goods and capital will be impossible without the active support of the United States; but

---

cent. (Marcus Diamond, "Trends in the Flow of International Private Capital, 1957–1965," IMF Staff Papers, Vol. XIV No. 1, Mar. 1967.)

[5] Those who believe that speculation would create wild swings in rates will challenge this statement. Needless to say, I am not in that camp, and believe that the statement above can be supported. For example, see Harry G. Johnson's paper "The Case for Flexible Exchange Rates, 1969," in Part II.

the United States will be in a position, both politically and economically, to provide the necessary leadership only if it does not have a weak balance of payments, which prompts it to erect substantial obstacles to the inward movement of goods and outward movement of capital across its own borders. Inasmuch as the United States, under the present system, generally is regarded as having little or no latitude for adjusting its parity vis-a-vis other currencies, and must rely on changes by other nations in their parities to bring about changes in dollar-exchange rates, it follows that the United States has a special interest in seeing to it that the other currencies adjust to the dollar with as little delay as possible. Two great defects of the present system are that it not only permits persistent disequilibrium to build up, together with all the resultant misallocations of resources, but it also substantially "ties the hands" of the only nation in a position really to provide effective world leadership toward freer movement of goods and capital. It is most difficult to imagine that this situation either reduces risks or increases the profitability of American business as a whole, both at home and abroad, in comparison with the circumstances that would prevail if exchange rates could adjust more frequently.

DIRECT INVESTMENT UNDER A WIDER BAND SYSTEM

If the present system were to be replaced by a system of floating rates within bands, how would direct investment be affected? Obviously, the first thing one can say is that there would be a new but essentially short-term element of risk, namely, the risk of short-term movements in exchange rates. (We consider the *new* element of risk to be *short-term* because, under the present system, there *are* long-term exchange rate risks, since parities do sometimes change).

Case III—The Wider Band with an Equilibrium Parity

Let us begin a review of the probable effects of a floating system on foreign direct investment by taking a situation in which the dollar *parity* of the currency is widely regarded as the appropriate one. Then, speculation should keep market exchange rates moving around parity as the center. During any given week or month, the rate might temporarily be below or above the parity, and this could occasion some unanticipated losses or windfall gains for foreign investors who repatriated earnings or capital in such periods. They could, of course, have covered this uncertainty by a forward exchange transaction undertaken in advance, but there would have been a cost. Or, if dollars were selling above the parity, they could borrow dollars short-term and use these funds as a substitute and, at a later date when the price of dollars had fallen back to parity, they could purchase spot dollars to repay the loan. Here again, however, there could be a cost (or a gain!) that would depend on the difference between the interest rate they had to pay on their dollar loan and the rate they were able to earn on the local currency holding during the period. In addition, in this example, there would be the exchange risk involved in the underlying anticipation that the price of the dollar would in fact soon return to the parity level. In any event, international interest rate arbitrage and currency speculation should make fluctuations of exchange rates very small, under the condition specified, namely, that the dollar parity of the currency is widely and correctly regarded as being the appropriate one.

One may note that, given the underlying assumption that the parity is fully appropriate and that, as a consequence, any deviations of exchange quotations from it will be temporary, the possibilities of exchange losses are fully offset by the possibilities to exchange profits. However, if direct investors on the whole tend to be risk averters in foreign exchange transactions, as observation seems to suggest they are, then the above-mentioned symmetry may not provide sufficient comfort to them to have a neutral effect on their investment decisions.

The real questions, therefore, become: What is the amplitude of the fluctuations likely to be? and How sharp will the movements be within the range? The issue thus becomes one fundamental to the potential success or failure of *any* international monetary system—namely, how stable are the underlying forces of demand and supply for the major currencies—and *any* system would be in serious difficulty if these forces are erratic, as Johnson has pointed out. It is interesting—perhaps ironic would be a better word—that critics of proposed floating-exchange-rate systems almost always assume that the underlying demand and supply forces would be inherently and strongly unstable, and then proceed to present illustrations that show how hopeless it would be for businessmen and bankers to operate under such a system; yet, they then proceed to describe the benefits of the present fixed-exchange-rate system within a framework of stability of underlying demand and supply forces. If such asymmetry would in fact prevail, the reasons why this would be so are not obvious and need to be explained by those who chose to make such an assumption.

Two issues come to mind, therefore, and they are crucial ones. First, are the underlying forces of demand and supply likely to be *independent* of the type of system in operation? Second, if there is a difference, which of the two types of system is the more likely to aggravate any tendencies toward a lesser degree of stability in demand and supply forces? Needless to say, one cannot do justice to these two issues in a few sentences; they deserve an entire paper to themselves. But I believe that a theoretically rigorous and practically relevant analysis would demonstrate that the forces that determine the stability or lack of stability of international demand and supply for goods and financial assets are reasonably stable under each of the two types of systems, but that, to the extent that the degree of stability would differ under the two systems, the present system is more likely to aggravate or create instabilities than would a floating-exchange-rate system.

The reason for this conclusion is that, under the present system, a currency can become substantially and quite discernibly overpriced or underpriced in relation to the fixed price at which the monetary authorities continue to act as residual sellers and buyers. The opportunities for profitable speculation mount, and can mount to a point at which the forecast of the speculators becomes self-fulfilling, unless the day of reckoning is postponed by drastic government intervention in the form of exchange controls, trade controls, or both, and these merely create further, though perhaps temporarily suppressed, elements of instability.

It is difficult to visualize the logic of an analysis that would hold that a run on any commodity, or currency, would be weaker if one seller stood ready to take on all comers at a rigidly fixed price than if the price could bend and, as it bent, have the capability of snapping back.[6] There is one clear exception to this, quite obviously: if the fixed-price seller has, and is recognized as having, an unlimited supply of the product. This is the case where national central banks and their *own* currency issues are concerned, and this is why they can break any run by depositors on their commercial banks. But it is not the case where the run is on the reserves of the central bank. Moreover, the more "efficient" the international monetary system becomes, in terms of a declining ratio of global international reserves to total world money supplies, the easier it tends to become for speculators against any currency to recognize that they can spark a drive that will attract enough of a following to "break the bank." Governments respond by setting up international swap arrangements and other credit devices in an effort to dissuade or defeat the speculators, or they impose exchange controls. But certainly neither the lure to speculators inherent in the system nor the efforts of the authorities to block them can be described as conducive to greater stability in the demand and supply forces that move the system.

In contrast, under a system of floating exchange rates, speculators would be set against speculators, instead of all speculators ganging up against the central bank. Since our underlying assumption, throughout this paper, is that we start from a position in which the initial parity is generally regarded as an appropriate one, any effort of any group of speculators to drive the rate down will be neutralized by other speculators' decisions to make a profit at the expense of the "nervous Nellies." The "nervous Nellies," on the other hand, seeing other businessmen will-

---

[6] The analysis immediately following deals with the intensity of a run *once it gets started*. The equally important issue of the likelihood of a run getting started in the first place will not be ignored more than momentarily, however.

ing to back their expectations with their money, are much more likely to be reassured quickly than they are under the present system, in which they see no evidence of any countervailing action except from the central bank, which is required by law to sell at a fixed price, bargain or not.

This is why, under the present system, a run on the monetary reserves can begin and feed on itself even if one starts with an assumption that the prevailing parity initially is generally regarded as an appropriate one. Since this belief has a dispersion, which we will assume is symmetrical (this is what, in fact, we mean when we say that the parity is regarded as appropriate), then the contenders, if turned loose, would fight to a stand-off, and the rate would stick at the parity level. But, if we take the present system, under which the central bank acts as a residual buyer and seller at a fixed rate, and, in addition, introduce an element whose existence practical experience verifies, then we arrive at a different outcome. This key element is that governments are loath to change their parities, but they are very much more loath to upvalue than to devalue; hence, if one is going to speculate against the central bank, one's chances of success, based on all past experience, are clearly much greater if one sells the currency short than if one buys it long.

In this circumstance, those who suspect the currency is overpriced are likely to act sooner and in greater force than those who hold the contrary opinion, and runs are more readily triggered. As the bears act, the central bank's reserves will fall and this may, under the right combination of circumstances, lead to a snowballing effect that never would have started if the system had been one that motivated the bulls to enter the game at the outset, which is what a floating-exchange-rate system does. In short, the present system provides greater motivation for bears to act than for bulls to act, and this creates an element of instability in underlying demand-and-supply forces, and, at times, a rather strong element.

In short, under a floating-exchange-rate system, it seems likely that, if the parity is generally regarded as appropriate, the fluctuation of exchange rates around the parity will be very small indeed. Foreign investors, by adjusting their leads and lags, and especially by some flexibility in the dates of remittances of earnings, could easily live with a floating-exchange-rate system in these circumstances.

Needless to say, by assuming that the parity is an equilibrium one, we have assumed away most of the problem. So we shall now proceed to relax this assumption.

Case IV—The Wider Band with a Slightly Overvalued Parity

The next case to be examined is one in which rates are permitted to float and events occur such that prevailing expectations that the parity is appropriate are gradually replaced by a preponderance of sentiment that the currency is slightly overvalued. A typical cause of such a revision of sentiment would be the appearance of inflationary forces unmatched by any confidence that the government would be entirely successful in halting them in the near future. As this change in sentiment developed, the exchange rate would fluctuate somewhat below the parity, on the average, and the rate rarely would exceed the parity. We also are assuming that the inflation appears sufficiently gradually, and opinions about its permanence are sufficiently dispersed, so that the rate reaches the lower boundary of the band once in a while, but bounces back off the floor quite regularly. Nevertheless, even in this situation there is some risk that the parity may have to be changed eventually, although, in this example, there is no crystallization of sentiment about imminent inevitability of this action. (It should be mentioned, in passing, that once sentiment of imminent inevitability crystallizes and is acted upon by speculators, the parity would have to be changed regardless of whether one is talking of the present IMF system or the wider band system, unless draconian controls are imposed).

In the situation described above, will foreign direct investment in the country be retarded, in the sense that it would be less than it would be in the equilibrium case? The answer is probably yes, for *some* of the reasons listed under Case I, which need not be repeated here. However, foreign direct investment should be discouraged to a lesser extent than in Case I because there should be no extended period of an adverse cost situation, since the exchange rate, and, if necessary, the parity, can be counted on to adjust fairly promptly.[7] Moreover, there should be less fear of exchange controls being imposed, because adjustment via a shift of the exchange rate would come sooner, instead of being blocked by official efforts to preserve an inappropriate rate by resort to controls. In addition, less tinder would be supplied to feed sparks of economic nationalism.

Thus, looking at the listing under Case I, it seems reasonable to conclude that points (1) and (2) will not cut deep, because the decline in the exchange rate will work toward offsetting the tendency of rising local currency costs to stimulate imports and to impede exports. Point (3), however, will hold and will cut sooner (because depreciation actually occurs instead of merely becoming a threat), but the risks, and hence the costs, of cover for short periods (say up to three or four months) should be less than those that would exist under the existing system once

---

[7] The assumption is made here that, if governments become willing to permit their rates to fluctuate within, say, a 5 per cent range on either side of parity, there will be no great reluctance to move the parity once market forces have clearly indicated that it is no longer appropriate. In effect, the parity would follow the market instead of, as at present, attempting to dictate to the market. This would be especially so, of course, if an automatic "sliding parity" arrangement accompanied the wider band.

a situation of overvaluation under the latter system had prevailed for an extended period of time. The reason for this is simply that, once the degree of overvaluation has mounted to a sizeable proportion, the market never knows when the day of devaluation will occur, although it knows that the devaluation is quite likely to be substantial. Hence, the risk and costs of getting caught with a long position in the currency on D day are great, and the forward exchange market's rates have to reflect this situation.

Contrast this with the comparable situation under floating exchange rates: inasmuch as the movement from the previous equilibrium rate is very modest in any given span of, say, three months, and since there is no "backlog" of overvaluation to be protected against, the amount one is willing to pay for cover is small, and there is unlikely to be any run on bank credit, with its own implications for creating instability, in order to obtain cash with which to buy foreign currencies spot in the hope of a "quick kill."

There is a further element worthy of mention: a *gradual* sagging of an exchange rate—which is the situation we are discussing here in Case IV—should lead to less *total* depreciation by the time the driving force (e.g., domestic inflation) has been halted. A reason for this is that foreign exporters would not have had a long period of overvaluation, as they do under the modus operandi of the present system, in which to establish a firm foothold in the domestic market, a foothold that would require the eventual devaluation to be even larger than would have been necessary if the foothold had never been achieved. Similarly, *mutatis mutandis,* on the export side: a *long* overvaluation produces a loss of export markets and thereby requires a greater eventual devaluation to make it worthwhile for the country's exporters to venture to reestablish the position they have lost in overseas markets—a greater devaluation than would have been necessary if the markets had never been lost (as they would not have been, presumably, if the rate had been free to move, or, at the very least, the loss would have been reduced).

Thus, we conclude that point (3) under Case I may come sooner, but the amount of risk over an extended period should be smaller, especially inasmuch as the total amount of depreciation necessary to restore equilibrium should be less.

Point (4) of Case I will be much less serious, because the ability of the exchange rate to move should reduce the likelihood of, and the need for, exchange controls.

Point (5) would hold, to *some* extent, but any attempt to accelerate remittances on a large scale would be self-defeating, since it would soon drive the rate down below a level many astute corporate treasurers would regard as sustainable, which would induce some treasurers to withhold remittances for a short time and would also induce some other treasurers in need of the local currency to accelerate their purchases. This sequence does, of course, assume that no panic is generated. Unless the underlying political and economic situation justifies panic, it is not at all clear why one should assume that the "sagging" situation depicted here in Case IV should degenerate into such a debacle, yet most opponents of floating exchange rates always seem to assume that this will happen. Simultaneously, they assume it will not happen under the currently prevailing system. While one may guess that there is somewhat less chance that a run will occur under the present system *during the initial interval in which the departure from equilibrium is small,* one would expect that the odds of a run would increase as the gap between the prevailing rate and the equilibrium rate became wider, whereas, under a floating rate, this widening would not occur. Hence, over a *number* of periods, the average likelihood of a run being generated should be far greater under the present system than under a floating-rate system.

One may challenge the foregoing by noting that the underlying political and economic conditions are made identical in the two cases, and it is only the response to them that is compared. This is true, so let us address this problem. Many critics of the present system allege that governments and central banks would be "less responsible" if they did not have to preserve a fixed exchange rate, and that, in the absence of this constraint, they would be much more tolerant of inflation than they are now.

This is a serious charge, and it is difficult to counter other than by expressing what can be no more than an opinion. Nevertheless, it is by no means clear why it should be assumed that electorates would hold their governments less accountable for persistent declines in the external value of their currencies than they presently hold them accountable for persistent declines in the nation's monetary reserves. Awareness of shrinkage in the external value of a currency will be especially strong in countries whose citizens travel abroad in large numbers, and in countries in which imports are a large component of total consumption. In fact, a decline in a country's exchange rate should be much more widely noticed than are declines in the central bank's reserves under the present system (and, unlike the latter, they would be impossible to conceal). Accordingly, it seems reasonable to suppose that the organs of influential public opinion would be at least as critical of fiscal and monetary irresponsibility as they now are. In addition, most of the painful domestic social consequences of inflation would remain unchanged, and these should act as a check on carefree political attitudes about inflation. Consequently, the argument that floating exchange rates would stimulate overt or latent inflationary proclivities of governments is far from being convincing. In any event, the present system has not been notably successful in avoiding inflation entirely, but it has enabled domestic inflations to produce a great many *international* distortions, in addition to the domestic ones. If greater variability in exchange rates can reduce international distortions, this should also be of some assistance in reducing domestic distortions in resource utilization.

Point (6) of Case I refers to the choice of timing of foreign investment. A floating rate would be helpful to direct investment in the sense that it would help investors to avoid the prospect of major errors (and fears of errors) in the timing of direct-investment transactions. The reason for this is simply that exchange rates at no time would deviate from the equilibrium rates by as much as they sometimes do under the present system, because the latter permits overvaluations to become quite large and persistent. Hence, the possibility of investing in a major country and suffering a 10 or 15 per cent devaluation a few months later would be reduced.

Case V—The Wider Band with a Substantially Overvalued Parity

This case is similar to Case IV except that the degree of depreciation of the currency is great enough to cause the rate to hit the lower end of the band and to move above it only infrequently and for short periods. The implications of this case would be largely analogous to those of Case I. The outcomes in both cases would depend on how soon the parity and the limits of the band were moved downward, and on how promptly the government dealt with the forces causing the decline. However, the decline in the currency's quotation would provide some of the needed adjustment even before the parity was lowered, and this would help to smooth the process of establishing and adjusting to a new parity.

Case VI—The Wider Band with an Undervalued Parity

In this case, the rates fluctuate consistently above parity, because it is generally believed that the parity is too low. This case is analogous to Case II of the present system. However, it will be less advantageous to direct investment than the present system because the rise in the rate will eliminate at least some of the subsidy to foreign direct investment, which the monetary authorities provide under the present system when they peg their currencies at a bargain-rate level.

Should the rate's upward movement be blocked by the upper end of the band, of course, then the situation becomes identical with that of Case II, except possibly for a difference in the willingness of governments to revise their parities upward under the two systems. Any such difference can be expected to be in favor of the floating-rate system, for the reason given in footnote 7.

Conclusion

By starting with an equilibrium situation under the present international monetary system, and by then introducing departures from the initial position, and by doing the same for the proposed wider band, we conclude that, on balance, the greater flexibility in rates permitted by the wider band (or floating exchange rates without a band) would create considerably more favorable conditions for sound international investment. By "sound" we mean investment that moves mainly in response to the workings of a competitive price mechanism, under conditions that minimize uncertainties.

· 15 ·

The Business View of Proposals for International Monetary Reform

JOHN H. WATTS

THIS paper attempts to outline, from the viewpoint of firms in the United States, the important implications of the proposed reforms based on "crawling pegs" and "wider bands" for trade and investment between countries with established parities.

The Paradox of Business' Position and Actions

The business view of crawling pegs and wider bands represents somewhat of a paradox. On the one hand, it is natural for businessmen to resist the uncertainty embodied in any change to the monetary mechanism, after recent record growth in international trade and investment. On the other hand, this strong growth indicates that a considerable degree of accompanying unrest and uncertainty is not necessarily inconsistent with vigorous expansion of international business activity. The same businessman who identifies with the popular rhetoric "we can't survive another year of monetary strain like 1968" is often pictured in the company's 1968 annual report beside graphs of escalating international sales and profits.

One may assume that businessmen recognize that the established parity system provides a subsidy to the international sector, and, therefore, they resist change.[1] Most business criticism, however, has centered on "reform" in the form of fully fluctuating currencies. With few exceptions, firms with international activities have not analyzed the impact of a limited increase in exchange-rate variability on their own trade and investment outlook. Another barrier to specifying the business view of these proposals is that, to a great extent, commercial banks have ended up with the role of spokesmen for business in monetary questions. These banks, which do create and operate the foreign exchange market, see, however, primarily the market itself. Most of their transactions are with other banks, and have little direct relationship to the array of business considerations involved in the underlying real transactions.[2]

[1] Anthony Lanyi, in Princeton Essay in International Finance No. 72, February 1969, discusses costs and benefits of the fixed-rate system by specifically treating governments' rate-stabilization as a direct subsidy to their external sectors.

[2] Though commercial banks usually know the business of their own clients in detail in a given currency transaction, especially in a future contract, they often do not know whether the firm simply is covering an open trade transaction, or is covering an asset "exposure." The bank may not even know how the corporation

Even wider than the dichotomy between past business opinions and results is the apparent contradiction between expressions of grave concern over recent monetary disruptions and actual business plans for 1969–1970. Recent broad surveys [3] indicate that American corporations expect a growth of trade between 10 and 15 per cent in 1969, and an even greater growth in the near future in investment abroad and in resulting sales by foreign subsidiaries. This apparent paradox results, however, to some degree because many such polls of intentions cover only major international firms, omitting many smaller enterprises that may be most seriously affected by wider fluctuations in currency quotations.

The Assumption of Greater Uncertainty

Lying behind business' resistance to proposals for "tinkering" with the currency rate mechanism is an aversion to what often is perceived to be the likely result—added uncertainty. Corporate treasurers typically assume that wider bands and automatic parity changes would produce wider fluctuations in the prices for spot and future currencies. Although this projection may be incorrect, it is unlikely to be changed until experience proves it right or wrong. Therefore, for the purposes both of understanding business response to reform proposals, and of separating the more from the less substantial objections, the assumption of wider fluctuation is accepted in this discussion.

As a backdrop for consideration of several kinds of business situations, I will presume that if intervention bands were widened to, for example, a total width of 5 per cent and a peg mechanism adopted, allowing up to 2 per cent parity change per year, there would result variations in dollar spot prices of major currencies of 3 per cent or more within a calendar quarter, as frequently as not. The corresponding figure over the past few years would, of course, be closer to ½ to ¾ of 1 per cent. In addition, I will assume that the annualized rate of premia or discount for three-month future currency contracts would, for the major

---

calculates its foreign currency exposure. Consulting the exchange experts at commercial banks on the implications for business of changes in the monetary system is, therefore, a little like asking a policeman at a traffic intersection to analyze why people drive through his station. He does see, of course, the drivers wishing to cross his intersection, but he is not immediately involved in the decisions to operate the autos, nor can he predict reliably what the volume of traffic would be if the roads were, for example, wider but rougher.

[3] For example, 200 executives were surveyed at the March 1969 conference of the International Executives Association. Those responding expected an average increase of 14 per cent in their international activities (*The New York Times*, March 29, 1969). An NICB survey of 182 international executives, reported in *The Outlook for Overseas Production and Trade*, found that half the men expected their exports in 1969 to grow by more than 10 per cent. The overwhelming majority expected growth in sales from foreign-based production to exceed export growth.

currencies, widen to a median (above as often as below) figure of 3 per cent for periods when rate change is not widely expected, compared to a typical cost closer to 1½ to 2 per cent over the past few years.

Severity of Impact

Three major factors should determine the impact on business of wider rate fluctuations of roughly the presumed magnitude: the types of firms involved in a transaction, including their location and the strength of their currency; the type of transaction; and the nature of the markets for traded goods.

First, a variety of *types of enterprises,* uses the international currency markets. Each may expect a different severity of impact from greater exchange fluctuations. One could distinguish between enterprises by function.

(1) Manufacturers (exporters or importers). These include producers of products ranging along the spectrum between "necessary" exports, which in effect must be sold abroad (these are raw materials for which the domestic demand is inadequate and foreign demand is fairly insensitive to price, such as metallurgical coal), to "optional" exports (in which only a small portion of production is exported and foreign demand is capricious, as in many chemicals). Importers also may deal in "necessary" imports (materials needed in manufacture for which there are no good domestic substitutes) or "optional" imports (products imported on the basis of price or other marginal advantage). Because the demand-elasticity for products and factors in the industrial sector varies widely, the impact of a higher cost of currency-risk protection in a specific country will vary widely among manufacturing firms in that country.

(2) Retail Goods Importers. Importers of products that are differentiated from domestic competition or other substitutes in varying degrees, ranging from Scotch whiskey to such commodities as coal. The less differentiated the product, of course, the more likely is greater fluctuation in currency-protection cost to result in a change in actual imports for a given country.

(3) Direct Investor-Producers. "Multinational" firms obtain labor and materials, and produce and sell a large part of their products outside their country of origin or ownership. One advantage they have over national firms is the ability to "trade" internally among subdivisions with little or no concern about rate fluctuation. Also, because such firms customarily make large long-term investments, their sights are raised above short-term costs. In addition, such firms have a variety of other means of insulation against currency risk, as will be discussed below.

(4) Traders. Firms that purchase in one country for sale in others, having little or no integration either backward into production or for-

ward into marketing and distribution. Traders stand to be affected by fluctuations more than any other major type of international organization. Depending on other characteristics, to be discussed later, they may find some of their trade to be severely limited under fluctuations of the presumed magnitude. Association with a producers' or governmental cartel or similar group would, of course, enhance individual traders' ability to withstand currency buffeting.

(5) Investors in Portfolio Securities. Including investment and pension trusts, these organizations can be less concerned about increases in short-term currency fluctuations. The market value of securities typically can be expected to fluctuate as much, or more than, the presumed degree of variability in exchange rates. Hence, like direct investors, portfolio investors are concerned with the long-run economic performance of a currency, not (within the range of uncertainty we have presumed) the parity or spot price mechanism.[4] Short-term trading in securities would, of course, be discouraged by greater short-run exchange rate uncertainty.

(6) Service Firms. This category particularly includes financial agents and intermediaries, such as banks and insurance firms. Impact on these firms would be the most complex, differing widely depending on their nature. A firm that arranges technical licenses may, for example, have profit margins sufficiently large, and underlying arrangements of sufficiently long term, to be insensitive to the rate mechanism. A manufacturers' representative firm might, on the other hand, suffer for the opposite reasons.

Other characteristics, such as size, can bear on a firm's sensitivity to currency market volatility. Small firms with little financial strength obviously face greater difficulties in financing fluctuations in the value of their foreign receipts and payments.

In addition to size, firms differ in degree of diversification. If the portion of an enterprise's activity involved in the foreign sector is small, its exposure to currency difficulties is less serious. And, within that portion, if the number of countries and currencies in which assets are held and denominated is large, and sufficiently spread throughout the world, the firm enjoys a portfolio effect providing some risk protection.

Another factor affecting sensitivity to currency fluctuation is location. A currency can be at various times "weak" (forward exchange rates at a discount vis-a-vis other currencies) or "strong" (forwards at a premium to most other currencies). If an exporter or an importer of a product is in a country whose currency's strength is roughly equal to that of its major competitors, he has an advantage over an exporter invoicing in a

---

[4] However, if sliding parities or wider bands increase a country's rate of inflation because of relaxation of the "discipline" of the present parity conventions, portfolio investors with less inflationary domestic currencies would be penalized.

stronger currency. Customers would prefer to owe a trade liability in the weaker currency because the cost of insuring against an exposure in the strong currency would exceed the premium available from covering trade liabilities owed to a weak-currency exporter. Therefore, although in a global sense it is difficult to say whether widening of forward rates would decrease total trade, it is clear that some exporters and importers would suffer. Although it is true that one trader's discount is some others' premia, these gains and losses will offset exactly only in rare cases when they are recognized by both sides of a trade flow in one good. Usually, one party in a trade will consider himself neither richer nor poorer when forward rates widen over spot since his trade-connected financial asset or liability remains unchanged, in his view, when it is denominated in his own currency. Hence widened future discounts and premia act as reallocators of trade flows, harming some firms while rewarding others. In addition, since the new equilibrium is determined by other than real factor costs, it often may result in less world production and trade in any one commodity.

Secondly, parallel to the variety of types of firm, different influences from greater rate fluctuation can be expected with different *types of exchange transactions*. These are, of course, generally related to the type of originating firm. They include:

(1) Trade transactions.

(2) Borrowing and investment of short-term funds. These two general transaction types are most likely to be affected by greater rate fluctuation, because the cost of added currency-uncertainty will often make domestic alternatives more attractive. In addition, the short period of turnover of funds in these types of activities means that returns on each transaction are small compared to the cost of removing or reducing currency risk.

(3) Long-term borrowings.

(4) Portfolio investments.

(5) Transfers for direct investments. Greater variability in spot price and forward costs should not greatly influence such long-term transactions, which must in any event depend on expected relative economic stability and currency purchasing power.[5]

---

[5] As an example of the long-term borrowers' view, it is interesting to note that a 1 per cent interest advantage has recently been sufficiently attractive to encourage American firms to engage in long, unhedged borrowings in German marks instead of in U. S. dollars. Though this violates the old rule of not borrowing in a "strong" currency during a period of monetary unrest, it could be a rational judgment even for one who expected a mark revaluation of, say, 10 per cent. Such an event would raise the cost of interest payments directly by about 0.65 per cent (10 per cent of a 6.5 per cent coupon). And, even at a very conservative corporate internal discount rate of 7 per cent, the cost of paying back 10 per cent more in twenty-five years would be equivalent only to 0.16 per cent more (at 7 per cent, an extra $0.0016 per year accumulates in twenty-five years

(6) Payments. Potential impact on this category of transactions, including dividends, royalties, interest, etc., is complex, since their time-cycle, or turnover, is short enough to be affected significantly by short-term exchange-rate trends across wider intervention bands. In addition, many corporations like to include planned receipts from foreign affiliates in their schedule of cash flows. Faced with greater uncertainty, more of these firms should enter the forward exchange market to insure against disruption of their plans.

(7) Hedging, or future currency contract, transactions. Distinction should be made between two types of hedges. Some are entered into for protection against any price fluctuation, even that within intervention bands. These typically are taken when the transactor's capital is small compared to the value of the transaction, as in commodity trade, or when the time-cycle of a receipt or payment is short. Other transactions, probably in the majority, are primarily hedges against a change in parity. Businessmen do anticipate a greater volume of hedging of the first type if the reforms under discussion are adopted, though not necessarily more of the second. Indeed, if risk of changes in parity were perceived to be lessened by greater flexibility, the volume of forward exchange activity of the second type should diminish.

Third, the impact of greater spot and future price fluctuation can also be expected to differ according to the *nature of the markets for the product* being exchanged in trade.

If, as indicated above, a good domestic supply or substitute exists for an imported good, the importer stands to lose more business because of the increases in his costs caused by increases in currency fluctuation. In addition to price-elasticity effects, wider fluctuations also would produce different influences on companies according to the currency used for invoicing in its markets. The exporter or importer whose trade accounts are denominated in his own currency, either because he is located in a "vehicle" currency country, or because trade in his product is traditionally denominated in his currency, usually considers himself (perhaps wrongly) to be protected from currency risks.

Prototype Views

It would be, of course, meaningless to attempt to catalogue the potential impact of greater rate fluctuation on each of the multitudes of different combinations of types of firms, transactions, and markets. Whether, for example, a medium-sized, well-diversified trading firm, invoicing in a weak currency, and dealing in relatively price-sensitive commodities, would be more disturbed than a small manufacturer with only a few

---

to the required extra $0.10 per dollar borrowed). So the effective interest cost after revaluation would be 7.31 per cent (6.5 plus 0.65 plus 0.16), less than many domestic alternatives.

plants abroad producing goods for export into highly price-inelastic markets, cannot be forejudged.

Extremes of the spectrum of sensitivity to currency-rate variability can, however, be placed in some perspective by focusing briefly on two prototype situations; the exchange dealings of a multinational manufacturer based in the United States, and those of a specialized commodity trader.

Thirty per cent of the assets of the large American multinational firm, typically, are located abroad. Although the firm is likely to execute almost every type of exchange transaction within a given year, none of the individual transactions as a rule is large enough, relative to the parent firm's earnings, to jeopardize overall corporate earnings, should moderate exchange-rate fluctuation or even devaluation occur. The firm's foreign assets, payments, and liabilities probably are denominated in a portfolio of currencies, and there usually are strong and weak-currency assets in their portfolio. The firm probably "hedges" via future contracts some of the net "exposure" indicated by its accounting conventions. It may, however, accept at times the full risk of its normal net asset position—that is, it may self-insure—when the cost of cover via local currency debt or forward exchange becomes judged to be excessive. The company also is likely to manage its currency risk with some sophistication, regularly reviewing its position in different currencies and trading off currency risks against the cost of insurance. It is, in short, relatively insensitive to the difference postulated between the pattern of today's spot and future prices and that pattern "reforms" might bring.

The trading firm, on the other hand, has assets (receivables) and liabilities (payables) that are very large compared to net worth, and are denominated, to a large extent, in only one, or at most a few, foreign currencies. It concentrates typically in a small number of related commodities that are likely to be undifferentiated and highly sensitive to price competition with domestic and foreign goods. Profit margins on transactions, in many instances, are less than the cost of obtaining the essential protection against currency fluctuations of the magnitude we have projected. In short, in many of its markets the firm could afford to accept neither the risk of remaining exposed nor the cost of cover. Of course, if in all of its markets its competition (domestic and foreign) were equally affected by greater fluctuation, prices would simply rise to include the new (presumed higher) insurance cost, and demand would fall somewhat. Because of the differences among firms discussed above, however, this is not likely.

Trends Affecting Business Accommodation

Looking beyond a transition period to how well businesses eventually might accommodate to the reforms, several trends stand out with reference to concerns headquartered in the United States. There is, for example, evidence in the record of recent international transactions (and in the expectation of executives of multinational firms) of an increasing reliance on the movement of factors for multinational production and a lessening emphasis on the exchange of final products.[6] Continued expansion of international production decreases the potential impact of moderate exchange-rate fluctuation, simply because multinational firms typically have the necessary financial strength and managerial sophistication to minimize exchange exposure. Associated with greater multinational corporate investment is a volume of capital flows across the exchanges that is, at least for the United States, growing over twice as fast as current payments related to trade in goods. As capital transactions, the long-term parts of which are less sensitive to exchange-rate variability, grow relative to trade transactions, the overall impact of greater rate fluctuation should be lessened.

Aside from this trend toward greater international production, however, there certainly appears to be an underlying growth in trade itself that exceeds that of the growth of world GNP. Hence, the number of firms, and the dollar amounts, exposed to difficulty if rates fluctuate more, are growing.

On the other hand, trading firms that are usually the most exposed to difficulty, are tending to integrate into production and distribution, thus providing both greater diversification of activities and financial strength. In addition, firms that in the past primarily produced for export are spreading their activities outside their own traditional products and countries.[7]

Too, there is a growing sophistication about foreign-currency risks and hedging in many international businesses based in the United States. One major change in this direction, which has reduced the reliance of many firms on the forward-currency markets, is a growing acceptance of a more realistic interpretation of the financial impact of currency devaluations.[8] Similarly, many firms are realizing that they have both

---

[6] This trend has been documented by Judd Polk (in *Producing in the New World Economy*, U. S. Council of the International Chamber of Commerce, October 1967), among others, whose findings lead me to conclude that the value of goods produced by all multinational firms in facilities outside of their own countries' boundaries approaches, and may even exceed, the total value of goods that move in direct trade.

[7] Mitsui's American president, for example, recently announced that a large and growing fraction of the (multibillion dollar) Mitsui-United States business relates to transactions that have no direct connection with Japan. Mitsui, in these transactions, is acting as a trading, financing, and even producing agent.

[8] Though complicated in detail, the essential point is that long-term debt in a foreign currency increasingly is being treated as an offset to "exposed" assets such as cash, receivables, and inventory. The older rules, which defined the way in which "losses on foreign exchange transactions" were reported to the public, were based on net current assets alone. By the old definition, most foreign sub-

the financial strength and a level of return on their own funds that makes self-insuring against currency risks appropriate. The days in which it was considered *de rigueur* to hedge all transactions and all exposed current assets, regardless of cost, appear to be waning, as more firms realize that buying currency insurance in the forward market may be a highly unprofitable investment.

The more serious risk to business, moreover, is quite often not that of somewhat greater fluctuations in currency prices, but the risk of controls, higher tariffs, blocked currencies, and the possibility of monetary disintegration and international economic conflict. More and more businessmen consider the devaluations and fluctuations experienced from 1967 through 1969, bad as they were, to be less of a threat to profits than the trade and investment controls that were erected during the same period.

Finally, there is the possibility that the private, professional speculator in currency may assume a more important role than the almost inconsequential one he has played in the past. This would require an acceptance in the commercial banking community, which makes and manages the foreign-exchange markets, of the view that taking positions in foreign exchange is neither rash nor immoral, but is desirable, and could be done in a professional manner, with controlled levels of risk.

Conclusion

In conclusion, therefore, it appears probable that most international business, including especially large, multinational direct investors, would not be seriously affected by such moderately wider currency fluctuations as we have assumed. Although many businessmen consider that any system entailing greater fluctuations would be dangerous for all forms of business, this review of some likely real effects of the more moderate reforms suggests that, in practice, the consequences might not be severe for the greater majority of American business.

Greater spot and forward rate fluctuations would, however, pose significant problems for some international businesses. There might be a shakeout among small or highly specialized firms, such as commodity traders, as the government "subsidy" of the costs of currency fluctuations is reduced. Though the proportion of world trade, and especially of world investment, conducted by such firms may well be small, this does not mean that the costs to growth and vitality of international and domestic markets would be proportionately small. For a disproportionate share of the driving force of domestic economic growth for many countries—the stimulus of their more dynamic external sector—may be at

---

sidiaries have a long position in a local currency, and would need to be hedged. By the newer method, many subsidiaries will measure even, or short, in the local currency. Thus, apparent hedging needs are smaller.

the margin where some export markets are lost, or foreign subsidiaries lose profitability, or foreign supplies become too costly. It is undoubtedly for such reasons, at least implicitly, that government and private efforts have for so long been focused on smoothing or reducing the costs of future currency contracts.

Finally, though many companies can expect to diversify, self-insure, or otherwise cleverly manage themselves over somewhat rockier exchange market roads, and though we might hope that markets or governments would move to supplement as required the currency protection required by others, there still remains the larger political risk that sliding parities might further stimulate a propensity to inflate in some countries. If this occurs, the sanguine outlook prescribed here for portfolio lenders, direct and portfolio investors, and many exporting manufacturers, would be ill-founded indeed. In this event not only would the international allocation of resources be diverted from their most productive directions, but many internal economies also would suffer from the effects of inflation. The greater concern of international business about the proposed reforms would, therefore, seem best to be focused on the outlook, under these reforms, for appropriately stable prices in their economy.

Part III. The Case Against Flexible Exchange Rates

IN HIS paper "The Outlook for the Present World Monetary System," Peter M. Oppenheimer expresses the belief that "neither SDRs nor the possibility of gradual alterations in exchange rates seems likely to bring about a decisive strengthening of the monetary system," though he admits that limited flexibility of exchange rates may make a contribution to the adjustment process. He fears, however, that a sliding parity adjustment would be neutralized by an offsetting trend of domestic wages and prices, would not rule out bigger jumps of exchange rates, and would actually heighten the conflict between internal and external objectives of monetary policy. The widened band might be still too narrow, and variations within the band would discourage shifts of industrial production between home and foreign markets. Oppenheimer argues for a doubling (or more) of the price of gold as "the one measure that could make a decisive contribution to the stability of the system." Thomas D. Willett's "Comments on Mr. Oppenheimer's Paper: A More Optimistic View" suggests that the present difficulties in the monetary system of the world come from deficiencies in the adjustment process, rather than from deficiencies in the supply of gold.

Max Iklé gives an entirely negative answer to the question asked in the title of his essay, "Could the Crises of the Last Few Years Have Been Avoided by Flexible Exchange Rates?": in no case would greater flexibility of exchange rates have been of any help. The system suffered from a premature transition to convertibility, excessive unilateral payments (United States), wrong domestic policies (Germany, France), lack of reserves (Great Britain), and a lack of confidence. Confidence would not have been improved by greater flexibility of exchange rates. Actually, the system had the flexibility it needed, only it was a flexibility of monetary reserves rather than of exchange rates.

In his "Notes for the Bürgenstock Conference," Antonio Mosconi considers a system with more-flexible exchange rates as incompatible with the aspirations of the European Economic Community. The EEC should establish fixed parities not only between its members, but also with third countries as "the only workable approach to a higher degree of international cooperation and economic growth." Mosconi admits that a "gradual modification of parities" might be better than discrete and large peg adjustments. But he objects to "mechanisms" as against "negotiations." Since he believes that the dollar can be strengthened and the international payments system stabilized, he warns against pseudosolutions, among which he includes greater flexibility of exchange rates.

Giuliano Pelli's paper, "Why I Am Not in Favor of Greater Flexibility of Exchange Rates," rejects both the widened band and the crawling peg, because they would introduce a further destructive element of uncertainty into the foreign exchange market without supporting the adjustment mechanism. Economic crises are the result of structural situations and often have nothing to do with the foreign-exchange rate. Pelli considers the uncertainties connected with widened band and crawling peg as *additional* to the uncertainties of large peg adjustments and foreign-exchange restrictions.

Emil Kuster's note, "Greater Flexibility of Exchange Rates: Effects on Commodities, Capital, and Money Markets," tries to show that a wider band might paralyze the international money markets, wipe out the relatively small profit margins in international commodity trade and insurance, and even disturb international issue markets. A band of a total width of 5 per cent would require constant central-bank intervention and "this would defeat to a large extent the benefits that the proponents of a wider band are expecting from greater flexibility." Furthermore, currency uncertainties produced by wider bands would lead to barter and clearing agreements in the attempt to eliminate currency risks. Kuster's "Selected Case Studies Relating to Foreign-Exchange Problems in International Trade and Money Markets" is meant to substantiate the claims made in the preceding paper.

In his "Comment on Mr. Kuster's Paper," Richard N. Cooper argues that transactions that become unprofitable through an equilibrating depreciation of the exchange rate should, from an economic point of view, not take place. He also suggests that a country that does not allow its currency to depreciate is, in effect, subsidizing its imports and, thereby, distorting international trade. It will then either lose reserves or introduce controls and artificially restrain some other international transactions.

The papers of Pelli and Kuster should also be considered in connection with Part V: "Exchange-Rate Flexibility and the Forward Market."

In addition to the five articles of Part III, three articles from Part VI should be counted as critical of greater exchange rate flexibility: Max Iklé's "The Problem of Floating Exchange Rates from the Swiss Viewpoint," Antonio Mosconi's "Comments on Mr. Kasper's Paper: Requiem for European Integration," and Tadashi Iino's "Japan's Twenty-year Experience with a Fixed Rate for the Yen."

• 16 •

The Outlook for the Present World Monetary System

PETER M. OPPENHEIMER

Symptoms of Disorder

TENSION and uncertainty in the world monetary system have shown themselves, during recent years, in three broad ways.

First, several countries have felt constrained by balance-of-payments weakness to adopt measures detrimental to free trade and payments. Earlier in the 1960s we had the Canadian and British import surcharges; later examples are the British and French limits on tourist spending, the increased tying of development aid by the United States and other countries and, most striking of all, the progressively tightening controls on capital exports from the United States since 1965. It is true that balance-of-payments problems did not prevent the successful conclusion of the Kennedy Round tariff negotiations in 1967, which means that a substantial further cut in import duties on industrial goods is now in progress. Nevertheless, recourse to restrictive measures has become too prominent to be overlooked, especially in the case of the United States, where such controls were regarded as unthinkable less than a decade ago.

Second, there is the tightness of international money markets in the last three or four years. This trend reached a climax in the second quarter of 1969 with the interest rate on three months' Eurodollars touching 13 per cent. It may be noted in passing that the Eurodollar market is more of a "perfect market" than are national credit markets, and the trend of interest rates is, accordingly, a better indicator of general market conditions than is the case in national credit systems. The major impulse to higher money rates after 1965 came from national monetary policies. The United States played the biggest part but several other countries contributed, including Germany, the U.K., France, and Japan. In March 1969, even the Italian authorities instructed their banks to repatriate their net overseas assets, thus further straining the situation in the Eurocurrency markets. It is true that these markets continued to expand without interruption and even at an accelerated pace, but one is still left with the impression that the major industrial countries were forced into ever more intense competition for a limited pool of hot money.

Third, the difficulties of the dollar and uncertainty over the source of future increases in world monetary reserves have called into question the Bretton Woods system as a whole. Ad hoc swaps and other credit arrangements have kept things going, and commercial confidence in the dollar has not so far been affected; but the failure of policy makers to rectify the underlying disequilibrium of the system and put the future growth of world reserves on a reasonably secure footing has made a breakdown look more and more likely. The major victim of the situation so far has been sterling. The lack of autonomous growth in world reserves is making it almost impossible for Britain to achieve the prolonged surplus that she needs in order to repay the short- and medium-term debts piled up since 1964.

Two further points may be noted in this connection. First, the problem has not been solved by the realignment of Common Market currencies in 1969. The upvaluation of the German mark and the devaluation of the French franc should certainly leave the balances of payments of the EEC countries in better shape; but they have not altered the underlying position of the dollar. Secondly, the move to a two-tier gold price in March 1968 has, in itself, made little difference to the situation. Obviously, it eased the immediate pressure on the dollar by putting a stop to the massive drain of gold from American reserves. But the suggestion advanced by some commentators that the world is now on a dollar standard and that the United States no longer has a balance-of-payments problem must be interpreted as either advocacy or forecasting. The system has taken a step toward a dollar standard, but so far the American authorities remain concerned about the external balance of the United States and see no real scope for easing the restrictions on international payments imposed in recent years. The official price of gold is still $35 an ounce and, in the last resort, foreign monetary authorities can obtain gold from the Treasury of the United States at this price. Moreover, while the Treasury may be reluctant to sell gold, no one claims that it is reluctant to buy—except, ridiculously enough, from South Africa.

Fashionable "Solutions"

A number of changes in international monetary arrangements, designed ostensibly to remove the tensions listed above, are being initiated or debated. They fall under two main headings: reserve creation and exchange-rate flexibility.

So far as reserve creation is concerned, the first $3½ billion of Special Drawing Rights have now been issued, and further issues of $3 billion are agreed for 1971 and 1972. However, the timing and scope of SDR creation over the longer run remain to be agreed; and, of course, until the scheme has been operating no one can be sure what effect it will have on national economic policies. It is quite clear, however, that major problems concerning the status and acceptability of SDRs as reserve assets remain unresolved, chief among them being the relationship between SDRs and gold.[1] SDRs are denominated in gold. They, therefore, preclude demonetization of gold and could not operate (except perhaps in a limited regional form not corresponding to present intentions) if the link between gold and the dollar were officially severed. If SDRs are to succeed in easing the dollar problem and the tensions related to it, they must have the effect of either (a) persuading the surplus countries to adjust their surpluses away more completely and effectively than hitherto; or (b) enabling the United States to finance a continuing deficit of, say, $2 billion a year without further deterioration in its international liquidity position. Neither of these alternatives looks likely—the first because the allocation of SDRs to surplus countries involves no additional inflationary pressure for them and no additional loss of real resources; and the second because it implies agreement to create not less than $5 billion and probably nearer $10 billion of SDRs a year (assuming SDRs are distributed in proportion to IMF quotas), and such agreement is highly improbable.

It has been suggested that limited flexibility of exchange rates combined with an inconvertible dollar may be another way of solving the problem of reserves, either in conjunction with SDRs or independently of them. This is the approach advocated by (among others) William Fellner.[2] I doubt, however, whether it can prove satisfactory, and for the reason stated by Fellner himself:

> No country should be pressured politically into holding or accumulating dollars, but I suggest that it is equally reasonable to lay down the principle that no country can complain legitimately of excess dollar-holdings or accumulations if it can reduce its holdings or acquisitions to the desired rate by an orderly, gradual revaluation of its currency in relation to the dollar.
>
> At any rate, if the principle expressed in the preceding sentence is rejected, then it is difficult to see how an increase of the price of monetary gold could be avoided. Indeed, an increase of the gold price would *reflect* the nonacceptance of the principle just formulated, and gold-revaluation would be a natural corollary of the nonacceptance of that principle.

In my view the "principle" enunciated by Fellner is liable to rejection on the simple Keynesian grounds that it confuses savings with liquidity preference. Whether or not countries want to add to their external reserves over time is a different question from the mix of assets that they

---

[1] A further important issue is how far drawings on SDRs will eventually be repayable. So far the "average use" formula has provided only for 70 per cent nonrepayability *during the first five years*.

[2] In his paper "A 'Realistic' Note on Threefold Limited Flexibility of Exchange Rates," in Part IV.

wish to hold in their reserve portfolios. Hardly any central bank at present considers that it has an excessive external surplus, but quite a number feel under pressure to hold more dollars than their own preferences would dictate. Currency revaluations are irrelevant to this problem. SDRs, on the other hand, may merely introduce further complications. It is unlikely that a reserve system comprising a fixed gold stock, dollars, and SDRs can function unless countries renounce sovereignty over the composition of their reserves. In return for this, however, they will probably claim a bigger voice in each other's financial policies, thus aggravating a major cause of present tensions. All in all, neither SDRs nor the possibility of gradual alterations in exchange rates seems likely to bring about a decisive strengthening of the monetary system.

Limited exchange-rate flexibility may, nevertheless, make a contribution to the balance-of-payments adjustment process in particular instances. Politicians and public opinion in several countries need to be convinced (a) that exchange rates sometimes have to be changed in the modern world and that premature decisions to abolish the possibility of changing them (such as by means of Common Market arrangements) can only lead to trouble and, ultimately, to a reversal of the decisions in question; and (b) that exchange-rate changes are not a political catastrophe but a normal technique of economic policy. If the advocacy and/or use of sliding parities or wider bands can in particular cases contribute to these objectives, well and good—though it does not seem to me obvious that they can.

In any case, there are also disadvantages attaching to both sliding parities and wider bands as alternatives to the present system of adjustable pegs.

With regard to sliding parities, three problems need to be considered. First, an exchange-rate adjustment of 2 per cent per annum for a period of years risks neutralization through an equal and offsetting change in the trend of domestic wages and prices. How real this danger is will depend on the extent to which money-wage bargains are constrained (from above or below) by world market prices of the home country's tradable goods. It is not difficult to imagine such a constraint operating in Germany or in several other European countries.

Second, even if this first worry proved unfounded, a sliding parity, particularly of the discretionary kind, could not rule out the need for bigger jumps in exchange rates in the event of large or obstinate disequilibria, and so would do little to alleviate the problems of speculation and hot money movements.

Third, a system of sliding parities would heighten the conflict between internal and external objectives of monetary policy. It is true, as Thomas Willett points out, that the various weapons developed in the 1960s to ease this conflict and to strengthen control over international capital movements—such as interest-equalization taxes, forward-exchange policy, regulation of the foreign operations of commercial banks and similar measures—could be further refined and adapted to a crawling peg system.[3] The point is, however, that many of these devices, which sooner or later give rise to economic inefficiencies, would have been unnecessary if the Bretton Woods system had been operated properly in the first place. To accept their indefinite continuance as part of a package for reform of the system is to forget what half the discussion over reform has been about.

Wider bands are free from the third and to some extent from the second of these objections. They would enlarge the scope for disparities between national interest-rate levels and, by increasing the size of possible losses from mistaken speculation on a change in parities, would help to deter speculative movements of capital. But their efficacy as a weapon of basic balance-of-payments adjustment is, like that of crawling pegs, open to doubt. Basically this is because of the comparatively narrow limits on automatic exchange-rate movements that would still obtain under a band system. To push the rate beyond the limit set by the band would obviously require some other type of exchange-rate flexibility. Moreover, exchange-rate movements within the band would be subject to quick reversal by random factors, and this would weaken the incentive for industry to switch production and marketing plans from home to foreign markets (or vice versa). In other words, industry could not be sure that a 4 or 5 per cent depreciation or appreciation within the band would be *held*.

Prospects

The difficulties enumerated in the first section of this paper have not so far halted the rapid growth of world trade and production, which has characterized the postwar period. International monetary cooperation has cushioned or offset short-term upheavals in the exchange markets, while regular consultations in Paris, Basle, and elsewhere have limited scope for mutual misunderstanding of national economic policies. On the other hand, such consultations have not prevented the gradual undermining of the Bretton Woods system. There is no reason why the monetary improvisations of the 1960s, which have culminated in SDRs, should not continue and develop further in the 1970s. The expansion of world trade would then be maintained, but the tendency to use direct restrictions on international payments would be confirmed rather than reversed. This seems, in fact, the most likely prospect.

Exchange rates will continue to be changed by one means or another from time to time, but fancy new techniques for sliding, spreading, or

---

[3] In his paper "Short-Term Capital Movements and the Interest-Rate Constraint Under Systems of Limited Flexibility of Exchange Rates," in Part IV.

hop-skip-and-jumping are unlikely to put the monetary system on an altogether firmer foundation.

The extreme tensions on world money markets will also subside, at least temporarily, with the next recession in the United States—which may be imminent. But this is a cyclical matter and again will not indicate a fundamental strengthening of the monetary system.

The one measure that could make a decisive contribution to the stability of the system for the next generation is a doubling (or more) of the price of gold. This has been clearly and, in my opinion, conclusively demonstrated by Milton Gilbert in his Princeton Essay in International Finance, No. 70, *The Gold-Dollar System: Conditions of Equilibrium and the Price of Gold*. Gilbert's analysis amounts to a restatement of the Triffin-Kenen model of the gold-exchange standard, drawing attention to the role of the price of gold as a national policy weapon governing the possibility of equilibrium in the balance of payments of the United States. Most economists still reject Gilbert's conclusion because, as Harry Johnson put it at the AEA meeting in December 1968, they are "professionally prejudiced" against it. The points usually put forward against a rise in the gold price are:

(1) the immediate benefits from it would be unfairly or inappropriately distributed;
(2) it would cause inflation;
(3) it would provide only "a breathing space," solving no long-term problems, and another price increase would be needed sooner or later; and
(4) the monetary use of gold (or any other real commodity) wastes resources.

Point (1) is a pure value-judgment with no analytical force. One could equally well maintain that it was unfair to hold the gold price down to $35 an ounce for many years while other prices doubled and trebled. As for American "promises" not to raise the gold price, central bankers should know better than to put their trust in princes. Rather, they should read their Tobin and choose their portfolio assets with a proper eye to the risks involved.

Point (2) may well worry the French or Swiss authorities, who might, indeed, find themselves with local inflationary pressures on their hands —similar perhaps to those faced by the Italian authorities at the time of the Italian "wage explosion" in 1963—but I cannot see why it should worry anyone in the United States. If the United States concentrated on managing its own economy and balance of payments and left it to other people to manage theirs, we should all get along much better.

As to point (3), if this means that a rise in the gold price now would not solve all international monetary problems forever, it is obviously true but hardly an argument. If, however, it means that a higher gold price would not make a serious contribution to world monetary stability for the next generation then I think it is false. Indeed, I do not see how anyone who has understood Gilbert's paper could advance this view. In this connection I want particularly to stress the point that the United States, contrary to what is often asserted, it not unable to alter its exchange rate in the present system. The dollar price of gold *is* an exchange rate. A substantial increase in it would help the United States to equilibrate its external accounts, and not merely to go on financing deficits. This is because it would lead to a substantial annual inflow of new monetary gold and would, thereby, relieve the pressure on the United States to act as a net supplier of reserves to other countries.[4]

Point (4) is correct as a matter of pure logic, but is of little quantitative importance—especially when account is taken of the fact that no one has a clear idea of how the world monetary system would actually work without gold. Demonetization would be a step into the unknown and could easily lead to wider restrictions on international trade and payments.

In conclusion, I should like to re-emphasize that the purpose of this note has been to discuss the prospects for the *present* monetary system and the possibilities of reversing the undesirable trends that have affected it in the past few years. I consider that the present system is perfectly viable if its rules are properly operated, and I doubt whether any coherent alternative to it is in sight. Whether it is the best possible system that human ingenuity can devise is, of course, quite another question.

[4] A detailed analysis may be found in P. M. Oppenheimer, "The Case for Raising the Price of Gold," *Journal of Money, Credit and Banking* (August 1969).

· 17 ·

Comments on Mr. Oppenheimer's Paper: A More Optimistic View

THOMAS D. WILLETT

I SHOULD like to register a more optimistic view than that of Peter Oppenheimer concerning the workability of a less golden international monetary system. Oppenheimer's case for increasing the price of gold rests upon a Triffin-Kenen view of reserve asset preferences under a gold-exchange standard.[1] However, as Lawrence H. Officer and I argue in our paper, "Reserve-Asset Preferences and the Confidence Problem in the Crisis Zone," [2] there have been several factors at work in recent years that have tended to reduce the likelihood of the instability of reserve asset behavior pointed to by the Triffin-Kenen model and analogies with Gresham's Law.[3]

As Oppenheimer amply documents, the operation of the international monetary system in recent years has certainly not been such as to inspire complacency. But Officer's and my thesis is that these difficulties have come more from deficiencies in the adjustment mechanism than from deficiencies in gold supply or the existence of multiple reserve assets. To the extent that our view is correct, greater flexibility of exchange rates may go a long way toward reducing the types of difficulty generally discussed under the heading of "the confidence problem."

---

[1] Robert Triffin, *Gold and the Dollar Crisis* (New Haven: Yale University Press, 1960); Peter B. Kenen, "International Liquidity and the Balance of Payments of a Reserve-Currency Country," *Quarterly Journal of Economics* (November 1960), and *Reserve-Asset Preferences of Central Banks and Stability of the Gold-Exchange Standard,* Princeton Studies in International Finance No. 10, 1963

[2] *Quarterly Journal of Economics* (November 1969). See also our longer paper, "The Stability of a Reserve-Currency System: The Interaction of Adjustment and Gold Conversion Policies," Harvard Institute of Economic Research Discussion Paper No. 74, May 1969.

[3] See, for instance, Robert Z. Aliber, "Gresham's Law, Asset Preferences, and the Demand for International Reserves," *Quarterly Journal of Economics* (November 1967). Also of interest is the comment by Henry N. Goldstein, "Gresham's Law and the Demand for NRU's and SDR's," *Quarterly Journal of Economics* (February 1969).

· 18 ·

Could the Crises of the Last Few Years Have Been Avoided by Flexible Exchange Rates?

MAX IKLÉ

I

BEFORE the present system is replaced with flexible exchange rates, the causes of the monetary crises in the recent past should first be analyzed and examined to see if a system of flexible exchange rates could have prevented them.

Since the change-over to convertibility at the beginning of 1959, the following crises or disturbing factors have arisen:

In the autumn of 1960, the price of gold on the London gold market rose to over $40 per ounce, which was taken as a sign of a coming devaluation of the dollar. The persistent deficit in the balance of payments of the United States repeatedly weakened confidence in the dollar and, therefore, in the Western monetary system.

Early in 1961, the German mark and the Dutch guilder were revalued by 5 per cent, a move that caused considerable disturbance on foreign-exchange markets and unleashed the first pound crisis.

In 1962–1963, Italy registered a sizable deficit in the basic payments-balance, which led to an undermining of confidence in the Italian lira.

The autumn of 1964 once again saw the pound sterling in crisis. After a brief recovery—from the autumn of 1966 to early 1967—the pound sterling again became subject to pressure, which led to the devaluation at the end of 1967.

In 1962, the Canadian dollar suffered a dizzy spell, but was able to overcome it thanks to American assistance.

In 1966, the credit restrictions imposed by West Germany gave rise to a recession that resulted in large surpluses in the balance on current accounts.

The rebellion in France in May–June 1968 sparked a crisis in regard to the French franc.

In November 1968, large funds flowed into West Germany in expectation of a German mark revaluation.

Since 1959, we have, thus, been confronted with problems affecting the two key currencies, the three principal European currencies, as well as the Canadian dollar. In the paragraphs that follow, I shall make an attempt to analyze the causes of these crises.

THE BALANCE-OF-PAYMENTS DEFICIT OF THE UNITED STATES

Except for the years 1957 and 1968, the United States has shown deficits in its balance of payments since 1950. Although from 1951 to 1956 the deficits remained at the $1–2 billion level, they rose to an average of $3.7 billion for the years from 1958 to 1960. The annual average for the years 1961 to 1964 was $2.5 billion, whereas it fell to $1.3 billion for the years 1965 and 1966. However, 1967 saw the deficit increase to $3.3 billion. The deficits in the United States are not traceable to a weakness in the American economy. The trade balance and the balance on goods and services always showed surpluses. The deficits are attributable solely to government grants and credits, military outlays, and capital exports. The American deficit is, therefore, a consequence of the dearth of capital in the rest of the world as well as of the United States' international position, which induced it to grant aid to developing countries and to defend the interests of the West in Asia and Europe. Since 1961, United States governmental aid has weighted down the balance of payments by an average of $2.9 million annually. Military outlays averaged $2.2 billion, and rose in 1967 to $3.3 billion.

The balance of payments of the United States has been adversely affected in recent years by capital exports, which in the last few years have usually exceeded $4 billion. In contrast, capital imports were insignificant up to 1965. Only since 1966, have there been capital imports worth mentioning. In 1966, they reached $2 billion, in 1967 $2.9 billion, and in 1968 no less than $7 billion. The mounting interest and dividend payments have in recent years offset the outflow of capital, with the result that capital and interest movements combined have not had an adverse effect on the balance of payments since 1965.

As capital exports were larger in most years than the balance-of-payments deficit, the United States's international position has steadily been strengthened since the end of World War II. In 1967, foreign balances reached $122 billion, which contrasts with deficit positions of $70 billion. In the long-term capital sector, the United States registers a sizable surplus. However, with respect to short-term funds, liabilities ($37.7 billion) exceed assets ($14.5 billion). The surplus of total assets over liabilities reached a sum equal to that of the monetary reserves of the rest of the world, thus making the United States by far the wealthiest nation in the world, despite the deficit in its balance of payments. American business continues to be competitive on the international markets. The modest surplus in the 1968 trade balance does nothing to lessen this fact. The worsening of the trade balance is due solely to the sharp increase in imports. This is coupled with the Vietnam war and the resulting excess demands placed on the American economy. The United States continues to boast a technological lead in a number of sectors, such as in aircraft and computer production, to cite only two examples.

As far as the significance of capital movements for the American balance of payments is concerned, 1968 proved a turning point. Up to the mid-sixties, the United States possessed the only truly efficient capital market. War and inflation destroyed Europe's capital markets, which had to be rebuilt during the postwar years. At the same time it was necessary, however, to meet the enormous demand for the capital needed to restore the ruined economies of Europe. The British capital market, which to some extent was still operative, was made use of in its entirety by the Commonwealth nations. The Swiss capital market is too small to exert an influence on the overall situation. I might add, however, that the European capital markets have recently been gaining in strength. The so-called Eurobond market, on which loan issues are placed at an international level, was able last year to launch more than $3 billion worth of bond issues. Europeans are beginning to become interested in American securities for reasons of risk distribution, and the European economy must make up its lag in direct foreign investments. Even if the volume of the capital flow to the United States reached in 1968 can scarcely be maintained, we nevertheless believe that the one-sided outflow of capital from the United States is coming to an end and that in the future large-scale inflows of capital will be observed. When the Vietnam war is settled, and if the inflationary forces are brought under control, there is good reason to hope that the American balance of payments can be kept at approximate equilibrium in the future.

A deficit of $700–800 million would be fully bearable, and would not exert an adverse effect on the United States's gold reserves, as the dollars would be maintained as working balances by the private economy in the presence of expanding world trade and not find their way to the central banks. There is, therefore, no reason for a pessimistic appraisal of the monetary position of the United States and, due to this viewpoint, arrival at rash conclusions that could have disastrous consequences for the Western monetary system. There is also no cause to eliminate the convertibility of the dollar into gold. The gold stocks of the United States are adequate to meet current requirements, especially since the principal trading partners are prepared to cooperate.

THE PROBLEM OF GERMANY'S BALANCE-OF-PAYMENTS SURPLUSES

West Germany, whose economy lay in total ruin at the end of World War II, has, over the last two decades, once again become the strongest economic power in Europe; thanks to continual balance-of-payments surpluses, it has been able to boost its monetary reserves to about DM 35 billion. This development has been facilitated by the following factors:

The internal debts largely disappeared because of inflation and the collapse of the Third Reich, while the external commitments could be reduced to a tolerable level on the occasion of the London Conference of 1952.

During the postwar years nearly 7 million refugees fled to West Germany. Consequently, there was no shortage of labor until the mid-sixties. The influx of refugees depressed wage levels, with the result that German wages were for many years lower than those of other countries.

Thanks to the Marshall Plan, the destroyed factories could be rebuilt relatively quickly and were equipped with the most modern machinery.

West Germany's entry into NATO led to the stationing of Allied troops on German soil, which meant an additional inflow of currency.

The establishment of the Common Market encouraged direct American investment in West Germany.

The sizable demand for capital on the part of the West German economy resulted in large volume of capital imports. On the other hand, the high interest rates in existence up to 1965 discouraged capital exports, quite regardless of the fact that the West German capital market was scarcely in a position to satisfy domestic requirements.

The fact that Germany had lost the war created positive prerequisites for a good working atmosphere. Everyone realized that the national standard of living could be raised only by doubling one's own individual efforts.

Owing to the fact that after the division of the country the industrial potential of West Germany was too large for the reduced area of the Federal Republic, a need to export arose.

West Germany's entry into the Common Market provided its industry with a substitute for the shrunken domestic market. The efficient industry of West Germany was able to benefit substantially from this circumstance. The economic upswing led, however, in 1965, to a sharp rise in imports. The trade balance registered a surplus in this year of only DM 1.5 billion. The exceptionally tight credit restrictions put an end to this upturn and, in 1966–1967 brought on a recession. Imports dropped in 1967 to the level recorded in 1965, whereas exports continued to rise. This led to a trade balance surplus in 1967 of DM 16.8 billion and one of DM 18.3 billion in 1968. Such a development, coupled with the weakening of the French monetary situation, gave rise to rumors of an upvaluation of the German mark and a devaluation of the French franc, which led to the massive capital movements witnessed last November (November 1968).

The surpluses in the balance on current account were largely offset in the past year by long-term capital exports. In 1968 these long-term capital exports reached DM 11.5 billion, whereby the basic balance of payments was almost brought into equilibrium. Without the rumors of a pending revaluation of the German mark, West Germany would not have constituted a disturbing element for the Western monetary system in 1968.

In retrospect, the economic measures adopted by Germany now appear to have been inadequate. With a more modest tightening of credit, the recession of 1966–1967 could have been avoided. Imports would not have declined so sharply and the trade-balance surplus could have been kept within more reasonable limits.

During the two decades since the end of World War II, the German capital market has regained a strong position. German interest rates have adjusted themselves to the international level, especially since interest rates outside West Germany have shown a rise. If the German boom at home continues to gain momentum, it should be possible to reduce the surplus in the trade balance to a reasonable level and the balance of payments could be kept in equilibrium by capital exports. Overcoming the German balance-of-payments surplus should, therefore, not present an unsolvable problem.

The German economy, which lost its foreign investments in the war and, during the last two decades, has had to devote its entire resources to reconstruction at home, has a pent-up need to make direct foreign investments. It is fully possible that in the coming decade West Germany may at times show an adverse balance of payments due to capital exports, as it has been the case with the United States in recent years. The German example indicates that it would indeed have been possible to prevent external equilibrium by internal economic policy measures.

ITALY'S BALANCE-OF-PAYMENTS CRISIS IN 1962–1963

At the beginning of the 1960s, the Italian economy was in the process of a sharp upturn, as was also true of other European countries. Whereas Germany and Switzerland had to rely on foreign labor to meet the demands of industry, north Italian industry could mobilize its labor reserves in the south of the country. The south Italians adjusted very rapidly to consumer behavior in the north. At the same time, wages were raised 15 per cent in two consecutive years. This led to a heavy demand for consumer goods and a corresponding increase in imports. The balance of trade registered large deficits, and the disequilibrium immediately become apparent to the outside, as the Italian banks incurred a heavy degree of indebtedness on the Euromarket. In this critical situation the Banca d'Italia made use of the assistance proffered by the Federal Reserve. Thanks to the vigorous measures on the part of the Banca d'Italia, it was possible to restore equilibrium both internally and externally in less than two years. Today the Italian balance on current account again shows substantial surpluses. It must be noted, however, that the political climate within the country is encouraging capital exports. In the past few years Italian financial circles have become increasingly interested in Eurobonds and other foreign securities.

The Italian example shows that it is possible to re-establish balance-of-payments equilibrium by maintaining stable foreign exchange rates. It also shows the elasticity of the Eurocapital market for the first time. The assistance extended by associated central banks remained relatively modest in this instance.

THE PROBLEM OF THE POUND STERLING

Within the Western monetary system, Great Britain's balance-of-payments situation presents the most difficult problem. During the postwar years it has been seen time and again that the steps taken to stimulate the economy of Great Britain have resulted in balance-of-payments disequilibrium. Every crisis in the Western monetary system has produced adverse repercussions on the pound sterling. The pound problem is too complex to permit detailed discussion in this study. Its roots can be traced back to both World Wars, during which Great Britain lost its position as a creditor nation. The so-called sterling balances, for the most part, came into existence during World War II. England, which among the Allies had to bear the greatest losses from the war, financed its war costs partly by taking out loans at home and partly by obtaining credits from the Commonwealth nations. It is true that many large shifts took place within the sterling zone during the postwar period; the prominent position occupied by India was taken over by the Mideast oil countries, for instance. Nevertheless, the external debt could not be reduced.

In contrast to the currencies on the Continent, the pound was not destroyed by inflation. As a result, the internal debt constitutes a far heavier burden than in other nations. This is one of the reasons why British taxes are so high. Steeply progressive taxes cripple the initiative of the people and the economy. Without a far-reaching tax reform, the restoration of the pound and the British economy to a state of health is hardly conceivable.

To counter inflationary trends, the interest rates in Great Britain have to be kept at relatively high levels. On the other hand, this also increases the interest burden vis-a-vis the sterling creditor nations. The pound sterling constitutes the currency of the entire sterling area. Balance-of-payments deficits on the part of any one sterling nation have an effect on the reserves of the entire sterling area.

The pound continues to be a currency used in international trade. Particularly in commodities trading, the customary method of invoicing is in sterling. If there is a lack of confidence in the British currency, the leads and lags become considerably more noticeable than in countries that have only a local currency. The British monetary reserves are in no way proportionate to the worldwide usage of sterling as a reserve and trade currency. The leads and lags alone could absorb three quarters of the British monetary reserves. Traditionally, the British trade balance has a deficit. Invisibles earned by British banks, insurance companies and international trading firms made up the difference in times past. Earlier, when international trust in the pound sterling existed, and England was the wealthiest nation in the world, the pound sterling could be managed without difficulty on the basis of modest monetary reserves. Today the latter are not even adequate to stem moderate crises.

Great Britain still has to bear the political responsibilities of a world power. Expenditures of the British Government for foreign aid and the military establishment debit the balance of payments by over £400 million annually. The Commonwealth nations employ British money and England's capital market for operations involving £100–140 million yearly. Although in the 1950s, the trade balance deficit averaging £260 million could be easily offset by invisibles averaging £327 million, the deficit has since increased, and invisibles have shown a rather stagnating trend; in this connection, government outlays, moreover, became an ever-more significant factor as time went on.

The devaluation of the pound has made the situation even worse—insofar as we can appraise it today. The trade balance deficit has risen from £637 million to £857 million, and the balance-of-payments deficit has climbed from £490 million to £587 million.

The British example indicates that even a 15 per cent adjustment of the exchange rate could not improve the balance of payments. A country that depends to such a pronounced degree on the confidence of the world around it cannot allow itself to experiment with its currency. The devaluation rocked the world's trust in the pound and led to withdrawals on the part of the sterling creditors. Imports, which had become more costly, could not be offset by increasing exports; nor could the difference be made up by a corresponding growth in earnings from invisibles. In view of the basic and structural problems confronting Great Britain, it is hard to believe that the difficulties can be removed by means of flexible exchange rates. Instead, it is to be feared that with a system of floating rates, confidence in the pound will be thoroughly destroyed. The banks, insurance companies, and international trading companies that today earn the invisibles would be placed in a grave position.

THE FRENCH FRANC

The French franc, which up to 1958 had for decades been subject to an inflationary process with only brief tapering-off periods, could be stabilized after the devaluation in 1958. Owing to a consistent monetary and economic policy, it was possible for France to raise its monetary reserves from zero to the respectable figure of $7 billion. The social uprisings in May and June of 1968 brought a sudden end to this development. Wages had to be increased 14 per cent, which in turn led to a 5.3 per cent rise in living costs. At the same time a substantial volume of credit was made available to the economy in order to inject new life into it. Faith in the French franc could not, however, be restored, a development that resulted in a flight of capital. The rumors of an impending devaluation of the franc and an upvaluation of the German mark subsequently caused a sizable flow of capital out of France and other countries into West Germany.

The crisis that gripped the French franc had its origins in domestic political sectors. It was not related to the French monetary policy, or at most was only very loosely connected with it, thus making further discussion of this factor unnecessary for us today. The sole question of interest to us in regard to the French franc and the German mark is whether or not a system of flexible exchange rates would have prevented the crisis in November 1968. This cannot be answered unequivocally. Of decisive importance would have been the actual rates of the German mark and the French franc applying before the outbreak of the crisis. If both currencies had been at parity in the beginning of 1968, with a spread of ±5 per cent, the flight out of French francs into German marks would have assumed the same or even larger proportions than was the case in 1968. In this connection, the franc would have dropped to the lower intervention limit and the mark to the upper, with the result that French speculators would have realized a gain of 10 per cent. However, if the franc and the mark had already reached the lower and upper intervention limits, respectively, the initial situation would have been similar to what it was in November 1968. Only rumors of a change in parities could have then given rise to sizable capital movements.

THE CANADIAN DOLLAR

The Canadian dollar is the only currency within the Group of Ten that was allowed to fluctuate over a 12-year period. The Canadian dollar was relatively well suited for an experiment of this kind. It was, nevertheless, restabilized. If the experiment had proved successful, it would surely have been continued. Canada's example, therefore, does not speak in favor of flexible exchange rates.

II

In the first part of our comments we have attempted to analyze the reasons for the crises that have occurred within the Western monetary system. It might be worth reminding ourselves that currency convertibility has existed only since the beginning of 1959. Before this date, payment transactions were carried out in Europe through clearing channels.

The step to convertibility in early 1959 involved a certain risk. In fact, it was held at that time, among the directors of the Swiss National Bank, that the time for the introduction of convertibility had not yet come. The repercussions of World War II were far from removed. France, for instance, found it possible to venture the transition to convertibility only if it was coupled with a simultaneous devaluation of the French franc, as its monetary reserves were virtually exhausted. England, in turn, had to shoulder the debts that it had incurred during the war. Europe's capital markets were performing with anything but efficiency. The international political situation led to a heavy burden being placed on the Anglo-Saxon nations in terms of foreign exchange and to benefits accruing to West Germany. Italy's economy suffered from chronic unemployment. It is quite understandable, therefore, that the temporary disturbances and crises did occur.

It is far more surprising that the ambitious system of convertibility was able to weather all of these crises. Surely one is also justified in saying that the global economy has undergone unprecedented growth in the ten years since convertibility has been in existence. World trade has shown a vigorous increase and has led to a certain degree of integration of the economies throughout the world, thanks to which the living standard could be considerably raised. This is perhaps more observable from the European viewpoint than from the American perspective.

None of the crises of the past ten years could have been avoided by a system of floating exchange rates. The underlying causes of disequilibrium in the various balances of payments go deeper than could have been cured by widening the band. The monetary system has suffered repeatedly from a lack of faith. Flexible exchange rates would not, however, have strengthened confidence, but would rather have weakened it. They would have triggered speculative movements until such time as the strong currencies reached the upper limit of the band and the weaker currencies the lower limit.

The convertible monetary system has not suffered from a lack of flexibility; only, it was not the exchange rates that were flexible, but rather the monetary reserves. It has proved possible in the last eight years to channel international liquidity, without any loss of time, to all places where it was required. On the occasion of the first pound crisis early in 1961, $1.2 billion were made available within a week; in the pound crisis of autumn 1964, $3 billion were granted within two days. The Monetary Fund and the General Arrangement to Borrow has functioned properly on repeated occasions. The central banks have developed techniques whereby they could channel liquidity rapidly without rate risks. A system of medium-term credits (the so-called Roosa bonds) was also developed.

The private economy, too, has equally contributed to the creation of international liquidity. In Europe, the Euromarket was developed. Even if it may display certain weaknesses, it has nevertheless made a substantial contribution toward directing global liquidity from surplus countries to deficit nations. Let us call to mind that the deficit in Italy's basic payments balance in 1963 was largely financed by means of the Euromarket. With the step-by-step return of the Italian balance of payments to normalcy, funds began to flow back into other countries. Short-term capital, which for reasons of security and other considerations found its way into Switzerland, was reinvested on the international money market by the Swiss banks. In Switzerland, the interest rate gradient itself took care of the outflow of capital. In contrast, the Swiss National Bank undertook swap operations in the opposite direction at year's end or also at quarter's end and reinvested the foreign exchange it had received on the Euromarket in order to prevent disturbances on the latter. Through a system of notification, bank positions were recorded. In this connection it was interesting to note that the bank's positions increased from year to year and finally exceeded central bank reserves. This means simply that surpluses and deficits in the balances of payments were brought into equilibrium to an increasing degree, with monetary reserves being largely preserved in the process. In this way the market contributed to the creation of international liquidity.

If there is a desire to initiate changes in the system, one might perhaps consider how this market could be made even more effective. It is difficult to understand why the market is centered in London and not in the United States, which today provides the key currency for the system. American laws, such as Regulation Q, would very likely play a significant role in this development. The fact that the international money market would get into serious trouble under a system of flexible exchange rates has already been emphasized on another occasion.

III

The question has been raised if, under a system of flexible exchange rates, the central banks should intervene or if the rates should be allowed to fluctuate within certain limits, so that the "proper rate" would be determined by market forces themselves. Anyone with a little experience in this sector knows that without the intervention of the central banks it would be impossible to maintain the system in functioning order. If it were merely a question of commodity flows, or long-term capital movements as well, it would be theoretically feasible that the play between supply and demand would culminate in the "proper rate." In recent years, however, the short-term capital movements among the industrial nations have acquired a dominant role. It would be irresponsible to leave the rates of exchange to the mercy of short-term capital movements. Under such a system, the rate of the Swiss franc would reach its upper limit at the end of the year because of the repatriation of short-term funds, whereas it would have to drop to its lower limit by spring and then perhaps climb again to its upper limit by mid-year. If such fluctuations remained within 1 per cent, they would not constitute a disturbing factor. However, if a spread of ± 5 per cent existed, fluctuations would result that would prevent any useful economic calculations.

If one is convinced that a system of fluctuating exchange rates could not operate without intervention, one must also consider that this would constitute a heavy degree of responsibility for the central bank officials in charge of foreign-exchange movements. Those responsible for the rate of the currency cannot estimate with any absolute degree of certainty which forces are at play on the foreign-exchange market. Whether an economy finds itself with a surplus or a deficit over the long run can usually be determined only after the passage of a lengthy period. In the meantime the short-term capital movements can completely cover or offset the basic tendencies. Most often, there is only one specialist in a central bank who, on the basis of long experience, is able to read the pulse of the foreign-exchange market. The fate of a flexible currency, therefore, lies virtually in the hands of one person, even if an official committee has to bear the responsibility.

IV

In conclusion, I would like to express the belief that the present system of stable exchange rates—which has now been in operation for only ten years—should be maintained, in view of the fact that the disturbing factors of the past will have less of an impact in the future:

(1) The strengthening of the European capital markets will lead to an exchange of capital, instead of a one-sided outflow from the United States. This turning point was reached during the past year and constitutes an important step in solving the American balance-of-payments problems. In addition, there are reasons to believe that the Vietnam war is coming to an end, which would also provide relief for the American balance of payments. A strong key-currency provides solid support for the system. The currency unrest of the past year is largely attributable to the fact that confidence in the dollar was shaken repeatedly.

Should the elimination of the American balance-of-payments deficit lead to a shortage of international liquidity, then the system of special drawing rights could be used. The resistance to it will subside just as soon as the American balance of payments again remains favorable. The system of special drawing rights would most likely provide vigorous protection for American monetary reserves and call forth increased readiness on the part of many countries to carry dollars. If one has to consider that dollars could be converted only into SDRs and not into gold, many central banks would prefer dollars to SDRs, as the dollar brings higher interest and is easier to sell than the SDR.

(2) The problem of the West German balance-of-payments surplus will be easier to solve in the future than in the past once the German capital market is made more efficient and the German interest rates are not higher than those prevailing in other countries.

(3) France will not record such large surpluses as in the period from 1959–1966, so that no disturbances should be forthcoming. On the other hand, it should be possible for France to overcome its current deficit.

(4) Italy will most likely continue to show a surplus in its current accounts over the long run, whereas Italian capital will seek investment abroad.

(5) The smaller European nations have not given rise to any monetary difficulties in the past and will not do so in the future.

(6) The only monetary situation that is difficult to appraise is that of Great Britain. However, one thing is certain in this connection: Great Britain will not solve its difficulties by means of flexible exchange rates. Auguring somewhat more optimistically for the future is the fact that the problem of sterling holdings was partly solved in the past year.

In view of this situation, it would seem unjustified to make any basic alterations in the present monetary system. In particular, we must warn that by means of flexible exchange rates a new factor of uncertainty would be created that would do nothing to strengthen urgently needed confidence.

· 19 ·

Notes for the Bürgenstock Conference

ANTONIO MOSCONI

I

THE international dimension of the monetary problem originates in the existence of many national currencies, each administered by a more or less independent sovereign state under different economic policies. This leads to unequal degrees of inflation in the various countries.

Rigid parities, to be adjusted only in the face of "fundamental disequilibrium," add an element of potential stability to the international monetary system because fixed parities compel each country to keep its inflation in line with that of other countries to avoid external imbalances and losses of reserves. However, inflationary pressures in certain countries may be so strong that their governments are politically unable to resist. Then the temptation becomes very strong to evade the strict discipline of the Bretton Woods Agreement and to engage in bold financial practices. A flexible exchange-rate system has the one great advantage of avoiding severe stabilizing measures and of tolerating high inflation, rather than being forced, now and then, to admit failure publicly through the devaluation of the country's currency.

II

Disregard of the obligations of membership in the Bretton Woods institutions means a serious step backward. It undermines the evolutionary process that Robert Triffin has clearly identified as the shift from "commodity currency" to "fiduciary currency," first within individual states and then on the international level. The ever-increasing international cooperation with its enormous benefits in terms of trade liberalization is attributable mainly to the Bretton Woods Agreement, by which inspired leaders tried to build a collective system on the ruins of World War II. At a time when the international monetary system shows some cracks, it is necessary to work toward strengthening the institutions designed to expand international cooperation, rather than revive policies that have proved to be conducive to unbridled inflation, fogginess in world trade relations, and competitive exchange depreciation.

III

In the postwar period it has been possible to achieve a far wider—though perhaps still not strong enough—international cooperation with more viable schemes for economic integration for specific multinational areas, such as the one set in motion in 1958 by the Treaty of Rome for the European Common Market—a process that I should like to call irreversible. Fixed exchange rates (or exchange rates varying within the smallest possible limits, if need be) between the EEC currencies constitute the first step toward a common monetary policy. The existence of different currencies is reduced to a simple matter of different names when these currencies are made reciprocally convertible on the basis of fixed rates, an agreed policy toward third countries, and strong solidarity in dealing with possible speculative assaults on a member country's currency.

A system of flexible or even only "more flexible" exchange rates would be incompatible with fixed agricultural prices within the EEC. In addition, it would compromise the progress made toward a common monetary policy, a common administration of reserves, and, ultimately, a common currency for the Six. The process of economic integration would be endangered. In negotiating monetary questions, the countries of the EEC cannot ignore the recommendations of the European Commission to the European Board of Ministers concerning the coordination of economic policies and monetary standards within the Community. The Commission moved that "member states should bind themselves to make parity changes subject to common consent," and that "day-to-day currency fluctuations around parity levels be eliminated among member states and equal variation margins be adopted in respect to third countries."

IV

With respect to inter-European relationships, the following conclusions seem in order:

> Should it happen that a nonmember country unilaterally lets its currency fluctuate beyond the present limits, the EEC currencies, while remaining fixed with respect to one another, should change together vis-a-vis the currency of any such country. Furthermore, the international efforts of the Community should, sooner or later, be directed to negotiating the re-establishment of fixed rates as the only workable approach to a high degree of international monetary cooperation and economic growth.

V

A few additional comments on the "technical" merits of the various proposals for limited flexibility of foreign exchange rates seem appropriate.

A widening of the band for permissible exchange-rate variations could only produce effects similar to those of a devaluation. In other words, wider fluctuations, if allowed, would temporarily replace currency devaluations and revaluations. In the absence of corrective policies, however, the leeway afforded by a greater flexibility would soon be exhausted and the situation would fall back into the present, rigid groove. For this reason the "crawling peg" has been suggested, meaning an automatic adjustment of the parity of a currency, frequently and in small amounts, when the rate has been, for a certain period, near the limits of permissible fluctuations. Indeed, gradual modifications in parities might become necessary and, in principle, I do not deny their advisability under appropriate conditions. What I do anticipate as dangerous is the use of "mechanisms" instead of "negotiations." Mechanisms have proved to be irrational and blind. In the postwar world, conditions for a "negotiated economy" have developed, in which freely contracted mutual engagements override the exercise of national sovereignty.

VI

The deficit in the American balance of payments, the reason why we question the Bretton Woods system, stems from the worldwide role of the greatest Western power. The United States' military engagements, her generous contribution to the development of the Third World, her ample support of all the institutions designed to promote cooperation among the peoples of the world, along with large foreign investments, have exceeded her current balance-of-payments proceeds, drained her gold reserves, and put the dollar under such pressure that only the two-tier gold market could relieve it. In 1968 inflation damaged the competitiveness of the United States and eliminated the traditional trade surplus, but attractive investment prospects encouraged considerable capital flows from the rest of the world that temporarily balanced the external account. These plus factors were of an exceptional nature, however, and are not expected to recur. Thus the problem of the deficit of the United States remains, and it cannot be solved by devices that are detrimental to international cooperation and above all to cooperation between the United States and Europe.

As pointed out so well by P. P. Schweitzer, the dimension of the international monetary problem is political rather than technical. The efforts of President Nixon toward an equitable negotiated solution of the Vietnam war and toward monetary stability will certainly benefit the foreign-exchange position of the United States, strengthen the dollar, and contribute toward a more stable international-payments system. If these endeavors will be as successful as they deserve, why then hasten the introduction of pseudosolutions whose negative effects have already been underscored? We ought to strengthen and not to weaken international cooperation.

An outcome of this spirit of cooperation was the introduction of Special Drawing Rights which Europe accepted, albeit suggesting gradualism and constraint in actual implementation, lest they become bad money driving out the good according to Gresham's Law. The European countries can only hope that the United States will withstand the temptations of isolationism that expresses itself not only in the form of protective tariffs, but also in competitive interest and exchange rates.

· 20 ·

Why I Am Not in Favor of Greater Flexibility of Exchange Rates

GIULIANO PELLI

THE points I had examined in my initial paper were the following:

(A) How much additional forward cover would be required?
(B) Would such an additional cover be forthcoming? How? Would new institutions be required?
(C) What would be the cost of the additional forward cover obtainable?
(D) How would these results affect the volume of trade, capital investment, liquid flows including the Euromarket?

I shall treat these points here again, but I should like to emphasize that they do not constitute the only negative aspects of a greater flexibility.

(A) *Let us suppose that the band be increased to 5 per cent on each side of the parity against dollars.*

As we know, the present band amounts—with the exception of the Swiss franc—to only ¾ of 1 per cent on each side of the parity. According to the rules of the IMF, the intervention points could have been fixed for the member countries at 1 per cent on each side.

Let us take an example from the present rates (Summer 1969):

	Lower intervention point	Parity	*Upper intervention point*
£/$	2.38	2.40	2.42
$/DM	3.97	4.00	4.03
£/DM	9.4486	9.60	9.7526

With *a band of 5 per cent* on each side of the $ parity, these rates would be:

£/$	2.28	2.40	2.52
$/DM	3.80	4.00	4.20
£/DM	8.664	9.60	10.584

As we see, a band of 5 per cent on each side of the $ parity means about 10 per cent on each side of the parity for cross-rates (e.g., £/DM). In other words, a possible total fluctuation of 20 per cent, as compared with 3 per cent for cross-rates today.

The answer to question A is, of course, not easy. But no doubt *the need for forward contracts would be increased considerably.* Today, many transactions, commercial and financial, are concluded without any forward cover. In times where the pound for example is under no pressure—in other words, when no devaluation is expected—a firm exporting goods to England, payable after ninety days, may decide to take the foreign-exchange risk and not sell the sterling forward. The same will happen for short-term investments in England.

With a 5 per cent band on each side of the dollar parity, on the other hand, everybody would feel obliged to cover the foreign-exchange risks. Supposing that the $/DM rate would be around the parity ($1 = DM4.00) and the £/$ rate around 2.39. This would mean a cross-rate £/DM of (2.39 × 4.00) 9.56. As we have seen before, the lower intervention point £/DM would be 8.6640. Obviously, with such a difference (DM0.896 per £, i.e., 9 ⅜ per cent), nobody will be ready to take the foreign-exchange risk. Supposing that, at the same time, the interest for three-months-fixed-deposits on the Euromarket would be 10 per cent for pounds and 4 per cent for German marks, the discount for three-months-forward pounds against marks would amount to 6 per cent a year. A forward sale of pounds against marks for ninety days would cost 1.5 per cent, as compared with a possible fluctuation downward of 9 ⅜ per cent. Of course, that is also true for fluctuations upward and, supposing there is no pressure on the pound, this currency would also be *bought* forward. But the result would be that the volume of forward cover required would be much higher than today.

The example of pounds against German marks might not be the best when we consider that, in the last few months, due to the rumors of upvaluation for the German mark and the still existing possibility of a sterling devaluation, the forward risk for pounds has probably been covered anyway. *But if we consider other currencies that are under no pressure whatsoever, we can be sure that in case of a widening of the band, two, three, or four times more forward cover would be required than it is the case today.*

(B) *Would such an additional cover be forthcoming? How? Would new institutions be required?*

The total of the additional cover required would hardly be provided. First of all, we should be aware of the fact that the commercial banks have already such enormous amounts of forward contracts outstanding that they would not be ready to increase them much more, even if we admit that the technical possibilities might be available. Why would this be so? What sort of risk is involved in the forward foreign-exchange transactions for the banks? We can admit that there are no *del credere* risks because the counterparts of the bank are either a bank, the standing of which is beyond any doubt, or a customer who has to pay an adequate margin. But troubles could arise from measures taken in one of the countries concerned.

Let us take an example which is, of course, purely theoretical. Bank

A in Switzerland has bought forward an amount of $5 million against Swiss francs from Bank *B* in London. Before the maturity date of the contract, the following might happen: England puts an embargo on all foreign currencies and *B* is not able to pay the dollars to *A*. In such a case, all the foreign exchange amounts bought from banks in England by *A*—and by any other buyer outside England—could not be paid. What would then happen? *A* would not pay the Swiss francs countervalue to *B* and, as to this point, would suffer no loss. But what about the other part of the transaction? The $5 million *A* bought forward from *B* had simultaneously been sold forward to another counterpart, say to *C* in Germany. At the maturity date, *A* will have to pay the dollars to *C*. To be able to do it, *A* will have to try and buy the dollars in the spot market, and might have to pay a much higher price. *A* will probably claim the price difference from *B*, and this will lead to discussions or even more.

This is only one of the possible cases and, fortunately, it is purely theoretical today. But a bank has to consider all the theoretical dangers and that is the reason why, in most banks internationally engaged in the forward market, a ceiling is fixed for the dealers as to the total of foreign exchange forward transactions that may be outstanding. *Considering these facts, I think that only part of the additional cover required would be forthcoming.*

I do not see how new institutions could be created. If by "new institutions" we think of the possibility of the central banks intervening, I think that such an intervention could be compared with a direct intervention on the foreign-exchange spot rates within the official intervention points, as this is the case today. Now, would it be worthwhile to widen the band if we assume that central banks would still intervene within the new intervention points? I do not think so. I will try to explain why.

Let us take the example of a currency under a heavy pressure. After the widening of the band, we would be faced with one of the following situations:

(1) the central bank still intervenes within a narrow band; or
(2) the central bank does not intervene within the official points.

In case (1), fluctuations would not be higher than the present ones, but, because of the possibility of a change in the policy of the central bank —which would no longer intervene within a narrow band—the uncertainty would be greater and the requirement for forward cover would be, as we have seen before, much higher. In case (2), the rate of the currency under pressure would soon drop to the lower intervention point and the situation would not be different from the one we have today with a narrow band. The defenders of a system with a wider band think that such wider fluctuations could replace devaluations and upvaluations that, for political reasons, would otherwise not take place. That might be true, but the advantages, if any—I shall come back to this point later on—of the possibility of having such automatic devaluations or upvaluations would be to a large extent compensated by the disadvantages connected with such possible fluctuations.

(C) *What would be the cost of the additional forward cover obtainable?*

As we have seen before, all the additional forward cover required *would not be forthcoming*. But let us examine what the part obtainable would cost. We have already considered the example for pounds against German marks. We would come to the same conclusions concerning other currencies.

Let us take Swiss francs against German marks. With a 5 per cent band on each side of the dollar parity, we would have the following new intervention points:

	Lower intervention point	*Parity*	*Upper intervention point*
£/$	2.28	2.40	2.52
$/SF	4.154	4.3728	4.591
£/SF	9.471	10.495	11.569

Now, supposing that, before the widening of the band, the rates of interest for short-term, fixed deposits on the Euromarket were 10 per cent a year for pounds and 6 per cent a year for Swiss francs. At the same time, the spot mean rates would have been, for example, £/$ = 2.39, $/SF = 4.30, and £/SF = 10.277. The discount for forward pounds against Swiss francs would have been (10 per cent . / . 6 per cent) 4 per cent a year, i.e., about SF0.41 for one pound and one year, or about SF0.10 per pound for three months.

Due to the new wider bands, the £/SF rate (10.277) could drop to the lower intervention point, which would be 9.471. As we have seen before, no doubt, even without any special pressure on the pound, *all* investors and commercial firms would want to cover the foreign-exchange risk. We could then have the following cases:

(1) neither pounds nor Swiss francs is under any pressure: the offer of forward pounds might be compensated by the demand for forward pounds, and the cost of the cover would not be increased. But we would have a highly increased demand on both sides for forward cover, which, as we have seen before, would not be available;

(2) there are rumors of, say, devaluation of the pound, upvaluation of the Swiss franc, or both: the discount for forward

pounds would grow considerably. It is true that this is already the case today as, when a currency is under a heavy pressure, its forward rate may drop below the lower intervention point. But when there are rumors of devaluation, we generally see that part of the potential sellers do not believe in the devaluation and do not sell forward. With a wider band, on the other hand, even the nonpessimist would require a forward cover, and it is to be expected that the pressure on the forward rate of the pound would be much higher than it is today even in a pound crisis.

(D) *How would these results affect the volume of trade, capital investment, and liquid flows including the Euromarket?*

I think, for the reasons described before, that the widening of the band would constitute an obstacle to expansion in all three cases. For in all three, the risk represented by possible wide fluctuations would prevent the conclusion of many transactions and, if not, would make every transaction more expensive.

As I think that all the additional cover required would not be forthcoming, and in many situations the cost of the cover would be much higher, I am also convinced that trade, capital investment, and capital movements in general would be made more difficult, and would be, in most cases, more expensive. *The increase in the cost of forward cover would automatically contribute to increasing the inflation.*

For this short study, I have taken the example of a band widened to 5 per cent on each side of the dollar parities. However, my remarks are also valid for a band of, say 3 per cent on each side. In such a case, the disadvantages would be smaller but they would still exist.

As we have seen before, the defenders of a system with wider bands think that it would give the opportunity to achieve de facto devaluations or upvaluations that, under the present system, are not made for political reasons. *Against this argument, I should like to say that it is very seldom that a change of parity of only, say, 5 per cent would be sufficient to rectify the situation. Very often, an economic crisis has nothing to do with the foreign-exchange rate. I think that this is the case, for example, with the pound sterling today. In other cases, on the contrary, the parity should be changed. But then, I think that a real devaluation—or upvaluation—should be used, and it would have to be, in most cases, of 10 per cent or more against dollars, and could not be replaced by wider bands.*

In the last few months, the crises involving the pound, French franc, and German mark have been widely interpreted as proof that the monetary system must be changed. *I do not agree with this view.* Just the fact that one takes such examples proves that they have nothing to do with the monetary system. Why? *Because the structural situations in England, France, and Germany are entirely different.*

Finally, could we assume that with a system of greater flexibility of foreign-exchange rates the present crisis could have been avoided? Certainly not. And this constitutes, I think, the best argument against a greater flexibility. Of course, the monetary system could continue to function even with a somewhat greater flexibility. But would this solve the present problems? I do not think so. On the contrary, wider bands and crawling pegs would introduce a further element of uncertainty into the foreign-exchange market—which would be destructive.

· 21 ·

Greater Flexibility of Exchange Rates: Effects on Commodities, Capital, and Money Markets

EMIL KUSTER

It seems to me that any expose on the possible effects of wider trading margins on the futures markets should particularly emphasize the problems that are most likely to arise in the *international capital* and, above all, in the *international money markets* (Eurodollar, Eurocurrency markets), which are all too often underestimated.

Wider trading margins for spot transactions would inevitably mean wider fluctuations for futures, which, incidentally, have neither an official "floor" nor an official "ceiling." Wider official trading margins alone could bring about a contraction of the present volume of Eurodollars because a great many holders of dollars would no longer be willing to face price fluctuations that are disproportionate to the return to be obtained on such short-term investments.

The "intercommunication" between the Eurodollar market and other money markets (German marks, Swiss francs, etc.) would be put under strain if not paralyzed. The swap-rates, which usually reflect the interest-rate differentials between the various money markets, could widen to such an extent that these operations would become impossible; that is, the costs of swapping from one currency into another or into Eurodollars would become prohibitive. This again could substantially reduce the available dollar supply. (Authoritative sources have estimated that today the equivalent of about $6 billion of nondollar currencies are in the Eurodollar market on a swap-basis.) Only a partial disappearance of such large sums of money could have serious repercussions on the international credit situation. They could easily initiate a chain reaction and lead to difficulties in the world's credit structure.

Added emphasis should also be placed on the likely effect of forward-exchange cover on *transit-trade* and on *international trade in commodities and other goods* as practiced by thousands and thousands of trading firms the world over. Profit margins for such trade are relatively small; therefore, even costs of, say, 2 per cent could "kill" this business.

The *international insurance business* would be another sector that could hardly stand the higher costs of hedging foreign currency commitments.

The *international issue market,* whether conducted on a dollar or other currency basis, could suffer by reason of the uncertainty of the currency situation.

Substantial discounts or premiums in the futures markets (a certain occurrence especially in times of stress and strain) would produce distortions in international trade that would make a shambles of trade and tariff agreements. The more integrated the economies are, the more severe the effect would be. (Price differentials for agricultural products in the Common Market are a particularly valid illustration.)

In my opinion, the widening of trading margins, even to 2½ per cent either side of parity, would create a situation that, even under "normal" circumstances (not to mention crisis situations), would be difficult to handle without constant intervention by the central banks. Aside from the problem of financing the huge sums of money likely to be involved, this would defeat, to a large extent, the benefits that the proponents of wider bands are expecting from greater flexibility. Furthermore, intervention could easily become the vehicle for "trade wars" and an instrument of trade policy in countries where the banks of issue enjoy only nominal independence.

Currency uncertainties produced by wider bands and the unpredictable gyrations in the futures markets would almost inevitably lead to barter and clearings transactions as exporters would want to sell in their own currency, and importers to buy in their own currency in order to eliminate the currency risks. So as to establish a cost-basis, essential to all international trade, an arbitrary, but fixed, exchange rate would have to be established, which brings us back to where we came from, with, however, a series of special headaches and handicaps. That such practices would hardly be conducive to maintaining, not to mention expanding, world trade is as obvious as two and two are four.

On the technical side of the exchange markets, one also has to bear in mind the effects of distortions or malfunctioning of futures markets on the central banks's reserve positions. If futures of a strong currency are not available in sufficient quantities, that currency will be bought spot and, therefore, increase the flow of weaker currencies into the central banks through the commercial banking system. On the other hand, a badly functioning forward market for weak or weaker currencies will cause the immediate drain on the respective country's exchange reserves, as prospective sellers of the currency will mobilize, by hook or crook, any spot exchange they can put their hands on. Stated a little differently, it also means that the "leads" and "lags" would become an even greater problem and more imponderable than they have been in the past.

· 22 ·

Selected Case Studies Relating to Foreign-Exchange Problems in International Trade and Money Markets

EMIL KUSTER

Exports and Imports of Capital Goods

CURRENCY problems of some magnitude arise in connection with trade in capital goods (heavy equipment such as machine tools, generators, farm machinery, computers, jet planes) which involve extended delivery and payment terms. This is a difficult situation to cope with even under our present system of fixed parities and narrow trading ranges. How much more difficult it would be under a system of wider trading margins, not to mention floating rates, may be illustrated by the following business, which actually has taken place:

The American subsidiary of a Swiss company contracted to sell heavy equipment to an American company (the amount involved was over $100 million) for delivery and payment over a three-year period. The subsidiary sold the equipment against U.S. dollars, but its contract with the Swiss parent was in Swiss francs. In so doing, the subsidiary incurred an exchange risk that it, of course, could not afford to carry. How was this problem approached and then resolved? The normal procedure of hedging the Swiss francs against dollars to coincide with delivery and payment terms proved to be unworkable. Neither the American nor the Swiss bank was in a position to provide the hedge because ordinarily the futures market is for three to six months, with occasional possibilities to arrange a forward transaction for one year. Attempts to engage the respective central banks in the transaction also proved to be impossible for a number of reasons. To buy the Swiss francs for spot delivery and to hold them until the respective payment dates would have been an intolerable burden on the American subsidiary (if it could have been arranged at all). To borrow the dollars in Switzerland and to sell them for spot delivery (in both cases, of course, to eliminate the exchange risk) would have been costly and probably difficult to finance. After long negotiations, parent and subsidiary finally came to an agreement whereby the parent, having a much greater profit margin than its subsidiary, declared itself ready to absorb 90 per cent of whatever exchange differential might be involved between the time of signing the contracts and final consummation of the entire operation.

It stands to reason that the foregoing compromise solution has been possible only because the Swiss parent company was satisfied that there would be no undue risk involved in assuming that the Swiss franc–U.S. dollar relationship would not be significantly changed for the period involved and, in any event, would not be changed to such an extent that the company's profit could be wiped out or that it would even have to face an overall loss.

If, in the future, the Swiss company were to face wider fluctuations for dollars against Swiss francs, certainly if the band should be widened to as much as 5 per cent either side of parity, it is most likely that the transaction under consideration would not have taken place unless either party involved could have covered the exchange risk through a not-yet-existing hedging or insurance mechanism.

What holds true of exports to the United States would equally apply to exports from the United States. If the United States were to export on a dollar basis, the importer abroad would have an exchange risk in his own currency, and if the importer were unprepared to deal against dollars, but could deal only in his own currency, because of his inability to shoulder the exchange risk or to hedge his risk (and at an acceptable cost), obviously the exchange risk would become the American exporter's problem. How it would be possible to resolve this in connection with the vast orders for American jets, with delivery and payment terms going well beyond the Swiss case cited above, is an even bigger problem than arranging the financing itself, which is difficult enough.

Attention should also be called to exports that require competitive bids from the United States as well as from other exporting countries. At the time the bids are submitted, the prospective supplier does not and cannot know whether or not his bid will be accepted. In a great many instances he is open on his bids for several days or even weeks. If he should be called upon to engage himself in a foreign currency, he incurs a wide open risk against which it is not practical to protect himself, for if he is turned down on his proposition he would have to undo his exchange contract, which could easily result in a loss.

To overcome unpredictable exchange risks in connection with export sales of various kinds of equipment (partly with extended-payment terms), some countries have tried to sell with so-called escalation clauses; others have endeavored to do the same thing in the case of imports. Devices of this type may work in some very exceptional cases, but are unworkable from a practical point of view because one side or the other incurs an unknown exchange risk.

Importation of Automobiles

Practices and procedures for importing automobiles vary considerably. One important importer estimates his need of foreign currency approximately three months ahead of payment date, covers about 50 per cent of his requirements and "stays open" for the balance until a few days before payment date. For the purpose of establishing his cost price and his wholesale selling price, respectively, he assumes the approximate parity rate of the foreign currency for the uncovered portion and the known rate at which he bought the other portion.

This method has worked well in the past. However, if the rates should fluctuate more widely or if the cost of forwards (if and when available) should increase considerably, the importer would try to increase his selling price, which, however, might price his product out of the market. To stay in business he might be willing, for a time, to forego his profit or even to operate at a loss. In any event, there would be additional hazards involved to hamper his and his suppliers' activities.

Steel: Imports and Third Country Trade

Some trading firms, aside from buying in the United States, purchase steel and steel products in Belgium and France against local currencies. Sales are effected in dollars in the United States and various Latin American countries against U.S. dollars. Delivery and payment terms are usually for four months.

To establish the dollar cost for offering in the United States or Latin America, the firms buy (hedge) Belgian francs as well as French francs for future delivery. In addition, the costs of freight in the respective currencies also have to be taken into account.

As profit margins for this type of business are traditionally small, even a fairly moderate increase in the cost of hedging could make this business unprofitable or impossible altogether. It is clear that under wider swings, except perhaps at the bottom of the trading range, these trading firms could not afford to leave the foreign-currency commitment uncovered.

U.S. Bankers Acceptances and Other Short-Term Investments

For a good many years, European central banks and commercial banks have been investing part of their short-term funds in the New York money market, notwithstanding higher yields to be obtained in the Eurodollar market. Central banks in particular have been in this market for very substantial amounts of Bankers Acceptances. Bankers Acceptances are also being purchased by European commercial banks (maturities up to ninety days), for their own accounts as well as the accounts of some of their clients, to employ surplus funds in a high-ranking bank paper with an established market. The dollars thus invested may represent unhedged balances held in the United States as working balances or for many other reasons. The dollars may also have been acquired against local currencies on a swap basis, the forward contract having been concluded to coincide with the maturities of the acceptances. The amounts involved are very sizable.

It is most questionable whether these investments would continue if the banks and their clients believed that the exchange risk involved would be out of proportion to the return to be obtained on the investment, or if the cost of hedging should make such an investment unattractive. Incidentally, greater exchange risks could also be a decisive deterrent to holding dollars on current or time accounts with banks in the United States. They could also discourage other types of investments in the United States. The effect of all this on American markets and, above all, on the balance of payments could be quite important.

The Grain Trade

The foreign currencies usually traded in by the grain companies are Canadian dollars and U.K. sterling. As a rule these companies buy Canadian dollars and sell sterling. Canadian dollars are bought for delivery in nearby or deferred positions to coincide with expected shipments of the Canadian grain. Intervals may be as long as nine months in the future.

Offers of Canadian wheat and feed grains are usually made in terms of U.S. dollars; the price for all offers being sent out by *Telex* is based on the closing price on the exchanges for that day, and is good (firm) for reply by 10:00 o'clock the following morning. In some cases offers to foreign governments or buying missions must be firm for forty-eight hours. Prior to the sterling devaluation in November 1967, one of the large grain houses in New York followed the practice of offering American and Canadian grain to their correspondents in the United Kingdom in sterling. Lately, with sterling again under a cloud, overnight firm offers are usually made in U.S. dollars. The rule for this is obvious; with vessel sizes getting larger every year, the amounts offered also tend to become quite sizable—LST 360,000 being just about the average value of a full cargo of grain. This represents a rather big risk in times of sharp currency fluctuations. Offers made by a grain house during the day for immediate reply, as well as bids received from their correspondents in London, are, on the other hand, made in sterling as this facilitates and speeds up negotiations with the buyers in the United Kingdom.

Unusually large amounts are occasionally at stake when some of the Eastern European countries are in the market for very large quantities of wheat, and offers worth several million Canadian dollars are made simultaneously by all major exporters, which, even in a currency such as the Canadian dollar, can cause rather sharp fluctuations in the exchange rate.

Considering the fact that margins in the grain business are traditionally very small, it is not surprising to learn that those businessmen firmly believe in the present system of fixed exchange rates moving within well-defined and narrow limits, because it is the best way to assure unhampered export trade at competitive prices.

Similar considerations apply also to exports and imports of other commodities that are traded internationally and involve two or more currencies.

· 23 ·

Comments on Mr. Kuster's Paper

RICHARD N. COOPER

EMIL KUSTER gives us several examples where wide actual or expected movements in exchange rates would discourage foreign trade. His remarks present a perspective very different from that of the economist, who is typically concerned with the operation of the system as a whole rather than with particular transactions. He cites three cases—machinery, grain, and steel—where profit margins are small relative to the possible movement in exchange rates within the period of contract. This relationship raises the possibility that a movement in the exchange rate will turn what was thought to be a profitable transaction into an unprofitable one, and the possibility of such an unfortunate turn of events, Kuster argues, will inhibit trade.

In assessing the merit of Kuster's point as an argument against flexible exchange rates, it is useful to distinguish two cases. The first arises when the exchange rate of a particular currency is expected to move in one direction within a period relevant to the transaction under consideration. The second case arises when the exchange rate is not expected to move one way or the other, but of course might move owing to unforeseen circumstances and thus give rise to uncertainty concerning the exchange rate that will prevail at the end of contract.

The difference in perspective comes out most clearly in the first case. If, under a system of movable exchange rates, the exchange rate is (accurately) expected to decline, then the economist would argue that those transactions that are not profitable to undertake at the new, depreciated rate should not take place. Such transactions not only will be discouraged, but ought to be discouraged. The country that does not allow its rate to depreciate under these circumstances is in effect subsidizing its imports and taxing its exports. Trade is distorted. Under fixed exchange rates, the country must either be losing foreign-exchange reserves or it must be restraining some other forms of international transactions that are perhaps socially more valuable. Britain, for example, has on occasion limited foreign travel of British residents so that foreign exporters could continue to sell profitably to the United Kingdom. But under the doctrine of consumer sovereignty, additional expenditure on foreign travel is worth more to Britain's residents than is additional expenditure on foreign goods,[1] and the country thereby loses by discour-

[1] This statement does not allow for the fact that many merchandise imports

aging travel while importing at the prevailing exchange rate. In short, a system of fixed exchange rates may foster the types of transactions with which Kuster is concerned only by inhibiting other international transactions.

It should also be pointed out that where a currency is expected to depreciate, which discourages certain imports into the country whose currency is depreciating, the same expectation will also encourage exports from that country, since some prospective foreign sales that are not profitable at the present exchange rate will be profitable at the expected future exchange rate.

In the second case, the exchange rate could go up as well as down, with no clear expectation regarding a movement in either direction. But the possibility of sharp, unforeseen upward or downward movements in the exchange rate introduces uncertainty into international transactions, and to the extent that businessmen are averse to this kind of risk, foreign trade might well be discouraged. In considering this possibility, it is necessary to distinguish between short and long intervals.

With short-run contracts, traders can hedge against uncertainty in exchange-rate movements by dealing in the forward-exchange market. Hedging will completely eliminate the exchange uncertainty for a particular trader. If the "cost" of forward cover increases,[2] that is, if a large premium emerges on the purchase of forward foreign exchange by an importer, this premium will normally reflect an expectation of a change in the exchange rate, and the argument given in the first case applies.

As Kuster points out, forward markets exist only for relatively short maturities. Markets would undoubtedly develop under the circumstances of greater flexibility in exchange rates, but they may not offer maturities for the long durations many commercial contracts would require for covering in this fashion. For a variety of reasons, traders may not always find it possible to cover in other ways either, for example, by borrowing or lending in foreign currencies. But here again the question of perspective becomes important. Over a period as long as several years, exchange-rate uncertainty exists under the Bretton Woods system, even with apparently fixed exchange rates. For such a period of time, there is no assurance under present arrangements that exchange rates will not change. Kuster mentions jet aircraft, which are typically sold on terms of seven or more years. With a purchase contract denominated in dollars, German buyers in late 1969 were paying less, and French and British buyers were paying more, each in their home currencies, than they

---

were also subject to restraints, especially tariffs. The statement would have to be qualified to allow for that.

[2] See the paper by Machlup (No. 34) on the difference between practitioners and economists in terminology. I use "cost" here in the practitioner's sense, as Kuster does.

217

would have at exchange rates prevailing when contracts were let in the mid-sixties. Unless the changes in exchange rates that in fact took place were anticipated at the time of purchase, German buyers are somewhat better off, and French and British buyers are somewhat worse off, then they expected to be, even under a regime of fixed but changeable parities.[3] Over a period of several years, there is little if any reason to believe that exchange-rate uncertainties in commercial transactions would be greater under a regime of somewhat more flexible exchange rates than under the Bretton Woods system.

[3] Actually, the position of these buyers is more complicated than this statement implies. Where fares are internationally determined, revenues in francs and pounds have gone up for French and British airlines, and revenues in marks have gone down for German airlines, other things being equal.

Part IV. Practical Proposals and Suggestions for Implementation

WITH the exception of the plan proposed by Donald B. Marsh, the following contributions are different versions of band and crawl proposals. However, two of them make use of variations of monetary reserves, which play a key role in Marsh's suggestions. Several papers favor a certain amount of asymmetry in band and crawl, with the purpose of building an anti-inflationary bias into the system.

Lawrence B. Krause's essay "The International Monetary Game: Objectives and Rules" deals with operating restraints resulting from the trade-off between price stability and unemployment. These restraints relate to the adequacy of the adjustment mechanism, the maintenance of discipline, the control of speculation, and the speed of institutional change. If the adjustment mechanism is to be improved through greater flexibility of exchange rates, the choice of the band will depend on the willingness to accept uncertainty. Immediate transition to freely-flexible rates would violate the rule that change must be slow and evolutionary. Parity adjustments of 2 per cent per year should be permitted. Interest-rate constraints would be necessary to prevent disequilibrating capital movements.

In his paper "When and How Should Parities Be Changed?" Robert V. Roosa emphasizes the fact that while deficit countries can be compelled to devalue, surplus countries cannot be forced to revalue. He suggests the rewriting of the Articles of Agreement of the International Monetary Fund so that an asymmetrical band and crawl can counter the inflationary bias of the present system. There would be no mechanical automaticity, but the dimensions of the permitted parity adjustments would be so small that the governments could delegate them to the central banks.

William Fellner's "A 'Realistic' Note on Threefold Flexibility of Exchange Rates" would limit the band-crawl flexibility not only in extent, but also to upward flexibility in relation to the dollar, and to a small number of countries with undervalued currencies. For these countries a slow and systematic upward crawl would be better than "jerky and disruptive peg adjustments in the midst of successive crises." Automatic flexibility would be very helpful in raising domestic resistance against inflation "because prompt exchange-rate movements are loud warning signals, easily noticeable by the public."

George H. Chittenden's paper "Asymmetrical Widening of the Bands Around Parity" proposes to give member countries the option to increase the upper bands to 2¾ per cent, but to leave the lower bands where they are under present regulations. Chittenden reasons that all countries with strong currencies have in the past objected to parity changes on political, psychological, and economic grounds. A modest widening of the upper bands would eliminate the fear of large jumps, make speculation a two-way proposition, and create a useful tool for domestic monetary management.

In his "Sliding Parities: A Proposal for Presumptive Rules," Richard N. Cooper proposes small but frequent *presumptive* changes in parities whenever variations in the official reserve position exceed some specified small amount. Admittedly, the sliding-parity system cannot cope with major disturbances and is not meant for the correction of already existing fundamental disequilibria. Adjustment of interest-rate differentials may be necessary to prevent disequilibrating capital movements. Problems connected with seasonal changes could be handled by exchange-rate variations inside a widened band.

In his paper "The Fixed-Reserve Standard: A Proposal to 'Reverse' Bretton Woods," Donald B. Marsh proposes that exchange rates should be left free to move (if desired), but that national levels of exchange reserves should be fixed within relatively narrow limits. The width of these limits should be sufficient to allow interventions for smoothing purposes. Exchange-rate fluctuations would reflect fundamental factors of demand and supply and eliminate the need for exchange control or complicated reforms such as the creation of SDRs or even the various species of band-crawl. Variations of reserves could be policed by the International Monetary Fund. The fixed reserve standard would free the members of the system of the obligation to adopt inappropriate policies of expansion and contraction in response to excesses by a few members.

In "Rules for a Sliding Parity," Thomas D. Willett addresses himself to the question of how a one-sided downward adjustment of parities (and a progressive overvaluation of the dollar) can be avoided. To eliminate this danger, he proposes a crawling peg that combines both discretionary and automatic elements. He uses Marsh's idea of keeping monetary reserves within a relatively narrow band and applies it to the crawling parity by making parity changes mandatory at the stipulated maximum whenever reserves fall outside the "band."

Constant M. van Vlierden discusses "Some Implications of Flexible Exchange Rates, Including Effects on Forward Markets and Transitional Problems." He favors a widened band of up to $\pm 2\frac{1}{2}$ per cent and changes in parities of ± 1 per cent when conditions warrant and the Fund approves. Parity-realignments are suggested as precondition for the introduction of the system. Van Vlierden believes that increased flexibility of exchange rates will improve the adjustment mechanism and, accordingly, lead to more stable exchange rates. Forward cover need not involve additional cost because both demand *and supply* would increase.

In "A Technical Note on the Width of the Band Required to Accommodate Parity Changes of Particular Size," Harry G. Johnson argues that the band would have to be substantially wider than the permitted discretionary parity changes to avoid disturbing the market.

In his essay "Short-Term Capital Movements and the Interest-Rate Constraint Under Systems of Limited Flexibility of Exchange Rates," Thomas D. Willett points out that limited flexibility would substantially reduce market expectations of major parity changes or impositions of market controls. However, a crawling peg presupposes the use of interest-rate differentials to compensate for the incentive to transfer capital from depreciating to appreciating currencies. Several factors tend to mitigate this interest-rate constraint. If the downward crawl is caused by inflation, "the real rate of interest would remain the same while nominal interest rates rose by an amount equal to the expected crawl." Furthermore, the interest rate constraint would not be very great in absolute terms once the initial portfolio adjustment has taken place. Finally, the country with the upward crawl would lower its interest rate, sharing thereby the adjustment burden with the deficit country. If desired, monetary interdependence of countries can be reduced by widening the band, by officially financing private capital flows, and by using selective measures to reduce such flows.

· 24 ·

The International Monetary Game: Objectives and Rules

LAWRENCE B. KRAUSE

CHANGES can be made in the present international monetary system by altering some of the rules by which it operates. Before setting down suggested "rules of the game," however, it would appear desirable to make explicit the "objectives of the game" in order to make the discussion meaningful. Also, it was found to be insufficient to merely state the "fundamental" objective of the international monetary system without also stating some operating constraints, for it may well be the latter that are determinants in a choice between alternative sets of rules.

Fundamental Objective of the International Monetary System

At the outset, one must decide whether the international monetary system has attributes that should be considered "ends or goals" directly affecting welfare, or "means to an end," only indirectly affecting welfare. My inclination is to treat the system as a means to an end, although some arguments might be made on the other side. Given this distinction, I examined three competing fundamental objectives for possible selection as *the* objective.

The first objective examined and the one selected, can be stated as follows: The objective of the international monetary system is to provide an institutional arrangement whereby individual countries can obtain maximum economic growth with full employment within a framework of price stability. To obtain maximum economic growth, economic efficiency must be encouraged by means that include promoting international trade and investment up to, but not beyond, the limits determined by comparative advantage. In a fundamental sense, price stability is not really an economic object, but merely a means of achieving economic objectives. However, the importance of price stability for social and political reasons is so great as to force one to consider it an economic objective in its own right. The three goals, economic growth, full employment, and price stability, are those chosen by the country itself. In such a system, if a country was able to achieve its selected economic targets, then the country should not be subject to pressures from the international side that would prevent it from continuing along its desired path. A further highly desirable attribute of such a system would be a

---

The views in this paper are those of the author and are not presented as the views of other staff members of the Brookings Institution.

consistency of pressures; international pressures would become operative when a country was not reaching its internal objectives and would push it toward attaining them.

One could alternatively have chosen as the objective of the international monetary system an arrangement that was concerned only with encouraging the most international trade and international investment. The rules of the game required to support such an objective presumably would emphasize exchange-rate stability to reduce private uncertainty and, thereby, enhance private trade and investment. Under the first objective, however, exchange-rate stability would be favored only if it promotes economic growth, full employment, and price stability.

Another alternative objective would be an arrangement that would put maximum pressure on individual countries to act "responsibly" in their choice of economic growth, full employment, and price stability. Responsible behavior might be defined as a bit better than the average of a country's peer group (either developed countries or LDCs) that is, what the average would be in the absence of irresponsible behavior, or, alternatively, as determined by a group of internationally-recognized wise men. Such an objective would be attractive if one distrusted the judgment of political leaders (or the political process) in choosing basic economic targets. This objective would be almost the exact opposite of the first objective.

Operating Constraints

The need for operating constraints comes from the requirement for an elaboration of the fundamental objective and stems from the fact that the separate economic targets themselves are sometimes competitive rather than complementary, the often observed trade-off between unemployment and price stability, for example. Operating constraints are required to help formulate rules in areas where choices have to be made between advancing one or the other economic goal. Indeed, a country might decide upon an inconsistent set of economic targets that are not obtainable simultaneously, given its economic structure and institutions. In such a case, the fundamental objectives become almost inoperative in practice.

Four operating constraints will be discussed, although these may not exhaust all possibilities and others might be usefully added upon further investigation. The four relate to the adequacy of the adjustment process, the maintenance of discipline, the control of speculation, and the speed of institutional change.

The first operating constraint is a direct attempt to link balance-of-payments adjustment to the fundamental objective. The international monetary system should have a mechanism for adjustment that, as a minimum, would be sufficient to compensate for divergences that occur among countries even though all were simultaneously attaining their basic economic targets. It would be highly desirable if the adjustment mechanism were automatic; however, a "policy" operated system might work if symmetry existed in responsibilities and willingness to deal with surpluses and deficits.

The second operating constraint relates to discipline and is operative when basic economic targets are not being met, and particularly when the inconsistent target problem is present. The international monetary system should exert discipline upon a country that is not meeting its targets because its failures upset other countries as well as itself. When a country incurs an inflation, for instance, some of the inflation spills over to other countries and likewise with deflation. Discipline should be put on the erring country to correct its domestic distortion. As a corollary of this proposition, there is some presumption that in domestic trade-off situations, the international monetary system should stand on the side of promoting price stability over full employment on the grounds that distortions of the former are less easily corrected than the latter, and, thus, will do greater injury to other countries.[1]

The third operating constraint concerns currency speculation. The international monetary system should be so ordered as to require currency speculators to bear the full risk of their speculation. It may (presumably) be desirable to actively discourage speculation if this can be accomplished without undermining other objectives. Given the amount and visibility of speculation in recent years, speculation is often given great prominence in plans for reforming the system.

The fourth operating constraint relates to the speed of institutional change. It is operative if changes are contemplated in existing institutions. Because institutional change is itself painful and does inflict adjustment costs that are not easily measurable, small changes are preferable to large ones, and slow evolutionary changes are better than abrupt dislocations. While this constraint would not necessarily affect the rules of the game for a revised system if one is desired, it may be very important in determining the rules for the transition from one system to another.

The Rules of the Game

The rules of the game, as they now exist, for the international monetary system, as it has evolved from Bretton Woods, are well known and need not be reviewed. The frequent financial crises of recent years have caused a great deal of dissatisfaction with the way this system has operated. The question to be answered is whether improvements in this per-

[1] It should be noted that irreversibility is the sole ground for elevating price stability as a goal. If institutions were such that excessive unemployment was more difficult to correct, then the ordering would be reversed.

formance can be made through changing the rules of the game and thereby altering the system. The two fundamental faults with the current system seem to be the lack of an adequate adjustment mechanism and the stimulation of debilitating currency speculation. Can rules be conceived to correct these faults while furthering the objective of the international monetary system?

It is well to recognize a limitation of the market-mechanism approach to the problem of adjustment. The market mechanism will react only to maladjustments in the demand for and supply of foreign currencies. If countries have particular goals for the trade balance or the current-account balance, then additional instruments will be required to achieve them.

There are at a minimum three types of rules that have to be specified. Rules obliging countries to intervene in currency markets (width of band), rules specifying the options of countries to intervene in exchange markets even when not obliged to do so (intervention within the band), and rules governing changes in exchange parities. In formulating these rules, both the spot market and the forward-exchange market must be recognized. In addition, rules might be desirable (under some conditions they could be necessary) concerning proper use of domestic monetary and fiscal policy instruments, and rules differentiating among countries might be considered.

WIDTH OF THE BAND

Possible rules concerning the width of the band extend from zero (currency union) to infinity (flexible exchange rates). The choice of a particular band depends on how much scope is desired for instantaneous adjustment to exchange-market forces, on the one hand, and the willingness to tolerate market uncertainty on the other. The Bretton Woods system reflecting the experience of the 1930s opted to minimize market uncertainty and, thereby, gave up automatic adjustments via exchange rates, leaving open the possibility of a policy-determined change in the exchange rate to correct a fundamental disequilibrium.

In order to solve both the adjustment and the speculation problem, the band would have to be widened sufficiently to make the limits inapplicable in practice, or essentially a flexible exchange-rate system. Fully flexible exchange rates, as the first modification of the present system, would seriously violate the constraint of gradual institutional change and this constraint would appear to be binding unless it could be demonstrated that such a drastic change was absolutely necessary. In all likelihood, only a more modest approach is likely to command enough support to be adopted, because a less drastic change may be sufficient to correct the defects in the present system and some experience is needed to permit institutions to become comfortable with a system having greater flexibility.

A moderate change in the width of the band is likely to have more effect on the speculation problem than on the adjustment problem. A wider band would not provide much room for immediate currency adjustment and would soon be exhausted if divergent trends in national economies persisted. Short-term speculative positions in currencies, however, might be greatly affected by the added risk of loss resulting from widening the band and, thus, speculation would be less attractive. But to be effective, central banks must let the spot rate move within the band with little or no intervention.

Central banks have usually intervened within the existing narrow bands, limiting changes in market rates to very small amounts. This suggests that if the speculation problem is to be treated through the exchange-rate mechanism, the first step must be to insure greater rate movements within the present band and only subsequently considering a widening of the band.

From this reasoning, one can conclude that little gain can be expected from a modest widening of the band alone, and only a modest change is at all likely. While a widening of the band might be desirable if combined with or subsequent to other changes, by itself it is unlikely to be very useful.

INTERVENTION WITHIN BANDS

As noted above, central banks habitually operate within the existing bands to reduce market-rate movements. The main rationale for such intervention rests on the desire to minimize uncertainty for exporters and importers. It is also argued that speculative fever can sometimes be headed off if a large market movement is prevented. Finally, there is a feeling that such intervention may economize on the use of central bank reserves, if it is begun before the floor is reached so that a downward movement appears more gradual.

If uncertainty for traders is to be minimized, as it is currently, then it must be recognized that intervention within a narrow band encourages speculation because the cost of speculating wrong is also minimized. However, there seems to be little reason to limit market uncertainty to this extent. The small amount of trade and investment that might be discouraged from greater uncertainty is unlikely to be very important in furthering the economic growth, employment, or price stability of developed countries. The cost that society bears in terms of foregoing the benefits of market adjustment may well exceed these small gains. Furthermore, the other benefits claimed for intervention are probably illusory. If market traders were ignorant of central bank intervention, then a deception of stability might be perpetrated upon them, but this is not the case. Indeed, speculators often take their cue from the government and build positions after action by a central bank has indicated a serious situation.

It would appear that speculation would be less of a problem if central banks entered the market only at the edges of the band; also, limitations on central banks would be a necessary part of a gliding-peg scheme of the self-adjusting variety. Some objections have been raised to letting "blind market forces" influence exchange rates, particularly if they would affect parity changes. "Blind" apparently refers to the belief that central banks have unique knowledge of temporary foreign-exchange demands or supplies and there is social benefit to offsetting such demands and supplies in the market. If this is the case, then one could amend the no-intervention rule to permit central banks to counter temporary situations. Intervention could be permitted if it occurred in response to transactions without regard to exchange-rate movements that prior agreement indicated should not be allowed to influence rates. It is only when central banks intervene in exchange markets in response to movements in exchange rates themselves or to influence rates that the price mechanism is destroyed.

CHANGES IN PARITIES

There are grounds for believing that changes in exchange parities should be encouraged in addition to or in place of those adjustments undertaken under existing rules. In recent years, trend deviations among developed countries have appeared that would be inordinately difficult to overcome by internal adjustments. Some countries, fulfilling reasonably well their internal economic targets, have found themselves in external disequilibrium (Germany), and others have found that external pressures were pushing them away from meeting internal targets (France). If all countries were achieving their internal targets, there is no reason to believe that the external situation would remain in equilibrium even if it started out that way. The present system seems least able to handle slowly evolving disequilibria very effectively. Small changes are unable to trigger the decision-making apparatus until they have accumulated to such an extent that all participants in the market are aware of a disequilibrium. At such times parity changes are politically difficult and very expensive.

A modest change in the rules could provide for some flexibility to permit market adjustments to correct this situation. If parities could have been adjusted by as little as 2 per cent per year, equilibrium probably could have been maintained during recent years for most currencies. There may be occasions when a fixed devaluation or appreciation will be required to correct for a sudden and substantial shift in competitive positions. No automatic system short of flexible exchange rates could adjust to this possibility. If countries should decide not to change parities in the face of such disturbances, as is often the case now, a more flexible system would be preferable because an adjustment process would be started that could eventually correct the imbalance.

An ideal system of flexibility would be one in which exchange rates appreciated and depreciated in exactly the right amounts to correct a disturbance immediately when it occurred. While such an ideal system is unlikely to be devised, the exchange market itself could be utilized to approach such a system even if fully flexible rates are not permitted. Movements in the spot exchange market could be utilized to signal a needed change in parities. Such a system would provide flexibility in both directions ending the devaluation bias of the present system.

The essence of the proposed change in rules would be to permit actual movements in spot-exchange rates to affect exchange parities through a continuous series of very small changes. The exchange parity at the beginning of any trading day would be made equal to the simple average of spot rates experienced during the previous year. Thus, exchange parities would be determined by a moving average of spot prices. The determination of spot prices must be left to market forces if the system is to be self-adjusting. Central banks would still have to intervene at the edges of the (moving) band and, therefore, changes in international reserves would still play an important role in disciplining countries that deviate from modal behavior.

Exchange parities would continue to be specified in terms of dollars. There are some problems involved in using the dollar as the numeraire, but the alternatives are much more difficult, if possible at all. With the dollar as numeraire, the United States itself can only be in equilibrium when all other countries are in equilibrium, or if there are exactly offsetting disequilibria of deficits and surpluses in other countries. Also, monetary policy in the United States would have to be geared to the needs of the world as a whole as well as to the domestic situation. But in reality, the current situation is not all that different, and all countries face similar difficult constraints in using monetary policy for domestic stabilization purposes.

The operating characteristics of a self-adjusting peg system cannot be exactly predicted, but much can be anticipated. At the point of departure, it might be just as well if exchange margins are maintained at the 1 per cent on either side of par permitted by the IMF (rather than the 0.75 per cent margin used in practice). Once central banks stop intervening to smooth day-to-day movements within the band, we can expect private financial institutions to perform stabilizing speculation to offset seasonal and other short-run problems in exchange markets, but some minor instability of the rate would be neither unusual nor harmful. If a country's price performance deviated from the modal behavior of other countries, then exchange parities would slowly reflect this in a corrective fashion. With continued deviations over an extended period of time, a change of 2 per cent per year in a parity is possible. Some analysts have expressed concern over the possibility of a sudden reversal of domestic price behavior and destabilizing movements of exchange parities. In such a circumstance, assume a currency was appreciating and suddenly suffered a substantial loss of competitive position; the spot rate would immediately move in a stabilizing direction and depreciate by 2 per cent within the band. The parity, however, would not respond immediately and further stabilizing movements of the spot rate would evolve only slowly, but the original spot movement would not be reversed.

In a self-adjusting peg system, as much attention would have to be devoted to the forward market as to the spot-exchange market.[2] The covered-interest-arbitrage mechanism cannot be allowed to be manipulated to influence spot rates. Governments would be required to support the forward market so that the price could not exceed conceivable spot rates at the maturity of the contract, and would have to constrain monetary policy to this end.[3] A strong case can be made for central banks doing most of their required intervention in the forward rather than the spot market. If, for instance, a currency were under downward pressure, the central bank could offer forward contracts to sell dollars at a rate sufficiently attractive so that arbitrage would keep the spot rate from piercing the floor.

A realistic appraisal would suggest that the self-adjusting peg might not be negotiable as the first alteration of the present system, although it might evolve in time. Too many international transactions still take place outside the exchange markets for the market signal to be completely reliable. Also governments would be reluctant to limit their freedom of action in monetary policy that might be required. But if a more discretionary scheme is considered, it should be designed to mirror the self-adjusting peg as closely as possible. In particular, care must be taken to ensure that appreciations will occur when needed, so that the devaluation bias of the system is overcome.

Conclusion

I have tried to outline changes in the rules of the international monetary system that would help to achieve what I believe is its objective. Some have argued that no change in the system is required if governments would behave as they should. If governments do design economic

---

[2] For expositional ease, it is assumed that only a one year forward market is needed.

[3] A 4 per cent spread between forward buying and selling rates would correspond to a 2 per cent spot margin.

policy so as to be responsible, and they have enough foresight and courage to make it effective, then the rule changes I have proposed are unnecessary, but they would not be destructive. A prudent man, however, would be forced to bet that democratic governments will not or cannot behave in this fashion.

Others have argued that such a modest change as I have outlined would not be sufficient to correct the disequilibria that will occur in international transactions. While that is a possibility (although I believe an unlikely one), it calls for even greater flexibility of exchange rates than is implied by this reform. If countries are not prepared to consider seriously a system of fully flexible exchange rates, better some flexibility than none at all.

· 25 ·

When and How Should Parities Be Changed?

ROBERT V. ROOSA

IN THE introductory section of this collection of papers, I wrote that there seemed to be a greater similarity among the objectives of various proposals for increased flexibility than in the mechanics of the proposals themselves. Indeed, sympathy for the underlying objective of releasing exchange-rate parities from the often perverse influence of political exigency, can be detected among many who are not in favor of any of the newer proposals. Perhaps the answer may lie in going back to one of the original conceptions of the International Monetary Fund, that of modest changes of par values by individual countries from time to time, without IMF scrutiny or opprobrium. The original provisions of the Fund Articles designed for that proposal have been overtaken and rendered inoperative by events. A few simple adaptations might, however, give the original provisions new life and meaning.

Section 5 of Article IV contemplates that changes of up to 10 per cent from the original parities, downward or upward, can be made by any country with simple notification to the Fund. It provides for an additional 10 per cent on conditions that require only a limited scope for delay or intervention by the Fund. Beyond that range, lengthy consultations and tightening surveillance by the Fund are to occur. However, the many parity adjustments of the postwar era have long since used all of the intended leeway for most of the IMF members who maintain current account convertibility. And arrangements for lengthy, international review procedures, where tried, have invited speculative distortions of money flows. As a consequence, in my view, the time has now come for a reinstatement in some form of the scope for, and presumption in favor of, moderate parity changes at the initiative of the individual countries, as visualized at Bretton Woods twenty-five years ago.

Whether or not a normalizing of parity adjustments should be accompanied by another change in the Fund Articles, to permit a wider band for the fluctuation of current exchange rates on either side of any given parity, is not to me as clear. Section 3 of Article IV specifies that actual exchange transactions "shall not differ from parity in the case of spot exchange transactions by more than 1 per cent." But it also specifies that "other exchange transactions" (notably forwards) shall not fluctuate outside the spot margins "by more than the Fund considers reasonable." In practice, the Fund has not attempted to limit the range of forward quotations and central banks have varied greatly in the extent of their attempts to influence or limit them.

This two-tier system of exchange quotations has, until now, seemed to me as well suited as any operational approach could be to provide an optimum degree of stability in the payments arrangements among nations that are inherently subject to change. However, the intractable performance of the German Government in 1968 and 1969, when facing a clear need to revalue the mark, both for inflation control at home and to relieve pressures on other currencies abroad, does raise a grave question. Must the international monetary system contain a built-in bias toward the aggravation of inflationary developments, wherever they occur, or can some way be found to inject a counterbias to help resist the international transmission and aggravation of upward costs and prices? That is, must there be acquiescence to the view that all changes in official exchange rates can only be downward? Or is it possible to hope for some averaging out in the other direction by creating a presumption and a structure in favor of currency appreciation by countries in strong payments positions?

One way to help redress the balance—in view of the inescapable fact that countries can be compelled by a weakened condition to devalue, but not forced by a strong condition to revalue—might be to build a bias into the IMF arrangements. Preferably this would be a facility to which governments might adhere as they do to the Fund Articles, but with the implementation left to central banks, so that the prestige of a government need not be engaged in the details of exchange parity determination. A rewriting of Article IV, at least of parts of Sections 3 and 5, as they relate to convertible currency countries, might include provisions along the following lines:

(1) Variations in spot rates above parity could rise as much as 3 per cent over parity, while the margin below would remain at 1 per cent.

(2) Parity changes in an upward direction by 2 per cent might be made by any country in a single year simply on notification to the Fund.[1]

(3) Upward parity changes in excess of 2 per cent would be reviewed for action by the Fund at any time within twenty-four hours of notification, and would have an "overwhelming benefit of the doubt" in their favor.

(4) Downward parity changes would be reviewed for action by the Fund within forty-eight hours of notification, but would

---

[1] Dr. Otmar Emminger of the Deutsche Bundesbank has made a somewhat similar suggestion for a "discretionary upward crawl" in his excellent article in *Euromoney* (August 1969), pp. 6–7.

ordinarily not be made at intervals of less than three years and be for no more than an average of 1 per cent per year since the date on which the previous parity was established.

(5) No devaluation in excess of the 1 per cent annual average might occur without introduction of a program for domestic monetary stability approved by the Fund, and access to the Fund's resources beyond the first credit tranche in the event of such devaluation would be dependent upon the Fund's approval.

These suggestions are, of course, meant only to illustrate an approach; they do not represent a hardened proposal. Moreover, very little could be accomplished by steps of this kind toward untangling an impasse such as the one that preceded the more sizeable revaluation of the German mark in October 1969. However, the recent German situation should not be viewed as cause for excoriation, but rather as a useful advance warning of problems that are likely to recur—a harbinger of other situations in which other countries may well find themselves in the future unless some changes are made in the IMF procedures.

There may be several advantages from reintroducing a modest degree of flexibility into the Fund's exchange rate provisions, with scope for ad hoc action that will generally be recognized as more frequent, but also as less sizeable, than the currency adjustments that have occurred thus far in the postwar period. Once the present German distortion is out of the way, there would be grounds for individual concerns everywhere to base their financial planning on the prospect that changes in exchange rates or in parities, in either direction, are likely to be relatively small. In such circumstances, the burden of providing hedges for exchange risks in satisfactory volume for a growing scale of world trade and financial transactions should be kept manageable, and the costs on either side of a transaction should be reasonable.

Yet changes in parity, when they come, would be genuinely ad hoc, the result of a reasoned appraisal by monetary authorities. There would be no mechanical automaticity, with its potential for perversity, and its inability to distinguish among relevant and irrelevant causes. There would be little basis for the kind of occasional projection of a pattern that has led at times in the past, to heavy speculation into or away from a currency in anticipation of a possible massive change.

In particular, there would be a clear and usually compelling business reason for major international corporations not to swing available liquidity into a premium currency at a time of international crisis or disruptive internal events in one country. The potential for loss, if funds were moved into a currency at a high premium and no subsequent parity change occurred, would be raised by a wider band on the upward side.

A test of the efficacy of such a wider band (though of course not an exactly parallel event) occurred during the currency storm of May 1969, when the Bundesbank restricted the sale of German marks, as is documented by Charles Coombs in the New York Federal Reserve Bank *Review* for September 1969. Because of this move, many corporate treasurers and others found that their open orders for spot German marks were executed at a 3 or 4 per cent premium on the day of the heaviest inflow into marks. Thus, a number of those who are identified as speculators when they act to protect their accounts from exchange losses found that the "one-way gamble," moving out of weak and into strong currencies during a crisis, could have two cutting edges.

Moreover, and this may be the greatest advantage, the scope and significance of any simple official action affecting exchange rates could be kept within dimensions that governments might be willing to delegate to central banks. Thus, apart from extreme situations (and no system can prevent occasional distress cases from occurring over the years), governments as governments could be shielded from the direct responsibility for making the immediate decisions concerning exchange rates. And because each central bank would have freedom to respond, by changing the parity itself as temporary situations seemed clearly to be merging into permanent conditions, many of the severe strains of the kind created by an extended malalignment of currencies might be avoided. There could then be renewed hope that the international monetary system would continue to be the assisting servant, and not the resisting master, of dynamic growth in the world economy.

· 26 ·

A "Realistic" Note on Threefold Limited Flexibility of Exchange Rates

WILLIAM FELLNER

This note is motivated by the belief that a specific variety of limited flexibility of exchange rates has a better chance of receiving consideration from policy makers in the near future than do other varieties. The flexibility I have in mind was, I believe, first described for Germany—and for that country alone—in the 1966–1967 Report of the Council of German Economic Experts.[1]

Disregarding for the time being the possibility of gold-revaluation—a possibility to which I shall return later—we will have to face the need to find monetary arrangements acceptable to the rest of the world, given the inconvertibility of the dollar into gold (its inconvertibility aside from what may be called fringe transactions). Such arrangements are likely to involve at least some degree of exchange-rate flexibility, in addition to close consultations among the leading industrial nations about monetary and fiscal policies of mutual interest. I will argue that, in view of the political attitudes dominant in the countries concerned, the kind of flexibility that has the best chance of becoming adopted before long is limited flexibility in three senses. I mean limited in *extent* (that is, presumably falling in the widened-band and crawling-peg categories), limited at the start to currencies tending *upward in relation to the dollar,* and limited to a *very small number* of currencies for which this gradual upward flexibility would be put into effect by specific policy decisions. The resistance to *general* systems of flexibility continues to be strong enough to suggest to me that in the *near* future such a system will not be introduced, though one or the other weak currency might conceivably be allowed to float for a while before a discrete peg-adjustment takes place. At a later stage, policy makers might give preference to a more comprehensive system of band-and-crawl flexibility. It is to be hoped that they will do so.

Why Upward and Why, for the Time Being, not also Downward Flexibility in Relation to the Dollar?

Most of us believe that to be in overall balance, the United States needs a significant current-account surplus, which it does not now have. This suggests that some countries would be apt to experience a sustained

[1] *Expansion und Stabilität,* Verlag Kohlhammer (Stuttgart und Mainz: 1966), pp. 152 ff.

dollar inflow of greater than the desired size even if their future rate of inflation were no lower than the American, and even if relative rates of inflation were the only important determinants of trends in competitiveness. Other countries have for some time been in a weak balance-of-payments position at given exchange rates. Along these lines, one arrives merely at an argument in favor of *once-and-for-all* adjustments of some rates (with a presumption that in some cases a temporary float would perform a useful function for finding the equilibrium values of currencies). The German mark is of course the strongest candidate for upward revaluation. At the present writing, it seems that by one method or another adjustments will indeed be made.[2] Yet it is quite likely that *some* countries will continue to have a lower rate of inflation than the United States; and it also seems that structural factors, rooted partly in differences between the income-elasticities of demand for various types of goods and services, and partly in differential sectoral productivity-trends, continue to work in favor of some countries that have all along had a very strong balance-of-payments record.[3] This takes the problem out of the context of once-and-for-all realignment.

The United States has a more heterogeneous population than many other countries. This is likely to result in continued efforts to generate favorable labor-market conditions for weak elements in the American labor force, even if such efforts create rather severe shortages in other types of labor. At the end such policies might well prove self-defeating, since ultimately they are based on money illusion, but we do not seem to have come to the end of the era in which inflationary methods of keeping employment high are used in a good many countries, including the United States. The present American rate of inflation will *have to be* reduced—of this the American policy makers are well aware—but it nevertheless seems likely that some major Western countries will remain located lower in the inflation spectrum than the United States, and it is likely that some of these countries will resist pressures to revise their policies in the direction of higher long-run inflation rates.

But even if this guess should prove wrong—that is, even aside from differential price-level changes—differences between income-elasticities of demand and other structural factors[3] also seem to produce an uptrend in the exports of some surplus-countries as compared to their im-

[2] This was written prior to the French move of August 1969 and the German move of September 1969.

[3] The income-elasticity argument is developed in H. S. Houthakker and Stephen P. Magee, "Income Elasticities in World Trade," *Review of Economics and Statistics,* May 1969. However, the statistical method used by these authors attributes to differential income-elasticities *also* the consequences of other factors, such as differential productivity trends between the export-goods sector and the other sectors within the economies considered, *coupled with* nonprice competition in the sale of an enlarged volume of exports (where the trend-differentials favor the export sector)

ports. Given the fact that balance-of-payments surpluses will continue to show largely in the form of dollar-accruals, and that the United States cannot, of course, devalue in relation to this particular medium, some countries—the least inflationary ones or those favored by the structural factors to which I referred—are likely to become faced with developments calling for gradual upward revaluation of their currencies relative to the dollar. These developments will manifest themselves in "unreasonably large" accumulations of dollar balances, which may assume either the form of official balances, or of private balances, to the purchase or repurchase of which central banks are committed. "Unreasonably large" means large enough to make it difficult to counteract major inflationary consequences, and/or large enough to raise, in a significant way, the question of risks in terms of the "real value" of the accumulating dollar holdings.[4]

The proposition that, quite aside from any once-and-for-all realignment, differential inflation rates and the structural factors on which we have commented will lead to a gradual upward-revaluation of a small number of currencies in relation to the dollar needs to be qualified in one respect. I do not believe that the qualification would be of decisive significance. Recently, foreign investment in the United States, and foreign lending of various types, has grown substantially, and if this change should express a *trend* in foreign lending, the adverse current-account effect of higher American inflation rates (as compared to *some* other countries), as well as of the other structural factors mentioned above, could become offset by increasing capital imports. However, when considering an extended period ahead of us, this generalization from the experience of 1968 seems distinctly implausible to me, not only because American capital imports were promoted by the two European political crises of 1968, but mainly because these capital imports may be expected to become reduced by the prospective dampening of inflation in the United States. With the present American rate of inflation, a given money rate of interest in the United States corresponds to a real rate that is several percent higher when viewed from the United States.[5] The prospective dampening of the American inflation will reduce the attractiveness of capital exports to the United States.

The number of currencies under "chronic" upward pressure is likely to be small. Indeed, Germany might at first act as the sole pioneer in recognizing that she is facing the situation so described, and that it is

[4] Also, to the extent that the inflationary consequences, which diminish reserve-inflows, can be avoided, continued large-scale accumulation of monetary reserves represents forced savings of a kind that is particularly hard to justify on economic grounds, and beyond some level even on "political grounds."
[5] See Chapter 11, by Friedrich A. Lutz, in William Fellner, Fritz Machlup, Robert Triffin, et al., *Maintaining and Restoring Balance in International Payments* (Princeton, N.J.: Princeton University Press, 1966).

preferable to face that situation by a very slow and systematic upward crawl than by jerky and disruptive peg-adjustments in the midst of successive crises.[6] Sudden peg-adjustments do not express what I mean by *flexibility:* they occur when a parity *breaks,* and it seems reasonable to expect that the small number of "chronically" upward-adjusting countries will prefer flexibility to repetitive breaks.

I would expect that for some considerable time a much larger number of major currencies will remain unchanged in relation to the dollar; and quite a number of currencies will become gradually and increasingly *overvalued* in relation to the American currency. But these latter countries —those with weak currencies—will make an effort to reduce their rate of inflation, and, whether or not this effort will prove successful, the policy makers of the countries in question will not want to introduce a measure that could be interpreted as foreshadowing highly inflationary domestic policies. Indeed, something can be said for changing over to limited flexibility relative to the dollar at a time when one's currency does *not* have a recent record of devaluations (such as follow overvaluation) and is *not* suspect of "needing," in the long run, *more* than a very slow crawl. The analogous suspicion may be disregarded for strong currencies with a record of undervaluation. These are not suspect of *running away* upward.

Under the circumstances here envisaged, provisions for a widening of the bands and for a potential crawl would have to involve a policy-declaration by individual countries. This declaration would have to state that within widened bands the specific countries in question will not suppress exchange-rate movements in response to market forces by interventions such as would result in *significant* reserve-movements (nor have them offset by special arrangements with commercial banks); *and* that if the exchange-rates of their currencies should remain in the vicinity of a band-limit for more than a short time, they will let a crawl go into effect in relation to the dollar with the intention of not stopping the crawl before the exchange rate of the country arrives in the vicinity of the center of the shifted band-width.[7] Whether the parity rate of a currency would actually move within the limits permitted by a band-and-crawl declaration would then depend on market forces.

An upward crawl of some "strong" currencies would make it easier for the policy makers of countries with a weak currency-record to acquire a record of greater stability, that is, a record that would enable

---

[6] However, such a move by any major country tends to increase the pressure of surpluses on other countries that are in a similar situation.

[7] Some amount of administrative discretion in the interpretation of such a clause is inevitable, and even desirable. As for the size of the band-width, 2 per cent or 3 per cent on each side of parity would seem sufficient to me, and I believe that the crawl could be limited to a *potential* rate of 2 per cent per year in weekly installments. For the problem in general, see my "On Limited Flexibility of Exchange Rates," Chapter 5 in Fellner, Machlup, Triffin, op. cit.

them to adopt band-and-crawl provisions without arousing suspicions in the currency markets. Moreover, the policy makers of these latter nations might, after a while, arrive at the conclusion that extension of a system of limited flexibility to their currencies would be distinctly helpful in raising domestic resistance against inflation. This is because prompt exchange-rate movements are loud warning signals, promptly and easily noticeable to the public, while reserve movements are not. It is, therefore, conceivable that even if the policy makers of countries with currencies now regarded as "weak" should find it impossible to avoid further jerky devaluations in the future, they will nevertheless arrive at the conclusion that limited flexibility would lead to more reasonable domestic policies. Adoption of a general system of limited flexibility might at some later stage seem desirable *also* to the countries with a record of exchange-rate stability in relation to the dollar, because the abrupt, major peg-adjustments of weak currencies in the midst of crises, and after largely ineffective attempts at enforcing measures of exchange control, are harmful to the international community at large.

In due time these insights might indeed result in the adoption of a general system of limited flexibility (band-and-crawl flexibility), with allowance for the formation of currency blocs within which exchange rates might remain fixed. But the change of attitudes required for such a comprehensive reform does not yet seem imminent *in the sense in which concern with a narrower aspect of the flexibility problem is imminent.* What will, I think, make it imperative for practitioners to concern themselves with a narrower aspect of flexibility—that is, with the threefold-limited flexibility of the present note—is a search for "safeguards" against being oversupplied with reserves under a system in which these accrue very largely in the form of dollars that are inconvertible aside from "fringe transactions," with the result that all deficit-countries other than the United States automatically tend to become depleted of reserve media, but the United States does not. It is in the nature of the problem that this particular concern should become focused on methods by which a small number of countries can allow their currencies to rise relative to the dollar, since the alternative course of placing the United States under an effective reserve-squeeze is not open to them. Moreover, given the fact that converting dollars into gold on any major scale would be as impossible at a gold price somewhat in excess of $35 as it is at the present price, the United States is in no position to play an active role in adjusting the structure of exchange rates which is, in reality, centered on the dollar.

What Would Be Accomplished?

By the standards of those of us who have been pleading for appreciably greater flexibility of exchange rates, the discretionary flexibility here considered would represent a modest reform. But the reform would be a highly desirable one, and it would be desirable *not only* because it would be a "step in the right direction." Assuming that American policies will become distinctly less inflationary than they have been in an atypical recent phase of development, the reform could in itself prove very valuable. On this assumption the reform could make a significant contribution to the solution of the one and only truly serious problem that is about to arise *as a specific result* of the gradual recognition of the inconvertibility of the dollar (or, as long as the status quo continues, we should say: as a specific result of the dollar's inconvertibility except for conversions that do not appreciably reduce the American gold stock). No country should be pressured politically into holding or accumulating dollars, but I suggest that it is equally reasonable to lay down the principle that no country can complain legitimately of excess dollar-holdings or accumulations if it can reduce its holdings or acquisitions to the desired rate by an orderly, gradual revaluation of its currency in relation to the dollar.

At any rate, if the principle expressed in the preceding sentence is rejected, then it is difficult to see how an increase of the price of monetary gold could be avoided. Indeed, an increase of the gold price would *reflect* the nonacceptance of the principle just formulated, and gold-revaluation would, I believe, be a natural corollary of the nonacceptance of that principle.

In the event of gold-revaluation by a substantial margin—say, a doubling of the price of monetary gold—the dollar would become truly convertible, and it seems likely that, in this case, countries with a long-run tendency toward a surplus could, without taking steps to revalue their currencies, avoid accumulating dollars beyond any desired amounts. If exchange rates were realigned at the time of the gold-revaluation—that is, if an initial revaluation relative to the United States *did* take place— then such *differential* gold-revaluation could, of course, initially reduce or turn around surpluses and deficits. In the long run, chronic balance-of-payments pressures could revive again, though it would be hard to predict in which directions they would develop. Genuine gold-convertibility of the dollar, after a major revaluation of gold, would, of course, not enable the present surplus countries, or any other country, to avoid inflation; on the contrary, one of the grave disadvantages of gold-revaluation would be that this measure would increase the inflationary pressures in all countries. The unpredictability of the future supply of gold would make it particularly difficult to devise rational policies for moderating the inflationary tendency. What genuine gold-convertibility of the dollar would enable the rest of the world to do is to reduce greatly its *dollar*-reserves and to expose the United States to a reserve-squeeze whenever the United States became a "chronic" deficit-country. "Chronic" surplus countries could then accumulate gold, and they could force the United States to devalue again in terms of gold, unless it balanced its accounts in time. To the extent to which reserves were held in gold, such a policy would involve a loss of interest earnings for the countries other than the United States, but an American devaluation would not reduce the real value of the reserves held by the rest of the world. Moreover, since, as compared to most other countries, the United States could in such circumstances prove relatively efficient in its gold-sterilization efforts, more than "gaining time" might be involved in this course for the United States. The American balance-of-payments position might become very different from what it has been over the past decades.

Yet I find it impossible to think my way through this problem without arriving at the conclusion that from the point of view of *all* Western countries the course so described would be distinctly inferior to that discussed in the main part of the present paper, namely, to increasing the flexibility of exchange rates within a rate-structure centered on the dollar. Gold-revaluation would not merely give rise to very significant inflationary difficulties, but it would prolong the life of the system of "adjustable pegs," which, after some time, would again lead to a series of jerky changes of exchange rates in the midst of crises and after lapses into exchange control. If gold-revaluation should take place, this would be because the present kind of gold-conversion pledge could give rise to a crisis, as a result of which conversion would have to be suspended at a time when the dollar would be under sharp attack; in such circumstances some countries, led by what I would consider misjudgment, could give preference to forming a gold bloc rather than adopting a system of dollar-centered, exchange-rate flexibility; the United States, also led by what I would consider misjudgment, might decide not to "fight it out" but to put an end to such economic warfare by resuming gold-conversion at an appreciably higher price. Therefore, I do not regard the present unrealistic gold-conversion pledge as harmless.

In principle, the disadvantages of gold-revaluation could be avoided, and the alleged advantage of exposing the United States to a reserve-squeeze could nevertheless be achieved, by making the dollar convertible not into gold metal but into paper-gold, the quantity of which would be regulated by international agreement. But it is very difficult to see what would induce rational American negotiators to accept such a system that would, indeed, make the United States vulnerable to a squeeze *and* would do so without even creating a presumption that the inflation rates of the other countries would exceed the American. Nor do I see any tendency on the part of other countries to make the acceptance and the use of dollars contingent on their convertibility into some jointly regulated, ultimate reserve asset, the value of which would depend exclusively on international treaty. The idea of making the dollar convertible into an ultimate reserve asset must, of course, be sharply distinguished from the idea that the *additional* reserves of successive periods should *in part* be created in the form of jointly regulated securities (or "drawing rights").

Hence, I suggest that given the facts of life, we should try to work toward a system under which the inconvertibility of the dollar is recognized,[8] and under which monetary and fiscal policies of mutual interest are properly discussed among the major countries, with the result that countries desiring to reduce their dollar-accumulations can do so by revaluing their currencies relative to the dollar. Assuming a reasonable reduction of the inflationary pressures in the United States, they should be able to do this *gradually,* by means of the "crawl," over periods of appropriate duration. In my appraisal, the only *realistic* alternative to recognized inconvertibility and orderly, gradual exchange-rate adjustments is the revaluation of gold.[9] Gold-revaluation would, however, create difficult problems of inflation control, aggravated by unpredictable changes in the supply of gold, and, in the long run, it would bring back the sudden and disruptive major changes of exchange-rates that now plague us. Therefore, I feel convinced that gold-revaluation would prove inferior to the policy line suggested in this paper. I believe that the two-tier system will prove a success only if in retrospect it will be possible to interpret it as a transition to arrangements such as those here anticipated, and if these arrangements will prove to be a transition to a more general system of limited flexibility.

[8] One cannot have very definite convictions about how long "recognized inconvertibility" may continue to mean *"de jure* convertibility such as does not *de facto* result in any appreciable reduction of the American gold stock." But, as I said, I do not consider the present American gold-conversion pledge harmless from *any* country's point of view, except if the policy makers of a country are "eyeing" with gold-revaluation as an alternative to the type of reform discussed in the main part of the present note.

[9] I consider this an "alternative" in two senses of the term. (1) Gold would, I believe, in fact be revalued if some solution along the lines suggested in the present paper were not found; (2) by increasing foreign inflation more than the American, gold-revaluation, combined with genuine gold-convertibility, might well lead to a strengthening of the American balance-of-payments position, and if this result should not show, the other countries would find it possible to place the United States under an effective reserve-squeeze.

· 27 ·

Asymmetrical Widening of the Bands Around Parity

GEORGE H. CHITTENDEN

ENCOURAGED by a comment in Harry Johnson's paper,[1] and particularly by William Fellner's recommendation of a formula for limited flexibility,[2] I should like to suggest that our group consider asymmetrically wider bands for the major currencies as one feasible step toward the long-range objective of increased flexibility for exchange-rate parities.

In brief, the idea is to modify the IMF Charter to give member countries the option to increase the upper bands, but leave lower bands where they are. Such freedom would be useful at the present time for the stronger European currencies; in the longer run most convertible currencies could benefit.

These notes are inspired by a belief that the monetary system does not need a complete overhaul, but that we do have a problem. My suggestion of wider upside bands is aimed at improving the market's ability to cope with the two aspects of the problem that I consider the most critical, namely, the recurrent crises of the undervalued currencies, and the increasingly large short-term capital flows connected with them. Assuming that the suggested change proves beneficial, the hope is that we will have started a process of experimentation that will make subsequent appropriate modifications of the system easier to accomplish.

I do not recommend downside wider bands because I feel they would provide only limited assistance to overvalued currencies; the strong ones do not need downward expansion room. Central-bank cooperation, IMF credit facilities, SDRs, and devaluations, when demonstrably valid, should continue to be the medicine for the chronically weak.

Historical Background

Developments since the sterling devaluation of 1949 have given us a markedly different world from the one contemplated at Bretton Woods. The story has two parts. The first is that, due to such numerous structural factors as European and Japanese economic recovery, the Common Market formation, technological advances abroad, major tariff re-

---

[1] "The Case for Flexible Exchange Rates, 1969," Paper No. 8 of this volume.
[2] ". . . . In the meantime, those persuaded of the case for flexible exchange rates would probably be better advised to advocate experimentation with limited rate flexibility, in the hope that the results will dispel the fears of the supporters of the fixed-rate system. . . ," Paper No. 26.

ductions, and others, the dollar has gradually given the appearance of being overvalued. Recent inflation in the United States during the Vietnam War period has accelerated this development. The picture has been blurred by the measures taken by the Kennedy and Johnson administrations (the Interest Equalization Tax and the balance-of-payments restraint programs), but it is becoming increasingly clear. The deterioration of the American balance of payments on current account is plain evidence that shows through the cosmetics.

The second part is that the 1958 move toward convertibility, the rapid development of the international money market, the increased linkage of the national money markets, and the sharp growth of privately held liquidity, have vastly increased the scope for movements of short-term funds in times of currency speculation and upheaval.

The first of these—overvaluation of the dollar—could in theory be dealt with by changing the parities of major stronger currencies vis-a-vis the U.S. dollar. With the gold price immutable, and as long as the dollar is tied to gold, a devaluation of the dollar can only be attained by revaluing other currencies vis-a-vis the dollar. With IMF approval, countries now have the freedom to move their parities either on a crawling basis or on a quantum-jump basis. It would indeed be helpful if countries would not delay changing their parities beyond the time when it has become clear that such moves are appropriate. However, practically all strong-currency countries have political, psychological, even economic objections to doing so. The Italians, while recognizing that their current account surplus is too large for their own comfort, are concerned with overt and covert capital outflows. The Germans, while acknowledging that their currency may be undervalued, appear to be willing to change their parity only as part of a multilateral arrangement, and no one else seems to want to deal. The Japanese, who have seen their trade accounts strengthen greatly in recent years, are concerned about political developments in 1970 and future policy of the United States. And so it goes, right on down the list. Although it is conceivable that other currencies, such as the guilder and the Swiss franc, might participate in a multilateral arrangement, no such movement is likely under today's conditions without the Germans and Italians and, therefore, it remains to be seen whether parity changes will occur. Perhaps the recent suggestions from the German and Italian central banks of some form of sliding peg is an acknowledgement of this situation.

The second aspect of the problem—that of short-term money movements—is likely to be with us even if a meaningful currency realignment took place. One needs only to recall the Canadian dollar crisis of 1968, when all the fundamentals indicated that 92½ cents was the right price for that currency, to realize that money is going to move in ever larger amounts at times of temporary uncertainty about currencies. The floods of money that wash up on Swiss shores at such times have become almost a way of life.

To deal with both aspects of the problem more effectively, I suggest a wider band on the upside only, as the near-term answer. What we are looking for is a formula the politicians can buy—a first stage experimentation, not too radical, but of enough significance to crack the present impasse.

The Numbers

Though the IMF permits a 1 per cent movement away from present parities for Article VIII countries, the effective swing for the EEC currencies is now ¾ per cent up and down, for a total of 1½ per cent. My prescription would be simply to change the upward limit to 2¾ per cent, leaving parities and lower limits unchanged. To use the DM/$ rate as an example, this would mean: parity 4.00/$, lower limit 4.03/$, upper limit 3.89/$. This 2 per cent enlargement of the upper band would be a shade more effective if it were added to the currently permitted but unused 1 per cent band, but I feel that the less ambitious figure would be sufficient to relieve pressures and would be slightly more acceptable politically.

Practical Market Application

One might question whether such a modest change would do the job. I believe it would, for the following reasons and in the following ways.

(1) It will dissuade those who become convinced that existing parities of specific currencies simply must be adjusted upward in a big way one of these days—thereby leading to a subsidence of flows associated with structural leads and lags. It is difficult to assess how much of the present bias toward the German mark is motivated by the expectation, or fear, of a major jump in the DM/$ rate, but certainly some of the general hedging in favor of that currency would be deemed needlessly expensive if the near-term and medium-term risks should be judged to be 2 or 3 per cent instead of 8–15 per cent.

(2) Having satisfied market expectations by permitting their currencies to appreciate modestly, and at the same time having satisfied domestic preference for the existing parity, these countries should also have improved the credibility of the bands themselves. One of the notorious disadvantages of the present narrow-band system is that hedging and speculation too often seem to be a very inexpensive exercise. A "downside risk" of, at most, 1½ per cent is small as against the potential gain if a parity is changed. To enlarge that risk to 3½ per cent would certainly discourage some portion of the present leading and lagging. This would be particularly so

after the market had gone up and down the ladder a few times. There is plenty of recent evidence, in the rate record of the German mark and Swiss franc, to indicate the probability of such price action.

(3) In fact, a review of the recent track record of the exchange rates of most of the undervalued currencies reveals that, except for periods of inflamed expectation of over-the-weekend revaluation, these currencies have floated well within their permitted band, the German mark itself having been more inclined to sell at or below its parity than above. This indicates that the monetary managers of these currencies are quite capable of keeping their external position in balance through one means or another in noncrisis times.

(4) Wider upside bands, with the increased cost of speculation and the improved credibility of the band that I envisage, would be a useful tool for domestic monetary management as well.

This surmise is based on the belief that permitted exchange rate fluctuations of $3-3\frac{1}{2}$ per cent can make a noticeable contribution to the adjustment process whereas fluctuations of $1-1\frac{1}{2}$ per cent do not mean very much. Translated into an equivalent change in the price of export and import commodities or manufactured goods, such a shift is bound to affect a country's trading accounts.

It should also motivate capital movements to some useful degree. Think of the amount of potential capital outflow that is backed up in Germany today waiting for an upward adjustment in the DM/$ rate! Looking a bit beyond the hangups of the present market situation, it is entirely conceivable that wider upside bands could fit the future needs of such countries as Canada and Japan. Many countries, including these, have learned to use the freedom they now possess regarding forward rates to influence or offset capital flows executed on a hedged basis. What about the funds that move through the spot market on an unhedged basis? I would argue that an exchange-rate movement toward a higher, more credible band would induce outflows of unwanted liquidity. Likewise, an exchange rate at or close to a dependable lower band, combined with high domestic interest rates would attract inflows if and as wanted. Thus, more freedom as to spot rates is a logical companion piece to existing official freedom in the forward market.

(5) Exchange traders are often accused of being positively Mammonic in their appetite for profit. Having lived a couple of joyous decades in their competitive company, it is my observation that years of trading enormous volumes of money at tiny spreads may not have cured the fraternal order of dreaming of 10–20 per cent profits on large positions, but it has made them susceptible to placid contentment when profits of 1 or 2 per cent are in hand.

This is just another way of suggesting that the movers and shakers in the market place would be better and happier citizens if the profit potential were enlarged somewhat from its present norm of 1–1½ per cent, and narrowed considerably from its present deemed potential of 10–20 per cent. Another way of expressing it would be to suggest that with wider bands the alleged "agents of disorder" might well become the "angels of order."

(6) This same quizzical reasoning could be applied to the concern expressed by many, both academics and practitioners, for the depth, health, and welfare of the forward-exchange market in the event of wider bands. Most of us agree that if exchange rates were permitted wider total swings, a somewhat higher percentage of current account exchange exposure would want to be hedged. The question is whether the existing market machinery and institutions could handle the increased demand for forward cover.

The answer to that one depends in the end on the answer to the question of whether an asymmetrically wider band, for a few of the undervalued currencies, will relieve existing strains in the market and help normalize international financial behavior. I believe it will. And if it does, the market banks will be able to handle the increased business with profit and pleasure.

· 28 ·

Sliding Parities: A Proposal for Presumptive Rules

RICHARD N. COOPER

A SYSTEM of "sliding parities" is among the proposals for improving the international adjustment process. This note attempts to indicate the nature, effectiveness, and limitations of a particular system of sliding parities.

The Proposal

A country would be expected to change its exchange parity weekly whenever its payments position warranted a change. The weekly change in parity would be fixed at 0.05 per cent, cumulating to about 2.6 per cent a year if changes were made in the same direction every week. A change in parity would be triggered by a movement in the country's international reserve position. If reserves rose more than a stipulated amount during a given week, the country would announce, at the end of the week, an upvaluation in its parity for the following week, and vice versa for a decline in reserves. The movement in reserves would determine whether the parity changed or not, but not the amount of the change in parity, which would be fixed at 0.05 per cent. Market exchange rates need not change by the full amount of the parity, however, for the country's central bank might adopt a strategy of supporting the market rates temporarily even after a change in parity.

Changes in parity would be presumptive rather than mandatory. Where special circumstances influenced reserve movements, a country might ignore the presumption that the parity should be changed. But a country that failed to alter its parity when an alteration was indicated would be required to explain and justify its decisions before other trading nations, which would meet on a regular basis several times each year to review international monetary developments. Any country that systematically ignored the presumptive rules and offered unacceptable justification would be open to sanctions: for a country in deficit, no credit from the IMF and other international sources of balance-of-payments support; for a country in surplus, discriminatory "exchange equalization" duties against its products.

Aims

An arrangement such as this would be suited for providing relatively smooth accommodation to certain kinds of disturbance to balance-of-payments equilibrium. In particular, it would prevent or inhibit payments disequilibrium arising from:

(1) gradual shifts in the patterns of demand, as incomes grow and tastes change, toward or away from the products of individual countries;

(2) gradual changes in international competitiveness or other supply conditions, such as might arise from exhaustion of natural resources or from small differential rates of change in labor costs due in turn to different national choices regarding tolerable increases in money wages;

(3) modest influences on trade positions due to alterations in national policies, for example, rates of indirect taxation and corresponding border-tax adjustments.

This arrangement would not be well suited for coping with large disturbances to international payments, such as very large wage settlements or engagement in major overseas military adventures. For this reason large discrete changes in exchange parities, as called for under the Bretton Woods System, could not be ruled out. (The cumulative effects of small changes in parity might of course obviate some large parity changes that would otherwise be necessary.) Furthermore, this arrangement would not limit much the need for international reserves, and, on some occasions, might actually increase the need for reserves. Finally, this arrangement would offer somewhat greater scope, as compared with the present, for independent national monetary policies, but monetary conditions would still be subject to strong international influences, as they are today.

Effects

Sliding parities would affect both trade and capital movements. The effect on trade would arise from the gradual change—upward or downward—in exchange rates, making goods and services in a country whose currency was appreciating less competitive than they otherwise would be, and the reverse for a country in deficit. In some cases these changes in exchange rates would merely neutralize opposite changes in other elements affecting competitiveness, for example, changing wage costs or small border-tax adjustments, and, thus, would be preventive of changes in price competitiveness rather than corrective. In other cases they would produce compensatory changes in trade flows to offset disturbing changes in trade or other international transactions. In the latter cases, trade flows would have to be sufficiently sensitive to relative price movements for the system to work well. Empirical evidence suggests that the required degree of price sensitivity exists for most countries.

Gradual changes in exchange parities would also influence long-term international investment, but the influence would be limited and, on balance, would mark an improvement as compared with the Bretton Woods System. Under fixed parities portfolio capital may inappropriately flow to countries with high nominal interest rates resulting from inflationary pressures—at least until a change in parity is regarded as imminent. Under sliding parities, exchange depreciation, appreciation, or both will offset such yield differences, without however inhibiting long-term capital movements inspired by real as opposed to nominal differences in interest rates. Similarly, sliding parities would help to neutralize inappropriate incentives or disincentives to foreign direct investment based on divergent trends in money wage costs or certain national tax changes under (temporarily) fixed exchange rates, while leaving uninhibited capital flows based on differences in real rates of return.

The impact of a sliding parity on short-term capital movements, and, hence, its implications for monetary policy, is somewhat more complicated. The case in which gradual parity changes are widely expected must be distinguished from that in which the financial public is unsure whether parities will slide and, if so, in which direction. In the first case, monetary policy will have to be governed by balance-of-payments considerations if large outflows of interest-sensitive funds are to be avoided. In the second case, monetary policy will have somewhat greater scope than under the Bretton Woods exchange-rate system for devotion to domestic stabilization.

Strong and one-sided expectations about the direction in which the parity and actual exchange rates will move will be reflected in forward exchange rates. For example, a currency at its floor and expected to depreciate at the maximum rate would trade at a discount of at least $2\frac{1}{2}$ per cent (annual rate) in the forward market vis-a-vis the intervention currency. Under these circumstances, strong interest arbitrage incentives would develop, and, unless the country in question permitted its relevant interest rates to rise above those prevailing elsewhere by a corresponding amount (or adopted restrictions), interest-sensitive capital outflows would ensue. In this respect, however, the sliding parity would not restrict the flexibility of monetary action any more than it is restricted at present under similar circumstances.

On the other hand, if expectations about future exchange-rate movements are diverse, a system of sliding parities would offer somewhat greater scope for national monetary autonomy than present arrangements. At present, a country whose exchange parity is not expected to change in the near future finds its flexibility to use monetary policy for domestic purposes increasingly circumscribed by a large and growing volume of interest-sensitive international capital.[1] While forward exchange rates are not technically pegged by official action, their movement is limited under these circumstances to a band hardly wider than

[1] Countries whose parities are expected to change also experience difficulty in preserving monetary autonomy, but for different reasons.

the band officially allowable for spot exchange rates, for movements outside the spot floor and ceiling rates evoke speculative forward purchases or sales of the currency. The practical limits on forward exchange-rate movements similarly limit deviations in domestic interest rates from those prevailing in major foreign financial markets, for deviations in excess of those permitted by the range of forward exchange rates would evoke large-scale inward or outward movements of covered, interest-sensitive funds, thus weakening or even vitiating the intended effects of tight or easy monetary policy on the domestic economy.[2]

Because, under a sliding-parity, exchange rates might move in the course of a year by as much as 2.6 per cent in either direction outside the band around parity (although less in practice, since the full 2.6 per cent would require movement in the same direction every week), forward exchange rates could also range outside the initial band without evoking large, one-sided, speculative forward purchases. To the extent that uncertainty prevailed about the direction and extent that the parity would slide, therefore, monetary policy would be given somewhat greater scope for pursuit of domestic objectives without being undercut by international capital movements.

Special Problems

The proposal outlined above would sometimes call for changes in parity even when no such change would be appropriate in the long run, and occasionally the direction of change would be the opposite from that called for in the long run. This would arise, for example, during periods of seasonal strength in a weak currency, followed by later depreciation, with larger reserve movements called for during the swing from strength to weakness than would have been required under fixed parities. This contingency would not arise, of course, to the extent that private exchange speculation compensated for the seasonal movements in trade and long-term capital movements. In the absence of such speculation, this problem might be handled: by keying parity changes to reserve changes adjusted for seasonal variation; by allowing countries with strong seasonal patterns in their net receipts to maintain a band around parity wide enough to absorb the seasonal changes; or by allowing countries to exercise the option not to change their parities on grounds that are demonstrably seasonal.[3]

---

[2] We are somewhat misled into exaggerating this problem by the practice of converting three-month-forward discounts into annual rates. An exchange margin of ¾ of 1 per cent around parity would permit an interest differential (at annual rates) vis-a-vis the financial markets of the country whose currency is used for intervention of up to 3 per cent before speculation would necessarily become heavily one-sided under the postulated circumstances.

[3] It is sometimes pointed out that a system of sliding parities would have led to perverse movements in the exchange rate of the German mark during the

SUGGESTIONS FOR IMPLEMENTATION

In times of internal instability (excessive economic expansion or contraction) leading to corresponding imbalances of payments, movements in the parity would aggravate the internal problem. A country with a recession-generated surplus of payments, for example, would be obliged to appreciate its currency, and this would further weaken demand for domestic goods and services. But in such circumstances appreciation would be appropriate, for it would inhibit the transmission of the recession to other countries. Furthermore, it would reinforce the need to pursue appropriate domestic policies, in this case to take expansionary measures.

So long as exchange rates of most currencies are supported by official market intervention in dollars, there would be an asymmetry between the dollar and other currencies: maximum movements in cross-rates between two nondollar currencies would be twice the maximum movements in exchange rates vis-a-vis the dollar, and under certain circumstances this would inhibit adjustment in the American balance-of-payments accounts. Such an asymmetry is unavoidable so long as the pivotal currency has "nationality"; exchange rates determined by reference to gold or some other "neutral" medium would be required for complete symmetry among national currencies. But this does not mean that the United States would not benefit from the arrangement; an even greater asymmetry exists today, when countries in surplus are under much less pressure to take steps to eliminate their imbalances than are countries in deficit. Major imbalances in the United States would result in a gradual appreciation or depreciation of many currencies against the U.S. dollar, yielding gradual elimination of the imbalance.

From a technical point of view, parity changes could be monthly rather than weekly, so long as the changes were smaller than the costs of transactions incurred in moving from the currency in question into other currencies and back again. The larger the parity change (0.20 per cent a month, to achieve 2.5 per cent maximum on an annual basis), however, the greater would be the incentive to lead or lag payments to take advantage of expected changes in market rates following parity changes. Weekly changes would be both smaller and less certain as far as the public was concerned, and would offer correspondingly less incentive to lead or lag payments.

---

winter of 1968–1969, when it was technically weak despite Germany's huge current account surplus and the need eventually to revalue the mark. But this episode supports rather than weakens the case for sliding parities. For external reasons, the German authorities maintained a degree of monetary ease (thereby stimulating capital outflows in excess of the current account surplus) that they themselves regarded as alarmingly expansionist from a domestic point of view, and which they later reversed, leading, in October 1969, to revaluation of the mark. Sliding parities would have made it somewhat easier to reconcile internal and external objectives.

Discretion vs. Automaticity

It is tempting to make the rules governing changes in parity automatic and mandatory. Too often domestic politics and national prestige become involved in government decisions regarding exchange parities, and a fully discretionary system would very likely result in less frequent changes in parity than would be desirable. Even apart from the difficulty of devising automatic rules appropriate to all circumstances, however, governments as a practical matter are not likely to bind themselves to courses of action that they may not always conceive to be in their best interests. This difficulty can be resolved by laying down *presumptive rules,* of the type indicated in this proposal, which no country is obliged to follow, but which each country would be expected to follow in the absence of sound and persuasive reasons for not doing so. A procedure could be established in the International Monetary Fund or elsewhere for close and continuing examination by other member countries of those cases in which the presumptive rules were not followed.

Rules Based on Reserve Changes

Presumptive rules for parity changes must be based on some measure of balance-of-payments performance. Movements in reserves, spot exchange rates, and forward exchange rates all convey some information about a country's payments position. No single indicator will always be appropriate. However, simplicity is a virtue, and presumptive rules will be less seriously deficient when they are based on reserve movements, tempered where necessary by other indicators on a discretionary basis, than on market rates in the spot or forward markets. Forward rates may be held at a premium or discount by differences in national interest rates, even when there is no net movement of funds, and such premia or discounts signify nothing about countries' balance-of-payments positions. The great importance of nonmarket transactions, such as the purchase of German marks for American forces under NATO, militates against major reliance on spot rates, since these large transactions, even when, by agreement, they take place at market rates, exert no direct pressure on the spot market since they occur outside the market. Thus, a country's currency could be technically weak even where the country had a strong payments position, and vice versa.

There is, moreover, some positive advantage in keying parity changes to reserve movements, since this would relate balance-of-payments adjustment explicitly to demands for reserves, and would thereby highlight any national inconsistencies in the global demand for reserves. Under the Bretton Woods System, countries declare exchange parities but do not declare their demands for reserves, with the result that global demand may exceed global supply (or vice versa) and balance-of-payments adjustment policies may work at cross purposes as many countries attempt, unsuccessfully in the aggregate, to increase their reserves.[4] Under the presumptive rules proposed here, changes in parity would be keyed to national reserve changes relative to some normal, desired reserve increase. The declaration of desired reserve increases would, in turn, assure that the total demand for reserves matched the total supply —if necessary by adjusting the supply (e.g., creation of SDRs).[5]

For the presumptive rules, reserves would be defined as gold, SDRs, liquid assets in convertible foreign currencies, and reserve positions at the IMF, net of liabilities to the IMF or to other central banks. Countries can always influence their reserve movements, just as they can influence market exchange rates, by making it attractive for commercial banks and other private parties to lend to foreigners or to borrow abroad by suitable adjustments in monetary and related policies, such as forward swaps. But unless the authorities are prepared to see a continual outflow or inflow of this type, in which case it may appropriately be regarded as a structural feature of the balance of payments, such shifts of funds are once-for-all and at worst may postpone changes in parities.

With parity changes keyed to reserve changes, yet severely limited in amount to 0.05 per cent weekly, countries might occasionally find it in their interest deliberately to concentrate their reserve changes in certain periods so as to limit changes in their parities. Persistent manipulation of reserve changes (by use of forward contracts with commercial banks, for example) would be subject to international censure. Countries experiencing deficits of payments that failed to reduce their parities adequately could be denied borrowing rights; countries in surplus that failed to increase their parities adequately could be subjected to internationally sanctioned trade discrimination, such as by the imposition of "exchange equalization" duties on its products at least as high as the currency appreciation that should have taken place.

Monetary authorities would be free, as now, to intervene in the exchange markets as buyers or sellers, but they would have an incentive not to, since intervention (implying reserve movements) would presumptively require a change in parity in the direction the authorities were resisting. Reserve sales to inhibit a market-induced fall in the exchange rate within the band would call for a reduction of the parity, for instance.

---

[4] Thanks to the reserve-currency role of the dollar and the relative indifference of the United States to its payments position, this problem was not acute during the fifties, since dollar outflows satisfied residual demand for reserves in the rest of the world.

[5] Each country would thus have two reserve "targets" under the scheme: (1) the target increase to allow for secular growth in reserves; and (2) the amount by which reserve changes would have to exceed or fall short of this target increase before a change in parity was presumptively triggered.

Countries imposing restrictions on foreign payments for balance-of-payments reasons would be encouraged to eliminate them in favor of changes in parity, and would be permitted to reduce parities as such restrictions were reduced, even before the appearance of reserve losses.

Coverage

The presumptive rules would apply to all countries with nationally-managed currencies. Members of de facto currency unions would be individually exempt, as might those of groups of countries with announced intentions of forming a currency union, although sliding parities among the members of such groups would not be inconsistent with close monetary cooperation among them. In these cases, parities of the currencies involved would be changed in unison, in accordance with the reserve movements of the group as a unit.

Any country that desires to maintain a constant exchange rate between its currency and some other currency can, of course, do so by following a monetary policy appropriate to that objective; its monetary policy then becomes fully dependent on conditions abroad, and monetary policy is truly (if one-sidedly) "coordinated," a necessary condition for a durable regime of fixed exchange rate without controls on international transactions.

Transitional Problems

A difficulty with any new proposal is the transition during which it is put into effect, especially when the initial situation may be characterized, in this case, by large actual or suppressed imbalances in payments.

It would be highly desirable with any innovation in the rules governing exchange rates to begin from a position of approximate payments equilibrium, at least among the major trading countries. As a practical matter, this may not be possible, even with some initial realignment of rates, since any changes may not be exactly right. Fortunately, however, transitional problems for a system of sliding parities are markedly less than for many other proposals regarding changes in the exchange-rate regime. In particular, initial equilibrium, while desirable, is by no means a necessary precondition for the introduction of sliding parities.

Inaugurating the system from a position of disequilibrium would, for a time, assure the direction in which certain exchange parities would move, and this assurance, in turn, would provide incentive for speculating on currencies expected to rise in value and against those expected to fall. But this incentive would not necessarily be greater than that before the introduction of sliding parities in what is, by assumption, a position of widely recognized disequilibrium. The only new element is the certainty of parity change, but with that certainty also comes the certainty that the rate adjustment will be made in small increments spread over a period of time (provided the new regime itself is credible) and the assurance of eventual correction (provided new sources of disequilibrium do not equal the corrective capacity of the parity changes). Moreover, the financial incentives of small changes can be compensated by corresponding differences in interest rates, lower on assets in an appreciating currency, higher on assets in a depreciating one. Thus, starting the arrangement in the presence of payments imbalances would require at the outset an adjustment in certain national interest rates to compensate for expected changes in parities. Since relative rather than absolute interest rates matter here, such an adjustment should be the subject of international discussion and agreement.

Conclusions

While a system of sliding parities would be highly novel institutionally, and in that sense would represent a sharp departure from present arrangements, its impact on trade and payments and on the need for close cooperation among major countries would be limited, and in that (more relevant) sense it would represent a modest but possibly significant step in the evolution of the present international monetary system. Relations among currencies would be relatively stable, movements in exchange rates would be severely limited, pressures for coordination of national monetary and other policies would remain high, and movements in foreign exchange reserves—augmented, when necessary, by official borrowing from the IMF and elsewhere—would continue to absorb the bulk of swings in payments positions.

Within limits, however, a system of sliding parities would prevent the cumulative imbalances that arise from disparate rates of growth or disparate rates of wage inflation—reflecting different national priorities—among countries, and by so doing, it would reduce the need to resort to import surcharges, tax devices to improve foreign receipts, and direct controls over international transactions that have once again become a common feature of the international economic landscape.

· 29 ·

The Fixed-Reserve Standard: A Proposal to "Reverse" Bretton Woods

DONALD B. MARSH

Scope of Paper

PROPOSALS for floating exchange rates or other reforms may relate to one country only. Thus, it may be argued that it is in Canada's economic interest, as I believe it is, to float the Canadian dollar against all other currencies.[1] This chapter deals, not with an exchange-rate policy for one country, but with an international system designed to achieve automatic external balance for all its members. Such a system will certainly require floating exchange rates on a fairly wide, but not necessarily universal, scale. The goal is not floating exchange rates as such, but automatic external balance for all countries within the system and, hence, for the system as a whole.

External Balance and the Mechanism of Adjustment

The mere suggestion that we might conceive of a system that involves the floating of even a few currencies of the relatively advanced nations is usually rejected out of hand because such a system would lead, allegedly, to manipulation, massive speculation, competitive depreciation, worldwide inflation, and, as a natural accompaniment, a chaotic fluctuation of exchange rates.

Nevertheless, a so-called "fixed-rate" system [2] that has managed to get involved in six major crises and three major exchange-parity adjustments in less than two years clearly leaves something to be desired as a model of international stability!

Concentration on so-called "fixed rates," under the present IMF system, has led to a corresponding concentration on international liquidity as a means of tiding over the inevitable periods of disequilibrium.

Under the old "gold-standard" system, the need for liquidity was minimal. Fixed exchange rates, in terms of gold, were maintained by appropriate adjustments in wages, prices, and employment, in the countries adhering to the system. This resulted in some incidental disasters for those

---

[1] I deal with this case for floating rates in one country in Part VI, Paper 41.

[2] The present IMF system is actually a band of (optionally) floating rates within plus or minus 1 per cent of "parity," with the further option of adjusting the parity itself, subject to certain rules and regulations.

261

most closely affected; but, undeniably, individual countries *were* in external balance, and the system as a whole was, therefore, in continuous balance-of-payments equilibrium.

Unfortunately or otherwise, the gold standard has, in recent years, come into direct conflict with certain national goals. The most important of these are the twin goals of "full employment" and "price stability": both of these, because they require national independence in monetary and fiscal policy, are inconsistent with the inexorable rules of the gold standard.

The fact that the twin goals of full employment and price stability may also be inconsistent with one another serves further to emphasize the dreariness of the human condition, but this in no way alters the fact that the gold-standard "solution" must now be ruled out.

The founding fathers at Bretton Woods recognized this fact, even though they preserved a nominal gold standard—a "gold standard" bereft of any pretence of power to bring about balance-of-payments adjustment.

Horrified as they were by the system of competitive exchange-rate manipulation and control that succeeded the breakdown of the old gold standard in the 1930s, they sought stability in a system of exchange parities fixed within narrow limits. And, instead of the mechanism of adjustment provided by the gold standard, they provided for certain credits to countries in temporary disequilibrium and for certain exchange-rate revisions (adjustable pegs) for countries defined to be in "fundamental disequilibrium."

Now, just twenty-five years after Bretton Woods, the whole IMF system is itself threatened by a major breakdown, unless its members can agree on fundamental reform.

Fundamental reform means much more than the creation of Special Drawing Rights or other devices to increase international liquidity. Indeed, the need for increased international liquidity reflects the lack, in our present system, of an effective mechanism of adjustment. The "law of demand" for exchange reserves, that is, for international liquidity, may be stated as follows: "For any country, the demand (need) for reserves (liquidity) varies inversely with the degree of flexibility of the exchange rate." In a system of floating rates, this demand would be zero (aside from the minimum required for smoothing operations), and there would be no liquidity problem. Conversely, with completely rigid exchange rates, demand can become insatiable; and the fundamental weakness of the SDRs and similar devices is that they concentrate only on providing liquidity, on filling this bottomless pit, instead of providing a mechanism of adjustment to achieve the international balance that would make additional liquidity unnecessary.

The Fundamental Condition of External Balance: Fixed Exchange Reserves

In our present system, the clearest sign of a gathering storm is the accumulation of reserves by one country or a few countries at the expense of other countries in the system. This may at first reflect a strong trading position or other "real" factors; but, in our fixed-rate, adjustable-peg system, the flow of reserves is greatly aggravated by speculative pressure based on the probability, or even the inevitability, that the pegs will have to be adjusted—upward for the strong, or downward for the weak, or some combination of adjustments in both directions.

Stability of exchange reserves is usually regarded as merely a symptom of external balance in the system: a sign that all is well. But it is, I think, much more than that. It is the necessary and sufficient condition for stability in the international monetary system. Fix each nation's exchange reserves (within narrow limits [3]) and, whatever type of exchange-rate policy the members of that system may adopt, each nation and the international system as a whole must be in continuous equilibrium.

Bretton Woods in Reverse: A Fixed-Reserve Standard

What we may call the "Fixed-Reserve Standard" is, in effect, the reverse of the Bretton Woods System. Instead of fixing exchange rates and leaving exchange reserves free to move, the Fixed-Reserve Standard would leave exchange rates free to move (if desired) and fix national levels of exchange reserves.[4] The essential condition is that exchange reserves remain essentially flat. Given this condition, nations may elect to float their rates, to fix their rates, or to adopt any of the recent proposals for "limited exchange-rate flexibility."

The Options

Let us first consider the two main options: floating rates and fixed rates.

FLOATING RATES

One of the strongest objections to flexible exchange rates is that nations would use them, as in the 1930s, to subsidize exports and penalize imports at the expense of their trading partners. This could not occur if the level of each country's exchange reserves were fixed within narrow limits, just as exchange rates are fixed under present IMF rules.

---

[3] To be defined below.
[4] "Exchange reserves" are defined to mean official reserves of gold and foreign exchange adjusted for any net credit or debit position with the International Monetary Fund.

The width of the limits on reserves should be sufficient only to allow a country to intervene on either side of the market for smoothing purposes, but not sufficient to buck a trend in the level of the exchange rate. As a result, the exchange rate would reflect fundamental demand and supply factors in the market, and exchange reserves over time would be essentially unchanged.

Fixed Rates

Some countries might choose to fix their rates relative to a key currency, presumably the U.S. dollar.[5] Provided always that they adhered to the Fixed-Reserve Standard, such a policy would be completely consistent with overall international equilibrium. However, the simultaneous fixing of exchange rates *and* exchange reserves would require that countries choosing the fixed-rate option would also have to tie their fiscal and monetary policies closely to those of the United States.[6]

Countries choosing to float their rates would be in automatic external balance, and, aside from minor smoothing operations, their exchange reserves would remain automatically at the fixed level set by the new IMF rules. Countries choosing to fix their rates relative to the U.S. dollar would achieve external balance by accommodating their internal policies to those of the United States. Under either option, therefore, all non-key-currency countries would be in external balance, which means that the key currency, and hence the whole international monetary system, would be in continuous equilibrium.[7]

The Roosa Objection

An objection to the Fixed-Reserve Standard was raised at the Oyster Bay Conference by Robert V. Roosa. His objection essentially was that published exchange-reserve figures may be misleading because of the many unpublished swap arrangements among central banks or other na-

---

[5] The key currency would of course appear fixed, with other currencies either adjusting gradually up and down in relation to it (the floating-rate currencies), or maintaining a constant relationship to it (the fixed-rate currencies).

[6] Countries choosing this option would be acquiescing in the questionable Mundellian thesis that the U.S. Federal Reserve Authorities should (or have?) become the centre of the international monetary universe. See Robert Mundell, "Toward a Better International Monetary System," *Journal of Money, Credit, and Banking,* I (August, 1969), p. 630.

[7] The "problem" of floating a key currency is really a nonproblem. With all nonkey-currency countries allowed to float, that is, with all nonkey-currency countries in external balance, the key-currency country must also be in external balance. Only $n - 1$ equations are needed for n unknowns, since the nth equation, the equation for the key currency or "numeraire," is implicit in the system. This rule still applies where some countries under the Fixed-Reserve Standard tie their exchange rates to the key currency, provided that they remain in external balance (that is, keep their reserves constant) by simultaneously tying their fiscal and monetary policies to those of the key-currency country. In effect, these fixed-rate countries then become part of the key-currency country's monetary system.

tional reserve authorities. However, when a similar point was raised, in another connection, at the Bürgenstock Conference, Stephen Marris replied indirectly to Roosa's original objection by stating that the OECD knows precisely what the reserve positions of its members are at any given time.

It would seem, therefore, that the IMF has, or could have, the same information. Thus, the IMF could, under the Fixed-Reserve Standard, turn its attention from the policing of fixed exchange rates to the policing of fixed exchange reserves.

Compromises

I have already referred to proposals for "limited flexibility" of exchange rates in relation to the proposed Fixed-Reserve Standard. Provided always that our fundamental condition is met—that exchange reserves for each country are fixed—the various proposals for limited flexibility may be subsumed as special cases under the Fixed-Reserve Standard. However, each special case poses special difficulties that, I would argue, arise, not from weaknesses in the Fixed-Reserve Standard itself, but from the inherently imperfect nature of the compromises. We can classify the compromise plans under four categories: the band proposal; the crawling peg (discretionary or nondiscretionary); a combined band and crawling peg; and Willett's plan (a combination of the combined band and crawling peg with a variant of the Fixed-Reserve Standard).

THE BAND PROPOSAL

We already have a "band" provided by the Bretton Woods Agreements Act; namely, ± 1 per cent of parity. The new band proposals would simply widen this band to, say, ± 2, 3, 4, or 5 per cent of parity. This might be dismissed as a mere difference in degree rather than a difference in kind, and the attractiveness of the band proposal may depend in part on its apparent similarity to the present system. However, a sufficiently wide band would mean a return to a system of completely floating exchange rates—not, in my opinion, such a bad idea!

Under the band proposal, once the exchange rate of any country has reached its upper or lower limit, it becomes in effect a rigidly fixed rate that presents speculators with a one-way option. At the top of the band, and given continuing upward pressure, the rate can only move upward through revaluation. At the bottom of the band, and given continuing downward pressure, the rate can only move down through devaluation. Either way, there is bound to be a wave of speculation.

Under present arrangements, the upper or lower limit of the band could be defended, just as exchange rates are now defended, by the build-up or running-down of reserves, combined with border taxes and similar devices for strong currencies, and miscellaneous credits and swap arrangements for weak currencies. In other words, by a return to the very conditions from which the band proposal was supposed to rescue us.

Under the Fixed-Reserve Standard, a country under these conditions could either: change the band by widening it or shifting it in the appropriate direction (that is, provide greater freedom for exchange rates to float); or accept the Mundellian Imperative, hold the rate at the prescribed limit, and join the Federal Reserve System of the United States. Either way, international equilibrium will be maintained; but the band proposal, *rigidly adhered to,* leaves only the second option, if we are to escape from the present disequilibrium system of international monetary arrangements.

THE CRAWLING PEG

The so-called crawling peg would allow a movement, up or down, in exchange parities, either on a discretionary basis or on the basis of some agreed formula.

We already have a discretionary crawling peg under the present IMF system. Under the original Articles of Agreement of the IMF, member countries were allowed to change their parities, cumulatively in either direction, up to 10 per cent by consultation, but not necessarily by agreement, with the International Monetary Fund. Unfortunately, most countries have, through large and infrequent changes in parity, already used up this degree of semiautomatic flexibility in the present system. Moreover, there have been no small and frequent movements of exchange rates to indicate that member countries ever took advantage even of the degree of freedom for small adjustments provided by the original Articles of Agreement.[8]

The crawling peg, like the band proposal, is consistent with the Fixed-Reserve Standard. But, if the "rate of crawl" is inappropriate, or seems inappropriate to the market, a country on the crawling peg may be forced either to adjust the rate of crawl (that is, to move toward a true floating rate); or, all else failing, to crawl itself into the protective arms of the Federal Reserve System of the United States!

COMBINATION OF BAND PROPOSAL AND CRAWLING PEG

A combination of the band proposal and the crawling peg has much to recommend it. Proponents of a combination of the band and crawling peg argue that disruptive speculation would not occur if parities were revised under the crawling peg, and if the band were then applied on ei-

---

[8] See Robert V. Roosa's strictures in "When and How Should Currency Parities Be Changed?," Paper No. 25.

ther side of the new parity. I am attracted to all proposals for increased flexibility of exchange rates and the re-establishment of an effective mechanism of adjustment. Nevertheless, I do not think that even the band proposal combined with the crawling peg will entirely rule out the danger of speculative pressure, upward or downward, on any currency. The band proposal alone clearly does not solve the problem. But even a crawling peg—whether announced by the government or indicated by formula—depends for its efficacy on whether or not the market thinks that the government can make the new rate stick. A credibility gap here would mean a return to the one-way option, real or imagined, and a corresponding wave of speculative pressure, upward or downward, on the nation's currency.

If we are to stop speculation and achieve international monetary equilibrium, the final answer, once more, is adherence to the Fixed-Reserve Standard. And the final result for each country, in this as in the two other cases, is either to move toward a true floating rate; or to give up all pretence of monetary and fiscal independence by, in effect, joining the Federal Reserve System of the United States.

WILLETT'S PLAN

Thomas D. Willett suggests a compromise plan, which incorporates some of the features of the Fixed-Reserve Standard into a combined band-crawling-peg arrangement. The band in this case would be determined by the Fixed-Reserve Standard's permissible range of reserve fluctuations for smoothing purposes. Within this range, Willett would allow a discretionary "sliding parity system." However, the discretionary crawl would become "mandatory at the maximum rate whenever reserve levels fall outside of their target range." [9]

Presumably, Willett's plan would also allow each country the option of adopting a fixed rate provided that the country's exchange reserves remained within the permissible range. In any case, discretionary rate movements within this range would ordinarily be small, and we should have, in effect, a fixed rate with a narrow band that could be maintained, as under the original fixed-rate option, only by tying the country's monetary and fiscal policy closely to that in the key-currency country.

However, the automatic crawling peg, applicable at either limit of the permissible reserve range, would not necessarily guarantee that reserves would be held within the permissible range. The mandatory rate of crawl might be too large or too small to restore equilibrium within the permissible range of reserves. Overcorrection of a strong currency could send it hurtling from the top of its reserve range to the bottom. Over-

[9] Thomas D. Willett, "The Rules for a Sliding Parity," Paper No. 30.

correction of a weak currency could send it flying to the top of its reserve range. Undercorrection, in either case, would simply fail to hold the line on reserves.

The only way to guarantee a fixed range of reserves, aside from the special fixed-rate case, is to float the exchange rate. Perhaps the general rule for the Fixed-Reserve Standard could be translated into Willett's terms as follows: "Any exchange-rate policy within the permissible range of reserves; mandatory floating rates as soon as the reserve range is breached." This would take care of both the fixed-rate and the floating-rate options under the proposed Fixed-Reserve Standard. Anything less would not meet the objections to the other compromise schemes; specifically, that they do not fully meet the problem of disruptive speculation and that they do not, therefore, eliminate the possibility of the recurring exchange crises that plague the present IMF system.

Conclusion

We are forced back, then, to the Fixed-Reserve Standard in its "pure" state.[10] One of the great advantages of that system, over even its best alternatives, is that there would be no need for exchange controls or all the paraphernalia of guidelines and other devices that we have come to associate with present international monetary arrangements. Indeed, controls and impediments of this sort should be outlawed under the new Fixed-Reserve Standard. Nor would there be need for such simplistic reforms as a rise in the official price of gold (*pace* Peter Oppenheimer!) or for such complicated reforms as those involving the creation of a new international currency unit, or of SDRs, or even for the adoption of one of the various species of band proposals or crawling pegs—whether or not geared to some ingenious and complicated formula.

None of these is necessarily inconsistent with the Fixed-Reserve Standard provided always that the fundamental condition—a permissible range of reserve variation—is accepted and fulfilled. But all become either unnecessary or irrelevant: even the band and crawling peg proposals could, as I think I have shown, lead either to the fixed-rate option, or to a breach of the Fixed-Reserve Standard and a return to the "bad old days" of disruptive speculation and recurring exchange crises.

[10] I see no obvious objection, however, to Willett's proposal to avoid temporary breaches of the permissible reserve band through the relending or recycling of funds. In fact, should two key currencies emerge (say, the U.S. dollar and the pound sterling) it might be desirable that they be fixed in terms of each other with losses of reserves by one key-currency country to the other counteracted by automatic loans in the opposite direction. Nevertheless, in the general case, the Fixed-Reserve Standard should be based on "owned reserves." Swaps and recycling, long continued, could result in the indefinite postponement of needed adjustment. Overvalued rates and undervalued rates could be maintained at the expense of equilibrium in the international monetary system as a whole. (See Willett, Paper No. 30, footnote 6.)

SUGGESTIONS FOR IMPLEMENTATION

Moreover, the discipline, which is supposed to be inherent in a fixed-reserve system, would be automatic and severe, and there would be no perverse effects, or enforced *lack* of discipline, such as we have seen in recent months, when a nation like West Germany, with a well-run economy, attempts to keep an undervalued exchange rate from rising above the upper limit set by the Fund.[11]

In sum, then, the Fixed-Reserve Standard would impose no specific exchange-rate policy on any country, provided that official exchange reserves are allowed to vary only within the permissible band. For some countries fixed exchange rates, and the consequent tying of their monetary policies to the policy of the key-currency country, may not impose an undue burden, and may, therefore, be the preferred option. But for others, and these would include most of the major countries of the West, such a condition would be intolerable. To stay within the permissible reserve band, they would, therefore, choose to float their rates in order to maintain a reasonable degree of economic independence. With each country in automatic balance, the system as a whole would be in an equilibrium sufficiently stable to be proof against the recurring crises of confidence that threaten the present international monetary order.

The proposed system is no panacea. It does not guarantee that a country bent on inflationary or deflationary excesses will be protected from the consequences of its folly. It *does* guarantee that the system as a whole will not suffer from the excesses of a few of its members. Indeed the penalties for failure to maintain discipline in such a system would be immediate and readily apparent.[12]

Perhaps most important of all, the Fixed-Reserve Standard would guarantee that the authorities in any country would be free of the obligation to adopt inappropriate policies of expansion or contraction—to import inflation or deflation—an obligation from which, under the present IMF system, they are seldom free.

Under the Fixed-Reserve Standard, therefore, folly would be punished; but wisdom would be properly rewarded. In other words, wise policy makers would be given sufficient discretion, sufficient freedom of choice, to translate well-planned economic strategy into effective action.

---

[11] The solution to Germany's problem finally adopted was to float the German mark temporarily rather than accumulate further exchange reserves. This is also the solution (on a permanent basis) that would be indicated under the Fixed-Reserve Standard—only much sooner!

[12] Inflation would be registered by a steadily falling exchange rate and a consequent worsening of the terms of trade, resulting in a further loss in welfare for the population of the inflating country. Inappropriate deflation and unemployment would be registered by a steadily rising exchange rate and further hardship due to a shrinking export market.

• 30 •

Rules for a Sliding Parity: A Proposal

THOMAS D. WILLETT

There has been growing interest in greater flexibility of exchange rates as a means of improving the international adjustment mechanism. Too often political decisions on exchange rates have been based on national prestige rather than economic reality. Greater flexibility of exchange rates offers the possibility of smoother, more gradual, adjustment in place of the jerky operation of the adjustable peg in recent years. As a result, changes of exchange rates might be depoliticalized to a large degree, and excessive rigidity might thereby be avoided.

Permissive changes in the IMF Articles of Agreement to allow more gradual adjustment of exchange rates can help only if countries avail themselves of the opportunities offered, however. Concern has been expressed in many quarters that without additional inducements, the excessive rigidity that characterized the operation of the present system would remain. On the other hand, it should also be remembered that the designers of Bretton Woods were more concerned that the postwar tendency would be a repeat of the excessive competitive depreciation of the interwar period, rather than the excessive rigidity that, in fact, developed. A purely permissive system of greater flexibility of exchange rates might display a systematic tendency for deficit countries to be more willing to allow their exchange rates to move down than for surplus countries to allow their rates to move up (a tendency that has not been altogether absent from the adjustable peg). In a system in which the dollar remained the pivot, such behavior could lead to a progressive overvaluation of the dollar and threaten the stability of the system.

Attention has been focused on the use of automatic formulas and on the rules for intervention within the permissible limits of exchange-rate fluctuation, in hopes that in this manner the likelihood of such results could be reduced. Probably no set of rules can be devised that would assure that their intentions will not be frustrated. A certain degree of willingness to abide by the spirit as well as the letter of any arrangement is necessary. But there are encouraging signs that the potential benefits of greater exchange-rate flexibility are becoming more widely understood, and a "good" set of rules could help nurture this spirit.

There is considerable attractiveness in proposals to simply prohibit government intervention within the band of permissible exchange-rate fluctuation as a means of assuring that a sliding parity based on a moving average of past exchange rates would not be manipulated in an antisocial manner. Countries do not seem inclined toward accepting such a restriction, however. Hence, the need for some sort of rules to govern intervention. Devising a workable set of specific rules for acceptable interventions in the exchange market would be no mean task. An alternative approach, recently suggested by Hendrik Houthakker,[1] is to include reserve changes in an automatic exchange-rate formula. If this were done, it is possible that the need for direct rules on intervention could be avoided. Again, however, it seems likely that there will be considerable resistance on the part of governments to the limits that the reserve-exchange rate formula variant might place on their week-to-week discretionary actions. Thus, despite the attractiveness on economic grounds of a formula variant of a crawling peg, it appears that a discretionary variant may be more likely to win political acceptance. These conflicting considerations suggest that a workable crawling peg may need to combine both discretionary and automatic elements.

A manner in which this might be done is suggested by Donald Marsh's proposal that we reverse the Bretton Woods procedure of fixing exchange rates and leaving reserves free to fluctuate. Instead, Marsh argues we should fix national levels of reserves and leave exchange rates free to move. This would limit the possibilities of "antisocial" government intervention. Reserve levels would not be absolutely fixed. There would be a reserve band, the width of which "should be sufficient only to allow a country to intervene on either side of the market for smoothing purposes, but not sufficient to buck a trend in the level of the exchange rate." [2]

While one would probably want to make provision for growth over time in usable reserve levels (perhaps tying these increases to the rate of SDR in total international liquidity creation), Marsh's proposal is extremely attractive to those of us who interpret the Canadian experience of the 1950s as an example of the workability of such a scheme. However, the absence of a limit on the maximum rate of exchange rate movement over a given period of time makes this scheme still too radical for general acceptance, I fear.

A workable compromise may be to adopt a sliding-parity system that is discretionary within Marsh's band of permissible reserve fluctuations, (that is, it is subject only to limitations on the maximum rate of parity crawl), but mandatory at the maximum rate whenever reserve levels fall outside their target range.[3,4] This would accomplish the major pur-

---

[1] "Some Reflections on the International Monetary System," speech at the University of Bonn, April 16, 1969.

[2] Donald B. Marsh, Submission to Canada's House of Commons Standing Committee on Finance, Trade, and Economic Affairs, February 6, 1969. See also Paper No. 29 in this volume.

[3] One could, of course, conceive of several bands around reserve parity, with the mandatory rate of crawl increasing in each zone up to the maximum rate as

poses of automatic formula variants—to keep exchange rates from remaining excessively rigid or being persistently manipulated in a beggar-thy-neighbor manner. For the system to work relatively smoothly, it is not necessary that all "inappropriate" intervention be eliminated, only that the effects of such actions not cumulate over time. Countries could be left free within the latitudes of the reserve band to make day-to-day decisions as they saw fit.[5]

The actual implementation of such a scheme is not without considerable technical difficulty. The definition of reserves to be used would have to be agreed upon (should private bank holdings of foreign exchange be counted, for instance) as would the criteria for setting reserve parities and band widths and provision for their change over time. However, these problems do not seem any more formidable than those connected with an exchange rate-reserve formula or a set of direct rules for intervention under a purely exchange rate formula, and I believe would probably be less so. Furthermore, the policing of the rules of the game should be easier under this approach. The violation of the reserve band would be a much cleaner cut triggering device than would periodic multilateral consultations to decide whether questionable behavior had continued too long.[6]

---

the final zone is entered. A single band should probably be sufficient, however, for knowledge of mandatory movements at the reserve band would probably be sufficient to induce discretionary parity movements before the reserve band was reached.

[4] This proposal is similar in some respects to one recently put forward by Robert Triffin at the international monetary conference at Claremont College. Triffin's proposal would also establish a reserve band (he uses the illustrative figure of 80 to 120 per unit of the normal level of reserves as a percentage of international trade), but countries would be obligated to keep parities fixed as long as reserves were within this band. In other words, a discretionary crawl would not be allowed.

When a country's reserves fell outside of the reserve band, it would be obliged to consult with the International Monetary Fund and could use reserves outside the band only to the extent permitted by the Fund. The Fund could, for instance, require certain internal policies if the country is to be allowed to maintain its exchange rate or it could prescribe a crawl, or discrete parity change, or even a temporary free rate. Thus, Triffin's plan would give the Fund greater power than would the proposal offered here, and would, perhaps, be subject to even greater political opposition than would a formula variant of the sliding parity.

[5] For interesting discussions of appropriate smoothing strategies for exchange equalization funds under flexible rates, see Paul Wonnacott, *The Canadian Dollar, 1948–1962* (Toronto: University of Toronto Press, 1965, Chapters 8, 9, and 12) and R. M. Goodwin, "Stabilizing the Exchange Rate," *Review of Economics and Statistics,* May 1964.

[6] In practice, some limitations on the sharpening of the trigger would probably be desirable, however. Richard Cooper has suggested in "Sliding Parities" (Paper No. 28) that the best way out of the discretion versus automaticity problem may lie in the use of presumptive rules. His point is well taken and is basically consistent, I believe, with the approach suggested here. The major difference is that Cooper's proposal calls for countries to explain their actions after the fact. Under my proposal, within the reserve band, no justification for actions would be

273

called for; outside the band, however, the crawl would become automatic, unless the country in question secured permission from some previously designated group to suspend the rules. In practice, the most workable way to handle the problem of avoiding rate movements, which it was generally agreed were undesirable, may be to make the rules always mandatory, but define the reserve band in such a manner that official borrowings and lendings of reserves may be used to keep a country's recorded reserves within the band. Thus, for instance, in the case of a large scale movement of speculative funds from the U.K. to Germany, relending or recycling of funds from Germany to the U.K., could be used to keep both countries' reserves within their bands if this was considered desirable.

• 31 •

Some Implications of Flexible Exchange Rates, Including Effects on Forward Markets and Transitional Problems

C. M. VAN VLIERDEN

AFTER consideration of some of the practical implications of a change in the international monetary system toward greater flexibility in exchange rates, we favor such a change. Specifically, we favor a widening of the trading bands around parities vis-a-vis the U.S. dollar, initially at least to no more than ±2½ per cent, with additional provision for changes in parities whenever conditions warrant, after consultation with, and the approval of, the International Monetary Fund, of no more than 1 per cent on each occasion. This change in exchange-rate policy should apply only to the major industrial and trading nations.

The transitional problems attending these changes should not be underestimated, but we believe that the benefits will clearly offset the short-term costs. Much of these costs, in any case, may well be incurred not because of a rational and orderly transition to a new system, but because of the almost inevitable crisis brought on by too long adherence to the present rules.

In order that the transition period be as orderly as possible, however, and to reduce the accompanying uncertainties, we recommend that the full trading bands not exceed 5 per cent. This spread (against the U.S. dollar) would permit variations in cross rates, under certain conditions, of up to 10 per cent. This variance should permit ample scope for the correction of discrepancies between national currencies.

The extent and severity of fundamental disequilibria existing today with respect to a number of major currencies, viz., the German mark, the French franc, and sterling, may dictate the need for some discrete parity realignments as a precondition for the successful introduction of more flexible exchange rates. Under present circumstances, even with a widened band, the rates for the three currencies mentioned (and perhaps others as well) may rest on the limits of the band for some time, giving rise to expectations of changes in parity. Changes in parities now should lend greater credibility to the new system, and increase confidence in it. In the end, of course, the success of this system (or any other) will depend in large measure on the confidence it inspires. Continued confidence must also be supported by the continued cooperation of the monetary authorities of the major countries.

The question of parity realignment may be decided by events. The introduction of the system under discussion will probably be the consequence of a severe crisis of confidence in the present system which is accompanied by changes in the par rates of the franc or the German mark or both, by attendant changes in a number of other par rates, and quite possibly, by the temporary abandonment of support for sterling parity. Even so, the question of the need for parity realignment raises a somewhat more fundamental problem. The possibility of a currency remaining for a considerable time on one of its support limits—even with a widened band—poses the same problems of destabilizing speculation and crises of confidence we are trying to avoid. Hence, many advocates of wider bands also favor arrangements for adjustments of parity.

Most of the suggestions for shifting parities signal too clearly the rate and direction of these shifts (see the proposals of John H. Williamson and James Meade) or are too dependent on past exchange market conditions (see the proposal of J. Carter Murphy). The optimum method would be one that minimizes the possibility of destabilizing speculation and adds to confidence in the stability and orderliness of the system.

To this end, we would suggest that there be incorporated into the system an allowance for changes in parity of no more than 1 per cent at any one time, and that arrangements for these parity shifts be made after consultation with, and the approval of, the IMF, with the fullest possible cooperation of the principal members. The limitation on the extent of parity changes at each occasion would virtually eliminate the cinch bet speculators now enjoy; at the same time it should encourage more frequent revaluations (in both directions) where these are necessary to prevent the build-up of large discrepancies. Coordination through the IMF should also minimize the fears of competitive devaluations.

This coordination through a central international institution, with the continued and strengthened cooperation between nations implied, is also important for another reason. The initial impression is that more flexibility in exchange rates would reduce the demand for increases in official international reserves, and, thus, make less urgent the issue of Special Drawing Rights. This is not the case. It will remain important that reserve policies be more closely coordinated in the future—under any system—and that SDRs become an increasingly important part of official reserves, eventually (although by no means soon) replacing other assets: gold and national currencies.

Contradictory as it may seem, the most desirable evolution of a system of greater flexibility in exchange rates will be toward more stable exchange rates, as the underlying adjustment processes are improved. In the immediate future, indeed, it is probable that some exchange rates may be truly *fixed* (e.g., the guilder-mark rate). Later, as and if financial policies in the European Common Market are harmonized, the potential for a common currency within this area is enhanced. It would be a stabilizing influence in the international monetary system if one of the European currencies became a "key-currency" in the same sense as the U.S. dollar is today, backed by an equivalent economic and productive potential. With greater flexibility in the exchange rate between key-currencies, the need for coordination of reserve policies is the greater, and the greater is the need for reserves to be held in an internationalized asset such as SDRs.

Effects of the Proposed System on Forward Markets and Some Implications

It may be argued that the greater the variation in exchange rates, the greater will be the variance of expected profits in all activities involving foreign-exchange transactions. If exchange-rate variations are increased in amplitude, frequency, and unpredictability under a system of widening trading bands, it is presumed that the cost of cover for exchange risk will be higher. The additional costs would eliminate exports and imports on the margin, and discourage marginally profitable foreign investment. More flexible exchange rates, therefore will, prima facie, have some damping effect on international trade and investment. This case rests on certain assumptions: that uncertainties about future exchange rates will be increased; that wider trading bands would result in less stable exchange rates than the present system; and that potentially greater short-term fluctuations in exchange rates will increase the costs of foreign trade and investment because of the greater necessity for hedging future commitments, and that the cost of this hedging will necessarily be higher.

In the initial period, it is true, trade and investment may be inhibited, largely because of uncertainties about the operation of the system, and the inevitable lack of confidence in what is essentially an untried system. After a time, however, and it need only be a relatively short time provided there has been a realignment of present parities beforehand, uncertainties should diminish markedly, and as noted above, exchange rates may well be more stable rather than less.

It is also our judgment that forward coverage under a system of wider trading bands need not involve additional costs. Any costs to exporters and importers who need to cover will be limited to brokerage or bank fees (except in the United States where fees are not charged). Given the anticipated increase in the volume of forward transactions, these costs can be expected to be rather small in relation to the anticipated profit margins on individual transactions.

If the system is accompanied by increased freedom for interest arbitrage, the difference between spot and forward rates will be limited to the interest rate differential. When spot and forward rates do diverge, forward discounts on one side of the market are offset by premia on the other. If, for example, the forward rate for the purchase of a foreign currency is at a premium over the spot rate, then importers who have assumed commitments to pay in the foreign currency will have to pay more for forward than for spot exchange, but exporters who sell their expected foreign exchange receipts forward receive more in exactly the same proportion.

The demand for forward cover will undoubtedly increase substantially, but the facilities of the commercial banks are basically adequate to handle the increase. The channels for this increase in business have increased substantially in recent years and can be expected to increase further under the proposed change. Many banks have integrated more closely their foreign exchange and money market activities, the number of commercial banks in the international field has increased and is still increasing, and relationships between international banks and large indigenous branch banks have been greatly improved.

Apart from an initial period of disturbance, therefore, the system proposed would not significantly affect the total volume of international trade. Such a system would necessarily affect the patterns of this trade; indeed, such is its *raison d'être*. The patterns would be altered so as to bring a greater measure of equilibrium in international accounts.

It is also our judgment that the greater permissible exchange-rate fluctuation would not in general deter international capital flows, although it may well affect the form and direction. We would expect, on the contrary, that the volume of capital movements for arbitrage (both interest rate and security arbitrage) would rise as the opportunities increase. Evidence from the Canadian experience with a floating exchange rate suggests that short-term capital flows tended to respond to both the covered and uncovered interest differentials. Both reason and the Canadian experience suggest, further, that arbitrage and speculative flows of short-term funds will be stabilizing for the exchange rate *if* the band of fluctuation (explicit or implicit) is expected to hold.

Just as flows of short-term funds between national money markets may be stabilizing or destabilizing, flows through the Eurocurrency markets may be stabilizing or destabilizing. Funds are transferred into the Eurodollar market for speculative reasons and to take advantage of interest-rate differentials. Insofar as the system of flexible exchange rates proposed enhances confidence in the system and in national currencies, destabilizing flows will be reduced. Where flows of funds, attracted to or from the Eurodollar market by interest differentials, will have an undesirable impact on national credit policies, the problem may be dealt with either by separate action of national monetary authorities or by cooperative action of the principal countries affected by the Eurodollar market.

The intervention in the forward-exchange markets that this would require should be made easier by wider limits for permissible fluctuation in exchange rates. The use of forward markets to encourage or discourage transfers into and out of the Eurodollar market would be less disturbing than direct capital controls and probably more effective.

It may be argued that flexible exchange rates would discourage long-term foreign investment (portfolio or direct) to a greater extent than short-term investment or foreign trade because of the difference in time horizons. It may also be that flexible rates will affect the form as well as the volume of international investment. Foreign portfolio investment under conditions that allowed wider fluctuations in exchange rates would tend to concentrate on equity shares rather than bonds, because of the expectation that any change in the exchange rate resulting from different rates of inflation would tend to be matched by corresponding changes in the money value of equity shares.

Again, the argument that flexible exchange will tend to be inhibiting to foreign transactions assumes that the alternative is exchange rates that are truly fixed and expected to remain fixed through the life of the investment. This is often not the choice under present conditions. Under the proposed system, the long-term investor will take into account and discount the possibility of a change in the exchange rate, *just as he does under the present system*. It is probable that if greater flexibility of exchange rates has an effect on the volume of international long-term capital flows, it will be rather to encourage these flows, insofar as the system promotes greater confidence in the world monetary system, and insofar as it reduces the need for direct controls on capital movements.

The question of the *form* of international portfolio investment is a rather more general one than we are considering here, and is related more to general inflationary conditions than to exchange-rate policy. It is perhaps instructive to note that the very large increase in the volume of foreign portfolio investment in the United States occurred in a period when the United States had one of the highest rates of inflation among the advanced countries.

There is one class of foreign investment that somewhat greater flexibility of exchange rates will not affect at all: direct investments by large international corporations (witness, for example, the extent of North American investment in Latin America).

• 32 •

A Technical Note on the Width of the Band Required to Accommodate Parity Changes of Particular Size

HARRY G. JOHNSON

DURING the discussion of band-and-crawl proposals, Marius Holtrop made a technical point that may be worth recording. The point in question is that, for smoothness of operation of the foreign-exchange market, adjustment of the parity value of the currency should not force a change in the market exchange rate. To ensure this, the band around the parity must be wide enough so that, when the parity is changed, the market rate of exchange prevailing just prior to the change falls within the new band around the new parity. Otherwise, the change in parity would force a change in the market rate, which forced change could be disturbing to the dealers and other participants in the market. This requirement imposes restrictions on the feasible combinations of band width and maximum rate of crawl under certain types of crawl proposals.

There is clearly no problem under an automatic crawling peg based on an average of past market rates with no official intervention other than market-smoothing. For the parity in this case can only shift by a small fraction of the band width, and the market rate prevailing before the parity change will necessarily lie inside the new band. For example, supposing a band width of 4 per cent (2 per cent on each side of parity) and a parity determined by the average of daily market rates over the past three hundred working days, a day's market rate below the parity by the full extent of 2 per cent permitted by the band would change the next day's parity by only $1/150$th of 1 per cent. The top of the new band would be 3 and $149/150$ths percentage points above the market rate that led to the change in the parity.

If, however, the crawl is discretionary, in the form, say, of automatic permission to change the parity by 1 per cent every six months, the possibility arises of a forced change in the market rate. In the first place, if the market rate happened to be atypically on the opposite side of the old parity to the new parity, a change in the market rate could be forced by the change in parity regardless of the width of the band. Presumably the authorities would prevent this from happening by intervening in the market before the parity change was made. Assuming that the market rate is at parity or on the same side of it as the new parity, to prevent a 1 per cent change in the parity from forcing a change in the market rate it would be necessary for the band to be at least ½ per cent on each side of parity, that is, for the band to be as wide as the permitted parity change, for the new band always to contain the old market rate. Since central banks typically intervene somewhat before the market rate reaches the outer limit of the band, the band would in practice have to be wider than the permitted percentage of parity change, to rule out the possibility of a forced change in market rate disturbing to the market. Further, since it would probably be desirable for the preceding market rate not to be too close to the relevant limit of the new band, the band should probably be substantially wider than the permitted percentage of parity change. (Holtrop suggested 1½ per cent for the case described.) Similarly, if countries were permitted to change their parities by a maximum of 2 per cent once a year, the band would have to be wider than 2 per cent—probably 3 or even 4 percent.

· 33 ·

Short-Term Capital Movements and the Interest-Rate Constraint Under Systems of Limited Flexibility of Exchange Rates

THOMAS D. WILLETT

ONE of the major areas of concern over the effects of limited exchange-rate flexibility, specifically of proposals for a crawling or gradually adjusting peg,[1] is that such systems might seriously constrain the ability of countries to use monetary policy for domestic purposes. If a country's currency were confidently expected to crawl down at (say) 2 per cent per annum, then, in order to neutralize this incentive to shift funds out of the country, interest rates would have to be raised by a corresponding amount relative to those in nondepreciating currencies.[2] Would the introduction of a crawling-peg system thus mean that greater exchange-rate flexibility was being gained only at the expense of monetary flexibility, with no net policy gain?

It is argued in this paper that there is a presumption that the answer to this question is no.

In the first section it is assumed for the sake of argument that the interest-rate constraint under a crawling peg would be as rigid as is suggested above. Even in this case it is argued, however, that it is not at all clear that the crawling peg would score badly, because the relevant comparison is not between the constraint that would exist under a crawling

---

This paper was included in *Interest Rates and Capital Flows under Limited Flexibility of Exchange Rates,* Princeton Essays in International Finance, No. 78, January 1970. The paper was written during time freed by a Ford Foundation International Studies Grant to Harvard University and revised while the author was on the staff of the Council of Economic Advisers. On this topic I have received stimulation and suggestions from people too numerous to name, but I should especially like to acknowledge helpful comments and criticism from David Bodner, William H. Branson, Ralph Bryant, William B. Dale, Samuel I. Katz, Edward Tower, Paul Wonnacott, and Ralph Wood.

[1] Somewhat arbitrarily, the term crawling peg is used throughout this paper to cover the whole range of proposals for gradually adjusting parities. The reader may at his pleasure mentally substitute sliding, gliding, groping, dynamic or any other named peg which he may fancy. Paul Wonnacott has recently suggested the name smoothly moving parity.

[2] For statements in this vein see, for instance, J. Black, "Proposal for Reform of Exchange Rates," *Economic Journal,* June 1966, James E. Meade, "Exchange Rate Flexibility," *Three Banks Review,* June 1966, and John H. Williamson's early writings on this subject, *The Crawling Peg,* Princeton Essays in International Finance, No. 50, December, 1965, and "Exchange Rate Policy and the Future," *Moorgate and Wall Street,* Spring 1967.

peg and no constraint at all, but rather between the constraints that would exist under a crawling peg and under the present adjustable-peg system. In the second section, the nature of the interest-rate constraint under a crawling peg is considered more closely and it is argued that it may be considerably less stringent than is assumed in section one.

Incentives for Capital Movements Under Jumping and Crawling Pegs

To facilitate comparison of the constraints that the international sector puts on interest-rate policy under these two systems, let us assume that monetary authorities always so adjust interest rates as to prevent any capital outflow and that the country under consideration has been running a deficit. Then our question becomes: under which system would interest rates have to be higher in the face of a given autonomous external situation. The answer depends upon which of two effects is greater. Under the crawling peg there will be a greater probability of a small decline in the spot rate (for example, 2 per cent per year) than there would be under the adjustable peg, but the probability of a large discrete change in parity or the imposition of controls should be less. Thus, on the first count there would be a tendency for interest rates to have to be higher under the crawling peg, but on the second count there would be a tendency for them to be lower. The net effect would depend upon the particular set of expectations that ruled at any point in time. There seems a strong presumption, however, that expectations of a major change in parity present the most difficult problem as far as liquid capital movements are concerned. If the additional scope for adjustment that would be provided by the crawling peg would substantially reduce market expectations of a major change in parity or imposition of controls, then it seems likely that the interest-rate constraint would be less of a problem under such a system.[3]

This can be seen in the following table, which gives expected appreciation values of the mark at annual rates under alternative assumptions concerning the expected amount of revaluation, the time period during which it is expected to occur, and the confidence with which the revaluation is expected. These would seem to be indicative of the range of expectations during the summer of 1969. If initiation of a crawling peg were to eliminate expectations of a discrete parity change, then even a certain crawl of 3 per cent per year would give less incentive to shift funds into the mark than any of the cases illustrated in the table. Of

---

[3] Black is of the same opinion. He argues that, "It is fairly certain that the present system involves the need for stricter monetary discipline (than the interest differential of about 2 per cent that the sliding parity might require) to counteract fears of sudden devaluation at times when fundamental disequilibrium is felt to be in the air." Op. cit., p. 294.

course the assumption of elimination or substantial reduction in the expectations of a discrete parity change is crucial. It seems likely that in the German case, starting from an initial sizeable disequilibrium, a 3 per cent certain crawl would be more stabilizing than, say, a 1 per cent crawl, for, in the latter case, expectations of a discrete parity change still occurring might not be significantly reduced.

Expected Appreciation Values of the Mark at Annual Rates Under Alternative Sets of Expectations

		Expected Revaluation = 7%	Expected Revaluation = 10%
Likelihood of mark revaluation during next 3 months	70%	19.6%	28.0%
	50%	14.0%	20.0%
	25%	7.0%	10.0%
Likelihood of mark revaluation during next 6 months	70%	9.8%	14.0%
	50%	7.0%	10.0%
	25%	3.5%	5.0%

Explanatory Note: This table gives the mathematical expected values of appreciation under alternative assumptions. Actual behavior would also be influenced by risk attitudes. Hence, a risk-averting speculator would prefer a sure gain of 2 per cent to a 20 per cent chance of a gain of 10 per cent. On the other hand, a risk-averting trader who views a change in exchange rate as a prospective cost would be less unhappy with a sure 2 per cent loss than with a 20 per cent chance of a 10 per cent loss. For a discussion of speculative behavior within the framework of von Neumann-Morgenstern expected-utility maximization, see Martin S. Feldstein, "Uncertainty and Forward Exchange Speculation," *Review of Economics and Statistics* (May 1968).

While a crawling peg would "work better" the greater the reduction in expectations of discrete parity changes or the imposition of controls, the complete elimination of such possibilities would not be a necessary condition for a crawling peg to improve upon the present system. Realistically, it is doubtful if any action short of monetary unification (or a return to a genuine gold standard) could bring about absolute confidence that there would be no discrete changes in parity. A creditable crawling-peg system could bring about a substantial reduction in the likelihood of such changes, however.

VARIABILITY OF INCENTIVES

This conclusion that the interest-rate constraint may be less of a problem under a crawling peg than at present is reinforced by the consideration that the variability as well as the level of interest rates needed to restrain undesirable international capital flows may be important. It would seem much easier to adjust the domestic economy to a relatively constant level of somewhat higher interest rates required by a downward crawl than to rates that could be somewhat lower most of the time, but which would have to be raised considerably higher during periods of speculative crisis.

Similarly, it should be easier to use selective measures to restrain capital movements where the incentives for such movements are not highly variable. As will be discussed below, it is only in cases where there are fairly confident expectations that the exchange rate will continue to crawl downward for some time that any substantial interest-rate constraint resulting from the crawling peg would become operative. Thus, difficulties with the flexibility of selective fiscal measures, such as a crawl-equalization tax, may not present as serious a problem under a crawling peg as they do under the present system. It should be noted that there does seem to be a presumption that, in the choice of selective measures for the purpose in question, policies that seek to operate directly on the interest rates relevant for international investors and borrowers and keep the domestic interest rate unchanged, would have advantages over those that allow domestic interest rates to adjust to external circumstances and then try to offset the domestic effects of these changes.

DISTORTED INCENTIVES WITH DISCRETE ADJUSTMENTS OF THE PEG

While a thorough discussion would go beyond the scope of this paper, it should also be noted that the presumption of distortions resulting from selective measures to reduce flows of *liquid funds* under today's system of managed national currencies seems much weaker than in the case of selective measures that inhibit *trade* or *direct investment*. Friedrich Lutz has pointed out how differential rates of price inflation under "fixed" exchange rates may stimulate capital movements that are not necessarily in the direction of the higher marginal efficiency of capital,[4] and the 1967 *Annual Report of the Council of Economic Advisers* lists differences in monetary conditions and financial structure, exchange-rate speculation, tax advantages and opportunities for tax evasion, all as motives for capital movements which may not lead to a "rational pattern of international investment." As Forte and Scott have argued, where the alternative is manipulating domestic interest rates to influence international capital movements, it is not at all clear that a selective tax on or subsidy to capital movements would have greater distorting effects.[5]

---

[4] "Monetary Rates of Interest, Real Rates of Interest, and Capital Movements" in Fellner et al., *Maintaining and Restoring Balance in International Payments* (Princeton: Princeton University Press, 1966) pp. 161–166.

[5] Francesco Forte and Ira O. Scott, Jr., "The Use of Selective Measures as a Means of Achieving Balance of Payments Equilibrium," *National Banking Review*, 1966. On the potentially distorting effects of aiming interest rate policy at international capital flows, see also Richard Ablin "Fiscal-Monetary Mix: A Haven for the Fixed Exchange Rate?" *National Banking Review*, December 1966; Harry G.

NOMINAL VERSUS REAL RATES OF INTEREST

Two other factors may tend to mitigate adverse domestic effects of the interest-rate constraint under the crawling peg. One is that the need to raise interest rates above those in nondepreciating countries need not necessarily imply that they should be raised above the level desired for internal reasons. For example, where an expected downward crawl was due to inflation of an equivalent amount, then the real rate of interest would remain the same while nominal interest rates rose by an amount equal to the expected crawl. One would expect that there would be a tendency for those countries whose rates were depreciating also to be having above average inflation. To the extent that this is the case, high nominal interest rates need not be high real rates that would have deterrent effects on domestic investment and growth, and under a crawling peg one would not have the distorted incentives for international capital movements discussed by Lutz.

COORDINATION OF POLICIES REGARDING CAPITAL MOVEMENTS

A second point is that the required change in the interest differential could be brought about by interest-rate declines in the countries with upward-crawling parities, as well as by interest-rate increases in the countries with downward-crawling parities. This suggests that when considering the various rules of the game under which the system would operate (such as the conditions on intervention in the foreign-exchange market) it might be useful to include coordination of interest-rate policy as well. The average level of world interest rates could be affected considerably by whether the countries with upward or downward-crawling parities took on the majority of the interest-rate adjustment that might be necessitated by the system. This point may remain of some importance, even though it is argued below that the interest-rate constraints induced by limited flexibility are not nearly as great as often imagined. Just as in the case of countries with downward-crawling rates, countries with appreciating rates could use selective measures to differentiate the interest rates paid on domestic and foreign deposits so as to reduce capital in-

---

Johnson, "Theoretical Problems of the International Monetary System," *Pakistan Development Review*, 1967; and F. Modigliani, "International Capital: Movements, Fixed Parities, and Monetary and Fiscal Policies," unpublished manuscript, 1966.

Elements of tax and subsidy may be combined to place a combined opportunity cost on capital movements. See Roger Sherman and Thomas D. Willett, "Regional Development, Externalities, and Tax-Subsidy Combination," *National Tax Journal*, June 1969. This type of approach is implicit in Benjamin J. Cohen, "Voluntary Foreign Investment Curbs: A Plan that Really Works," *Challenge*, March/April 1967.

flow. This already occurs to some extent under the present system, for example, in Germany and Switzerland.[6]

Thus, even if it would be necessary for countries with downward-crawling parities to keep their interest rates correspondingly above those in countries with upward-crawling parities, there seems to be considerable question whether such a constraint would more seriously hinder accomplishing domestic policy objectives than would the constraint which would exist in the same circumstances under the adjustable peg. Furthermore, on the external side one would be gaining a more potent policy instrument for adjustment and the gains from this would also have to be counted against any greater constraint on interest-rate policy, if this did indeed turn out to be the case in a particular situation.

The Nature of International Flows of Liquid Funds

Now let us consider more closely the likely effects of an expected downward crawl in a country's parity. For an expected downward crawl of X per cent a year to require an equivalent X percentage point increase in domestic interest rates to prevent a disruptive flow of capital, either one or the other of the following two conditions would have to hold:

(1) There is perfect international mobility of uncovered funds in response to differentials in the country's interest rates adjusted for any expected upward or downward crawl of its spot exchange rate. (Such funds could be moved by leads and lags in payments as well as by direct arbitrage.)

(2) The covered-interest-arbitrage schedule and the speculative-backwardation schedules are both perfectly elastic.

A perfectly elastic covered-arbitrage schedule implies that capital will always flow in response to any interest differential, so that in equilibrium the forward discount would have to adjust fully to the interest differential. The speculative-backwardation schedule relates the forward commitments of nonarbitragers to the difference between the present forward and expected future spot rate. If this schedule were perfectly elastic, then the current forward rate could not diverge from the expected future spot price. With both schedules perfectly elastic, equilibrium would require both that the forward rate be at its interest-parity level and that the forward rate equal the expected future spot rate.

[6] For discussions of the techniques used by European countries to discourage short-term capital imports and encourage exports see W. D. McClam, "Interest Rates: Their International and Domestic Linkages" in *Capital Markets Study Part III, Functioning of Capital Markets* (Paris: Organization for Economic Cooperation and Development, 1968) and Samuel I. Katz, *External Surpluses, Capital Flows, and Credit Policy in the European Economic Community*, Princeton Studies in International Finance, No. 22, February 1969.

These two conditions could be simultaneously met only where interest differentials are brought into line with the expected change in the spot rate.

With perfect capital mobility, a country could not follow an independent monetary policy even under the present system. But capital is not perfectly mobile internationally. The covered-interest-arbitrage schedule is not perfectly elastic over all of its relevant range, much less the schedules of backwardation (forward speculative) and uncovered arbitrage.[7] Sizeable differences in interest rates frequently exist between national money markets, and uncovered differentials are often even greater.

From the theory of portfolio choice, one would expect changes in interest differentials to lead primarily to a stock-adjustment reallocation of funds rather than a continuing flow. A capital flow would appear in the balance of payments during the transitional stock adjustment, but after their adjustment was substantially completed, continuing interest-induced capital flow would be much smaller and would result primarily from the growth of portfolios over time.[8]

We may view interest sensitivity in a broad sense as the responsiveness of funds to differentials in interest rates corrected for any confidently expected gradual appreciation or depreciation of the exchange rate. For convenience this combination of interest rate and expected crawl will be referred to as the effective interest rate. While all uncovered capital movements are in one sense speculative, funds influenced by expected small changes in exchange rates would seem better treated as interest-motivated in a broad sense. In this vein the phrase "speculative capital flight" from a country would seem more appropriate to describe large outflows motivated by anticipations of a major parity change than to describe outflows induced by a combination of interest rates and expected crawl below that combination that ruled abroad.

The effects of an expected crawl would be analogous to a change in the interest differential.[9] If a country's currency began to crawl down

---

[7] For a discussion of why one would not theoretically expect the covered arbitrage schedule to be perfectly elastic, see L. H. Officer and T. D. Willett, "The Covered Arbitrage Schedule: A Critical Survey," *Journal of Money, Credit and Banking*, (forthcoming). An earlier version appeared as Harvard Institute of Economic Research, Discussion Paper No. 73.

[8] For further theoretical and empirical discussion of the stock adjustment theory, see T. D. Willett and F. Forte, "Interest Rate Policy and External Balance," *Quarterly Journal of Economics*, May 1969; William H. Branson, *Financial Capital Flows in the U.S. Balance of Payments* (Amsterdam, North-Holland, 1968); and William H. Branson and Thomas D. Willett, "Capital Flows, Exchange Rate Systems, and Economic Policies" prepared for the National Bureau of Economic Research Conference on International Mobility and Movement of Capital, January 1970.

[9] Presumably an expected crawl of X per cent a year would not change the effective interest differential by fully X percentage points, because the change in the future spot rate that would face the transactor would still not be completely

and was expected to continue to do so, then, unless compensating policy was undertaken, capital would flow out of the country. The initial size of such a flow, however, would exaggerate the longer-run effects. After the stock adjustment of funds had taken place, a continued crawl of the exchange rate at the same pace should have a much smaller continued further impact on the balance of payments. Furthermore, the capital movements induced by expected crawls would be reversible. If the rate of crawl slowed, investors would begin to shift funds back into the country. If other conditions remained the same, then one would expect that when the crawl ceased there would be a substantially full return of the funds which had flowed abroad. In other words, these flows would be a function of expected changes in the exchange rate rather than its level, and it would not be necessary for the currency to begin to crawl upward to make it attractive to shift funds back into the currency.

This reversibility applies to the continuing flow effects of a change in effective interest rates (due to portfolio growth) as well as to the initial stock adjustment. A numerical example may make this clearer. To make the numbers easier, assume that only citizens in A allocate funds internationally. Citizens of A have a total portfolio size of 100 as. Ten per cent, or 10 as, is invested in B. Now A begins to crawl down and the incentives to invest in B are increased. A reallocates its portfolio to hold, say, 15 per cent in B, and there is a stock-adjustment capital outflow from A to B of 5 as. Now over the next time period (during which the crawl continues) A's portfolio size grows by 10 per cent, or 10 as. Without the crawl, 10 per cent, or 1a, would have been invested in B, but with the crawl 15 per cent, or 1.5 as, is invested. The "flow" due to the crawl is $1.5 - 1.0 = 0.5$ a. In total 5.5 as have flowed out of A. Now the crawl stops and the incentives to invest in B return to their original level. Citizens in A reallocate their portfolios again to hold 10 per cent in B. Since portfolio size has now grown to 110 as, the 5 per cent reduction equals 5.5 as, the quantity that flowed out in response to the crawl.

THE CASE FOR OFFICIAL FINANCING

The nature of such effective interest-induced capital movements would seem to make the use of reserves or some form of official borrowing, such as recycling, particularly advantageous methods of handling them. However, recycling of this type of capital movement might imply a willingness to extend credit over a longer period of time than would probably be required of the type of recycling of speculative funds during crises that has been the topic of considerable recent discussion.

It is true that, because of interest costs, one would not expect reflows

---

certain even under a crawling peg with bands no wider than at present. As will be discussed below, a widening of the bands may be used to further increase the uncertainty about the future spot rate.

at the end of a crawl to fully repay official borrowings, but there is a strong presumption that this interest cost would be much lower than would have had to be paid to keep the private funds from shifting. This is because the interest cost of official financing is only that paid on the newly borrowed funds, while, when domestic interest rates are raised to influence private capital, an important element of the cost is the increase in the interest that must be paid on funds already in the country. For countries with sizeable liquid liabilities to foreigners, this "rent" cost of an increase in interest rates may be quite large.[10]

Would the size of the stock adjustment caused by a depreciating exchange rate be so large as to make official financing impossible? We do have some clue of magnitudes involved from the econometric work which has been done on the interest sensitivity of international capital movements. Interest-induced shifts of funds are far from negligible, and their size appears to be increasing rapidly over time. But their magnitude is definitely finite and it will be some time, if ever, before their magnitude is such that they become technically impossible to manage.[11] The major economic rationale for suppressing rather than financing such movements would seem to be the difficulties for domestic financial management to which sizeable flows might give rise. Difficulties of political agreement of course might well arise before such economic considerations become important. But it is important to remember that the general problem of controlling capital movements is due to the increasing capital mobility per se.[12]

---

[10] For further discussion of this and other considerations affecting the relative attractiveness of official versus private borrowing, see Thomas D. Willett, "Official Versus Market Financing of International Deficits," *Kyklos*, fasc. 3, 1968. The changing foreign currency value of interest payments resulting from a depreciating exchange rate does not alter the relative cost of official versus private financing.

[11] The most recent (and highest estimate of the interest sensitivity of American short term capital movements is a stock adjustment of $1.5 billion in response to a one percentage point change in American interest rates relative to those abroad. See Branson, op. cit. For the results and criticisms of earlier studies for the United States, see Jerome L. Stein, "International Short-Term Capital Movements," *American Economic Review*, March 1965, and comments by H. P. Gray, D. G. Heckerman, A. B. Laffer, P. H. Hendershott, and T. D. Willett and the reply by Stein, June 1967. It should be noted that we would expect the relationship between interest-rate changes and capital shifts to be nonlinear. Consecutive increases in interest rates after some minimum should attract progressively less additional capital because of the disadvantages of growing portfolio concentration. See, for instance, Willett and Forte, op. cit. p. 246 and Herbert G. Grubel, *Forward Exchange, Speculation, and the International Flow of Capital* (Stanford: Stanford University Press, 1966) pp. 20–21.

An expected crawl might, of course, have some effects on longer-term capital also, but there should be substantially less unless there were strong expectations that a substantial crawl would continue for a number of years.

[12] There are of course both costs and benefits to higher mobility of capital. For discussions of the potentially beneficial role high capital mobility may play

THE EFFECTS OF CRAWLING PEGS AND WIDER BANDS ON THE INTERNATIONAL MOBILITY OF CAPITAL

Of course, the nature of the exchange-rate system itself affects the international mobility of capital. Because of the diminished likelihood of controls and major parity changes, a narrow-band crawling peg would probably increase the international mobility of liquid funds in response to effective interest-rate incentives. As argued above, however, it seems unlikely that the shifts of funds in response to, say, a 2 per cent change in the effective interest differential would be as great as the speculative shifts that now occur when parities come under suspicion. For a surplus country such as Germany, the major alternative route out of surplus (inflation) would also be likely to induce in time substantial capital inflows due to the higher interest rates which generally accompany inflation.

The reduced likelihood of convertibility controls that might accompany a crawling peg would have asymmetrical effects on capital mobility. The fear of controls tends to increase the interest-rate constraint under the present system. It is in deficit rather than surplus countries that the fear of controls is most relevant. Thus, the fear of controls (as opposed to controls themselves) tends to accelerate the movements of funds from deficit to surplus countries. Insofar as the crawling peg would reduce such fears, it should prove easier *ceteris paribus* for deficit countries to attract capital. This is, of course, the general characteristic of high-interest sensitivity of capital movements. A country's interest-rate policy is constrained in that an effective interest rate below that abroad will lead to a sizeable capital outflow, but on the other hand, by moving its effective rate somewhat above that abroad, it may attract a sizeable inflow.

As contrasted with a narrow-band crawling peg, a widened band would tend to lower the interest sensitivity of international capital movements. Unless there were strong expectations that the spot rate would stay at or very near the floor (ceiling) of its permissible fluctuation, even the certainty of small depreciations (appreciations) in parity would not imply that actual spot rates would move with the parity. The greater the permissible band of fluctuation and the greater the likelihood that fluctuations would in fact occur, the less elastic would become the speculative-backwardation schedule, and the less likely would become uncov-

---

when exchange rates are not in doubt see, for instance, James C. Ingram, "A Proposal for Financial Integration in the Atlantic Community," in Joint Economic Committee, Factors Affecting the United States Balance of Payments (Washington, D.C.: U.S. Government Printing Office, 1962), pp. 175–207, and Tibor Scitovsky, *Money and the Balance of Payments* (Rand McNally, 1969). It seems likely that in this respect a crawling peg would more closely approximate the genuine fixed-exchange rates of the gold standard or monetary unification than does the present adjustable-peg system.

ered movements of funds. Because of the greater freedom of the spot rate to adjust, substantial deviations from interest parity would be less likely. Covered-arbitrage movements would tend to reduce the incentive for further arbitrage movements more quickly than would uncovered movements and, hence, would reduce the total quantity of funds that would be transferred as a result of a change in the effective interest-rate differential. Similarly, the potential opportunity cost of speculating on a possible major change in parity would also be greater, thus tending to reduce to some extent the amount of speculation that would take place when a country's ability to maintain its parity was in question. The reduction in movements of uncovered funds would give an additional benefit in that the efficacy of forward intervention to control capital movements would be increased.[13]

Concluding Remarks

For the various reasons discussed above, it appears that fears concerning the interest-rate constraint under a crawling-peg system have often been exaggerated. Even with a narrow-band crawling peg, gearing interest-rate policy to mitigating undesired capital flows would probably not lead to a more serious constraint on domestic financial policy than exists under the present system. Furthermore, if it is desired, the monetary interdependence among countries may be reduced by widening the band of permissible exchange-rate fluctuation, by officially financing private capital flows, by using selective measures to reduce such flows, or by some combination of the three. Any of these types of measures would be perfectly compatible with a crawling peg.

It also is clear, however, that crawling parities would be most likely to place constraints on domestic policy in situations where a country's currency was considerably overvalued and there were strong expectations that the spot rate would continue to bump along the bottom of the band for some time. A crawling-peg system is more effective where it can keep substantial disequilibrium from building up as a result of differential balance-of-payments trends, than when it must seek to reduce a substantial disequilibrium that already exists.[14]

This suggests that such a system will work better both the more

[13] This is not the argument (which has correctly been criticized by Goldstein in "A Further Comment on an Aspect of The 'Band' Proposal," *National Banking Review*, June 1967) that forward intervention becomes more effective under a wider band because there is greater room to move the rate. It is rather that a given movement in the rate would have a greater impact because a higher proportion of transactions would be going through the forward market.

[14] As is argued by Samuel I. Katz in "The Interest-Rate Constraint and the Crawling Peg," Part II of Thomas D. Willett et al., "Exchange-Rate Systems, Interest Rates, and Capital Flows," Princeton Essays in International Finance No. 78, January, 1970, adjustable pegs and crawling pegs may be thought of as complements rather than substitutes.

closely its initial position corresponds to equilibrium and the more quickly it begins to respond to disequilibrating forces. This latter point suggests that some form of self-adjusting peg that responds automatically to market forces may be preferable to a variant that depends on deliberate policy decision to initiate a crawl.

That the crawling-peg system will work better the more closely its initial position responds to equilibrium does not imply that it would not work where there is substantial initial disequilibrium or that it would place an intolerable constraint on domestic policy, but only that problems would be greater in such a situation. There, of course, would also be circumstances under which a defense of parity under the present system would most interfere with desired domestic financial policies. Thus, for comparative purposes it will make quite a difference whether one considers the relevant alternatives under the present system to be a prompt parity change in response to the disequilibrium or a concerted effort to maintain the initial parity.

A second implication concerns how fast parities should be allowed to crawl. It seems to be a common view that the maximum feasible rate of crawl is set by the interest-rate constraint. Hence, perhaps, the popularity of 2 per cent as an illustrative figure. To the extent that the interest-rate constraint is less of a problem than has previously been thought, a faster rate of crawl should be feasible. Indeed, given the importance of substantially reducing expectations of discrete parity changes for the smooth working of a crawling-peg system, a 3 per cent maximum rate of crawl might yield a lower interest-rate constraint than would a one per cent maximum.

In closing, let me bring up one further consideration. The discussion of the interest-rate constraint has been concentrated on the case of deficit countries. Would we expect crawling pegs to lead to a higher level of interest rates in the system as a whole? This is, of course, a complicated question and I cannot offer to answer it here. But let me mention one consideration that suggests that the average level of interest rates may not be higher under a crawling-peg system. A number of observers have discussed the interest-rate competition to influence the balance of payments under the present system.[15] To the extent that the crawling peg would add a more efficient adjustment technique to countries' policy arsenals, one might hope that the upward thrust of international interest-rate competition would be reduced.

[15] See, for instance, Richard N. Cooper's discussion of "International Competition in Economic Policy" in *The Economics of Interdependence*, (New York: McGraw-Hill, 1968) pp. 160–173; and Jurg Niehans, "Monetary and Fiscal Policies in Open Economies Under Fixed Exchange Rates" *JPE*, Supplement to the August 1968 issue, pp. 908–912.

Part V. Exchange-Rate Flexibility and the Forward Market

IN HIS article "The Forward-Exchange Market: Misunderstandings between Practitioners and Economists," Fritz Machlup gives examples of remarkably different uses of terms by members of the two groups. He then goes on to show how these different definitions of demand for, and cost of, forward cover can lead to conflicting theoretical conclusions and attitudes toward policy questions, such as the question about the capacity of exchange dealers to satisfy an increasing demand for forward cover or the problem of social cost involved in maintaining fixed exchange rates.

In "Forward-Currency 'Costs': A Zero Sum Game?" John H. Watts takes issue with Fritz Machlup's statement that in cases where the forward-exchange rates between currencies differ from the spot rates, one man's gain is another man's loss. Watts argues that for the loser it is hollow comfort that somebody else is gaining, and that the reactions of both may shift trade to a less productive position. In his "Comments on Mr. Watts's Paper," Fritz Machlup answers that gains and losses are essentials of real economic adjustment and that "the only safe generalization is that long postponement of adjustment is probably against the interest of all nations."

Egon Sohmen's paper "Exchange Risks and Forward Coverage in Different Monetary Systems" takes issue with the view that with wider margins for exchange-rate variations risk premia would be higher and that, with freely floating rates, they would become so high that international transactions would cease. This view overlooks the fact that a system with floating rates would never need the convertibility restrictions that the present system of adjustable pegs requires. These restrictions make covered interest arbitrage impossible and forward cover excessively expensive. Sohmen argues for unlimited rather than limited flexibility of exchange rates, because widened margins and shifting parities imply that a country still *may* have to intervene. "Acceptance of proposals falling short of full exchange-rate flexibility should be conditioned by this consideration."

W. F. J. Batt studies "The Effect on the Foreign-Exchange Market of More Flexible Rates," and concludes that a widened band would increase both the forward risk and the demand for forward cover. The cost of forward cover would rise and, at times, would exceed the profit margin of the commercial trader and become prohibitive. The same would be true for short-term capital movements. All of these statements are challenged in Fritz Machlup's "Comments on Mr. Batt's Paper."

Edwin A. Reichers and Harold van B. Cleveland, in discussing "Flexible Exchange Rates and Forward Markets," assume either a wider band of a total width of 4 to 5 per cent or a regime of floating exchange rates, and distinguish between normal and crisis situations. Greater flexibility of exchange rates would improve the adjustment process and would mean fewer and less serious exchange crises. Under normal conditions, any increased demand for forward cover would be met by an increased supply. The effects that greater flexibility may have on forward markets "are probably not a major consideration in deciding upon the desirability of greater flexibility of exchange rates."

Other papers in this volume that concern themselves with the problem of forward cover are Giuliano Pelli's, "Why I Am Not in Favor of Greater Flexibility of Exchange Rates"; Emil Kuster's, "Greater Flexibility of Exchange Rates: Effects on Commodities, Capital, and Money Markets"; Donald B. Marsh's, "Canada's Experience with a Floating Exchange Rate"; and Max Iklé's, "The Problem of Floating Exchange Rates from the Swiss Viewpoint."

• 34 •

The Forward-Exchange Market: Misunderstandings Between Practitioners and Economists

FRITZ MACHLUP

As they listened to the foreign-exchange dealers talking about the "supply and cost of forward cover," the economists were bewildered by the practitioners' theoretical pronouncements. The economists soon realized that they did not understand the language of the trade, and that their own language was probably equally strange and confusing to the practitioners. Perhaps I can render a service to members of both parties—especially persons who did not have the benefit of hearing the discussions at Oyster Bay and Bürgenstock—if I attempt a confrontation of the two technical jargons and an interpretation of the misunderstandings that arise from the linguistic chasm.

Economists theorizing about supply and demand in the forward-exchange market think of the supply of and demand for a particular foreign currency for future delivery in exchange for another (usually the domestic) currency. For example, exporters invoicing in a foreign currency may offer the future proceeds from their exports for sale in the forward market, and importers ordering products from abroad, payable in foreign currency, may seek to buy the needed foreign exchange in the forward market. If supply and demand happen to increase by the same amount—for the same currency and for delivery at approximately the same future dates—the exchange rate (in the theorists' model) will remain unchanged. If supply increases more than demand, the future price (forward rate) of the foreign currency will fall to a level at which (a) importers, (b) speculators, (c) dealers, (d) money-market arbitrageurs, or (e) the central bank find it attractive (or "desirable," in the case of the central bank) to purchase the excess supply, that is, the excess of the amount offered over what would be demanded at the higher price (the higher forward rate). [See Comment 1 at the end of the paper.]

Foreign-exchange dealers describe these affairs quite differently. Assume that the additional supply of forward exchange from exporters is worth $100 million at the slightly reduced price that brings forth an equal increase in the quantity required by importers. Making forward contracts with both exporters and importers, a dealer would say that he was "supplying forward cover" for $200 million, thus meeting the increased "demand for forward cover" by both exporters and importers. It

---

This paper was conceived after the Oyster Bay meeting, but written only after the Bürgenstock conference.

would be unlikely, however, that the same dealer would serve the exporters as well as the importers. If an exporter sells his future currency proceeds to dealer *A,* while an importer buys the currency from dealer *B,* causing *B* to purchase from *A,* each dealer would say that he supplied forward cover and, adding the increased commitments of *A* and *B,* dealers would say that they had supplied forward cover to the tune of an additional $400 million worth. Since it is unlikely that the currencies as well as the maturities that the clients of one or two dealers offer or seek are even approximately matched, three or four dealers may be involved in the intermediation between exporters and importers, especially if none of the dealers wants to change his "net position," that is, the net of his total purchase and sale commitments of various currencies, and especially if many of them attempt also to match approximately the maturities of their contracts. As a result the sum of the commitments of the dealers involved in these transactions may increase by a multiple of the $100 million sold by exporters and purchased by importers. [See Comment 2.]

The clash of terminologies is remarkable. No matter whether clients want to sell or to buy forward exchange, in the dealer's language the clients seek (demand) forward cover; and no matter whether the dealer buys or sells forward exchange, in his language he supplies forward cover. For a while the economists, or this economist for one, thought that "supply of forward cover" meant that dealers were willing to change their positions, for example, to add to their net holdings of a weak (suspect) currency or to reduce their net position in a strong currency. But this hunch quickly proved wrong: even if his net position remained unchanged, and the maturities of his forward contracts were nicely matched, the dealer, having increased his sales and purchases by equal amounts, would report that he had provided additional forward cover to his customers. He means that his total commitments for future delivery have increased.

Theorizing about the consequences of a system of greater flexibility of exchange rates, practitioners and economists were inclined to agree that the volume of transactions in the forward market would most likely increase. Economists would express this by speaking of expected increases of both the supply of and demand for forward exchange; practitioners would say that they expected the demand, or need, for forward cover to increase. Economists would expect no difficulty if both supply and demand of forward exchange were to increase, especially since slight movements in the rates would most likely equalize the amounts offered and sought. Practitioners, at least some of them, would expect difficulties from the increase of customer requirements for forward cover, because their ability to supply that forward cover would be limited. Their capacity to supply forward cover would be limited partly because the increase in the volume of transactions might call for more personnel, but chiefly because the increase in their commitments would imply greater risks (chiefly the risk that some clients might fail—perhaps find it impossible—to deliver the currencies they had sold).

The economists, having learned the practitioners' language, raised serious doubts about the practitioners' theory of the limited capacity of the dealers, or rather the theory that this capacity could not be expanded with ease and at nearly constant average cost. It may be true that trained personnel are scarce at any moment of time, but it would be ridiculous to hold that people capable of learning the trade could not be found at appropriate salaries. It may be true that increased volumes of transactions may involve increased risks of default or nondelivery, but there is no reason why these risks should increase more than proportionately. (If they increase proportionately, average risk per dollar of transactions is constant, and unit cost does not increase.) It may be true that the total of commitments that the management permits the foreign-exchange department of a bank to undertake at any point of time may be "set," or fixed, but these internal limits can be (and have been) raised to meet an expanding demand. (If they were really fixed over longer periods and remained unresponsive to demand, this would be indicative of grave incompetence or of monopolistic restraint of trade. We have recently observed the failure of the New York Stock Exchange to deal with increasing turnover. The explanation lies clearly in the oligopolistic arrangements that exclude entry of new competitors and, by prescribing fixed commissions, restrict competition among the existing brokerage houses.) I shall return later to the theory of nonexpandable capacity for dealing in forward exchange.

Another semantic difference led to misunderstandings that were cleared up only after a good deal of talking at cross-purposes. The expression "cost of forward cover" meant very different things to economists and to practitioners when they began their conversations. Economists think either of the costs *firms* incur as they produce the goods and render the services they offer for sale or of the cost to *society* resulting from such activities. Apart from the effects of risk and uncertainty—to which we shall address ourselves presently—higher cost to society means that increased amounts of scarce resources (labor, land, capital, enterprise) are taken away from more productive uses or that inefficiencies in the allocation and use of productive resources become worse.

None of these things is implied in the exchange dealers' expression "cost of forward cover." It means merely the difference between the spot rate and the forward rate of a particular currency. This difference may be either a premium or a discount. A seller of forward exchange, say, an exporter, may view a premium as a gain and a discount as a loss (or cost); a buyer of forward exchange, say, an importer, may view a premium as a loss (or cost) and a discount as a gain. (In fact, neither exporters nor importers need have the feeling of unexpected gains or losses, since they may have taken full account of premium or discount when they made their calculations for the business transactions in question.) In any case, the exporters' gain would be the importers' loss, and vice versa. To speak of cost in both cases may be harmless as long as no association of business cost or economic cost is aroused in anybody's mind; but to interpret a premium or discount as if it really were a net cost to business or to society would be highly misleading.

It is my impression that this was recognized by all or most participants of the Bürgenstock conference; however, there may be many people who are misled by the semantic difference in the meaning of the term in the trade language, on the one hand, and in the economists' language, on the other. Some of the practitioners had actually been snared into concluding that an increase in the "cost of forward cover" would lead to a reduction in the volume of trade. A conclusion from increased cost to reduced quantity traded would be legitimate. But an increase in the premium or discount of forward over spot rates is *not* a net increase in the cost of trade. If it encourages imports, it discourages exports, and vice versa. It thus affects the *balance* of trade for any particular country, but there is no presumption that the *volume* of trade will be reduced.

The fallacious conclusion from forward premium or discount to trade volume must not be confused with a conclusion of a very different nature, relating risks and uncertainty to trade volume. An increase in (insurable) risks and (noninsurable) uncertainty in international trade is very likely to reduce the volume of trade; yet, such an increase is *not* involved when the *actual, known* differentials between spot prices and forward prices of foreign currencies increase. An increase in uncertainty is an uneasy feeling about the likelihood of unknown changes occurring in the future.

It has been argued, correctly I believe, that the social risks and uncertainties regarding future changes in foreign-exchange rates are the same under fixed and under flexible exchange rates; they are merely borne by different people. Fixed exchange rates "socialize" some of the risks, shifting the burden from firms engaged in foreign transactions to other groups in society. Under flexible rates the incidence of short-term exchange risks falls upon the activities which in the absence of government intervention would have to bear them, that is, foreign trade and short-term capital movements. Under fixed-exchange rates, the long-term exchange risks are still on export industries and on long-term capital movements—because exchange rates are fixed only until they have got to be changed—while some of the short-term exchange risks are transformed into social costs of various types. Among these costs are, first of all, the opportunity cost of the capital invested in official foreign reserves, earning low interest or none at all, while the same capital would yield much larger returns in productive investment; and, secondly, the wastes and inefficiencies involved in the monetary and fiscal policies forced upon the nation by the authorities trying to accumulate reserves or to avoid their depletion or to avoid the consequences of their accumulation or depletion. Moreover, systems of so-called fixed exchange rates not only leave the risks and uncertainties regarding abrupt changes in pegs or parities with the foreign-trade sector of the economy, but add the considerable risks and uncertainties pertaining to the imposition, aggravation, and discretionary operation of exchange controls and to more severe restrictions on trade, payments, and capital movements. However, this note is not designed to deal with such issues. Let me repeat only that the costs just referred to bear no relation to the magnitude of the premium or discount of forward rates compared with spot rates.

The risks, uncertainties, and other costs borne by forward-exchange dealers are not reflected in the differences between spot and forward rates but rather in the differences between buying and selling rates. If anything deserves the name "cost" of forward dealing, it is this margin between "bid" and "asked," though, of course, it includes profits that are probably above normal, as can be inferred from the obvious imperfection of competition among dealers. This imperfection is most evident where entry into the trade is closed by licensing or other devices or where conventions or agreements fix the margins between buy and sell rates; it can also reasonably be deduced from the nonacceptance of some types of clients even where the rejected business would be profitable and fully secured by collateral. (Most dealers in New York and London reject what they do not consider "legitimate business.") Businessmen who can afford to refuse unquestionably attractive and profitable orders, sticking to some conventional (noneconomic, however "ethical") principles of selection, undoubtedly enjoy a monopolistic position. (Firms under heavy pressure of unlimited competition cannot afford the luxury of turning away customers with profitable business.)

In judging limitations or imperfections of competitition in the forward-exchange market, various distinctions have to be made before one can arrive at sound conclusions. That there is effective competition among customers, that is, among ultimate buyers of forward exchange and also among ultimate sellers of forward exchange need not be questioned, since their numbers are too large to allow concerted action, let alone conspiracy. Some giant corporations may at times have large shares in the total market but probably not enough to give them oligopolistic positions, except if the masses of individuals and smaller firms potentially in the market are excluded by governmental restrictions or by voluntary restraints observed by dealers acting in concert. A well-functioning forward-exchange market also needs well-functioning money markets, if fully competitive "covered interest arbitrage" is to equalize the premiums or discounts in forward-exchange rates with the differentials in interest rates in the countries concerned. Competition among ultimate lenders and borrowers of money is surely fully effective, but competition among financial intermediaries may be restricted either by cartel agreement or by government regulation. The flexibility of interest rates is sometimes severely limited, especially in countries whose currencies are suspected of being overvalued at the exchange rates in the spot market, and are traded with the appropriate discounts in the forward market. (The fact that interest rates in such countries are not permitted to reflect the demand for credit can be inferred from a simple consideration: the confident expectation of a devaluation by 10 per cent in less than a week would make speculators eager to borrow at an interest rate of anything less than 10 per cent per week or nearly up to 520 per cent per annum. The monetary authorities and the commercial banks prevent interest rates in this order of magnitude by rationing and outright refusals of credit.)

The degree of competition among dealers in at least one country with a highly developed foreign-exchange market is indicated by a description of the spot market that was published in a booklet freely distributed by one of the largest Swiss banks. The essential passage reads as follows:

> In Switzerland, agreed rates for buyers and sellers are established each day jointly by the principal Zurich banks in cooperation with those of Basle and Geneva. According to a gentlemen's agreement every bank in Switzerland is pledged to adopt these respective rates towards customers for the whole of the next day. Each month one of the major banking institutions in turn assumes the task of printing the list of quotations and its despatch to even the smallest of local banks. This arrangement was created to put an end to competitive rivalry between banks which had caused profit margins to sink below tolerable levels. However, so as to discourage large clients from effecting their exchange operations abroad, banks are released from adherence to the agreed rates for amounts exceeding a consideration of Sw. Frs. 250,000.

It is clear from this statement that the exchange rates for all traded currencies and the margins between buying and selling rates are regularly fixed in a manner which in the United States would be prosecuted as criminal conspiracy in monopolistic restraint of trade—if this business is not exempt from the Antitrust Laws. It is quite likely that in most European countries the practices are similar to those in Switzerland, that is, regulated by cartel or cartel-like agreements. Whether competition among foreign-exchange dealers in the United States is significantly less limited, I do not know. Analogies such as the fixed interest rates on bank deposits and ceiling rates on certificates of deposits stipulated by the Federal Reserve Board and the fixed commissions charged by stock brokers under the auspices of the New York Stock Exchange (and up to now with the indulgence of the Securities Exchange Commission) may suggest that competition among American exchange dealers is likewise restricted. [See Comment 3.]

Practitioners of the forward-exchange market have made contradictory statements about the capacity to satisfy an increasing demand for forward cover. Some have doubted that capacity could be expanded sufficiently if the demand for cover (that is, supply of and demand for forward exchange) were to increase at a fast rate. A few have suggested that the demand for cover has been fully satisfied most of the time in the past and would without fail be served in the future, no matter how much it increased. None of these statements can be supported (just as, for example, the oft-repeated contention of the steel industry that they have always satisfied the demand cannot be taken seriously as long as no reference is made to price). Since the quantity demanded depends on price, it is always possible to suppress potential purchases by the simple device of raising the price. The demand for forward cover depends on the price charged for the service.

In reflecting on the possibilities of meeting an increasing demand for forward cover, we must, before all, realize that exchange risks can be covered also by operations other than forward-exchange transactions. Large corporations doing business in foreign countries, especially international corporations having and making direct investments abroad, often find it preferable to protect themselves against losses from devaluations (or revaluations) by borrowing (or lending) the currencies in question. The use of this simple technique can be expanded without impinging on any limitations that may exist regarding the capacity of the forward-exchange market.

Before one judges such limitations, a full discussion of the possibility of developing a broader forward market requires the consideration of establishing new institutions as well as expanding the operations of existing banks. The rapid growth in recent years of the foreign-exchange operations of American banks, the increased number of foreign branches and subsidiaries, and the increased interest of banks in a number of countries trying to get a share in the international "currency business" support the view that the capacities of the existing banks can be expanded rapidly to take care of additional business. But it would be wrong to think only of the capacity of the existing exchange dealers to take on additional business and to carry the increased risks that are involved in increased commitments. One must also examine alternative or supplementary ways of organizing the forward market. It stands to reason that some such alternatives or supplements can be developed. Practical experts may be able to present many reasons why all suggestions of novel practices and new institutions for a broadened exchange market are "impractical." It would be enlightening to hear these reasons and I shall, therefore, boldly provoke them by pointing to new ways that may be open toward broadening the forward-exchange markets.

The forward-exchange dealers today are departments of large banks; they do most of the business as principals, buying and selling for their own account. Occasionally—on days of crisis, when the volume of business is overwhelming and more of it would seem too risky, especially when the market is "all one way"—they confine themselves to acting as mere intermediaries in the sense that they take business only "on an order basis," that is, only when they have found offsetting transactions somewhere in the market. At such times, the dealer's role becomes more like that of a broker, though he still acts as a principal and does not bring clients together to deal directly with each other. Actual brokers who, for a commission, find matching partners (of impeccable credit rating) and leave all the risks to them, operate in some centers, such as New York and London. Such brokerage business may well develop, if total activity in the forward markets expands, in all countries in which governmental restrictions do not place obstacles in the way of this development.

Brokerage business would evolve especially—with no institutional limitations—where organized exchanges are established for foreign-exchange transactions in all maturities, spot as well as future. In view of the risks of nondelivery or default, the bourse would have to adopt rules requiring collateral as adequate margin to protect against losses from nondelivery. The existence of a bourse, however, does not guarantee effective competition. If only the same oligopolistic group of banks that now run the market as dealers are admitted to membership on the exchange, it probably makes no difference whether there is a bourse or not. Free access to the exchange, a large number of members acting either as brokers or as dealers, and absence of regulations or agreements fixing minimum charges and commissions—these would seem to be prerequisites of making the market really competitive. But if effective competition can be secured, could not a foreign-exchange exchange take care of practically any amount of business that should be forthcoming? Could such a market in major currencies ever be "thin"? Even if monetary authorities did not intervene within a wide band, but allowed private speculation to do the job of "stabilizing" the rates, would not the elasticities of both supply and demand be high, and the fluctuations of exchange rates, spot and forward, therefore, be quite small, at least for major currencies?

FLEXIBILITY AND THE FORWARD MARKET

I have put in the form of questions what I should have liked to advance as affirmative propositions if I had the necessary factual information. To attempt some of the answers, practitioners experienced in the working of organized exchanges (securities and commodities) and in forward-exchange dealing will have to put their heads together with those of economists knowledgeable in international trade and finance. I do not think, however, that all the answers are needed before we make a determined move toward greater flexibility of exchange rates. We may learn some rather disappointing lessons as we adjust to a novel way of doing business; but whatever shocks a system of "gliding parities within a wider band" may have in store for us will hardly be as disturbing as those we are getting under the present system of jumping parities— jumping far out of a narrow band around parities fixed until further notice.

Comments on My Own Paper in Response to Comments from Especially Knowledgeable Specialists

COMMENT 1

I do not assert or assume that all five groups of potential buyers will respond to the reduction in price resulting from an increase in supply of foreign exchange. Many central banks deal only in the spot market, not in the forward market, so that arbitrage would have to "intervene." Dealers may find themselves insufficiently liquid or perhaps restrained by self-imposed limits regarding their net positions. Speculators (a category that should be understood to include business firms with net positions which they cover only when the forward rate is sufficiently attractive) may not be alert enough to act immediately. Importers may not be waiting in the wings to appear on the scene immediately at their cue. And the men at the trading desks of the banks may be slow to accept the decline in the rate that is required to clear the market and may, thus, leave some of the "excess supply" without takers. Yet, if the suppliers of a major currency are willing to accept lower exchange rates, it is not conceivable that really no takers would be found. The notion that the demand for a major currency may have a zero elasticity (if you allow a few days for the demand to react) is not believable.

COMMENT 2

That the foreign-exchange dealers talk in terms of the total of forward contracts whoever the counterparty may be does not mean that they fail to distinguish between different delivery risks or credit risks according to whether the counterparty is, for example, (a) a bank in their own country, (b) a major bank abroad, (c) a large corporation in their own

GREATER FLEXIBILITY OF EXCHANGE RATES

country, (d) a large corporation abroad, (e) a small domestic corporation, etc.

COMMENT 3

My friends among New York foreign-exchange dealers assure me that competition among them is very much less limited than competition in most foreign countries. I have no reason to doubt them.

· 35 ·

Forward Currency "Costs": A Zero Sum Game?

JOHN H. WATTS

EXPERTS in the theory of international finance have made the tautological, although not widely understood, observation, that in a global sense there is no real factor "cost" incurred when businessmen insure against exchange risk via the forward market. In this view, when the forward-exchange rate between two currencies differs from the spot rate, one man's gain is another's equal loss. Therefore, the price mechanism for traded goods could be expected to equate conditions to those obtaining when spot and forward rates were equal. Fritz Machlup, in the preceding paper, notes, in addition, that in order to gauge the impact that a decrease in one country's forward-exchange rate relative to others may have upon the trade volume, one would have to know the constellation of elasticities for all items in its external sector, since exports would be stimulated and imports discouraged.

As Machlup notes, however, major changes in the usual pattern of forward rates can be expected to affect the balance, or allocation of trade. No sure conclusion can be drawn about the impact on the volume of world trade, or even one country's trade, of greater discounts and premia, because elasticities are not known. There would be no disagreement with this view of the role played by the forward market among international financial specialists in corporations and institutions.

More particularly, however, from the point of view of any one businessman, the assertion that all costs and benefits should net out somewhere, that his loss is some other's gain, can be hollow comfort indeed. In those cases in which the gain offsetting his loss falls entirely on his client, he can expect that the transaction price can simply be adjusted to reflect the change. Usually, however, the additional cost or revenue accruing in their own currency to one or the other party in a trade channel, as a result of an increase in the spread between spot and future prices, does not net out completely.

Consider, for example, a German firm exporting to France a commodity with a high demand elasticity, and invoicing in marks. When the franc-mark forward rate widens under the spot rate, French importers find accounts payable liabilities from German purchases to be considerably more expensive when translated into francs, since the forward franc-mark rate has fallen sharply. Two types of offsets to this "cost" are at work, of course. The German exporter has an asset of increased worth, since his mark-denominated account receivable can be sold forward for more francs than before; but since his accounts, and frame of reference, are in marks he individually perceives no offsetting gain, and, therefore, is not inclined to lower his price. Second, German importers find franc-involved goods to be cheaper, since they can sell marks forward at a premium for payment of their payables. However, this advantage is not directly transferred to the exporter, so again he does not immediately lower his price.

If there is a competitive world market in the commodity, therefore, the French importer turns to sources that invoice in currencies for which the forward rate is less expensive. The German firm finds its French business has shrunk. Depending, of course, on elasticities of both short- and longer-term supply, there is either an increase or decrease in world business in that commodity. Intuitively, however, many would suspect that world trade, and world production, in most commodities would more often shrink than expand as these reallocations take effect, since they are based on other than a shift in real factor costs. More important, however, is that many holders of the "gain" from a widening in the future rate do not feel enriched, since their score is in any event kept in their own currency. And, though importers gain when exporters lose, it can be expected that the political expression of the discomfort of the losers will make itself more clearly felt in various national councils.

Finally, much, if not most, hedging is done outside the forward market. When a country's forward-exchange rate weakens, importers from that country find it convenient and profitable to buy forward the exchange with which to settle their trade accounts. However, exporters to that country often take other measures, such as borrowing in the weaker currency, to offset the imbalance that they perceive to be caused by the trade financing assets they hold. Of course, the interconnectedness of markets should equilibrate the real effect of various alternatives if markets were perfect and arbitrage robust. Since these conditions do not apply, particularly in many domestic capital markets where hedging via borrowing is done, an increase in forward/spot spread may at times produce gains, losses, and reallocations of trade, which do not quickly offset each other.

Therefore, while increasing the mean spread between spot and future currency prices may prove to be a near-zero-sum game for all trading participants taken as a whole, it is clear that many individual firms will gain and many will lose. And, it may be that the productivity of the players as a group is not unchanged, but rather reduced, from the introduction of rules that shift the assignment of players away from that position they play best to another, however slight that shift may be, and however equally the rules affect the other teams.

· 36 ·

Comments on Mr. Watts's Paper

FRITZ MACHLUP

MR. WATTS is perfectly correct in saying that an exporter losing previously profitable business will not be comforted by any gains that importers may make when exchange rates change in the forward market, or, for that matter, in the spot market. Such losses (or reduced profits) in some industries and profits (or reduced losses) in others are the essentials of real economic adjustment.

If German exporters scream about a serious loss of business as a result of an upward adjustment of the German mark, this is circumstantial evidence of "real adjustment at work." This adjustment—retrenchment of export industries and import-competing industries, and expansion of industries catering to the domestic market—is unavoidable. Indeed, it is high time for it to take place, after several years in which the undervalued German currency has produced an export surplus unsustainable in the long run and, for the time being, financed in part by artfully engineered exports of long-term capital and in part by involuntary foreign lending through accumulations of monetary reserves. Real adjustment is eventually accomplished either through upvaluation of the German mark or through inflation of costs and prices in Germany—or a combination of both. In any case, some industries must suffer in the process and no one knows whether their losses will be equaled by increased profits of others.

I doubt that this is a zero-sum game regarding profits and losses, or regarding exports and imports, or regarding gains and losses of productivity. The only safe generalization is that long postponement of adjustment is probably against the interests of all nations concerned.

These comments have purposely disregarded the question of the spread between spot and forward rates. What matters in connection with foreign trade is the exchange rate at which exporters and importers transact their business. An increase in the premium or discount is simply a change in the exchange rate that many traders use as the basis of calculation.

· 37 ·

Exchange Risks and Forward Coverage in Different Monetary Systems

EGON SOHMEN

GREATER scope for exchange-rate variability is almost universally associated with greater risk for international trade and capital movements. Greater risk of trading and investing abroad would, in turn, reduce economic intercourse between nations, a most regrettable development.

Let it be remembered, to begin with, that increased variability of exchange rates is never recommended for its own sake, with everything else remaining unchanged. The abandonment of official manipulation of exchange rates within narrow limits is primarily intended to reduce or remove the substantial risks that now arise in connection with balance-of-payments maladjustments: economic stagnation that may be forced upon a country if its domestic policies have to be geared primarily to the requirement of external equilibrium at fixed exchange rates; sudden and unpredictable interference with the freedom of international trade and payments; and finally, as a last resort, large and unpredictable changes of supposedly "pegged" exchange rates themselves. Since the last possibility is by no means excluded under the Bretton Woods System, it is difficult even to maintain that exchange rates are now more stable and predictable than they would be under a system of continuously adjusting rates. Would we accept the view that a dictatorship is a more "stable" form of government in any relevant sense by comparison with a democracy, even if it could be demonstrated that the people in power change, by bloody revolution, only every twenty years on the average?

It has often been emphasized that flexible exchange rates are not necessarily unstable. By appropriate monetary policy, undesirable oscillations can always be eliminated even without any direct interference in the exchange markets. The relevant magnitude of the exchange risk with which traders are confronted can nevertheless not be measured merely by the *actual* variability of exchange rates that is observed. Even if it turned out *ex post* that flexible exchange rates had oscillated only very mildly over a certain period, traders might *ex ante* have felt paralyzing anxiety over what might have happened. This kind of uncertainty can

---

The arguments discussed in this paper are treated more fully in *The Theory of Forward Exchange*, Princeton Studies in International Finance, vol. 17, 1966, reprinted with minor changes as Chapter IV of the second edition of my *Flexible Exchange Rates* (Chicago: University of Chicago Press, 1969).

only be removed by the existence of well-developed forward-exchange markets.

Many argue that forward markets might not function well enough, however, to provide suitable covering opportunities for commercial traders when exchange rates are not stabilized within narrow bounds by official exchange-market intervention. If I understand the conventional view correctly, it rests on the argument that traders can now more easily find partners to relieve them of the exchange risk because this risk is narrowly limited. With wider bands, the risk of greater variability is more pronounced, and the risk premia that will be demanded by the "underwriters" on forward markets will be the higher the wider the margins. According to this view, risk would be at a maximum when there are no limits at all, and the risk premia demanded of commercial traders might then be so high that most international trade, not to mention capital movements, would cease.

At first sight, it would seem that these conclusions are well corroborated by the empirical evidence. Whenever the continuity of a currency parity appeared to be under a cloud, and the future range of possible exchange-rate variation consequently was greater than the customary margin of 1½ per cent around parity, forward premia or discounts became excessive (as they are at the time of writing for the French franc). Occasionally, forward markets broke down altogether (after the revaluation of the German mark of 1961, for example). It appears plausible to deduce that chaos would result if exchange rates were allowed to fluctuate without limits.

The basic flaw in this reasoning is the unwarranted extrapolation from the present system of *adjustably pegged* exchange rates to one of *free* foreign-exchange markets. Perhaps the most crucial difference between the two is that there would never be any necessity for convertibility restrictions in the latter case. At present, the authorities of deficit countries frequently see themselves forced to restrict the freedom of international payments because they might otherwise be confronted with the danger of almost immediate exhaustion of their reserves. Convertibility restrictions, and even the mere possibility that the freedom of payments might be jeopardized in the future, imperil the viability of one essential ingredient of well-developed forward markets: covered interest arbitrage. Only the absence of this factor (and not asymmetrical speculation by itself) can explain the occasional occurrence of forward discounts substantially exceeding the relevant interest differentials. Brisk arbitrage, an operation entirely free of exchange risk, would always step in whenever an appreciable difference between the two tended to arise ("appreciable" in terms of the notions of foreign-exchange traders, usually microscopic by the standards of ordinary trade). Even without anybody taking an exchange risk, exporters and importers would always be able to cover their expected forward proceeds (or commitments) in foreign currencies, and would be able to do so without having to pay anything that could be called a "risk premium." This verdict holds *even if* there is speculation in the foreign-exchange markets, for whatever difference between spot and forward markets may arise in general market equilibrium at full convertibility would only be explainable by: interest differentials; banking and brokerage fees for covered interest arbitrage transactions; and the opportunity costs of interest arbitrage funds.

The last component is undoubtedly a rising function of the size of total arbitrage transactions. The gap between interest differential and forward discount may consequently be larger the more arbitrage funds are required to bridge any differences between supply and demand of other market participants on individual forward markets. I would nevertheless expect that, since covered interest arbitrage, at least between the major currencies, is a type of transaction that involves very little risk, its supply should be unusually elastic. This would suggest that forward discounts and interest differentials will always be very close to each other when currency convertibility is not in danger.

These arguments are not limited to the closer forward exchange markets, which are the most active ones at this time. With the assurance of complete currency convertibility, there is no reason why banks or other financial intermediaries, or any other businesses, should not also profitably take advantage of arbitrage opportunities in more distant forward markets with maturities of several years. The thinner these markets, of course, the higher may be the transactions costs that are charged for this service. It can hardly be emphasized strongly enough, however, that opportunities for long-term hedging will always be *more* readily available in a system of *flexible* rates—a system that does not require convertibility restrictions—than in the present one, in which fixed parities with narrow margins can all too often be sustained only by various more or less subtle ways of interfering with the free play of foreign-exchange markets. It would not appear too far-fetched to argue—in sharp contrast to the conventional view—that the exchange risk properly speaking may be substantially *less* in a system of completely unrestrained exchange-rate movements than in the one we now have.

Even when the invalidity of the "insurance theory" of forward coverage is recognized, it might seem that a case could still be made for the traditional view that traders' costs are increased by greater flexibility of exchange rates on the grounds that banking charges for forward deals are higher than for spot, and that most traders might nevertheless want to cover forward if exchange rates were not pegged.

If banks, indeed, charge more for forward-exchange deals at the present time, this can only be due to the fact that forward markets are less developed than spot markets, and that the use of thinner markets is always more expensive, primarily as a result of the increased "search time" that is necessary to find partners in it. But this shortcoming will automatically be repaired if, as is assumed by all participants in this debate, many more traders will be inclined to hedge on the forward-exchange markets when rates are flexible. There is nothing in the nature of a forward market that would make transactions in it more costly in terms of economic resources used up (exchange dealers' time, cost of telecommunications, etc.) than transactions in spot exchange. It should also be realized that these costs do not have to be incurred *in addition* to the costs of spot transactions by those who hedge on forward markets. When an exporter sells his expected foreign-exchange earnings forward to his bank, the transfer of the amount in question when it is due is the end of the matter for him.

An additional argument that might be raised is that, with an increased total volume of transactions on each forward market, (1) the net balances per unit of time on each forward market and also (2) the random balances in the hands of each bank at the end of each business day would normally be larger. Larger net balances on each forward market (argument 1) will require more interest arbitrage, and with less than perfectly elastic supply of arbitrage funds, the potential divergence between interest differentials and forward discounts might also be larger. With larger random positions of forward exchange in each bank (argument 2), each bank will, on the average, have a larger foreign-exchange position—or so it seems—and the returns for this kind of service (a genuine risk premium in this case) will inevitably find its way into the costs of foreign trade.

The second of the two arguments is the more easily answered. With a given total volume of foreign trade, an increased volume of forward hedging will be accompanied by a reduced volume of spot transactions. Without systematic sources of bias, the random net balances of spot exchange in each bank will be correspondingly smaller, and the average foreign-exchange risk carried by banks at the close of each business day is not likely to be affected at all.

Concerning the first of the arguments above, there is, first of all, the question of the quantitative importance of the crucial factor, the supply of arbitrage funds. I would tend to believe that the importance of insufficient elasticity of arbitrage funds is negligible when convertibility is assured. If we sometimes have different impressions today, the reason must again primarily be the danger of future inconvertibility of one or more of the currencies involved, a factor that derives essentially from the faults of the present system.

Another consideration should also not be overlooked. Even if, as a result of insufficiently elastic supply of arbitrage funds, an appreciable deviation of the forward discount from the interest differential should develop at a certain time, this will make forward coverage more expensive only for *one* side of the market (say, exporters). Covering will become cheaper for the other side, and foreign trade as a whole does not, on balance, become more expensive.

All the analysis so far applied to the case of *unlimited* exchange-rate flexibility, a system that does not seem to be the wave of the immediate future. Systems of widened margins for exchange-rate variations, with or without a shifting parity, will differ from this limiting case in that it is not excluded that a country may have to intervene by sales of foreign exchange to an extent that endangers its reserves. Since it may, as a consequence, have to resort to convertibility restrictions, there is an increased likelihood that covered interest arbitrage may occasionally become impossible. As a consequence, forward coverage by traders may become unbearably expensive. It would follow that the exchange risk for trade may be the greater the *narrower* is the band, and the more *rigid* is the parity. Acceptance of proposals falling short of full exchange-rate flexibility should be conditioned by this consideration. Band limitations should be no more than a psychological device, a safety net below the flying trapeze of free-exchange markets, in the expectation that monetary acrobats, at least in the central banks and governments of the major countries, will exhibit enough skill to render the safety net superfluous. The enjoyment of the show will necessarily be impaired if the artists perform in the safety net most of the time.

· 38 ·

The Effect on the Forward-Exchange Market of More Flexible Rates

W. F. J. BATT

I

THE Forward-Exchange Market reached saturation point at least twice during 1968, once in March and again in November when the market became completely one way. For banks in England this situation was reached, for the first time, in November 1964, when their purchases of forward sterling began to exceed their sales of forward sterling by amounts greater than the limits imposed by the Bank of England. This was only one reason why the Bank of England came into the market as a buyer of forward sterling, thereby enabling the London banks to sell forward sterling and reduce their net position to the limits laid down.

At the height of the sterling crisis in November 1967, many banks, both in London and overseas, were endeavoring to reduce their overall commitments since their forward liabilities were becoming too large in terms of either credit risks or political risks (i.e., blocking of balances, exchange control imposed by the countries with whom deals had been done). My estimate is that total forward sales and purchases of all currencies for all banks throughout the world must have reached between $60 billion to $90 billion in November 1967.

Some banks at present calculate the forward risk to themselves in the event of nonfulfilment of the contract by their counter party to be the width of the present band plus the price of the forward margin. If the band were widened, then the forward risk, in their reasoning, would be increased proportionately and might necessitate a reduction in the limits granted to commercial clients and banks. The amount of additional forward-exchange cover that would be required would depend upon the maximum width of the band. At the present, sterling can effectively fluctuate 1½ per cent against the dollar and 3 per cent against Continental currencies. A 2 per cent band either side for the pound against the dollar is 8 per cent overall for the pound against Continental currencies. A potential maximum loss of 8 per cent is too much for a commercial trader to risk.

Assuming all currencies were around parity with each other and no devaluation or revaluation were expected, then with a 2 per cent band either side against the dollar and 4 per cent either side against Continen-

317

tal currencies, the maximum loss would be fixed at 2 per cent or 4 per cent respectively. The demand for forward cover should not be greater under these conditions than it is at the present time. But where the rates were not in parity, the demand for forward cover would be greater and would increase considerably as the bands grew wider. I believe that the amount of additional forward cover that would be required is in the region of 25 per cent and 50 per cent above present figures, which are themselves rather inflated because of present currency uncertainties.

II

I consider that at least an additional 25 per cent of the present forward cover should be forthcoming for the following reasons:

(1) New international banks that have been, and are being, formed can trade in the forward markets.
(2) Smaller banks are merging into larger units and presumably are willing to take larger risks in the international markets.
(3) Many limits within banks have been imposed by domestic credit managers; as they become more educated in international matters, they should increase the limits. Too many of them, at the present time, tend to look upon forward-exchange risks as 100 per cent liabilities instead of marginal (1–15 per cent) risks.
(4) A change in the American banking system in assessing forward risks would be helpful, for the present method applies limits to the gross outstanding forward commitments, rather than the net difference.
(5) The creation of new institutions to provide forward cover poses problems.
  (a) Any commercial institution would have to be creditworthy in the eyes of those with whom it did business.
  (b) Such institutions would need considerable risk capital and would be, in some respects, speculative ventures.
  (c) If such institutions were formed by the IMF, World Bank, Group of Ten, etc., then it is likely that the eventual risks would come back to the Central Banks of the currencies most in demand or supply. It is possible that such central banks would be unwilling to provide more forward cover (however indirectly) than they do at the present.
(6) Relaxation of Exchange Control regulation in various major countries would enable more of the indigenous banks to play a larger part in providing forward cover, but as the tendency is for such regulations to increase rather than diminish, there

is no hope for further expansion of the forward market arising from the removal of such regulations.

III

Obviously the greater the demand for forward cover the greater become the premia. When there was lack of confidence concerning a currency the forward margins in 1968 and 1969 rose (for short-term forwards) to 10–15 per cent per annum. For very short periods (up to one month), the cost has risen to 25 per cent per annum. I believe that at times the cost of forward cover would be greater than the profit margin available to the commercial trader.

IV

If forward cover became unavailable, or too costly, then some commercial traders might cease their international operations rather than enter into a risk that could involve them in considerable loss. On the pessimistic side, one could visualize a snowball effect whereby many smaller traders withdrawing from international trade could lead eventually to a decline in world trade.

Concerning short-term capital investment, at the present time most forward cover is restricted to a maximum of two years, although some sterling-dollar contracts have been entered into for five to seven years. It follows that any restrictions on forward cover (as given above) could impede short-term capital investment. Long-term capital investment cannot be covered forward except on a yearly basis with annual renewals. I do not believe that the investors are concerned with exchange rates, but more with annual yield and capital appreciation. The exchange risk is comparatively unimportant and almost always ignored.

In the 1920s there was a modified form of forward market and an elementary form of the Eurodollar market. During the 1930s, because of floating rates, the forward market contracted and the Eurodollar market vanished. One of the main factors in the present Eurodollar market is the existence of the forward market. A reduction in the latter could seriously affect the former. The major currencies, which are not dealt in in the Eurocurrencies markets, are those for which there is no forward market of any size.

A move to wider bands could probably mean that depositors would swing around wildly on the basis of economic and political fears from one currency to another and tend to retreat to domestic holdings with a consequent run-down of international financing operations.

• 39 •

Comments on Mr. Batt's Paper

FRITZ MACHLUP

THE first sentence in Section III of Mr. Batt's paper reads as follows: "Obviously the greater the demand for forward cover the greater become the premia." I do not understand why this should be obvious, since the opposite may happen just as well. Assume that the forward rate of the pound sterling has a discount of 10 per cent. Someone intending to import from England may wish to secure this cheap price of the pound for his future payments and, therefore, gives an order to buy pounds sterling forward. This is clearly an increased "demand for forward cover," but it will tend to reduce the discount on the pound. Similarly, the German mark may command a premium in the forward market. A German importer of dollar goods (or, for that matter, Italian, French, or other imports) may wish to secure for himself the cheap rates of the dollar (lira, franc, etc.) that are implied in the premium on the forward mark, and he, therefore, sells his marks in the forward market. This "greater demand for forward cover" would tend to lower the premium on the forward mark.

In other words, whether "greater demand for forward cover" will increase or reduce the premium (or discount) on particular currencies depends on *who* demands forward cover. If it is one who seeks protection against the premium (or discount) becoming *larger,* his covering transaction will tend to raise the premium (or discount). On the other hand, if it is one who wishes to take advantage of the current premium (or discount) and to seek protection against its becoming *smaller,* his covering transaction will tend to reduce the premium (or discount).

In the same passage, Batt writes: "I believe that at times the cost of forward cover would be greater than the profit margin available to the commercial trader." If by "cost of forward cover" Batt means premium or discount in the forward market, then the statement is, of course, perfectly obvious. Indeed, it would hold not only "at times" but most of the time. Very rarely would anyone buy or sell forward exchange if the difference between the forward and spot rates were smaller than the margin between selling and buying rates, let alone the net profit margin of the forward dealer.

In the first paragraph of Section IV, Batt theorizes about the probable consequences of forward cover becoming "unavailable, or too costly." He fears that commercial traders—exporters and importers—might cease operations, and the withdrawal of traders might lead to a decline in world trade.

Batt is right in expecting a decline in foreign trade when forward cover becomes unavailable. Just how much this decline would be is difficult to estimate. The relevance of his statement, however, is puzzling. Why does he speculate on the effects of unavailability of forward cover in a paper on "the effect on the forward-exchange market of more flexible exchange rates"? If he thinks so, he did not tell us why. Of course, foreign-exchange restrictions usually prohibit or restrict forward dealing in currencies. But the chief purpose of greater flexibility is to reduce the governments' propensities to impose direct controls and restrictions. The system of so-called fixed rates has led to foreign-exchange restrictions as a means of keeping exchange rates at fixed levels as long as possible. More-flexible rates are wanted so that we can get rid of restrictions.

One more comment. In the third paragraph of Section IV, Batt asserts that "during the 1930s, because of floating rates, the forward market contracted." He may be correct in the statement that the forward market contracted, but I doubt that this was so "because of floating rates." Some of my personal experience, apart from theoretical reasoning, makes me think that floating rates tend to expand the forward market. The firm I helped manage before and during a part of the 1930s had until 1931 never offered the expected proceeds of its exports in the forward market. Soon after the pound sterling went off its gold parity, we felt it necessary to seek cover and we were able to cover all our export business without difficulty. World trade declined rapidly in the early thirties, but this was chiefly because of worldwide deflation, higher tariffs, and the imposition of restrictions on exchange and payments; I should think, however, that the proportion of foreign trade that was covered through forward operations increased "because of floating rates."

· 40 ·

Flexible Exchange Rates and Forward Markets

EDWIN A. REICHERS AND HAROLD VAN B. CLEVELAND

THE conference has requested our views concerning the effect of greater exchange-rate flexibility on forward-exchange markets. The particular questions asked are: whether more forward coverage would be required; whether the additional coverage would be forthcoming; what its cost would be; and what the effects might be on trade, international investment, and the international movement of liquid funds.

This memorandum contains our tentative replies to these questions in relation to two hypothetical exchange-rate regimes: (1) a regime of "wider bands," in which the agreed margins of intervention have been widened to 2–2½ per cent on either side of parity; and (2) a regime of "floating rates," in which there are neither official parities nor agreed margins of intervention. The present regime is sometimes referred to as "narrow bands."

We have not considered the effect on forward markets of a regime of crawling or sliding parities. However, we believe that the basic conclusions reached would also apply to such a regime.

Under a regime of floating rates, central bank intervention in the spot market is assumed to be limited to smoothing operations, with no attempt to resist the trend of market forces. In the case of a regime of wider bands, it is assumed that apart from smoothing, central banks will permit the spot rate to move in response to market forces until it closely approaches the edge of the band.

Normal versus Crisis Situations

For the purpose of this discussion, it is necessary to distinguish between a crisis situation, in which a currency is under strong, one-sided selling or buying pressure in the spot market, and a normal situation, in which the spot market is relatively evenly balanced between sellers and buyers.

A normal situation may be defined as one in which the spot rate remains well within the limits of the band, be the band narrow or wide. Under floating rates, a normal situation is one in which the spot rate has no sustained upward or downward trend.

Under the present regime or with wider bands, a currency will be under strong, one-sided buying or selling in spot markets when the parity is widely regarded as precarious and subject to change. Such a currency would be at or close to the edge of the band, and massive intervention by a central bank would be taking place in the spot market. Under a regime of floating rates, one-sided speculation would bring about sustained depreciation or appreciation of the currency in the spot market over a period of weeks or months—assuming that the central bank did not intervene to arrest the movement.

A question central to this inquiry is whether or not greater responsiveness of exchange rates to market forces would increase or decrease the frequency or the severity of exchange crises. The answer to this question turns on whether or not greater flexibility of rates would improve the balance-of-payments adjustment process in the short run. If, as we believe, greater flexibility would tend to improve the short-run adjustment process, at least to a limited extent (primarily through its effect on short-term capital movements), greater flexibility of rates would mean fewer or less serious exchange crises.

We also incline to the view that exchange crises would be less frequent and serious under a regime of floating rates than under a regime of wider bands. Under a regime of floating rates, the more usual causes of balance-of-payments trouble, including differences among countries in rates of inflation, would not be so apt to lead to exchange crises, because the greater freedom of the spot rate to move would tend to maintain balance. One-sided speculation would, however, develop in more extreme disequilibrium situations, such as when international confidence in the country's government was low, or the country had embarked on a grossly overexpansive monetary or fiscal program. This was, for example, the case of France in 1937–1938, when the franc floated briefly. The combination of a Popular Front government and large budget deficits led to a persistent flight of capital and a sustained depreciation of the franc. The depreciation was self-aggravating because it contributed to internal inflation.

Activity in Forward Markets

Business firms and individuals buy and sell foreign currencies in the forward markets in order to cover (hedge) exchange exposures arising out of ordinary commercial transactions and foreign investments, or to speculate, or to engage in covered interest arbitrage. So far as hedging and speculation are concerned, the amount of activity in the forward-exchange markets depends chiefly on the difference between the present forward rate and what traders think the spot rate may be on the date the forward contract matures. It depends, in other words, on the degree of uncertainty about the future spot rate.

If spot rates were subject to wider swings, as they might be with wider bands or floating rates, uncertainty about future spot rates would increase. Accordingly, the volume of hedging and speculative activity in the forward markets would also increase, as firms and individuals reacted by covering a larger proportion of their foreign currency exposure. If uncertainty about future spot rates increased greatly, the volume of activity in the forward market would also increase greatly.

It is unclear, however, whether *under normal conditions,* spot rates would in fact swing much more widely under a regime of wider bands or floating rates than they do now with narrow bands, assuming smoothing operations by central banks. It would depend in part on what currencies were involved and in particular whether the country was large or small. It would also depend on whether currency blocs were formed. Presumably rates would fluctuate less as between large currency blocs than if individual currencies floated separately. We are accordingly uncertain whether the volume of activity in the forward markets would increase greatly or only a little.

Since firms and individuals normally cover only a fraction of their foreign currency exposure, the volume of potential additional demand for forward cover is large—a good deal larger than the present size of the forward markets, under normal conditions. We have no hard information on the proportion of present exposure in the various trading currencies which is now covered. Our rough guess is that under normal conditions, the business community as a whole covers about 25 per cent of its aggregate foreign currency exposure in liquid balances and receivables. During the last eighteen months, when several European parities have been continually under suspicion, this figure may have been on the average as high as 40 per cent, except in periods of acute crisis when it was much higher.

Under the present exchange-rate regime, when a currency is under strong, one-sided pressure, the proportion of commercial exposure covered rises steeply, and many customers also cover a part of their investment exposure. Thus, during recent exchange crises, activity in the forward markets has increased enormously. However, the increase in activity in crisis conditions under the present exchange-rate regime is not a good indication of the volume of activity in the forward markets that might be expected with wider bands or flexible rates under normal conditions.

Nevertheless, it seems likely that even under normal conditions, the demand for forward cover would increase to some extent under wider bands or floating rates, unless the currency in question had demonstrated marked stability on the exchanges for a considerable time—as was the case, for example, of the Canadian dollar when it was allowed to float freely in the 1950s.

Availability of Forward Cover

Under normal conditions, any increase in demand for forward cover under wider bands or floating rates would probably be met by an answering supply. For example, a fall in the forward rate due to more offers by exporters to sell the currency forward would tend to widen the forward discount and make it more attractive to importers to buy the currency forward. It would also attract more speculators and interest arbitrageurs into the forward market on the buying side. This equilibrating process presupposes the absence of interference by the authorities with the movement of short-term funds across the exchanges for speculation and interest arbitrage. Under normal conditions, such interference would presumably be unlikely, at least in the case of important currencies.

However, there are institutional obstacles to a large, sustained increase in the total activity of forward markets. For example, banks normally have rules about the total volume of forward contracts they will undertake. Foreign exchange trading is a highly specialized and concentrated business; its total "capacity" in the short run is necessarily limited. Given sufficient time and a sustained increase in demand, these obstacles would presumably be overcome.

In sum, under normal conditions, greater rate flexibility in the form of wider bands or of floating rates might well mean a larger forward market but not a disorderly or one-sided market. Any increased demand for forward cover would call forth an increased supply, so long as movements of short-term funds for exchange speculation and interest arbitrage were not unduly restricted by official action.

This conclusion is subject to an important qualification. The supply of forward cover for long-term commercial commitments would probably fall well short of demand if it turned out that rates do in fact fluctuate considerably more widely under wider bands or floating rates. Even in present circumstances, long-term forward cover is usually difficult and often impossible to obtain. If the demand were substantially increased, this problem would be aggravated.

Under crisis conditions, the forward markets would be one-sided under a regime of wider bands or of floating rates, as they are under the present regime. The pertinent question, therefore, is whether exchange crises would be more or less frequent or serious if rates were more flexible. Our views on that question have already been indicated.

Cost of Forward Cover

The preceding discussion of availability of forward cover under the more flexible exchange-rate regimes also answers the question of its cost. Under normal conditions, the cost of forward cover would not be substantially different with wider bands or floating rates than it is with narrow bands, because any increased demand for forward cover would bring further a corresponding supply. Both practical experience and economic theory (the interest-parity doctrine) support the view that the cost of forward cover is very largely determined by interest differentials, except under conditions of one-way speculation. We believe this would be as true with wider bands or floating rates as it is with fixed rates.

Under normal conditions, the spot and forward rates would stay close together (as long as the movement of funds is not restricted) regardless of what exchange-rate regime was in effect, because the spot and forward markets are alternatives equally available to the trader, who wishes to cover his exchange exposure, or to the exchange speculator. Moreover, the interest arbitrageur operates in both the spot and forward markets at the same time.

Under a regime of wider bands, if a change in the parity was expected, there would be the same sort of trouble in the forward markets as under a regime of narrow bands. If a devaluation were expected, for example, the forward rate would fall well below the band, and the forward discount would be much larger than the interest differential, as sellers greatly outnumbered buyers in the forward market. In such crisis conditions, moreover, covered interest arbitrage is apt to decline, and the authorities are also likely to restrict the movement of short-term funds, further aggravating the disequilibrium of the forward market. Thus, under crisis conditions, the cost of forward cover would rise steeply under wider bands, just as it does under narrow bands.

Both past and recent experience amply demonstrate the effect on forward discounts and premia of the one-sided speculation that occurs when a currency is under severe pressure and is pressing against the floor or ceiling of its band. The accompanying charts (Figs. 40.1 and 40.2) show how discounts or premia for sterling, the French franc and the German mark have increased sharply in recent crisis periods.[1] In the 1930s, when the fixed parities of the gold bloc countries were under suspicion, forward discounts were also very large. For example, during 1935, the discounts on three-month forward French francs, Dutch guilders, and Swiss francs reached 27, 22, and 29 per cent per annum, respectively.

Under a regime of floating rates, it might appear at first blush that the cost of forward cover would not be much affected by crisis conditions. Even with a sustained downward movement of the spot rate, would not interest arbitrage and speculation still keep the spot and forward rates close together?

This may be true in theory but it is of doubtful practical importance. Under crisis conditions, the authorities would probably intervene in the

---

[1] In interpreting Fig. 40.2, it should be kept in mind that the parity of sterling was under suspicion throughout the period covered by the chart, so that the relatively small forward discounts of sterling, except in extreme crisis periods, reflect to some extent the fact that the Bank of England was supporting the forward rate most of the time.

GREATER FLEXIBILITY OF EXCHANGE RATES

spot market to retard the movement of the spot rate, and would also restrict the outflow of short-term funds. Thus, even under a regime of floating rates, a crisis would produce disorderly conditions and high premia or discounts in the forward markets. The critical question, again, is which of the alternative exchange-rate regimes is least—or most—crisis-prone.

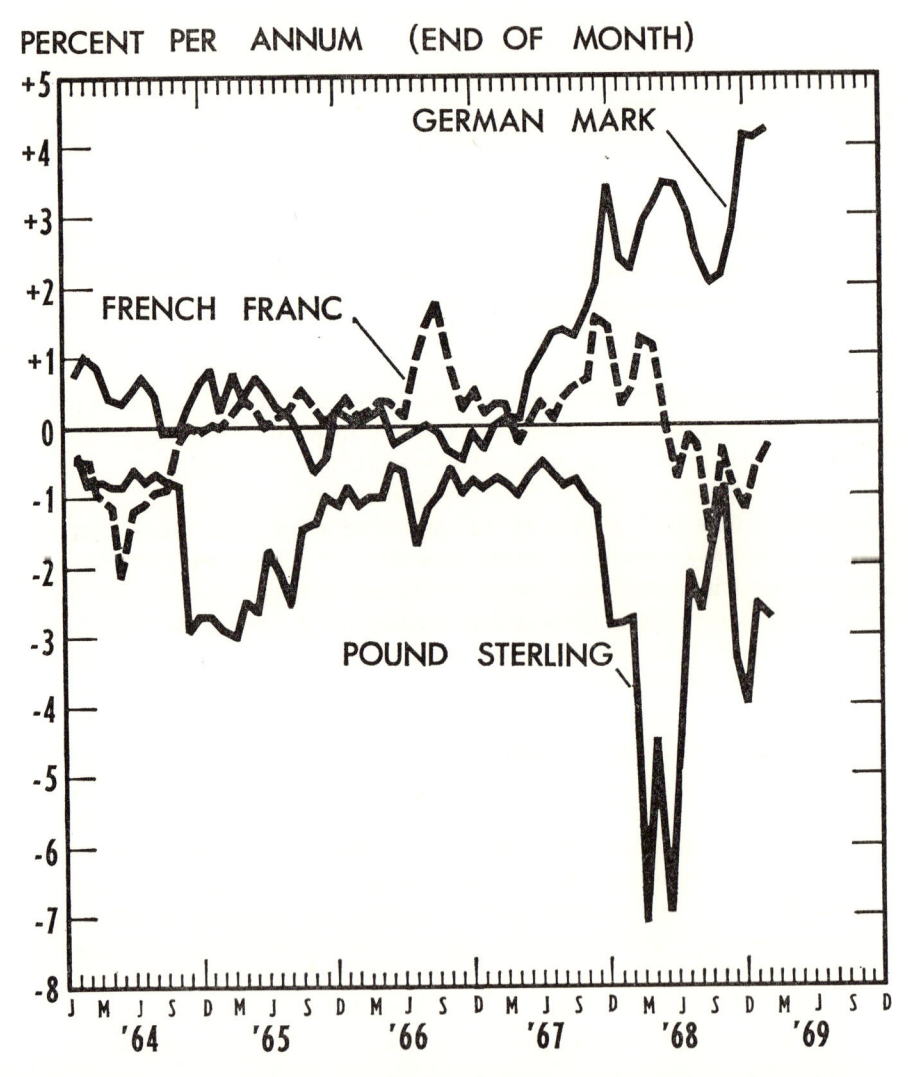

Fig. 40.1. Cost of forward cover of selected currencies. (Source: International Monetary Fund)

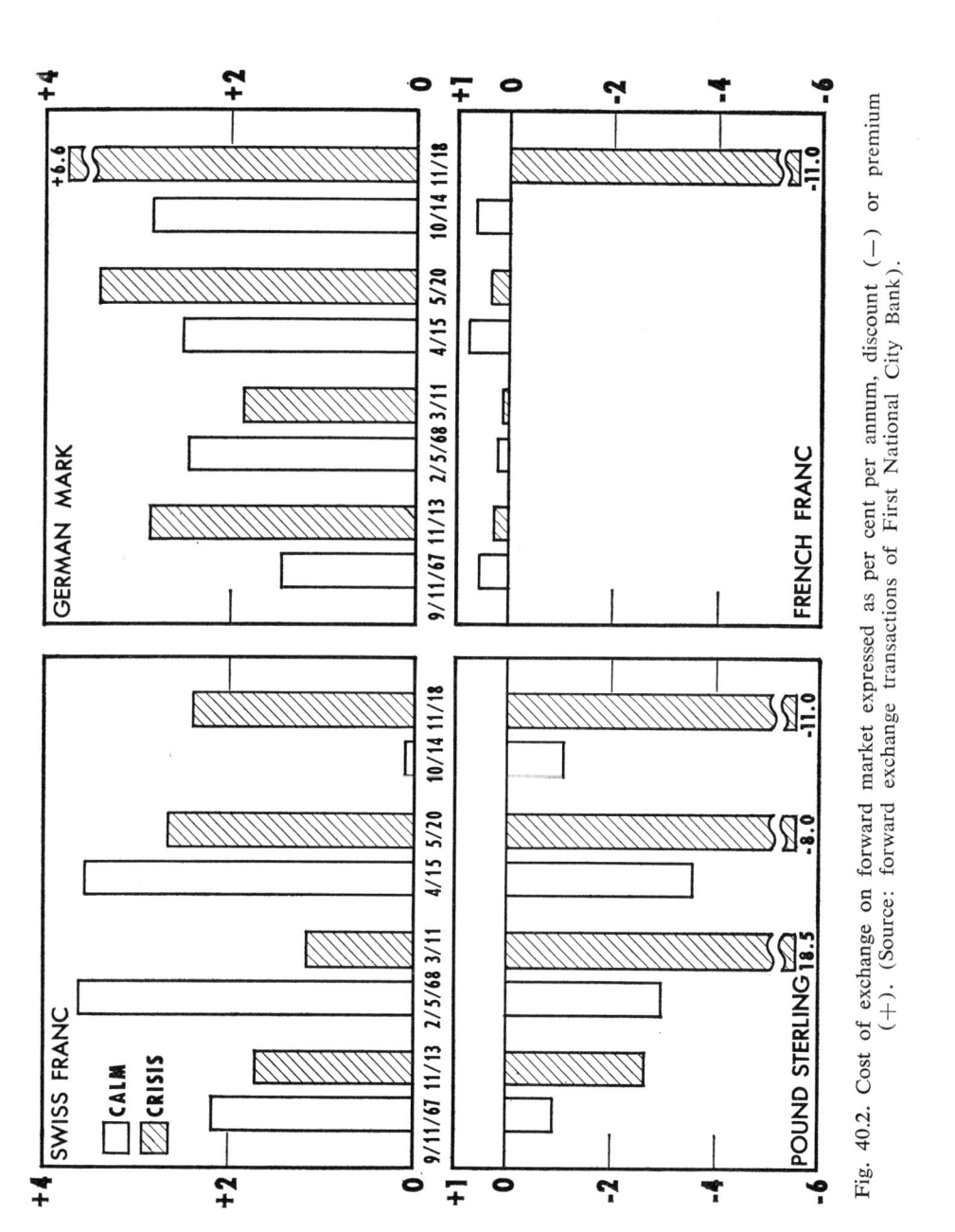

Fig. 40.2. Cost of exchange on forward market expressed as per cent per annum, discount (—) or premium (+). (Source: forward exchange transactions of First National City Bank).

Economic Effects

The significance of the changes in forward markets outlined above for international trade and capital movements would obviously depend on what and how many currencies were involved. If IMF rules were changed to permit wider bands, it is quite possible that few countries would take advantage of the opportunity. Another possibility is that currency blocs would form. For example, the European Common Market members might maintain fixed rates among their currencies, and a number of other Continental European countries might join them, while the pound and other sterling area currencies, along with the Canadian dollar and the yen, would peg to the U.S. dollar. In that event, greater flexibility of rates would exist between the blocs, but not within them. If a substantial number of countries adopted floating rates, currency blocs would be virtually certain to form.

The changes in forward markets that might occur under wider bands or floating rates would have relatively small effects on international trade, short-term money flows, and foreign investment, under normal conditions. The possible increase in the proportion of commercial and investment transactions covered would not, presumably, have much economic effect, since the normal cost of forward cover would be no larger than it is now. In crisis conditions, however, the sharply increased cost of cover and (often) its unavailability, would inhibit or distort trade, investment, and interest arbitrage, just as they do under the present regime. Once again, the critical question is whether crisis situations would be more or less frequent or serious under the more flexible exchange-rate regimes.

If, under wider bands or floating rates, spot rates fluctuated substantially more than they do under the present regime, the shortage of long-term cover would have greater economic importance than it now has. If this proved to be a serious deterrent to international trade or investment, ways might be found to mitigate it, although probably not to eliminate it altogether. Effective markets for long-term cover might gradually develop, and governments could assist this development by providing low-cost, long-term, forward cover directly to firms or by establishing or supporting a secondary market for long-term forward-exchange contracts.

Conclusion

Under a regime of wider bands or floating rates, the forward markets might be larger under normal conditions than they are today, but the normal cost of forward cover would be much the same as it is now. In crisis conditions, under wider bands or floating rates, there would be much the same kind of trouble in the forward markets as now, with one-sided markets and large premia or discounts. Crises, however, might well be less frequent and less serious, particularly under a regime of floating rates. Thus, our consideration of the effects of greater flexibility of rates on forward markets leads to the conclusion that effects on forward markets are probably not a major consideration in deciding upon the desirability of greater flexibility of exchange rates.

Part VI. Potential Impact of Exchange-Rate Flexibility on Different Countries or Groups of Countries

IN HIS paper, "Canada's Experience with a Floating Exchange Rate," Donald B. Marsh undertakes to show that the Canadian experiment worked well at first, but was, in the end, the victim of incompetent monetary policies. Canada enjoyed an unprecedented increase in international trade in the 1950s, and between 1955 and 1957 the appreciation of the Canadian dollar supported the anti-inflation policies of the central bank. From 1957 to 1961, however, the government continued its policy of monetary restraint in spite of growing unemployment. High interest rates attracted foreign capital and caused an appreciation of the Canadian dollar, which discouraged exports and encouraged imports when the state of the economy would have required opposite policies. The results were then blamed on the floating exchange rate.

"A Floating German Mark: An Essay in Speculative Economics" by Herbert Giersch and Wolfgang Kasper discusses what might have happened had West Germany, in the summer of 1964, introduced a combination of widened band (± 5 per cent) and gliding parity (2 per cent per annum). The authors come to the following conclusions: inflationary disturbances from the outside could have been neutralized and near price stability achieved; over the five-year period from mid-1964 to mid-1969 the German mark would have appreciated by about 10 per cent and would have lost only 5 per cent of internal purchasing power instead of 13 per cent; the market exchange rate would never have come nearer the limits of a 10 per cent band than by about 2 percentage points, thus permitting the assumption that one-way speculation could have been avoided.

In "Japan's Twenty-Year Experience with a Fixed Rate for the Yen," Tadashi Iino argues that Japan's fixed-rate system was a great success, and that there is no reason why Japan should change to a flexible rate. The success was the more remarkable because the rate constituted at first an overvaluation and had later to be maintained against the devaluations of other currencies. Iino gives several reasons for Japan's accomplishment: assistance of the United States, deflation and austerity policies, belated liberalization, elimination of much of the public debt, low cash-liquidity of private enterprise, modest wage increases, and a very high rate of saving and investment.

Max Iklé's paper, "The Problem of Floating Exchange Rates from the Swiss Viewpoint," tries to show that for a small country such as Switzerland a fluctuating exchange rate—even within the range of ± 5 per cent —would not be acceptable because of the increased risks and costs for international trade and money-market operations. If all other currencies were to become flexible, while the dollar retained its present gold convertibility, the Swiss franc would maintain its dollar parity. Abolition of the gold convertibility of the dollar would lead to the collapse of the present system and the split of the Western world into a dollar bloc and a gold bloc, with Switzerland most likely belonging to the latter.

In "Balance-of-Payments and Exchange-Rate Problems in Sweden, Denmark, and Finland," Erik Lundberg and Åke Lundgren investigate whether alternative exchange-rate policies would have produced better results in Scandinavia. In Sweden, fixed exchange rates did not lead to balance-of-payments difficulties, but they could be maintained only through policies that conflicted partially with domestic aims. Had flexible rates prevailed in the 1960s, repeated depreciations would have reduced the need for restrictive policies, and would have increased the employment level. The Danish situation in the 1950s and 1960s was one of continuous fundamental disequilibrium at fixed exchange rates. Nevertheless, greater flexibility of exchange rates was rejected with the argument that it would weaken the resistance against inflationary tendencies. The vulnerability of the Finnish balance-of-payments position (five devaluations during the postwar period) is explained by persistently inflationary budget and incomes policies. After the devaluation of 1967, cost-of-living clauses in wage and loan contracts were abolished with the intention of keeping the new rate stable and to "use this fixation as a disciplinary support for a stabilization policy." Interesting is the belief "that exchange-rate changes have to be big and of a shock-nature to have efficient results."

The paper "European Integration and Greater Flexibility of Exchange Rates," by Wolfgang Kasper, interprets economic integration as "the welding together of national markets, so that potential buyers have an undiscriminated choice between homemade and imported goods." From this point of view, the fixing of exchange rates is a disintegrating factor. Kasper, therefore, suggests greater flexibility of exchange rates even inside the EEC to overcome the misallocations caused by large and discrete peg adjustments.

Antonio Mosconi's "Comments on Mr. Kasper's Paper: Requiem for European Integration" contradicts Kasper's view. Only rigid exchange rates will lead to the needed integration of the monetary and fiscal policies of the Six. The EEC needs community-wide legal and political instruments. More flexible exchange rates would cause the failure of integration, and would be incompatible with the Agricultural Common Market.

Stephen Marris' note, "Comments on the Papers by Messrs. Mosconi and Kasper: Red Herrings, Carts, and Horses," suggests that greater flexibility of exchange rates inside the EEC would favor progress toward integration. It also points out that flexible rates would be more compatible with common agricultural policies than the present adjustable-peg system, because in *real* terms the support program will be uniform only to the extent that the exchange rates are in line with the relevant purchasing-power parities. Marris believes that it would foster monetary integration if the members of the EEC were prepared to honor a commitment not to alter parities by more than 1 or 2 per cent in any one year.

The problem of a common agricultural policy is also being investigated by Friedrich A. Lutz in his paper "The Agricultural Regulations of the European Economic Community as an Obstacle to the Introduction of Greater Flexibility of Exchange Rates." Lutz shows that greater flexibility of exchange rates and the present agricultural policies of the EEC are indeed incompatible, but finds that "this conclusion is not so much an argument against flexibility of exchange rates as against the present agricultural setup in the EEC, a setup that is, for many other reasons also, to be regarded as misconceived."

Thomas D. Willett and Edward Tower discuss "The Concept of Optimum Currency Areas and the Choice Between Fixed and Flexible Exchange Rates." They find that the concept is of considerable importance and tends to raise the level of discussions of fixed versus flexible exchange rates. Countries differ in downward flexibility of wages and prices, factor mobility, openness of their economies, and diversification. Disagreements concerning the relative desirability of fixed versus flexible exchange rates can frequently be traced to these differences. For instance, in the EEC, the economic ties between the members are such as to rule out both free rates and a full-fledged currency area, so that "a sliding parity might be the most efficient mechanism at this state of these countries' integration."

Probably the best additional source for discussion of historical experiences with greater flexibility of exchange rates is Leland B. Yeager's *International Monetary Relations* (New York: Harper and Row, 1966). The volume contains numerous references. References to more recent literature may be found in "The Empirical Evidence" in Egon Sohmen's *Flexible Exchange Rates,* revised edition (Chicago: University of Chicago Press, 1969), pp. 224–239. Several discussions of experiences with flexible rates, not cited by Yeager or Sohmen, may be of particular interest; they are: the discussion by Romulo Ferrero in *International Payments Problems* (Washington, American Enterprise Institute, 1965), pp. 94–99; Milton Friedman's discussion of Robert Z. Aliber's *Yale Economic Essay* "Speculation in the Foreign Exchanges: The European Experience, 1919–1926," Spring, 1962, in Milton Friedman and Robert V. Roosa, *The Balance of Payments: Free Versus Fixed Exchange Rates* (Washington, American Enterprise Institute, 1967), pp. 105–107; G. Hartley Mellish and Robert G. Hawkins, "The Stability of

Flexible Exchange Rates: The Canadian Experience," in *The Bulletin* of the Institute of Finance of New York University, Graduate School of Business Administration, No. 50–51, July 1968; William Poole, "The Stability of the Canadian Flexible Exchange Rate, 1950–1962," *Canadian Journal of Economics and Political Science,* May 1967.

· 41 ·

Canada's Experience with a Floating Exchange Rate, 1950-1962

DONALD B. MARSH

CANADA is not, of course, the first or only country to have a floating exchange rate. To cite only the outstanding examples, we have the famous "paper pound" of the Napoleonic period,[1] the Austrian gulden and the Russian rouble of the late nineteenth century,[2] the variously floating and manipulated rates of the 1930s and the floating-rate "concessions" granted from time to time by the IMF to underdeveloped countries in exchange difficulties. However, Canada is the first country, at least in the twentieth century, to embark on a floating rate from a position of strength, not weakness; and Canada is also the first country in this century in which the floating-rate system operated in the environment provided by a sophisticated, smoothly operating foreign-exchange market.[3]

A short history of this floating-rate period and of the events leading up to it is, I think, essential to an understanding of Canada's floating-rate system and to an evaluation of its implications for future policy.

Wartime Exchange Control

On September 16, 1939, Canada fixed her exchange rate under wartime exchange control at 110 (buying) and 111 (selling) in cents per U.S. dollar. Except for narrowing the spread to one-half on October 15, 1945, the exchange rate remained unchanged until July 5, 1946, when the authorities revalued the Canadian dollar to "par,"[4] or 100-100½ cents per U.S. dollar.[5] This led almost immediately to difficulties, and the Canadian dollar had to be supported in 1947 by import restrictions and exchange controls. With the 30 per cent devaluation of ster-

---

This chapter is an adaptation from Section II of my paper, "Canada's Experience with a Floating Exchange Rate," prepared for the Conference on the Foreign Exchange Market, sponsored by the University of Chicago Graduate School of Business, at Ditchley, England, March 17-20, 1967. I am indebted to Norman Heimlich who set up the appended tables.

[1] See Edwin Cannan, *The Paper Pound of 1797-1821* (London: P. S. King & Son Ltd., 1919).

[2] See Leland B. Yeager, "Fluctuating Exchange Rates in the Nineteenth Century," in Robert A. Mundell and Alexander K. Swoboda (eds.), *Monetary Problems of the International Economy* (Chicago: University of Chicago Press, 1969), pp. 61-89.

[3] The second country to float, under similar conditions, is, of course, West Germany, for a short period, September 30 to October 24, 1969.

[4] "Par," of course, is what you make it, but there is a special notional concept of parity with the U.S. dollar that means only one thing: $1 U.S. = $1 Canadian.

[5] Bank of Canada, *Statistical Summary*, Supplement 1965, p. 143.

ling, on September 18, 1949, the Canadian authorities felt themselves exposed to overwhelming pressure and, on September 30th, returned once more to the immediate postwar level of 110–110 1/2 cents per U.S. dollar. As it turned out, the Canadian devaluation of September 1949, undervalued the Canadian dollar. This was reflected in massive inflows of capital, largely in the form of U.S. dollar investment in Canadian government securities registered with the Foreign Exchange Control Board. Speculators had what they considered to be a one-way option. The Canadian dollar could move only in one direction—upward. Thus, in addition to interest income on their investment, they stood to make a sizeable capital gain owing to upward revaluation in United States funds of their Canadian dollar assets.

Since 110 Canadian dollars had to be raised by the Foreign Exchange Control Board to buy every $100 of U.S. dollar inflow, Canadian interest rates were subject to continuing upward pressure, the higher rates attracted still more interest-sensitive capital, thus creating a vicious circle. Previous experiments with the Fund's "adjustable-peg" system since the end of the war did not encourage the authorities to try once more to find the equilibrium level through revaluation. Instead, on September 30, 1950, the Canadian government abandoned its official rate and set the Canadian dollar free to find its own level in the exchange markets of the world.

The Era of the Floating Rate

The machinery of wartime exchange control continued in existence until 1952,[6] even though Canada had abandoned the fixed rate two years earlier.[7] However, the Foreign Exchange Control Board removed all remaining restrictions on dealings in exchange on December 14, 1951;[8] and the era of the "true" floating rate, free of direct or indirect government interference, began, therefore, on that date.

THE PERIOD OF ADJUSTMENT

The period of adjustment of Canada's undervalued dollar began with the initial freeing of the rate, announced on September 30, 1950, and may be said, rather arbitrarily, to have ended when the Canadian dollar finally rose to "parity" with the U.S. dollar on January 22, 1952. From that time on, with minor exceptions for fractional amounts, the U.S. dol-

---

[6] It was finally dismantled by The Currency Mint and Exchange Fund Act (proclaimed October 15, 1952), Part III.

[7] Perhaps this is another Canadian "first," a floating rate combined with exchange control!

[8] Foreign Exchange Control Board, *Annual Report to the Minister of Finance for the Year 1951*, Ottawa, May 1952, p. 17.

lar was at a discount in Montreal throughout the rest of the floating-rate period.[9] After the initial adjustment period, the floating rate fluctuated about 3 percentage points above and below the mean discount on U.S. funds.[10] This is the clearest evidence from Canadian experience that, contrary to the widely held view, floating rates are not necessarily widely fluctuating rates.

THE FLOATING RATE IN ACTION

Sometimes the very stability of the floating rate has been used as an argument against it because, it is alleged, the floating rate should move contra-cyclically in order to stabilize the economy.[11] The error here, I believe, lies in assuming that the floating rate is a policy variable. On the contrary, the main policy variable in achieving stability at a high level of employment is the appropriate mix of monetary and fiscal policies. The floating rate responds to a variety of forces, but, in general, it will be appropriately high during periods of inflationary pressure, provided that the mix of monetary and fiscal policy is appropriately restrictive. Similarly, the rate will be appropriately low in recession provided that the mix of monetary and fiscal policy is appropriately expansionist. The rate adapts to monetary and fiscal policy and overcomes balance-of-payments obstacles, which might otherwise inhibit policy, by keeping the economy at all times in a position of external balance.

For example, during the investment boom of 1955-1957, the floating rate was a strong ally of the Central Bank in its attempt to curb inflation. In spite of high interest rates in Canada, the authorities were not embarrassed by a large increase in exchange reserves as they were in 1950—instead, the capital flows pushed up the exchange rate. Imports were encouraged—exports, discouraged—not by an inflationary rise in Canadian prices, but by the effect of this higher exchange rate upon the prices and profits of international traders and investors. Since, under the floating rate, the government did not buy or sell exchange except for smoothing operations in the market, our foreign exchange reserves remained virtually flat over the whole period;[12] thus, we saw an excellent example of a floating exchange rate in action during the 1955-1957 investment boom.

---

[9] Strictly speaking, the floating-rate period ended with the "Baby Budget" of December 16, 1960, which announced tax measures discouraging capital inflow and ushered in an unannounced policy of government intervention in the exchange market.

[10] See Tables 1, 2, and 3, appended to this paper, for detail.

[11] This seems to be suggested in some of Professor Wonnacott's analysis. See Paul Wonnacott, *The Canadian Dollar* (Toronto: University of Toronto Press, 1965), Chapters 4 and 5.

[12] See Tables 4, 5, and 6, appended to this paper, for detail.

However, a period of slack in the economy occurred in 1957–1961 that called for an easing of monetary policy as compared with the tightness of the previous period. Instead, the monetary authorities continued their policy of monetary restraint even during this period of slack, overcapacity, and unemployment. This meant that inappropriately high interest rates in Canada attracted inappropriately large amounts of interest-sensitive capital, which, in turn, pushed the exchange rate to an inappropriately high level. Exports continued to be discouraged, and imports continued to be encouraged—when the state of the economy called for precisely the opposite policy. However, instead of reversing monetary policy, tight money continued, and the floating exchange rate was blamed for a set of conditions that really reflected only the ineptitude of the monetary authorities.

Decline and Fall

When, with a change in monetary management, the tight-money policy was finally reversed in mid-1961, this compulsive and baseless concern with the exchange rate induced the Minister of Finance to announce the government's intention of forcing down the external value of the Canadian dollar to a "significant [but undisclosed] discount." [13]

Even without this announcement, the Canadian dollar would have reacted to monetary ease by moving gradually and smoothly down to a point consistent with equilibrium under the monetary policy of the day; but the announcement of the government's intention to manipulate the rate by direct intervention so upset the market that the U.S. dollar, in Montreal, immediately rose to a "premium" of about 4 per cent over the Canadian dollar.[14]

Up to October 1961, this "premium" on U.S. funds seemed like an equilibrium rate. However, in October, the Canadian dollar showed embarrassing strength, so far as the government was concerned, when a speech by the Minister of Finance was interpreted to mean that the government was content with the existing 3 per cent premium on U.S. funds and would presumably withdraw from the market.[15] To keep the Canadian dollar from climbing back toward "parity" with the U.S. dollar, the authorities were forced to support the U.S. dollar by buying $186 million U.S., of which $50 million was bought in one day following the Minister's speech.

The Minister hastened to correct any misapprehension by announcing

---

[13] Canada: House of Commons, *Debates* (Ottawa, Queen's Printer, June 20, 1961), p. 6649.

[14] In the four months July to October inclusive, the premium on U.S. funds in Montreal reached a high of 4 per cent (in July) and a low of 3 per cent common to all four months. Bank of Canada, op. cit., Supplement 1963, p. 146.

[15] *The Gazette,* Montreal, October 27, 1961.

that the government intended to force the Canadian dollar down still further relative to the U.S. dollar. This final effort on the part of the government's open-mouth (or foot-in-mouth!) policy not only had the desired effect, but shook confidence in the Canadian dollar to such an extent that an attempted pegging at about 95 cents U.S., early in 1962, could be supported only by running down Canadian reserves of gold and U.S. dollars. A formal peg of 92½ cents U.S., filed with the IMF on May 2, 1962, proved also to be unsupportable.

Finally, after losing $1.1 billion in exchange reserves, and after an undue delay occasioned by a general election, the 92½ cent U.S. parity rate for the Canadian dollar (or Canadian 108. 108 cents per U.S. dollar in Montreal) was supported by an austerity program, announced on June 24, 1962, consisting of tight money, import surcharges, and foreign aid. These austerity measures soon proved effective and, by the fall of 1962, the Canadian dollar had achieved a buoyancy that it has maintained ever since.[16]

It is clear, therefore, that the decline and fall of the Canadian dollar in 1961–1962 was the result of government policy in 1961; and it is also clear that the unfortunate consequences of that policy occurred after the floating exchange-rate system of 1950–1960 had, with much fanfare, been completely abandoned by the authorities. Nevertheless, in the popular view, and even in the official view, the exchange crisis of 1962, in spite of all the evidence to the contrary, is usually considered to be the inevitable result of weaknesses inherent in a floating exchange-rate system!

Canada's ill-starred effort to engineer a devaluation in 1961–1962 was the first "1930s type" devaluation since World War II. The currency was under no threat from speculation in mid-1961. In fact, it took a great deal of exchange-rate manipulation and mismanagement before speculation became a destabilizing force (after October 1961). The effort to bring down the dollar by manipulation was a clear case of a beggar-my-neighbor attempt to increase home employment and cut the current-account deficit at the expense of our trading partners. Nevertheless (so compelling is the mystique of the fixed exchange rate!), our action was welcomed by the United States and the IMF. Canada was at last back in the fold!

---

[16] I am not, of course, unaware of the Canadian exchange crisis in the first quarter of 1968. The Canadian dollar was basically strong even during this period: speculation was based on a complete, and, in the event, costly, misreading of Canada's real economic position.

TABLE 1

Range Between the Lowest and Highest Canadian Exchange Rate,
1952–1960, Expressed as Percentage of the Yearly Average Rate
(Canadian Cents per U.S. Dollar)

Year [a]	High Spot Rate (1)	Low Spot Rate (2)	Range High-Low (3)	Annual Average [b] Noon-Spot Rate (4)	Range as % of Annual Average (5)
1952 [c]	100.00	95.88	4.12	97.41	4.23
1953	99.78	96.75	3.03	98.34	3.08
1954	98.75	96.34	2.41	97.32	2.48
1955	100.06	96.47	3.59	98.63	3.64
1956	99.97	95.66	4.31	98.41	4.38
1957	98.63	94.22	4.41	95.88	4.60
1958	99.16	95.75	3.41	97.06	3.51
1959	98.19	94.56	3.63	95.90	3.79
1960	99.81	94.94	4.87	96.97	5.02
1952–1960 period [d]	100.06	94.22	5.84	97.32	6.00
1952–1960 average [e]			3.75	97.32	3.85

Source: Figures are derived from data published in the Bank of Canada's *Statistical Summary Supplement,* issues of 1955–1962.

[a] For business days during year.
[b] Average of business days.
[c] March 1st to December 31st.
[d] The annual rates are not averages or monthly highs or lows, but the highest and the lowest rates recorded in the 1952–1960 period, beginning March 1, 1952.
[e] These are averages for the 1952–1960 period based on annual 12-month averages of highs and lows for each year. Only the 1952–1960 annual average noon-spot rate in column 4 and the high-low range in column 3, and the results in column 5 were computed. All other figures were given in the source.

TABLE 2

The Ten Months of the Widest Range of Fluctuation
in the Canadian Exchange Rate, 1952–1960

*Range Between Month's Highest and Lowest Quotation
Expressed as a Percentage of the Monthly Average*

May	1960	2.46
December	1960	2.35
February	1955	2.18
November	1952	2.18
March	1954	1.77
December	1957	1.76
July	1952	1.74
November	1956	1.59
September	1957	1.53
February	1953	1.47

Source: Figures derived from data published in Bank of Canada's *Statistical Summary Supplement,* issues of 1955–1962.

TABLE 3

Range Between the Lowest and Highest Canadian Rate for U.S. Dollars, Business Days, Within Each Month and Each Year, Expressed as Percentage of the Monthly and Yearly Average Rate, 1952–1960

Number of Months in which the High-Low Range Percentage was

Year	Between 0 & ½%	Between ½ & 1%	Between 1 & 1½%	Between 1½ & 2%	Over 2%	Average Range Within Months as % of Annual Average	Range Within the Year as % of Annual Average
1952 [a]	1	5	2	1	1 [b]	1.05	4.23
1953	3	6	3	—	—	.78	3.08
1954	4	6	1	1	—	.69	2.48
1955	5	4	2	—	1 [c]	.70	3.64
1956	3	7	1	1	—	.65	4.38
1957	4	3	3	2	—	.83	4.60
1958	2	7	3	—	—	.77	3.51
1959	2	8	2	—	—	.76	3.79
1960	2	5	3	—	2 [d]	1.10	5.02
Totals (No. of Months)	26	51	20	5	4	—	—
Averages	—	—	—	—	—	Within Months 0.81	Within Years 3.85
No. of Months as Percentage of the 106 Months in Period	24.53	48.11	18.87	4.72	3.77		

[a] March 1st to December 31st.
[b] November 1952, 2.18%.
[c] February 1955, 2.18%; (May 1960, 2.46%).
[d] December 1960, 2.35%.

TABLE 4

Range Between the Lowest and Highest Month-End Level of Canadian Official Holdings of Gold and U.S. Dollars Within the Years 1952–1960, Expressed as Percentage of the Yearly Average Rate, Millions of U.S. Dollars

Year	High Month-End Level (1)	Low Month-End Level (2)	Range High-Low (3)	Annual Average [a] Month-End Level (4)	Range as % of Annual Average (5)
1952 [b]	1,860.2	1,787.2	73.0	1,833.1	3.98
1953	1,866.8	1,750.1	116.7	1,801.8	6.48
1954	1,942.6	1,810.5	132.1	1,872.7	7.05
1955	1,938.3	1,840.0	98.3	1,902.3	5.17
1956	1,936.2	1,865.1	71.1	1,895.0	3.75
1957	1,973.0	1,828.3	144.7	1,916.9	7.55
1958	1,939.1	1,857.1	82.0	1,900.9	4.31
1959	1,938.3	1,863.0	75.3	1,902.4	3.96
1960	1,861.6	1,740.3	121.3	1,826.4	6.64
1952–1960 period [c]	1,973.0	1,740.3	232.7	1,872.4	12.43
1952–1960 average [d]			101.6	1,872.4	5.43

Source: Figures are derived from data published in the Bank of Canada's *Statistical Summary Supplement*, issues of 1955–1962.

[a] Average of month-ends.
[b] March 31st to December 31st.
[c] The annual rates are not averages, or month-end highs or lows, but the highest and lowest rates recorded in the 1952–1960 period, beginning March 31, 1952.
[d] These are averages for the 1952–1960 period based on annual 12-month averages of highs and lows for each year. Only the 1952–1960 annual average month-end level in column 4 and the high-low range in column 3, and the results in column 5 were computed. All other figures were given in the source.

TABLE 5

The Ten Month-Ends of the Widest Range of Fluctuation in the Level of Canadian Official Holdings of Gold and U.S. Dollars, 1952–1960

Month-End's Level Expressed as a Percentage of the Annual Average

May	1960	4.71
December	1957	4.62
December	1954	3.73
January	1953	3.61
April	1954	3.32
February	1955	3.28
July	1957	2.93
June	1960	2.87
June	1953	2.87
May	1954	2.70

Source: Figures derived from data published in Bank of Canada's *Statistical Summary Supplement,* issues of 1955–1962.

TABLE 6

Month-End Level of Canadian Official Holdings of Gold and U.S. Dollars, Within Each Year, Expressed as Percentage of the Yearly Average Rate, 1952–1960

Number of Months in which the Month-End Level Percentage was

Year	Between 0 & ½%	Between ½ & 1%	Between 1 & 1½%	Between 1½ & 2%	Between 2 & 2½%	Between 2½ & 3%	Over 3%	Range Within the Year as % of Annual Average
1952 [a]	2	2	4	1	—	1	—	3.98
1953	1	3	—	1	4	2	1 [b]	6.48
1954	—	1	3	2	2	2	2 [c]	7.05
1955	2	2	1	6	—	—	1 [d]	5.17
1956	3	5	1	2	1	—	—	3.75
1957	3	3	4	—	—	1	1 [e]	7.55
1958	1	2	4	2	3	—	—	4.31
1959	1	5	2	3	1	—	—	3.96
1960	2	4	1	3	—	1	1 [f]	6.64
Totals (No. of Months)	15	27	20	20	11	7	6	
Average	—	—	—	—	—	—	—	5.43
No. of Months as Percentage of the 106 Months in Period	14.15	25.47	18.87	18.87	10.38	6.60	5.66	

[a] March 31st to December 31st.
[b] January 1953, 3.61%; (April 1954, 3.32%).
[c] December 1954, 3.73%.
[d] February 1955, 3.28%.
[e] December 1957, 4.62%.
[f] May 1960, 4.71%.

· 42 ·

A Floating German Mark: An Essay in Speculative Economics

HERBERT GIERSCH AND WOLFGANG KASPER

Purpose and Major Conclusions

PROPONENTS of fixed parities frequently argue that greater flexibility of exchange rates would most probably end up in something near chaos. In order to investigate whether this fear is justified, it appears useful to discuss what might have happened, had a major industrial country adopted a floating rate:

What new difficulties might have arisen?

What policy conflicts would have disappeared?

What policy adjustments would have been necessary?

The case of West Germany suggests itself as a good example for such a speculative study on the grounds:

that the country has enjoyed stable political and economic conditions for over two decades,

that the German mark had a tendency to be undervalued, and that Germany could, therefore, have moved to some sort of flexible exchange rates from a position of strength rather than weakness, and

that, as a matter of fact, it had been suggested by the German Expert Council to the Federal Government early in the summer of 1964 to safeguard internal price-level stability more than temporarily by introducing flexible exchange rates.[1]

It will be assumed that, by mid-1964, only West Germany made its exchange rate flexible within a band of, say 10 per cent around a gliding parity of some sort. The subsequent considerations will suggest that the medium-term band-shift would have amounted to 2 per cent annually and that a minimum band width of 6 per cent would have sufficed. A somewhat wider band would, however, seem preferable, in order to avoid one-way speculation, which must be feared whenever the rate stays near the edge of the band.

---

[1] Reprinted in: Sachverständigenrat: Stabilität im Wachstum (Jahresgutachten 1967–68), Stuttgart-Mainz, 1967, Appendix II. See also the Expert Council's 1964 Report (StabilesGeld—StetigesWachstum, Jahresgutachten 1964–65, Stuttgart-Mainz, 1964, Paras 236–258 and Appendix IV, F. A. Lutz and E. Sohmen: Wie kann sich ein Land der importierten Inflation entziehen?)

Seen with the benefit of hindsight, mid-1964 may be considered the phase of the cycle best suited for the transition from a fixed to a floating mark:

> With the early phase of the upswing just left behind, business outlook would not have been upset excessively by the decontrol of the exchange rate.
>
> Internal demand had gained sufficient strength to reduce West German reliance on export demand.
>
> Compared to earlier and later phases of the cycle, the cost situation was relieved by big gains in productivity due to increasing capacity utilization. The wage push had not yet set in, and price expectations were, hence, not yet twisted upward.

In any other phase of the cycle, there might have been more reason to fear distortions in the demand structure owing to an alteration of the exchange-rate system; stronger expectations of price and wage increases might have stood in the way of internal price stabilization.

The Actual Background

Before showing what would probably have happened, it is necessary to sketch in short the actual course of events:

> Following its traditional cyclical pattern, the West German economy received strong stimuli from outside demand in the course of 1963. This started off a boom during 1964, which had its upper turning point in the first half of 1965. Afterwards, the utilization rate of the productive potential remained comparatively high through 1965.
>
> With wages lagging behind, productivity increases and demand-induced price increases led to a profit inflation in 1964–65, followed by a cost-push and a heavy profit squeeze in 1966, which led to the recession of 1966–67.
>
> Monetary restriction was ineffective during the 1964 export boom. The Bundesbank gained some space to maneuvre, after the so-called coupon tax on gains from German bonds held by foreigners was announced and later introduced, after the tax on bond issue by foreign lenders on the German market was abolished, and after a ban on interest payments to foreign depositors had been introduced. Monetary policy became fully effective only in late 1965 and early 1966, after the balance of payments had dipped into a sizeable deficit and the discount rate could be raised to 5 per cent.
>
> The subsequent recession brought the inflationary spiral to a halt and made the supply of export goods highly elastic with prices

much below world market levels, so that, as in 1963, a strong demand from outside helped to pull the economy out of the recession.

The pull of export demand was, however, still too small to restore a balance-of-payments equilibrium at the prerecession exchange rate.

The cost-of-living index had gone up, measured from trough to trough, at an annual rate of 3.2 per cent on average, a figure much too high for the goal of price level stability as interpreted by the German public, but still too low for the goal of balance of payments equilibrium (Fig. 42.1).

The Medium-Term Rate of Appreciation

Which medium-term rate of appreciation of the mark would have enabled the West German economy to achieve price level stability? An answer may be inferred from the following facts:

West Germany's main industrial trading partners, as a whole, had experienced a rise in consumer prices, from 1963 to 1968, of a little over 3 per cent, in export prices of a little less than 2 per cent, and in industrial labor unit costs of a little over 2 per cent.

If inflationary disturbances from abroad could have been neutralized by exchange-rate variations, internal socio-political conditions in West Germany (due to the experience of two hyperinflations within one generation and to a good stability record during the 1950s) would have permitted to achieve near-stability, i.e., 1 per cent in the medium term.

The gap of roughly 2 per cent between the internal price level objective and external prices could have been closed by a parity sliding upward with a medium-term trend of 2 per cent per annum.[2]

There is no reason to believe that a rate of appreciation of 2 per cent annually would have harmed the long-run competitive position of the West German economy. According to past experience with German cost behavior, aggregate labor unit costs in industry would have remained stable; interest rates and capital costs could have been lower due to the

---

[2] The 2 per cent rate of exchange-rate appreciation compares to a 2.5 per cent rate of revaluation incorporated in a proposal to introduce a (preannounced) parity slide, which the German Expert Council submitted to the Federal Government in the summer of 1966 (published in Sachverständigenrat: Expansion und Stabilität (Jahresgutachten 1966–67), Stuttgart-Mainz, 1966, Paras 268 to 274). The divergence between the ex-ante estimate of 1966 and the ex-post calculation seems only slight, particularly if one considers that the steeper trend was intended to exert some pressure against the price wave under way in 1966.

THE PERFORMANCE OF THE ECONOMY[1]

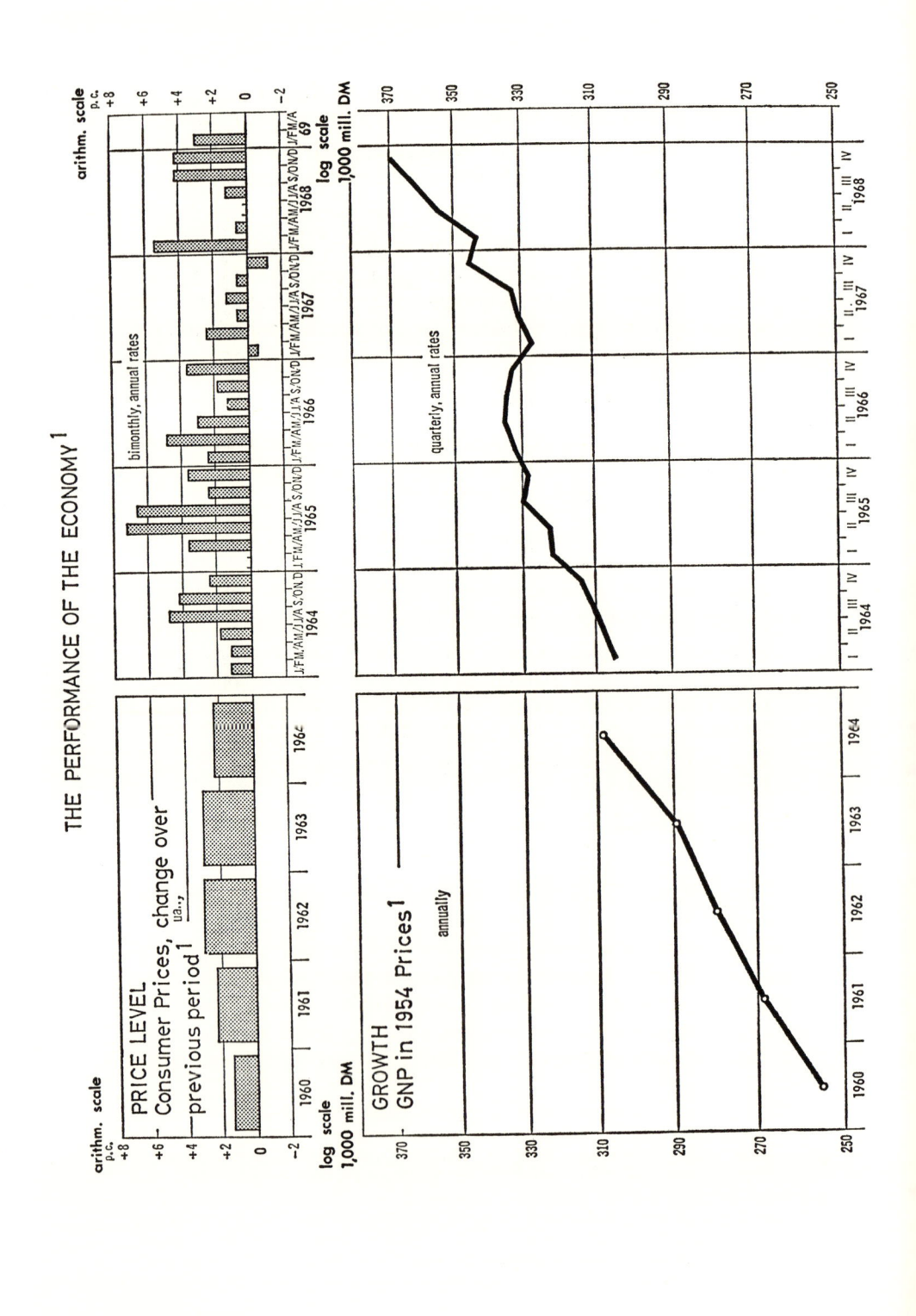

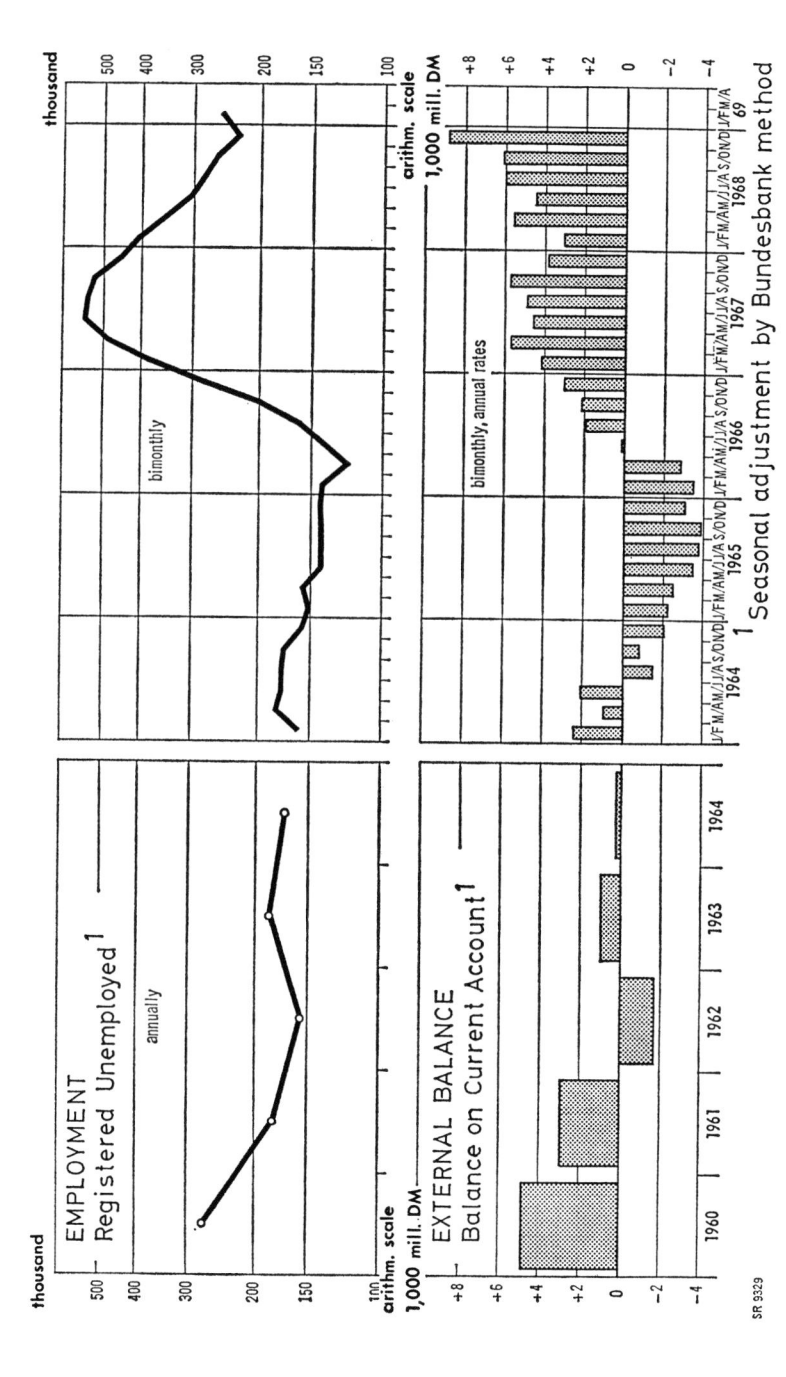

Fig. 42.1.

2 per cent parity slide and greater internal stability. Export prices in marks could have gone down a little due to the observed fact that productivity gains in the export industries is between 1 and 2 per cent above the productivity increase in the economy as a whole.

Cyclical Swings of the Exchange Rate

What cyclical swings of the exchange rate around this medium-term trend would have come about? Immediately after the transition, probably nothing dramatic would have happened, since the mark was, if at all, only slightly undervalued. The undervaluation that had prevailed in the late 1950s had been reduced by the 5 per cent revaluation of 1961 and by the sizeable inflation in 1962 and 1963 (cost-of-living index: +3.5 per cent in each of the two years). The thesis that the German economy was in the neighborhood of external equilibrium is backed by the observation that the balance of payments easily turned into deficit when internal investment demand began to replace export demand and when imports rose quickly in pace with the increasing pressure on internal resources. (This contrasts with the experience of sticky external surpluses during the steep internal upswing of 1968–1969.)

To ensure the success of the experiment, it appears essential that medium-term price expectations would be altered in the period of transition. An officially announced pledge that the Government was determined to follow, from then on, a fiscal and monetary policy geared to price-level stability would have seemed useful. And such an announcement could have been made in mid-1964 without the risk of killing the boom.

The adoption of a monetary policy of Friedmanesque lines—with increases in the volume of money equivalent to the growth rate of potential production plus 1 per cent for tolerable price increases and an adjustment for growing liquidity demand—would seem best suited to give the public a fixed medium-term standard of orientation. Alternatives could be (a) a wage standard based on an agreement with the trade unions to keep wage claims in line with productivity increases; or (b) a rule laid down in the Bundesbank Act that stipulated orientation of central bank policy at internal price stability and permitting the exchange rate to take care of the balance of payments.

During the first weeks after transition, temporary variations of short-term interest rates with the aim of avoiding hectic exchange-rate fluctuations, would possibly have been helpful. Whether permanent direct interventions in the foreign-exchange markets would have been advisable seems at least open to doubt, since the rules of a free-exchange market can probably best be learned if the market forces are left to work undisturbed.

Once the public had become confident that the price level could be expected to remain stable in the long run, the mark would have appreciated gradually during the second half of 1964 by more than the 2 per cent trend. This rise would have been reinforced by

the rise in export orders for German goods caused by the boom in world trade that started during the second half of 1964,

absence of (signs for) an immediate consumption boom, which has always been coupled with strong import demand, and

an inflow of capital invested in Germany, despite comparatively low interest rates, by people with a strong preference for price-level stability.

The German mark may, therefore, have appreciated during the autumn and winter of 1964 by 2 per cent, i.e. at an annual current rate of about 4 per cent. Forward rates would have been quoted at a premium that expressed the expected degree of price stability in West Germany relative to the rest of the world.

Smoothing the Boom

The effect of this appreciation of the mark would have been

to let export prices in marks fall slightly (whereas in reality they were pulled up at a 3 per cent annual rate during the second half of 1964),

to dampen the steep rise of DM import prices (which actually went up by 6 per cent) and, thus, to intensify internal price competition,

to put a mild brake to export demand (which actually accelerated until the spring of 1965),

to correct bullish expectations of investors (which actually led to an increase in investment of more than 15 per cent in the first half of 1965), and

to trim wage increases (which set in strongly in the autumn of 1964, after the wage drift had started going up by an exceptional 2½ per cent and after the metal workers' union had negotiated a 9 per cent pay rise).

The dampening effect on production would, however, have been only marginal. Assuming a short-run price elasticity of import demand and export supply of 1 [3] and some immediate effects on investment, domes-

---

[3] This value of a short-term price elasticity is suggested by past experience with stepwise parity changes (1961 DM revaluation; 1967 £ devaluation). It is, however, open to doubt whether it is at all permissible to make use of such data, since: conventional parity changes aim at correcting sizeable disequilibria, which would not arise with more flexibility; and interest rate effects could work unimpaired under a flexible rate to supplement the direct price effects due to exchange-rate variations.

tic production in the second half of 1964 might have been some DM 2,000 mill. (or 0.8 per cent of GNP) lower than otherwise.

During 1965 the demand pressure would have been somewhat less than it actually was. Monetary policy would have been restrictive with credit demand rising above the medium-term trend. A tendency of interest rates to rise would have come about. This would have worked to appreciate the exchange rate of the mark further and, hence, to back and supplement the restrictive effect of high interest rates. Had fiscal policy been as expansionary as it actually was before the elections in September 1965—income tax rates were cut, there was a public spending spree —interest rates would have gone up considerably, powerfully backed by a further upward movement of the exchange rate. But probably the fiscal boost of 1965 would not have come about to the same extent as it did, since taxes would not have come in quite as abundantly, and since parliament would probably not have been carried away by an economic euphoria.

Wages policy would probably have remained closer to the productivity line in 1965, in spite of a tight labor market (in reality nominal incomes per employee went up by 9 per cent, real incomes by 4.5 per cent). The trade unions would have demanded less, if government had made it clear, through the adoption of more flexible rates, that the danger of imported inflation was to be banned and that excessive wage claims would only produce unemployment. With more certainty about the future course of economic policy the employers' association and the trade unions would possibly have committed themselves in 1965, in a concerted action, to a stability-oriented incomes policy, which employers and unions had actually welcomed in 1965 and which did not come about, since the government refused to commit itself.[4]

For the exchange rate, all this would have meant that it appreciated at an annual rate of 4 per cent in early 1965, and that appreciation would have tapered off in the course of the year to something below the medium-term international inflation differential of 2 per cent, when business expectations became more moderate. A tendency to increase capital exports due to some fall-off in the prices of German shares might have worked in the same direction. With the easing of demand pressures, interest rates would have come down in the latter half of 1965. Forward marks might have even depreciated in the short run.

It is possible, however, that the price rise during 1965 would have somewhat exceeded the medium-term goal of 1 per cent, since the har-

---

[4] A stability-oriented incomes policy in a small country is doomed to fail if it is not shielded against inflationary pressures from outside. The Dutch postwar experience with an incomes policy, and its final fiasco, appears to demonstrate this.

vest was exceptionally poor. Such a price rise might have further contributed to reducing the rate of DM appreciation. It may be assumed that the rate of appreciation would have been about 1 per cent in late 1965 and during 1966. It seems, however, unlikely that the mark would have appreciated by less than that, since it became clear at the same time—mainly because of price developments in the United States—that world inflation was accelerating.

Avoiding the Recession

In the course of 1966, the slow rate of DM appreciation would have stimulated exports. Interest rates would have gone down and thus contributed to stabilizing the weak trend in investment both directly and through the effect on the exchange rate (whereas in reality the Bundesbank increased restrictive pressures as late as May 1966). There is no reason to assume that something like the recession of 1966–1967 would have occurred. What was actually lost during the recession ($12,500 mill. or almost 10 per cent of one year's potential GNP) was by far more than what would have been cut off during the boom in 1965 through the counter-cyclical DM appreciation and through an interest-rate policy that would not have been condemned to rest for a long time in a fixed-parity deadlock.

Over the five-year period from mid-1964 to mid-1969, the mark would have appreciated by about 10 per cent:

```
1964/II: + 2 per cent
1965   : + 3 per cent
1966   : + 1 per cent
1967   : + 1 per cent
1968   : + 2 per cent
1969/I  : + 1 per cent
```

The market exchange rate would never have come nearer the limit of a 10 per cent band than 2 percentage points (Fig. 42.2). The dollar would have been worth only about DM 3.60 (instead of DM 4.00) in the summer of 1969. The mark would have lost only 5 per cent in terms of internal purchasing power (instead of 13 per cent). A period of five years would probably have been enough to orient expectations around a fairly stable price trend, so that destabilizing speculation against the mark would no longer have to be feared. Interest-rate policy would have become freer to serve the task of flattening cyclical swings.

Possible Qualifications

One objection to what has been outlined above might be that some possible complications have been disregarded and that too wise an eco-

GREATER FLEXIBILITY OF EXCHANGE RATES

nomic policy is assumed. Of course, a series of policy blunders could wreck an economy with flexible rates as it could one with fixed exchange rates. But the exchange rate is certainly a more precise indicator of policy mistakes than changes in official reserves, which can be disguised and hidden from the public. Apart from this, the description of the assumed ideal policy was to serve one of the major purposes of this paper, namely to illustrate what policies would seem necessary to supplement greater exchange-rate flexibility. Another objection may be that our harmonious picture might have been harshly upset by some unforeseen exogenous disturbance.

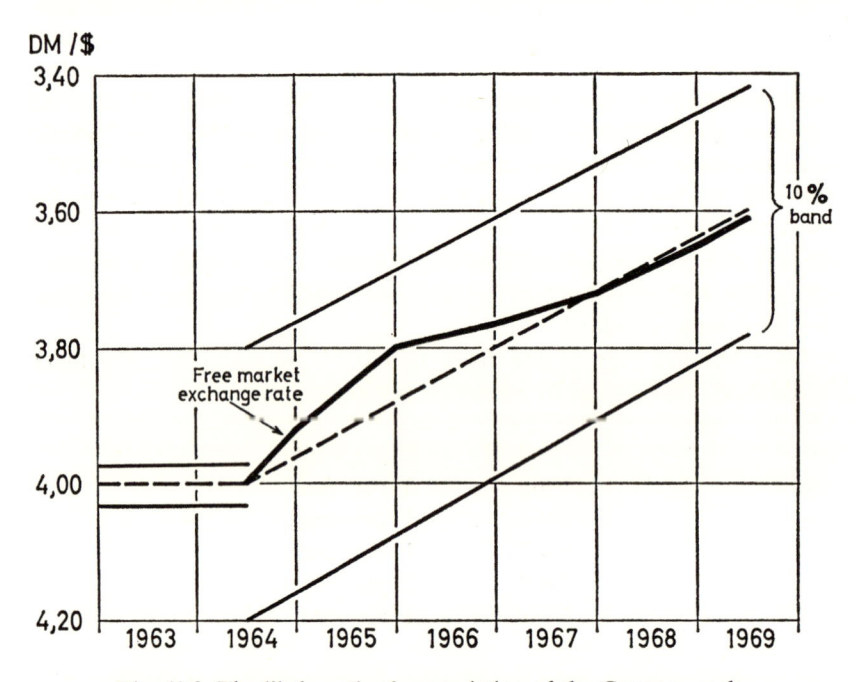

Fig. 42.2. The likely path of appreciation of the German mark.

For example, an overly expansionist fiscal policy in an election year like 1965 may possibly not be dismissed as easily as it was done above. But a band of 10 per cent would have left room for interest-rate and exchange-rate variations to overcome such an inflationary threat (as a last resort, the $7,500 mill. hoard of gold and foreign exchange that Germany had accumulated by mid-1964 would have permitted, if necessary, bidding the exchange rate up, in order to restrict exports and thus create room for a more stable internal expansion).

A devaluation like the one of the pound sterling in November 1967 might be considered another possible disturbance. However, one must first observe that the need to devalue the pound would have been less pressing, once Britain's main competitor had neutralized the consequences of a policy of internal stability through a gradual revaluation. But even a sizeable stepwise devaluation of the pound cannot be imagined to have upset the proper functioning of a more flexible mark: the shock of an abrupt sterling devaluation to the German economy would probably have been cushioned by a certain interim depreciation of the mark's rate. There would have been as much room as 5 percentage points for such a move at that time; German interest rates would have reacted, too. After a while it would have become clear anyway that the pound devaluation had had but little effect; the result would have been that the mark would have been written up more quickly in the foreign-exchange market. Similarly, the German economy could have been insulated against the consequences of the May events in France by an additional appreciation of the mark's rate.

A further disturbance one could imagine might have been a major crisis in Berlin. So far, no political crisis in Europe has brought the mark into serious difficulty. It can, therefore, hardly be assumed that this would be any different with the mark floating within limits. But even if a Berlin crisis acted to depreciate the mark, a certain "crisis discount" on the mark would be the most powerful medicine against a major exodus of capital. Another would be a short-term increase in the interest level.

None of those disturbances can be expected to affect the rate of return on capital invested in Germany by more than, for example, a wage increase, the actual devaluation of the pound in 1967, or the consequences of the quasirevaluation of the mark in November 1968. The hazards of a major crisis in the international monetary system and the reintroduction of controls on trade and payments would harm German export industry more. On the other hand, the combination of price stability with a high rate of growth—which seems possible under the socio-political conditions that prevail in the Federal Republic—would not only be an enormous welfare gain to West Germany. It would also be an instructive experiment, perhaps leading to imitation by other countries.

· 43 ·

Japan's Twenty-Year Experience with a Fixed Rate for the Yen

TADASHI IINO

THE exchange rate of the Japanese yen against the U.S. dollar was set at Y360 in April 1949, after a runaway inflation following World War II. This exchange parity has been maintained in all the years since then. In other words, after the war, Japan adjusted her economy properly on the basis of the par value of 360 yen to the dollar, and achieved a remarkable economic growth as well as a surplus in her international balance of payments. In the case of Japan, the fixed exchange parity, thus, has demonstrated itself to be a desirable system.

The following is a brief review of the circumstances leading to the establishment of the Y360 rate and the conditions under which the same rate has been maintained unchanged and stable.

Circumstances Surrounding the Establishment of the Y360 Rate

Japan's export and import transactions in the immediate postwar period were conducted exclusively through the medium of the General Headquarters of the Supreme Commander for the Allied Powers (GHQ) and the Board of Trade. A fixed rate for the yen did not exist. During and after 1947, the path for private trade was reopened gradually. In October 1948, the price-ratio system, fixing the exchange rates of the yen against the U.S. dollar on a commodity-classified basis, was adopted for settlement of trade accounts on the basis of *multiple* exchange rates. This system fixed the yen-dollar exchange rates individually for export-import commodities (ranging from Y37 to Y600). *The average exchange rate* under this system at the end of fiscal 1948 stood at Y340 to the dollar for export commodities and Y160 for import commodities.

On the other hand, during this period the domestic prices of commodities were officially fixed regardless of their production costs. This official price system was revised in July 1948, under a new formula aimed at stabilizing commodity prices at a level 110 times the prewar equivalents. When production costs of basic commodities were found to exceed such levels, a price difference subsidy was granted by the government to cover the excess costs.

Price control operations on the basis of governmental subsidies for exports and imports were conducted through the Trade Fund Special Account (the account handling yen currency receipts and payments based

357

on exports and imports as well as invisible transactions). Yen proceeds from American relief goods to Japan was the major source of the export encouragement subsidy.

On December 8, 1948, the GHQ announced the policy of "9 basic economic principles" for consolidating conditions for an early establishment of a single foreign-exchange rate. The policy aimed at making Japan economically independent on equal terms with other countries. In other words, the policy was designed to prepare Japan's domestic economic structure sufficiently for a single exchange rate.

On April 23, following the Diet approval of the fiscal 1949 budget, the General Headquarters issued a directive to the Japanese Government for establishing the yen exchange rate at Y360 to the U.S. dollar as of April 25. *GHQ did not reveal the reason for fixing the rate at Y360.*

The purchasing-power parity of Japan and the United States, calculated on the basis of the yen exchange rate in 1935 at Y3.50 to the dollar, with the advance of wholesale prices up to 1949 taken into account, is as follows:

$$Y3.5 \times 104.1 = Y364.35$$

The purchasing power of the yen in calculating the above Japan-United States purchasing-power parity was based on official prices, and such official prices were artificially supported by the price difference subsidy and the ration system. In other words, it is noted that the *yen was overvalued* at Y360 when commodity prices were evaluated at the level of prices in the free market.

It was under such circumstances that a disinflationary policy formulated by Joseph M. Dodge, American Minister to Japan, had to be used to exert acute deflationary pressure on the domestic economy in order to maintain the new single exchange rate.

Conditions Supporting the Maintenance of the Y360 Rate

Establishment of the Y360 exchange rate marked the prelude to the direct linking of the Japanese economy with the international economy after the war.

However, as the price difference subsidies, which offered a major prop to the official price structure at that time, were discontinued one after another, *it was not easy for Japan* to maintain the new exchange rate. To make the situation worse, in 1949 the United States began to suffer from the first business recession after the war, followed by a global business slump. As a result, the British pound sterling was devalued by 30.5 per cent in September 1949. Other countries followed suit by sharply devaluing their currencies. In December 1958, France devalued the franc by 17.55 per cent. More recently, Britain devalued the pound sterling again by 14.3 per cent in November, 1967.

In contrast, Japan has succeeded in maintaining the Y360 exchange rate of the yen unchanged for the past twenty years. At the same time, Japan's recent overall balance of payments has continued to register a sizeable surplus due to a large excess of receipts in visible trade and a brisk inflow of foreign capital.

How was the Y360 exchange rate maintained during the periods of postwar inflation and economic rehabilitation, and how was the value of the yen steadily enhanced in the process of Japan's rapid economic growth later? The following remarks refer to some specific factors that were responsible.

A DEFLATION POLICY BASED ON THE "DODGE LINE"

With the single exchange rate adopted for the yen, it became necessary for the Japanese economy to bear the brunt of acute deflation in order to adapt itself to the level of the exchange rate. Under the circumstances, enterprisers were required to streamline and rationalize management and the public had to bear the effects of an "austerity" policy. The government's program to squeeze domestic demand and earmark an increased portion of production for exports under the overbalanced budget in fiscal 1949 failed to materialize due to the international business slump.

As a result, monetary stringency for private enterprise grew. Unemployment increased due to corporate bankruptcies and management rationalization. Wage payments were delayed or became overdue. Consequently, the Japanese economy was plunged into an acute state of deflation. It must be said, however, that this was the inevitable consequence of the maintenance of an overvalued exchange rate.

AMERICAN ASSISTANCE TO JAPAN; THE KOREAN WAR

Japan's balance of payments in 1949, the year in which the single exchange rate was enforced, was extremely unfavorable. The balance of visible trade registered a deficit of $200 million, and the shipping and insurance accounts recorded an excess payment of $160 million. Thus, the balance of commodity and service transactions registered a deficit of over $300 million. However, receipts in the form of grants to the government (assistance to Japan from the United States) in the same year reached $530 million, more than enough to cancel out the deficit in commodity and service transactions.

Meanwhile, with the outbreak of the Korean War in June 1950 as the turning point, Japan's balance of payments began to improve rapidly. Due to the increase of exports in the wake of the war in Korea and purchases of war materials by the United Nations forces under overseas procurement contracts, the balance of commodity and service transactions in 1950 turned to the black to the extent of $50 million. As American assistance to Japan, amounting to $360 million, continued, the balance of payments in the same year registered a comfortable surplus. As a result, the United States discontinued assistance to Japan as of June 1951.

RIGOROUS EXCHANGE AND TRADE CONTROLS AND
THE GRADUAL CHANGEOVER TO LIBERALIZATION

GHQ continued to exercise overall controls on trade and exchange even after the establishment of the Y360 exchange rate.

Countries in Western Europe, which had completed their postwar economic rehabilitation programs earlier than Japan, started moves for trade liberalization. Convertibility of their currencies was restored, almost in unison, at the end of 1958. Japan followed suit by establishing the free yen account for nonresidents for partial liberalization of the yen exchange in July 1960. However, trade liberalization was deferred. Japan acquired the status of an Article VIII country under the Charter of the International Monetary Fund in April 1964, about three years later than the member countries in Western Europe.

Strict exchange and trade controls and the gradual changeover to liberalization, thus, indicate the relatively belated start of Japan's economic rehabilitation after the war, as contrasted with the recovery of Western Europe. However, it also may be said that *the timely and progressive schedule for liberalization* was one of the essential conditions for maintaining the Y360 exchange rate.

MANAGEMENT OF FISCAL AND MONETARY POLICIES

Japan's foreign trade expanded sharply due to the Korean War. However, following the United States's suspension of purchases of strategic goods in March 1951, the Japanese economy entered a period of an overall business slump. Besides, the government had to use fiscal and monetary policies to cope with inflation in progress since the outbreak of the Korean War, and the domestic economy was exposed to rapid deflation.

In its operation of fiscal and monetary policies since the end of the Korean War, the government has continued to repeat the same procedures alternately—stimulating economic growth as much as possible within the purview of the balance of payments, shifting to a tight money policy immediately when the balance of payments began to show signs of deteriorating, and slackening tight money when the balance took a turn toward improvement.

What was particularly noteworthy was the fact that such fiscal and monetary policies took quick effect in both phases, and the balance of payments turned favorable within a short period.

What enabled the tight money policy to take rapid effect, was *the excessively weak cash liquidity of private enterprises and the negligible fiscal burden of government debt* owing to the runaway inflation after World War II.

Due to a sharp increase of government bond issues before and during the war, the outstanding balance of government bonds at the end of the war reached a large total of Y118,400 million, consisting of Y117,500 million of domestic bonds and Y900 million ($442 million) of foreign currency bonds. The government's debts were almost equal to Japan's national income at that time.

The rapid rise of runaway inflation in Japan after the war, however, literally liquidated the huge amount of government bonds. With the outstanding balance of government bonds at the end of March 1946 indexed as 100, the comparable index at constant prices declined to 17 at the end of March 1949.

Flotation of government bonds was banned in principle under the provisions of the Finance Law enacted by the government in March 1947. Under the balanced budget in fiscal 1949, redemption of governmental debts was carried out. Postwar liquidation of government bonds thus made tangible progress.

Under these circumstances, the burden of the public debt on the Japanese economy has been extremely light as compared with the case of the United States and Britain. With the debt burden lightened by virtue of the postwar inflation it became *relatively easy for Japan to operate her monetary policy*. At the same time, *the effectiveness of monetary policy* was enhanced by the excessively weak cash liquidity on the part of private enterprise.

THE HIGH SAVING RATIO AND THE RAPID GROWTH
OF PRIVATE INVESTMENTS

The Japanese economy after the war thus achieved the highest possible growth permitted by the balance of payments. The principal factor giving support to the high economic growth was the rapid progress of capital accumulation, in particular the phenomenal expansion of investments in private plant and equipment.

Accumulation of capital at a swift pace has been made possible by *an extremely high level of personal propensity to save*. During the period from 1951 through 1959, the average saving ratio registered 15.1 per cent, surpassing the comparable ratio of West Germany at 13.5 per cent, the highest among Western countries. The saving ratio, which increased further since 1959, has been around 18–20 per cent.

New private investments in plant and equipment have served to strengthen sharply the international competitiveness of Japanese industries and to enable a large increase of exports. The rising tempo of private plant and equipment investments has been further accentuated since the end of a series of postwar economic rehabilitation programs. The ratio of such investments to the gross national product reached around 20 per cent in fiscal 1960–1962.

The progress of technological innovation based in part on foreign technologies and the increasing weight of heavy and chemical industries in Japan's economic structure were the two major factors contributing to the swift expansion of private plant and equipment investments. The latest incentive was the capital liberalization schedule enforced by the government in July 1967, which has stimulated further investments for streamlining equipment and expanding production.

The continuously brisk expansion of private plant and equipment investments over a long period after the war has propelled high economic growth, supported to a great extent by the large domestic market based upon the vast middle class of the nation. At the same time, the international competitiveness of Japanese industries has been swiftly bolstered as such investments have begun to bear fruit in the form of new production capacity. Exports, accordingly, have continued an energetic increase. The elasticity value of Japanese exports vis-a-vis world import trade has continued to stand high at 2 since 1960.

Stability of *wholesale prices* over a long period was one major factor responsible for the increase of Japanese exports at a pace faster than the gain of world trade. Comparing the price advance in Japan with that in other major countries in the West during the 15-year-period ending in 1968, Japan registered the highest increase of 78.6 per cent in *consumer prices,* or about double the comparable gain in the United States or West Germany. However, during the same period, the advance of the *wholesale price* index in Japan was restricted to 7.5 per cent, or about half, the comparable hike in West Germany. Japan's export prices were even more stable than its wholesale prices.

Several factors have worked to help maintain the stability of wholesale and export prices. In the first place, active plant and equipment investments at a rapid tempo, coupled with the progress of technological innovation, resulted in an increase of labor productivity exceeding the rise of wages. In the second place, the ratio of costs for imported raw and processed materials to total production costs has fallen gradually along with *the rise of heavy industrial and chemical products in the industrial structure.* As a result, the increase of imports has been kept at a level lower than the gain of exports. Accordingly, the increase of exports has begun to outstrip the gain of imports, resulting in the expanding surplus in visible trade to the eventual improvement of the overall balance of payments.

Conclusion

During the twenty years since the establishment of the Y360 exchange rate in April 1949, Japan has managed to adjust its economy on the basis of this fixed exchange rate. In the initial stage, Japan endeavored, and succeeded by its own efforts, to conquer runaway inflation after the war and to carry out its economic rehabilitation program, although the country in the interim was fortunate enough to receive American assistance and to benefit from offshore procurements in the wake of the Korean War. Ever since then, Japan has achieved a high economic growth without experiencing a destructive crisis in its balance of payments. Japan's economic structure, thus, has been greatly strengthened. In the process of its high economic growth during the 1960s, *the surplus in its visible trade* has increased steadily on the basis of a *sharp gain of exports and a modest hike of imports.* The balance of payments has continued to become more favorable.

In sum, the experience of the Japanese economy after the war is considered to have demonstrated the possibility and success of an attempt to adjust the domestic economy to a fixed-exchange parity.

Apart from the problem of the propriety of the Y360 exchange rate set twenty years ago, specific attention should be paid (1) to the success of the government in having managed fiscal and monetary operations in a manner suitable for the maintenance of the fixed exchange rate, (2) to the solidarity and discipline of the Japanese people, and (3) to their marked propensity for saving as well as their investments in new equipment. No system can be expected to function smoothly and efficiently in the absence of sound policy and discipline on the part of management.

· 44 ·

The Problem of Floating Exchange Rates from the Swiss Viewpoint

MAX IKLÉ

To A small country like Switzerland with a heavy volume of export trade, as well as a banking system closely tied to foreign money markets, with insurance companies operating internationally, and world-wide commercial and industrial firms and groups, a fluctuating rate of exchange, even within a range of, say, ±5 per cent, does not offer a workable solution. Countries with a small domestic market have to aim at the integration of their economies with those of other countries to the maximum extent possible. This integration is made more difficult by customs barriers and currency crises, just as it is facilitated by tariff reductions and stable exchange rates. Switzerland's interests are, therefore, closely tied to a stable rate of exchange, and our country is unlikely to permit any fluctuations of its currency. The considerations discussed below have been decisive in reaching this point of view.

EXPORT INDUSTRY

In making its calculations, it is not possible for the Swiss export industry to take account of currency risks in addition to normal commercial risks. Invoices are normally prepared in Swiss francs and, until now, our clientele has been willing to pay in Swiss francs, this currency having always been considered to be a stable one. If the Swiss franc were to begin fluctuating by ±5 per cent, with similar fluctuation ranges set in other countries, the customers of goods manufactured in Switzerland would demand that invoices be prepared in their own currency. This was clearly shown by what happened after the revaluation of the German mark in the spring of 1961. Believing that they might be faced with a further upvaluation of the mark, foreign customers were no longer willing to purchase German goods with German marks. They began asking for invoices made out in dollars or in their own currency. The German industry, being unable to incur the exchange risks involved, found itself obliged to engage in large forward sales of dollars. The German Bundesbank and the Federal Reserve Bank had to intervene vigorously on the forward market in order to prevent forward rates from collapsing.

In 1968, Swiss exports amounted to about 19 billion francs, or 25 per cent of the gross national product (GNP). In Belgium (36 per cent) and the Netherlands (32 per cent) the position is roughly the same. As a rule larger countries are less dependent on exports (France, for example, with 10 per cent, or the United States with 4 per cent).

Additional foreign currency supplied by the export industry on a forward basis would not be counterbalanced by corresponding demands from importers. Even at present, the latter are often obliged to pay in foreign currency. Importers whose position is very strong, and who have always been able to buy for Swiss francs, will undoubtedly be able to do so in the future. It would, therefore, be unrealistic to count on a new equilibrium developing on the forward market, especially inasmuch as the outflows of money at short notice will also have to be covered against exchange losses on the forward market and formerly found the counterparties among the importers. Even at present the Swiss forward market shows 35 billion in sales as compared with 30 billion in purchases. The German example does, in fact, show that the additional foreign currency supplied by the export sector was not compensated by corresponding demand from the import trade. This was precisely the reason for which the Bundesbank was forced to take the aforementioned support action.

TRANSIT TRADE

Floating rates of exchange would have a particularly negative effect on the transit trade, where profit margins are extremely low, especially in raw materials and groceries. In the case of some transactions, foreign exchange hedging costs of only a few per cent per annum make a major difference.

INSURANCE INDUSTRY

The Swiss insurance companies also operate with relatively low margins of profit. They have been able to build up international business only on the basis of a stable currency. A ± 5 per cent difference in the exchange rate would have very damaging effects on the insurance business.

INTERNATIONAL MONEY MARKET

The international money market, in particular, would react sensitively to a floating rate of exchange. A total of 30 billion francs (34 billion francs in the form of assets and 28 billion francs in the form of liabilities) links Swiss banks to both the Euromarket and other money markets. To a large extent the sums involved are one- to six-month loans that are secured against foreign-exchange losses. Nothing would be solved if these loans were made in the other currency because the burden of hedging costs would then merely devolve on the other party. If no other risks have to be taken into consideration, short-term financial transactions develop a swap-rate, reflecting the difference between the interest rates on the money markets involved. With a system of flexible rates of exchange, the exchange risk would be reflected in the swap-rate. Costs for the swap-operations would have to go up with correspondingly harmful effects on short-term investments. We had some experience of this kind in 1961, when, at times, swap-costs were as high as the money-market rates on the Euromarket, bringing short-term export of money to a complete standstill. We can barely gauge the effects of a fluctuating rate of exchange on the Euromarket. Presumably it would have to collapse, setting off a chain reaction of credit calls. This brings to mind conditions at the beginning of the 1930s, when Germany and Austria cancelled short-term loans. A collapse on the Euromarket with loans totaling roughly $30 billion might have similar effects. No one who has studied the history of the depression in the 1930s, and who knows conditions on the Euromarket, would wish to shoulder the responsibility of causing the collapse of this market by introducing flexible rates of exchange.

The countries whose currencies are considered to be weak would be the ones to suffer most from a floating exchange rate. Such a system would be especially devastating for Great Britain, a borrower on the Euromarket, whose banks, insurance companies, and international trading firms, just like their Swiss counterparts, have to earn the invisibles to offset the deficit in the trade balance. Financial centers can exist only in countries with a stable rate of exchange.

INDUSTRIAL COUNTRIES

If we have understood it right, the doctrine advocating flexible rates of exchange is based on the idea that the deficits and surpluses in the basic balance of payments are reflected in the rate of exchange. It is a fundamental assumption that the exchange rate falls whenever a country has a deficit, thereby increasing the country's ability to compete commercially and facilitating compensation of the balance of payments. In countries with a big surplus, a rise in the rate of exchange will have the opposite effect. This theory may, indeed, apply to primitive countries whose goods move only across the borders. Totally different forces are at work, however, in highly industrialized countries, such as those belonging to the "Group of Ten." With today's integration of all money markets, due to the existence of the Euromarket, the situation on the home money market is the main factor determining the rate of exchange. In Switzerland, the country most closely linked to foreign money markets, the rate of exchange is *determined exclusively by the state of the domestic money market.* If there is a great deal of liquidity on the money market, short- and long-term capital is poured into foreign countries. Whenever there is a shortage, the money is repatriated. In the first instance the exchange rate of the Swiss franc falls; in the second, it rises irrespective of the state of the balance on current accounts at that particular time. In other words, the basic payments balance is completely overshadowed by the operations on the international money market.

For all those who are familiar with the Swiss economy, there is no doubt that Switzerland cannot permit its currency to fluctuate. The consensus is that Switzerland owes its prosperity largely to a stable parity. In the past 120 years the Swiss franc has been devalued only once, and this happened in 1936, after all other currencies had been devalued. Never once since 1936 did Switzerland's stable currency rate affect the economy negatively. Quite on the contrary, it has been the very basis for the development of foreign trade, banking, and the insurance business. World trade could never have expanded as much as it has since 1959, unless the most important countries had maintained convertible currencies with a stable rate of exchange. A concomitant of international trade has been a far-reaching division of labor along with increased productivity, from which the smaller countries were not the last to benefit.

Not unlike the dollar parity, the parity of the Swiss franc is laid down by law. Only parliament and not the government can change this law. But it would be difficult to conceive that any Swiss parliament elected in the coming decades would allow itself to be convinced of the advantages of a floating exchange rate.

In Switzerland currency is not considered a commodity, which follows the law of demand and supply, but a *yardstick*. The German word for currency *Währung* is derived from the word *währen*, which means to last. Nobody would have much understanding for a currency subject to daily fluctuations.

On the other hand, stability is only a relative concept. In the event that all currencies should begin to fluctuate, even a stable currency would become a flexible one in relation to the others. In order to predict what policy might be followed by national monetary authorities in case the present system were to be replaced by a flexible rate of exchange, one has to proceed on the basis of certain assumptions.

POSSIBILITY NUMBER 1

Members of the International Monetary Fund are released from their obligation to keep exchange rates within a spread of ±1 per cent, while the *dollar* would *preserve* its *gold convertibility* on the same basis as the present one.

A system of this kind would make it possible for the Swiss franc to preserve its dollar ratio, which corresponds to a gold price of $35 per ounce. It would also mean that the present flexibility range of 1¾ per cent would be kept, though it would become legally possible to extend it to 2 per cent, as in the days of the pure gold standard. In this case the upper intervention limit for the Swiss franc would be set at $4.2850 as compared to the present rate of $4.2950. In actual fact, the Swiss franc would undoubtedly continue to fluctuate with a margin of 1 per cent.

The countries of the Common Market cannot tolerate fluctuating currencies vis-a-vis each other, as such fluctuating would constitute an obstacle to further integration. The stability of their exchange rates is best preserved, therefore, by means of buying and selling the key currency. As a result, we may assume that the Common Market countries will stick to their present policy without making use of the right to employ flexible exchange rates. At least this is what would be considered desirable from the Swiss point of view.

Inside EFTA, Switzerland would most likely exert all the influence at her disposal to induce member countries to keep their currencies at a stable rate of exchange also. On the other hand, it is quite conceivable that the present British Government would seek its salvation in a flexible exchange rate, although the effects of such action on the City would necessarily have to be very damaging indeed. The pound sterling would lose its character as an international currency. Countries of the sterling area would recall even greater amounts of money from England, thus weakening the financial position of the City of London.

Even if the Scandinavian countries were to follow Britain's example, Switzerland would keep her fixed exchange rate in the hope that sooner or later her EFTA partners would return to stable currency practices.

POSSIBILITY NUMBER 2

If the United States were *to abolish the convertibility of the dollar into gold* under a system of floating exchange rates, a situation of such gravity would develop that it would be quite difficult to foresee the consequences and to anticipate the measures that governments might take. A step in this direction would be tantamount to the *collapse of the existing monetary system*. The western world would lose its present key currency. There would no longer be an official price for gold, only a free-market price. The Swiss franc, whose parity is based on the existing official price of gold, would lose its standard. Currency convertibility, at present brought about by exchanging foreign currencies against dollars, would become increasingly difficult. Non-American countries would be faced with the alternative of either joining a dollar bloc of nations, or of building up their own monetary system.

Joining the dollar bloc would be equivalent to giving up sovereignty in monetary matters. In the field of monetary policy the countries belonging to the dollar bloc would find themselves in a state of complete dependency vis-a-vis the United States. An inflationary policy on the part of the United States would automatically extend to the other countries in the dollar bloc. If the United States were to have a deficit in its balance of payments, these countries would have to accumulate dollar reserves without being able to convert them. In this case the objection raised even today, according to which key currency countries enjoy undue privileges, would, indeed, be justified.

The convertibility of the dollar into gold is rooted in the Agreement of Bretton Woods. It would be extremely difficult to conceive of any United States Government that would break this agreement and, thus, confront the rest of the world with the kind of alternative outlined above. If this fateful step were to be taken nonetheless, it is to be feared that the western world would be split into two blocs from the point of view of monetary policy, that is, a dollar bloc and a gold bloc. The dollar bloc would probably be joined by the countries of the Americas, as well as a number of countries that are dependent on American aid, and where the dollar is the standard even now. For political and monetary reasons, the European countries would not be able to join a dollar bloc, as they cannot simply give up their national sovereignty in the realm of monetary policy. Most likely they would set up a gold bloc, although at present no one has any clear conception as to how it would function. Most probably the countries belonging to such a gold bloc would introduce fixed rates of exchange.

Even if a solution could be found to the problems within the gold bloc, further difficulties resulting from relations between the gold and the dollar blocs would be bound to arise. It would be going beyond the scope of this paper, if I tried to outline all the problems that might present themselves. They would be so numerous that all one can do is to hope that the western world will never be confronted with such a decision.

If two monetary blocs were to be formed—of which one were to have gold and the other the dollar as a standard—Switzerland would most probably join the gold bloc, in spite of the disadvantages involved.

· 45 ·

Balance-of-Payments and Exchange-Rate Problems in Sweden, Denmark, and Finland

ERIK LUNDBERG AND ÅKE LUNDGREN

THE common feature of these countries is their close dependence on foreign trade. The present value of their imports as a percentage of GNP may be taken as a rough indicator: Denmark 30 per cent, Finland 20 per cent, Sweden 25 per cent. The volume of imports tends to rise more rapidly than real GNP—both in the short run during the expansionary phase of the cycle and in the longer run. Measurements of import-propensities and elasticities are apt to be hazardous for a number of reasons. But the order of size of the longer-run import-elasticities (with regard to real GNP) varies between 1.5 and 2.

There is a great variability of the elasticities in the short run. But in the later phases of the boom, there is a tendency of imports to rise relatively more rapidly (in relation to GNP). However, this tendency is frequently disturbed by policy restrictions—mostly determined by actual or potential balance-of-payments disturbances.

The volume of exports, as well as the other items in the balance of payments, will not automatically develop in such ways that an equilibrium in the balance-of-payments position is reached or maintained. To what extent and how the payment problems are managed is our problem. In this respect the three countries are quite different. (In fact, we have here different cases of the problem of imbalances of payments, which illustrate rather well how varied may be the problem of exchange-rate policy.)

Sweden has had hardly any actual balance-of-payments troubles since 1947, when a serious crisis occurred following the appreciation of the Swedish crown in 1946. However, fixed exchange rates (to the dollar) have implied a development pattern in partial conflict with the targets for the internal economy.

Denmark repeatedly had foreign-exchange difficulties that implied serious economic disturbances and internal policy restrictions.

Finland had the experience of strong waves of inflation followed by balance-of-payments disequilibria, which have been solved by big, discontinuous devaluations of the Finnish mark.

In all three cases we may ask if and how alternative exchange-rate policies might have given better development results or more stability. According to our view, the foreign-exchange policy must be studied in close relationship to connected issues of short- and long-run economic development and corresponding policy questions. The exchange-rate problem cannot be treated in isolation. It is our purpose in this survey to demonstrate how closely the balance-of-payments problems, and, therefore, the question of an exchange-rate policy, are interconnected in these small countries, with income and employment targets in particular.

It might make sense to start with Sweden. Some issues common to all three countries can best be presented against the Swedish background. It is in a way more difficult and challenging to explain why *no* severe foreign-exchange troubles have appeared over a twenty-year-period with fixed exchange rates (to the dollar) than to account for repeated exchange crises (as in Denmark and Finland).

Sweden

SOME GENERAL FEATURES

The absence of serious balance-of-payments disturbances has been a favorable conclusion to the relatively stable and rapid growth of the Swedish national product. Despite the fact that Sweden has experienced periods of strong inflationary expansion over the past twenty-two years, with the economic balance being significantly upset in other respects, it has still been possible to maintain external equilibrium. It is remarkable that Swedish exports and imports have been increasing at such an equal pace over the years that the relatively low but stable foreign-exchange reserves (corresponding to about three months' imports) have been more than adequate to cover the balance-of-payments deficits that have actually arisen. During the majority of the postwar years, foreign-exchange reserves have grown at roughly the same rate as imports. No long-term change in the terms of trade has taken place during the postwar period. A fact particularly worth noting is that the growth rates for the volume of export and import kept pace with one another during shorter periods also. The acceleration of the growth rate, which took place after 1959, has thus affected both series to roughly the same extent. This is not the result of controls. Since 1952 imports into Sweden have in the main been unrestricted; no controls of any importance have impeded the free development of imports, either long-range or during cyclical fluctuations. We find that the income elasticity of imports has been around 1.7 over the whole period.

One can, however, discern a slight trend in the development of the balance of payments on current account: the years 1949–1953 witnessed surpluses of, on an average, 6 per cent, but varying between 2 and 11 per cent, of the value of imports. Since then it has mainly been a question of smaller deficits, averaging 2 per cent and reaching a maximum in 1965 of 5 per cent. The effect of these deficits on exchange reserves has been largely neutralized by the growing relative values of the residual in the accounts. Another question has to do with cyclical variations. The balance on current account tends to weaken during the more extreme boom years: 1947, 1950, 1955, 1960, 1965. In these years, steep increases in total demand, leading to excess demand in the labor market, have resulted in such a marked growth of imports as to weaken the balance of current payments. During the major part of the period, however, these setbacks were so relatively insignificant that there was no question of serious balance-of-payments strains. Their impact on foreign-exchange reserves was practically negligible. This harmonious pattern of development is bound up with the import of capital that has been a consequence of the relatively restrictive credit policy pursued in Sweden during the inflationary boom periods.

One way of interpreting the long-term, very slow deterioration of Sweden's balance-of-payments situation is to put emphasis on *the inflexible exchange-rate policy* since 1949. The devaluation in 1949 (when the crown followed the pound sterling) was clearly much too big. In the Korean boom, profits of the export industries were excessive, and there was a large balance-of-payments surplus. At that time arguments were raised for *an appreciation of the crown,* but the bad experience of the 1946 appreciation militated against this. Instead, a wage explosion followed (wages per hour rose by about 20 per cent per year in 1951 and 1952) that did not apparently eliminate the undervaluation of the crown as the wage and price inflation in Sweden continued to be relatively strong during the 1950s without causing the balance-of-payments deficits. There remained a leeway in the international accounts for this inflation. The inflation development during the 1950s may be taken as *a kind of equilibrating process* following upon the excessive devaluation of 1949. During this period the government budget deficit was large and business profits were relatively high.

The long-term development of the 1960s is more interesting and complicated from the point of view of exchange-rate policy. The elbow room has become narrow—given price and cost development in foreign markets. In fact, after 1965, there appeared an actual balance-of-payments restriction on the expansive tendency of government policy. Ambitions as to full employment had been brought down slightly (with an increase in the unemployment rate by about ½ per cent) during 1966–1968, and the main reason for this was a more vulnerable foreign-exchange position.

THE POLICY MODEL

The emphasis in the discussion of stabilization policy is focused on the issue of wage-cost development. The policy model currently used gives emphasis to the *dual character* of the economy. At given exchange rates—and given developments in other countries—the prices of export and import goods have been rising by 1 to 2 per cent per year during the 1960s. The sector of the Swedish economy (calculated to correspond to about one-third of the economy) that is directly exposed to world market competition (on the export and import sides) has to adjust to this "given" price development. As production per man hour in this sector has been increasing by 7.5 per cent per year, there has been scope for a yearly rise of about 8.5–9 per cent in hourly wages (and salaries).

From a narrow point of view, such a wage-cost rise may be taken as a "quasi equilibrium" condition. At given exchange rates, a lower rate of wage increase than this would, *ceteris paribus,* have involved profit inflation and a demand disturbance consequent upon it. This equilibrium development would also fit rather well, but not quite, into the condition of a balanced labor market. The full-employment policy pursued by the government—with unemployment in the range of 1–1.5 per cent—has been accompanied by an average growth rate for hourly wage costs varying between 8 and 11 per cent annually. It looks as though a Phillips curve, which expresses the statistical relationship between the labor-market situation and the rate of wage increases, quite accurately reflects the situation in both the 1950s and 1960s. Total hourly wage costs (in industry) thus tended to rise by 9–10 per cent during years of full employment; it does not look as though the active labor-market policy carried out by the government in the 1960s has been able to modify this kind of relationship significantly. It is only during the recession years of 1953, 1958–1959, 1967–1968—with unemployment close to 2.5 per cent—that the rate of wage-cost increase has been dampened to around 6–7 per cent.

The average rate of wage-cost rise (per hour) during the 1960s (9.5 per cent per year) has, however, been a little too high from the point of view of unchanged distribution between gross profits and wages. There has been a certain squeeze of profit margins within this sector working under international competition. At the same time, of course, a substantial rise of prices has occurred in the protected sectors of the economy (building, private and public services, etc.) where the rise of productivity also is much slower than in the goods sectors under foreign competition. The total result was a rise in the GNP deflator of about 4 per cent per year.

SOME CONCLUSIONS AS TO EXCHANGE RATES

The simplest way to start a discussion about how and to what extent more flexible exchange rates might have improved the development is to try to imagine the effects of other exchange-rate conditions. It is, in any case, the beginning of an analysis. We have already concluded that the Swedish crown was devalued too much in 1949; or, rather, that the crown should have been appreciated substantially at the beginning of the Korean boom. This is easy to say when looking at the ex-post results of keeping the rates fixed. When the problem was discussed in 1950–1951, the situation was complicated by the fact that the boom and the price rise were very unevenly distributed. A substantial appreciation would have struck important sectors of industry severely. From that point of view, a complicated system of export taxes and import subsidies was preferred, to be successively abolished after 1951.

Exchange-rate problems appear in a new guise with the new development trends of the 1960s. It is easy to argue that fixed exchange rates under given conditions of inflation in other countries must imply a corresponding rate of inflation in Sweden. A yearly appreciation of the Swedish crown would have been a necessary, but insufficient, condition for a stable (or more stable) price level. A strongly deflationary internal policy, with a substantial rate of unemployment, would have been needed to support such a policy. This is from a political point of view a completely unrealistic alternative.

A more realistic setting of the problem would be to take the full-employment policy for granted and to ask for the ultimate consequences of too high a level and too rapid a rise of wage costs (in Sweden in relation to other relevant countries). It has repeatedly been maintained (especially from the side of Swedish export industries and industries under heavy import competition) that Sweden's competitive position (with total wage cost per hour about 50 per cent above the Western European average level and rising more rapidly) is weak and getting successively worse. Leading economists and the Government Economic Research Institute have repeatedly warned of a coming exchange crisis as a result of too high demand pressure along with too rapidly rising wage costs.

It is of some interest, for an understanding of the exchange-rate problem, to mention the main factors that explain why Sweden has so far (up to the beginning of 1969) not had the balance-of-payments troubles it has deserved. The main explanation seems to be the remarkable boost in industrial productivity during the 1960s (the rate of rise being about half again as high in the 1950s). This result should partly be seen as an outcome of the increased pressure of competition. Under the pressure of *given* world market prices (rising very slowly and in several branches falling) and rapidly increasing wage costs, firms have been forced to become more efficient. The inflationary years of the 1950s may have implied waste and inefficiency that could be eliminated when the challenge came. One condition for the survival of corporations has been to increase their share in export markets (the home market mostly being too limited). The incentives as well as opportunities to raise productivity, offer competitive prices, introduce new products, and explore new markets apparently have been strong enough for a sufficient number of firms to save the situation. One very important aspect of this process has been a structural reorganization of industrial branches. In fact, the rapid rise in productivity during the 1960s has, in large measure, been the result of closing inefficient firms and production units, radically restructuring production and sales, dismissing workers and transferring labor to other units and areas, and so forth. The steep upswing in wage costs has, without any doubt, helped to accelerate this process.

As mentioned above, there have been some short-term pressures on the balance of payments during the 1960s. A substantial deficit appeared in 1965 and again in 1967–1968. An inflow of short-term capital has worked as an equilibrating mechanism—a function of the relatively restrictive credit policy that the Riksbank has been pursuing during booms, making exporters and importers shift the financing of trade from home to foreign sources. One result is, of course, that Swedish credit conditions and interest rates had to be pushed up in accordance with the conditions in other countries. Certainly, there is no given harmony between the credit policies dictated by monetary policies in other countries (and the Eurodollar market) and the needs with reference to internal balance. This potential conflict did not become a serious actual problem during the 1960s up to 1966. Only to some extent during 1967–1968 was this the case, when, as mentioned above, economic policy was somewhat more restrictive than would correspond to the full-employment target.

COULD MORE FLEXIBLE EXCHANGE RATES HAVE IMPROVED THE CONDITIONS OF THE 1960s?

From the above description of the developments, one *could* draw the conclusion that the Swedish crown has been fixed close to an *equilibrium position* during the 1960s. The argument for a change of parity during the period is not strong—anyhow not as compared with the apparent needs of other countries (such as Finland and Denmark). Such a conclusion implies a realistic disregard of a need for successive appreciation in order to eliminate price inflation, on the grounds presented above. Given the full-employment targets, as well as the system of free collective wage bargaining, there is a built-in revealed preference in Sweden for a certain amount of inflation in order to attain other more important aims. But, of course, there are no strict rules. A more restrictive policy setup could have implied a movement to the right on a Phillips curve—and have been followed by, say, only 6–7 per cent increase in yearly wage cost. A rising tolerance in this direction might be the consequence of an unemployment policy that becomes progressively more humane so that, for instance, the unemployed get better stipends while training for new jobs. This possibility has become a fact during 1967–1968, under the pressure of existing exchange-rate parities.

A specific Swedish line in policy-thinking should be mentioned at this point. The squeeze of business profits during the 1960s, being a result of the pressure of rising labor costs at given prices and exchange rates, is not only a government target as such (from the viewpoint of income and wealth distribution), but is also an element of an ambitious type of *selective* fiscal and credit policy. A lower degree of self-financing within private industry and a relatively high frequency of closing-down of firms, gives room and power to the government for actively directing investments in preferred channels (by means of government financing and subsidies of various kinds). Obviously there are rather close limits to this type of selective policy. But there is in Sweden a clear trend in this direction, and exchange rates fixed at the "squeezing point" give a good basis for this type of selective policy.

It is, however, quite reasonable to question the notion that the exchange rates of 1949 should be regarded as equilibrium rates during the 1960s. What would have been the result of more flexible rates eventually finding their own levels during the periods of disequilibrium? With apprehensions that the Swedish crown was overvalued during boom years, it is probable that a system of flexible rates would have resulted in repeated depreciations (1960, 1965–1966, 1968–1969) whose size and cumulative nature, however, remain open questions that cannot be answered. It is easier to see that the consequences, in the form of higher profit in export industries, a more rapid rise of prices, less need for restrictive policies, and lower average unemployment rates, would have "justified" the depreciations. Less pressure for a rise in productivity and less structural change might have worked in the same direction.

This type of guesswork is certainly not worth much—except as a setting for policy problems. It is, however, also possible to *imagine* a more successful policy where the Riksbank actively uses the flexible exchange rate as a *policy parameter*. We can, with some difficulty, imagine that the Riksbank could have used flexibility of exchange rates within a band to carry out a smoother monetary policy. Instead of raising interest rates so much and rather abruptly at the end of the booms it could, under these conditions, have let the crown rate depreciate toward the lower end of the band, managed forward rates so as to create the right expectations, let speculative reserves flow in to cover the rising deficit, and let this process continue (at a possibly stronger rate) after the turn of the boom until a new revival is started. Then let a crown appreciation moderate the start of a new boom.

Certainly we can imagine a policy where the band is skillfully used for first moderating the start and dampening the first stage of the boom and then prolonging it and giving elbow room for a more expansionary policy during the recession. The depreciation and consequent expectation of appreciation of the crown would make it possible to moderate interest-rate fluctuations. Of course, there would be great practical difficulties in realizing the potentials of the *greater autonomy* that the Riksbank would have when managing the exchange rate within a wider band. If possible, the management should mean actual interference in the market by the Riksbank only around the limits of the band. We, thus, consider it quite reasonable to argue for a wider band as an important condition for the improvement of a stabilization policy in Sweden.

Denmark

GENERAL SURVEY

The Danish balance-of-payments situation has developed in a very different way from that in Sweden. It can be said that there has been a more or less fundamental payments disequilibrium at the exchange rates prevailing during most of the years in the 1950s and 1960s. But, again, the conditions have been fundamentally different during the two decades.

During most of the 1950s—until 1958 or 1959—the National Bank had hardly any exchange reserves at all. The rate of growth and the degree of employment were narrowly restricted by the balance-of-payments position. The rate of unemployment varied around 9–10 per cent. Yet this was the period when industrial production and exports increased very rapidly.

There was what may be rightly called severe *structural inertia* in the economy, which brought about high short-term inflexibility. At the beginning of the 1950s, about 60 per cent of Danish exports were agricultural products with low income and price elasticity. The transformation of the economy went on at a fast rate, so that at the end of the 1960s industrial products represented 60 per cent (and agriculture 30 per cent). In the boom years, from 1959 on, industrial production, investment, and exports went up explosively, unemployment declined to between 2–4 per cent, and wages and prices rose very rapidly. During the 1960s, the foreign balance problem changed character. Total export volume was then able to rise sufficiently rapidly to cover nearly the whole of the import rise following the expansion. But not quite. The deficit in the current balance varied around 10 per cent of the import value and was covered by capital imports, starting systematically from 1959. The National Bank even acquired substantial exchange reserves. However, the balance-of-payments situation was quite vulnerable, and experienced serious trouble in 1962 and 1967–1968. Rapid wage inflation (10–14 per cent wage-cost increase per year) tended to endanger the competitive position, so that repeated, severely restrictive, policy measure had to be applied. The result was that in the last exchange crisis (1967–1968), a dampening of the growth rate and a rise of unemployment to 5 per cent had to be accepted.

THE EXCHANGE-RATE PROBLEM

Against this background what can be said about the exchange rate of the Danish crown and the possibilities of attaining better results by means of greater flexibility?

It is an unsettled question of the Danish debate whether a deeper devaluation of the Danish crown in the 1950s could have made it possible to carry out a more expansive policy and reach a more rapid transformation process. The argument against this view is supported by the notion that the Danish economy was quite inflexible to an extra stimulus. Industrial profits and the degree of self-financing were high during the 1950s, as in Sweden. The actual rate of growth of industrial production and exports was surprisingly rapid; each additional percentage point of industrial production would probably have meant so much extra inflation and imports that devaluation could not have helped. This view cannot be proved, but is a representative opinion.

It is again more interesting to turn to the 1960s. The weak foreign-exchange situation has prompted severe restrictions on growth and recurrently on employment. It can be maintained, therefore, that the strong rate of inflation of wages and prices in Denmark at full employment should have been accompanied by successive devaluations—either continuously or in the recession periods when the exchange difficulties became acute. Again we meet the argument (typically, it is presented more strongly in Denmark than in Sweden) that successive devaluations would weaken the resistance to inflationary income increases. In fact, the more or less successful attempts to stabilize movements in prices and wages have, to a large extent, been agreed upon on the basis of the fixed exchange rates and with reference to the weak balance-of-payments position. It has been a problem of trade-off between inflation and unemployment—and the Danes have revealed their preference for a marginal rise of unemployment. The inflexibility argument of the 1950s is, however, disappearing. With the economy considerably transformed to a well-diversified industrial state, the responses to changes of exchange rates are expected to function more efficiently. In fact, Denmark followed the United Kingdom part way in its devaluation of November 1967 (by 8 per cent). Part of the strong export revival of 1968, but also the deterioration of the terms of trade (by 6 per cent), is attributed to this change.

Responsible Danes show little understanding of exchange-rate variations within a wider band, and still less for completely free rates. One —not very important—reason is the country's dependence on foreign borrowing, which to a considerable degree also refers to private corporations. For a small country like Denmark, it is expected that there is negligible room for independent maneuvering within the big markets for short and long capital funds. From this point of view, only the tying of the crown to the pound sterling *or* the dollar could be imagined. However, as in the case of Sweden, the introduction of a wider band could improve short-term stabilization policy *if* the parity rate were close to a long-term equilibrium.

Finland

GENERAL SURVEY

Finland presents the case of a country with a rather flexible exchange-rate policy, having had five devaluations during the postwar period. Here we shall pay attention mainly to the conditions and consequences of the last depreciation of the Finn mark (by 24 per cent in October 1967; the previous depreciation, by 28 per cent, occurred in 1957).

The main factors determining the vulnerability of the Finnish balance-of-payments position seem to be connected with a structural weakness of the economy combined with persistent inflationary budgets and income policies. Exports are dominated (to about 60 per cent) by wood products, with heavy cyclical fluctuation in volume and prices. Terms-of-trade changes tend to become large. A boom in wood products, which, indeed, has occurred since 1959, quickly tends to exert a strong inflationary impact on the large sector of peasant forest owners, with strong transmission effects over the entire economy. Competing trade unions, cost-of-living clauses built into the economy to a very high extent, and on top of this a succession of rapidly changing weak governments with relatively little power to carry out stabilization policies, complete this picture.

There is a structural shift taking place in the Finnish economy that will work in the direction of more stability, a movement from agriculture, forest, and wood industries in the direction of metal industries and engineering. The reparation payments to Russia gave a strong impetus in this direction and expanding trade with this big neighbor (representing a share of foreign trade a little below 20 per cent) has supported this trend.

THE 1967 DEVALUATION

In many ways the Finnish experiences give good support to a flexible exchange-rate policy. First we can note that the devaluations of 1957 and 1967 worked out with remarkable short-term efficiency. Take the 1967 case. The current balance of payments began to weaken in the

1963 recession. The deficit became serious with the strong income inflation beginning in 1963, and remained at a level corresponding to between 10–15 per cent of the value of imports during the years to 1968, a deficit that was partly covered by foreign loans. Exchange reserves disappeared more or less completely. This weak exchange position called forth a restrictive monetary policy causing substantial unemployment (4–5 per cent) and a deceleration of economic growth (to 2–3 per cent per year, compared with a 4–5 per cent potential or normal growth rate). But fiscal policy continued to be weak, incomes rose by about 7–8 per cent per year, and the cost-of-living index by about 4 per cent per year.

As mentioned above, the fundamental disequilibrium in the foreign-exchange situation was met by depreciation in October 1967 (a month before the devaluation of the pound sterling). In order to dampen the inflationary effects of windfall export profits (foreign exchange rates rose by 31 per cent; by 26 per cent if correction is made for the closely following depreciations of the pound sterling and other currencies), a system of levies on export earnings (ranging between 6–14 per cent) was introduced as a transitory measure. But the profitability of export industries was restored. On the other hand, the effects from the rising import prices were accepted; the aim was to get a quick impact on import volume (which fell by 4 per cent from 1967 to 1968) and on the internal price system. In fact, the cost of living rose by 6 per cent in the six months before April 1968. At that time, after the shock effect had worn off, a general agreement on income stabilization was reached, including as an important element a complete abolition of cost-of-living clauses in wage and loan contracts. Restrictive credit and fiscal policy were important conditions for the stabilization achieved.

The Finnish devaluation of 1967 gives an example of a very successful policy, at least in the short run. The result was a considerable surplus in the current balance-of-payments account for 1968. The decline of the terms of trade was modest (by 3 per cent up to first quarter of 1968), and there was an improvement as compared with the fourth quarter of 1968. An important condition for the effective shift of resources to exports and to import substitution was the fiscal and monetary restrictions that had quick dampening effects on domestic demand (a decline in volume by 1 per cent from 1967 to 1968) and meant a short-term rise in unemployment (to 4 per cent). The price index for total domestic product (the GNP deflator) rose by 9 per cent in 1967–1968. Since the second half of 1968, total production has again been rising rapidly (estimated at 6 per cent per year), unemployment has returned to 3 per cent, and the rise in the price level has been brought down to 2 per cent per year.

QUESTIONS AS TO EXCHANGE-RATE POLICY

When considering this immediate success of the 1967 depreciation, the following two questions are naturally raised:

(1) Would it not have been better if the depreciation had been made earlier, say, in 1964? In that case, "unnecessary" welfare losses during 1965–1967 could have been avoided.

(2) Could the Finnish Government avoid the recurrence of big depreciations by introducing a smoother series of small devaluations —some kind of managed crawling peg? The disturbances some time before and after the depreciations have been serious and should, if possible, be avoided in the future.

There were certainly voices in Finland for an earlier devaluation. The same was the case with the 1957 devaluation. All the usual arguments of economists are on the side of shortening the time lag in the government's reaction pattern. The difficulties refer mainly to *political conditions* in a broad sense. Given the inflationary boom conditions of 1963–1964, including the system of cost-of-living clauses, the inflationary forces would have been aggravated if the Finn mark had been devalued in 1964. Nobody can prove that there would, as a consequence, have been more space for real expansion. The economist can of course *assume* an adequate stabilization policy supporting a more flexible exchange-rate policy and, thereby, excluding some of the main characteristics of the Finnish scene. The tragic "fact" is that some years of bad experience seem to have been a needed precondition for the type of efficient policy that was carried out in 1957 and 1967–1968. But perhaps this type of "learning process" will help next time!

This argument involves an answer to a second question also. The Finnish authorities will not accept the argument that the big (possibly too big) devaluation of 1967 will in due time be followed by a new one and that, therefore, it would be wise to consider a more continuous pattern of rate changes and, perhaps, even to start with a small step in 1969–1970, before any balance-of-payments restrictions have been applied. The policy intention is, with great determination, to keep the new exchange rates stable and to use this as a "disciplinary support" of stabilization policy. On top of this argument comes a belief that exchange-rate changes have to be big and of a shock nature in order to have effective results. Small and more continuous rate changes might not be sufficiently effective for real adjustment; they also carry the risk of inducing inflation. Finland has the privilege of causing minimum embarrassment to other countries by devaluing and, therefore, should be allowed to change its foreign exchange rates substantially at short notice (there being very little foreign holding of Finn marks).

Concluding Remarks

This survey of Scandinavian experiences of changing exchange rates gives no direct support for policies with crawling pegs or freely floating rates within or without a widened band. Our emphasis has been on actual experiences with fixed and changing exchange rates, and we have discussed possible ways of improving the policies by means of some pattern of more flexible exchange-rate policy than has actually been the case. It seems to us that foreign-exchange rates determined in a free market are unacceptable for our small countries. The stock of foreign-exchange holdings that potentially could be thrown on the market is so large relative to the flows originating from the current balance of payments over shorter periods that direct or indirect governmental interference must be taken for granted. From such a lack of market determination would follow speculation on future government policies, a factor that must put emphasis on skill and strength of policy.

From this point of view, Sweden with its strong government and high propensity for manipulation of policy parameters should be a good case for introducing spot and future exchange rates as new parameters within a rather wide band. A combination of market determination and skillful government manipulation of the exchange rates might create space for autonomy of a more independent business cycle policy than was the case in the 1960s. Denmark and Finland seem to need more flexibility in exchange rates than Sweden. But their sensitivity to inflationary disturbances is higher, while the built-in stability of their balances of payments is lower. To this may be added the fact that the Danish and Finnish governments are usually much weaker than the Swedish (a serious handicap in this particular respect).

In all three countries the arguments are strong for appreciation and depreciation of the currencies in order to cut out inflationary and deflationary impulses from abroad. But the management of such policies will never be easy—except ex post for economists. In a future world with a more flexible exchange-rate system, these Scandinavian countries would find a place—probably binding their currencies to some important key currency.

· 46 ·

European Integration and Greater Flexibility of Exchange Rates

WOLFGANG KASPER

IT IS frequently maintained that pegging exchange rates is a legitimate and forceful tool to achieve greater international integration. This view appears to be particularly popular with "professional Europeans," who hold that balance-of-payments disequilibria and the frictions of internal adjustment have to be borne as a price for the EEC.

In my view, the concept of integration behind this standpoint is too much centered around an institutional, organizational, and legalistic, not to say bureaucratic, notion of what international integration means. Rather, international integration should first of all aim at the welding together of national markets, so that potential buyers have an undiscriminated choice between homemade and imported goods—with the organizational and legal superstructure to come later.

If functional integration (in the sense of larger markets with equal competitive opportunities throughout) is the prime concern, the fixity of exchange rates may, rather, be seen, in the light of past experience, as a disintegrating factor. The clamp of fixed parities is far too weak to hold together the forces of diverging historical experience, of different national vices and virtues, of divergent preferences, ambitions, and traditions. To change these factors behind divergent price-and-cost trends appears to require generation-long efforts and experiences. Should we continue to ignore how deep-rooted the causes of international divergences still are, we face the risk that the pendulum of European public opinion swings farther back from integration-mindedness to a selfish stressing of petty national sovereignties. Apart from this, there is the economic consideration that distorted exchange rates work as a disintegrating factor, since they create—temporarily—competitive advantages and disadvantages that are not caused by such economic factors as productivity or location, and hence misallocate resources.

It is, therefore, my view that basic international divergences inside the EEC, too, should be evened out by an elastic monetary device. What, for example, is wrong with the Germans wanting to have more stability than the others—on the basis of their national historical experience, not shared by others? And why should the Germans impose their idea of monetary "discipline" on the French national temperament?

The consequence of completely banning exchange-rate adjustments within the EEC would be either more controls and artificial obstacles at the borders, which we once had wanted to make disappear, or

unwanted, outside inflationary and deflationary pressures on the various national economies, which will only reactivate dormant, nationalist notions.

If we admitted, instead, stepwise parity changes of the conventional kind, we would retain the unpredictable currency risk that bothers producers and investors now, and that works as an extra impediment to economic activity between the national "regions" in the Common Market. The rationale of this system would be, in the case of revaluation, first to encourage producers of a more stable EEC country to expand exports in accordance with the signals set by the ever-increasing distortion of the exchange rate, and then to shock them, all of a sudden, out of the export markets.[1]

As to import substitution, a stepwise revaluation would abruptly attract outside competitors, who would then be gradually eliminated, until the next parity jump "sucks" them in again. This consideration seems to be one important reason for official Europe's opposition to exchange-rate policy. It is overlooked that it is not exchange-rate policy as such, that causes disintegration, but rather the suddenness, the unpredictability, and the clumsiness of exchange-rate policy in the present system (in which officials have been trained).

An important advantage of increased flexibility inside the EEC would be that national business cycles were not "integrated" so easily. National cycles would more probably balance out, instead of reinforcing each other (as is happening in 1969).

Common Agricultural Policy is probably considered by many as one of the major obstacles to greater flexibility. CAP was devised when the first-hour optimism still prevailed in the EEC, that monetary, wage, and structural policies would be quickly harmonized and that political union was soon to come. History has proved that European integration has produced a table with only one leg—CAP. Since the complementary policies will not come for a long time, the table was already prone to tumble, even before greater flexibility of forward rates handicapped the common agricultural market. Solutions to reconcile the objectives underlying CAP with a system of limited flexibility can be found. Unit of account prices could, for example, be converted by a gliding parity into national intervention prices. Another solution would be to guarantee, at

---

[1] The disadvantage of such parity jumps may partly be outweighed by the advantage that they reactivate competition between producers, who tend to form international EEC-wide (quasi-) cartels. But a more elastic international monetary system, which would facilitate more frequent changes in international prices, would probably tend to further competition across borders and equally impede Common-Market-wide collusion of producers.

some cost of subsidizing, a certain unit-of-account/national-currency ratio for the next crop year and then to adapt it to recent variations of the market's exchange rate.[2] The reform of CAP, which is overdue anyway, could well be combined with the introduction of a new exchange-rate regime.

British entry would be easier, if smooth and frequent exchange-rate variations were permitted to neutralize divergent national cost trends: fears of many people inside Smaller Europe that British trade unions would "contaminate" the other EEC countries, and that the present EEC members would have to support the British balance of payments even more than they have up to now would lose much of their grounds.

It would, instead, become clear that the European nations with the rich diversity of their historic differences to be considered—in many respects an asset worth preserving—could live harmoniously together:

> without being forced into one rigid regime, which would be contrary to European traditions, and
>
> without having to forego the advantages of a common market as wide as the Old Continent.

[2] The German Expert Council has asked Dr. Timothy Josling of the London School of Economics to elaborate in a paper on CAP under exchange-rate flexibility.

· 47 ·

Comments on Mr. Kasper's Paper: Requiem for European Integration

ANTONIO MOSCONI

I CONSIDER Wolfgang Kasper's ideas on European economic integration highly controversial. Disillusioned by the yet unfulfilled promises of the ten-year-old Treaty of Rome, and using classical economic analysis, Kasper holds a rather pessimistic view of the integration process in the Old Continent. He seems to think that European integration can proceed by slow and almost imperceptible steps. I, on the contrary, believe that this process is one of transformation set in motion by the will of men who, confronted with the obvious failure of nationalist policies, want to do away with these policies.

While waiting for European integration to come about by itself or by some heavenly design, Kasper would consider it wiser to dismantle the ties already established between the Six, such as comparatively rigid exchange rates, so that each country could regain national sovereignty. I will discuss here, individually, his arguments for greater exchange-rate flexibility.

First, Kasper dreams of a vast market in which commodities, capital, and people can move freely without any control whatsoever. He calls this market Europe. This dream amounts to wiping out with a single stroke the forty years of economic history and the history of economic ideas since the Great Depression in order to go back to a pre-Keynesian and paleoliberalistic concept of economic relationships.

It should be obvious that such a leap into the dark, from national neocapitalism to a European paleocapitalism is not practical. The economy of Europe must be steered. And, as the European economy transcends individual countries, it can be controlled only by a statutory Europe-wide power. It is not utopian to think in terms of political European integration. Rather, it is utopian to think that in the twentieth century an economically integrated area could be established without community-wide legal and political instruments that are the sine qua non conditions for making it viable. It is utopian to think that we can go ahead with European integration without European planning, a European monetary policy, and so forth.

Without these instruments, the vast market that Kasper calls Europe would inevitably degenerate. Then the choice between nineteenth-century, individual, national states and a European Federation worthy of this century will have been made at the cost of catastrophe. The Eurodollar market illustrates the results of a "free international market" without political constraints. Cries for some regulatory action are by now heard from several quarters.

If, as I believe, there can be no durable economic integration without supporting political integration, the problem of monetary policy ought to be viewed first in the light of its effect on the political integration process. Exchange-rate rigidity, then, appears to be a basically necessary condition toward that end. It limits national sovereignty in the area of monetary policy—a critical factor in the achievement of internal economic and social equilibrium, particularly in the choice of a country's position on the Phillips curve.

What Kasper considers to be a serious fault of the present system I regard as a formidable booster for the integration process, the development of federalism, and the unmasking of the shameful inadequacy of nation states to manage the European economy individually. More flexibility in exchange rates among the Six would lead to the failure of integration, the "requiem" for Europe. Ours is the time when historical alternatives must be assessed realistically in their dramatic impact: nationalism versus federalism, decline of European civilization versus European independent growth, and colonization versus equal partnership for Europe.

Second, the argument that fixed exchange rates could distort competition and, consequently, impair the optimal allocation of resources, rests on the assumption that the economy is governed by immutable natural laws. Naturalism as applied to the social sciences belongs to the past. It has done enough grievous damage, especially in economics. It is anachronistic to think of applying natural laws to a science of man in our age when the very physical postulates are changing: the moon landing, for instance, could never have been achieved within the framework of Euclidean geometry.

The economy is being "negotiated." It reacts more to enforceable relationships among individuals, classes, and people than to unchanging natural laws. None of this can be found in the Walrasian equations of general economic equilibrium, which were based on a system of pure and perfect competition that can be found only in story books and in the writings on economics of the nineteenth century.

If we cannot base our analysis on the assumption of perfect competition any more, as I maintain, then we must recognize that the subject we are discussing is devoid of all substance in a complex system of monopoly, oligopoly, and imperfect competition. Exchange rates, as other economic relationships, are "negotiated"; they answer historical situations and other changing factors. As important pawns on the political chessboard, they cannot any longer be left to the sway of "market forces." For the European Community, exchange rates are a tool of integration and verification of the political will to walk together toward the objectives set by the word and the spirit of the Treaty of Rome.

The Phillips curve does not give us a new "natural law" of the economy. It merely expresses the inverse relationship between inflation and unemployment as experienced in capitalist countries in a given historical context and at a given stage of economic knowledge. It mirrors the inability of our economic system to solve the problem of combining reasonable monetary stability with a bearable rate of unemployment. Indeed, this is, first and foremost, a political problem, one that ultimately points up the failure of nation states. European economies, which are more advanced than the economy of the United States in the application of Keynesian tenets, could, if given a better political framework, more easily realize a better social balance expressed in terms of the Phillips curve.

A sound application of the Bretton Woods institutions would be sufficient, anyway, to avoid the most serious strains, should delays in integration cause fundamental disequilibria within the Community. The recent devaluation of the French franc proves that the remedy is available.

Strains that nevertheless may develop would serve—let us reiterate it—to force a historical choice that must be made by forfeiting a degree of national sovereignty.

Third, I believe we are too preoccupied with economic cycles that, in a fixed exchange-rate system, tend to affect all countries simultaneously. The problem of modern economies is one of growth. The cycle was the problem of the preceding generation. That problem has been solved as progress in the science of economics gave man a stronger control over the economy.

That economic cycles are transferred from country to country and spread the danger of economic and social dislocations, only confirms the need for cyclical adjustment policies on a Europe-wide basis similar to those that have been adopted by individual countries where major economic swings have been successfully avoided.

Fourth, I can agree with Kasper's contention that the Agricultural Common Market has been launched in a moment of enthusiasm, when all of its prerequisites had not yet matured. History, however, is made in this way. If anything, we should regret that such history-making moments of enthusiasm are only too few and far between.

Right now, in the face of mournful recitations about the European Green Plan following the French devaluation, I believe we can and ought to work to create the prerequisites that were not present when the plan was established. I do not mean to defend the plan as it is, for it clearly has serious faults. But I believe that it is a simplification if we make the Green Plan responsible for overproduction and all the rest. Instead, we must go back to the birth of "subsidized agriculture," a phenomenon that existed on the national state level. It is clear, then, that the Agricultural Common Market is not to be indicted for what it did and could not do otherwise; rather, it should be assessed for what it represents on the road to integration and for the role it can play in the future.

Flexibility of exchange rates is incompatible with the ACM, for renegotiation of all commodity prices each year—as Kasper seems to suggest—is impractical. The adverse effect of currency depreciation on the cost of living and wages would be heightened by an automatic price increase for internally produced commodities. Conversely, currency appreciation would call for price reductions, and this clearly is politically not feasible.

Finally, Kasper argues that a greater flexibility of exchange rates would favor the entry of Great Britain into the Common Market. This theory was also embraced by Dr. Carli in his report to the Monnet Committee in which he said: "The divergencies experienced within the EEC in cost and price trends seem to temper the impact of the arguments against British entry. However, it has been noticed that inflationary pressures within the Community reportedly are stronger than similar pressures within some of its members. But this may not constitute a good enough reason to reject the participation of Great Britain if at the same time mobile parities were introduced within the area to give an element of flexibility apt to protect the countries more prone to defend monetary stability against inflationary pressures from the other countries."

The core of this argument is that the entry into the Community by another country would be made easier if the ties that keep it together were relaxed. We must ask the question whether in such a case Great Britain would be entering a community proper, or just another "free trade area," one devoid of all substance and politically ineffectual.

In this case it might be more exact to say that the EEC enters EFTA rather than the other way round. I believe that there can be no question that under contemporary economic conditions, a free trade area lacking political power would invite back all the crises and woes of pre-Keynesian capitalism and lead to another 1929, this time made in Europe.

· 48 ·

Comments on the Papers by Messrs. Mosconi and Kasper: Red Herrings, Carts, and Horses

STEPHEN N. MARRIS

PROBABLY no two papers in this volume contain so many emotive and ideological overtones as those by Mosconi and Kasper. This is very understandable. The cause of European integration inspires—and requires—an emotional commitment. But it also requires careful analysis of the economic and political processes of integration, and a willingness to modify preconceived ideas in the light of evolving experience. The instinctive reaction against somewhat more flexible exchange rates may be a case in point. The purpose of this note is to suggest that if the studies now underway lead to a consensus that a more flexible interpretation of the exchange-rate rules would be both workable and an improvement for other countries, then it is quite possible that the adoption of similar rules by the EEC (perhaps with some modifications) would favor rather than retard real progress toward integration.

Red Herrings

It is clear that Kasper and Mosconi stand a long way down opposite slopes of the divide between those who believe that prices are or should be determined by free-market forces, and those who believe that in the modern world analysis based on this assumption has little validity. But is this issue really relevant? Mosconi would presumably agree that, however determined, exchange rates have a significant impact on international transactions; he admits, implicitly, that they may have to be changed from time to time. Kasper would probably agree that exchange rates are—and are likely to remain—essentially "administered" prices. The issue is whether they could be administered *better* under a different set of rules.

I have set down in Part I of this volume the arguments of those who believe that the adoption of a system of limited flexibility should lead to a significant improvement in decision-making on exchange rates at the governmental level. One point may bear repeating, because it does not seem to have received enough attention. Under the present arrangements, as recent experience has shown, international bodies can have very little say when it comes to exchange rates—even when they possess the strong institutional powers of the Commission in Brussels. With a large-change-or-not-at-all system too much is at stake; like it or not, national sovereignty rears its ugly head. But under rules that encouraged small and more frequent changes, it would be much easier to insist on proper consultation within the Community, and more likely that effective pressure could be brought to bear to insure that the exchange-rate policies followed were consistent with the interests of the Community as a whole.

Would more flexible exchange rates be incompatible with the common agricultural policy (CAP)? The fact is that the reverse may be true. The CAP has two interrelated but distinct aims. The first is to support agriculture within the Community as efficiently as possible at a level representing an acceptable compromise between the conflicting interests of domestic producers, domestic consumers, and foreign suppliers. As Mosconi remarks, the well known problems this involves date back long before the formation of the EEC. But far more important in the present context is the second aim, which is to provide support as far as possible on a *uniform* basis in the different member countries of the Community. This is the original and specifically EEC feature of the CAP and is where it becomes inextricably linked with the exchange-rate system.[1]

To demonstrate this linkage one must strip off the technical complexities and political horse trading incorporated in the CAP and concentrate on the basic economic mechanism. To rationalize European agriculture on a Community-wide basis requires that farmers in similar circumstances in different member countries face roughly the same relative inducements either to stay on the land or to seek employment elsewhere; that is, it requires uniform "terms of trade"—or more accurately relative income-earning opportunities—between the agricultural and nonagricultural sectors in each member country. Among various alternatives, the method chosen was to set uniform market support prices, denominated in units of account and converted at going exchange rates, with a built-in preference favoring first domestic and then other EEC suppliers. The heavy reliance on market support prices and the level at which these were set has been much criticized on general grounds. But it must be recognized that the arrangements provided a relatively simple and entirely logical approach to the specifically EEC objective of supporting agriculture at the same level throughout the Community. For what follows, however, it is important to note that in *real* terms the level of support will be uniform only to the extent that exchange rates are in line with the relevant purchasing-power parities.

---

[1] This is an ambitious and essentially "integrationist" aim, which also provides the only legitimate basis for shifting the financing of agricultural support onto a Community-wide basis. It would have been possible to decide that the different values implicitly attached to rural life in different member countries was part of the diversified European heritage, cherished by Mr. Kasper, which should be preserved. National policies could have been adapted to be compatible with free trade in agricultural products, but the level of support could have been left to be determined by national governments.

The fatal weakness was, of course, that no allowance was made for the distorting effect of diverging trends in national price levels within the Community. Agricultural support prices remained fixed and uniform in money terms at the prevailing (unchanged) exchange rates. But other prices rose faster in France than in Germany. In both countries the terms of trade for agriculture deteriorated, but German farmers did better than French farmers; relative to those in France their terms of trade *improved* by perhaps 10 per cent.[2] Then came the exchange-rate changes of 1969, with the cross-rate between the French franc and the German mark going down by about 20 per cent. To have restored the uniformity of agricultural prices at the new exchange rates would have necessitated *deteriorating* the terms of trade for farmers in Germany relative to those in France by 20 per cent. This could have been done by raising farm prices in France in line with the devaluation and lowering them in Germany in line with the revaluation; or more of the gains could have been given to French farmers or more of the burden placed on German farmers by altering the support prices in terms of the unit of account (or the parity of the unit of account itself). In the event it is hardly surprising that any solution along these lines was considered unacceptable either to the agricultural sector in Germany or the nonagricultural sector in France. Instead, the principle of uniform prices has had to be put into cold storage. Several lessons emerge:

(1) A difficult situation became impossible because the exchange-rate changes, when they came, were significantly greater than the change in relative national price levels over any relevant period. (Maintenance of uniform prices at the new exchange rates would have involved giving French agriculture, in real terms, substantially *better* terms relative to German agriculture than was implicit in the original pre-1967 political bargain.) Many would regard this as an inherent characteristic of the present exchange-rate system.

(2) The problems would still have been acute if the exchange-rate changes had been roughly in line with relative price levels. An overnight change of 10 per cent in all agricultural prices is at the least bad economic management, and, in reality, likely to be politically impossible.

(3) In considering how to get out of this mess, it becomes apparent that the most serious criticism of the present arrangements is that the timing and magnitude of changes in the terms of trade for

---

[2] Between July 1967 and July 1969, consumer prices rose by 4 per cent in Germany and 11 per cent in France. It should be noted that in setting the initial support prices some allowance was made for erosion due to subsequent inflation, and that agricultural productivity has improved more rapidly than expected with resultant excess production.

agriculture in the Community as a whole—with vital implications for agricultural surpluses, financing, etc.—have become inextricably entangled with the vagaries of the exchange-rate system, that is, with factors having nothing to do with agriculture at all. Suppose it is agreed that in real terms the average terms of trade for agriculture in the Community are, if anything, too favorable, but at the same time it is accepted that support prices cannot be lowered in Germany. Then one could only hope for such a rapid rate of inflation in France that it soon became possible to increase prices paid to French farmers by 20 per cent without improving their real position at all. By adjusting support prices in terms of the unit of account, it would then be possible to re-establish the unity of the agricultural market and abolish the subsidies now to be paid to German farmers. Talk about the tail wagging the dog!

The problem of how to maintain roughly uniform terms of trade for agriculture throughout the Community will remain with us until the conditions for full monetary integration have been achieved. But they should be *easier* to solve with a system of limited flexibility of exchange rates. As Kasper suggests, it would not be difficult to devise technical arrangements under which prices in national currencies could be guaranteed for one crop year ahead. Periodically—almost certainly each year—it would be necessary to adjust Community support prices, and the movement of exchange rates would be one of the relevant factors.

Mosconi has two objections. First, this would involve renegotiation of all commodity prices each year, which he regards as impractical. One can only reply that experience in other countries, and with the CAP itself, suggests that some kind of annual price review is essential in any way to deal with the evolution of supply and demand in the agricultural sector. Such a review, of course, needs to be carried out within a longer-term framework that provides appropriate guarantees for agricultural incomes and guidance concerning future price policy. But it also needs to be sufficiently flexible to permit price changes in any one year as large as, and in fact probably larger than, those resulting from the operation of a system of limited flexibility of exchange rates. Mosconi's second objection is that this would involve price reductions in countries whose currency had appreciated, which he claims is politically unfeasible. For large and unpredictable reductions, such as those theoretically called for under the present exchange-rate system, he is clearly right. But if this is to be accepted as a basic law of nature, even when extended to gradual changes, it follows from the analysis given above that the level of agricultural prices would over the longer run become a function of the rate of inflation in the most inflation-prone member of the Community. A surer recipe for disaster could hardly be imagined.

In practice it would seem likely that the whole question of exchange-rate changes would become of secondary importance if a system of limited flexibility worked as smoothly as its proponents suggest. At annual review time the real debate would be about the evolution of agricultural incomes in real terms, and supply and demand for individual products —as it should be. It should come to be regarded as normal, indeed equitable, that when translated into national currencies the decisions taken on these grounds would also reflect the relatively small exchange-rate changes that had taken place since the previous review.

Some of those who are aware of the problems discussed above nevertheless go on to suggest that the real trouble lies with the CAP itself, not with the exchange-rate system. It is worth stressing, therefore, that whatever the other merits of different methods of agricultural support, similar problems related to the exchange-rate system would arise in one form or another whatever method were adopted.

(1) With a system based on deficiency payments, it would be technically easier to handle exchange-rate changes (large or small) because of the separation between support prices and market prices. But over time there would be exactly the same question of how to adjust support prices to maintain uniform terms of trade in the face of divergent movements in national price levels.

(2) With a system based mainly on non-output related subsidies, direct income support, subsidies favoring structural reform, or a combination of these, for example, the problems would at first sight be less acute. Nevertheless, the trade-distorting effects of large exchange-rate changes would probably be unacceptable. More important, the principle of uniform income-earning opportunities in real terms would still require some mechanism for adjusting the subsidies, paid in national currencies, for diverging national price trends.

With either of these alternatives one could envisage the use of a system of indexation to help maintain the uniformity of support in real terms. This would really amount to inventing something to measure changes in purchasing-power parities as a substitute for exchange rates, because it was felt exchange rates could not be trusted to fill this role. In a general sense, therefore, it is clear that so long as national price levels continue to diverge, and so long as one rejects exclusive reliance on mandatory production controls, then the design and operation of the CAP would be facilitated by an exchange-rate system that eliminated large abrupt changes and tended to produce gradual adjustments roughly in line with purchasing-power parities.

To those who find it hard to accept this conclusion, one can only point out that to spotlight fixed support prices and fixed exchange rates while ignoring divergences in national price levels is to mistake illusion for substance; this is a money illusion, something we all suffer from as private individuals but which should never fool us as economists.

Carts and Horses

Putting aside the red herrings, the real issues concern basic objectives, priorities, and timing. Kasper's prime concern is to achieve what he calls *functional integration,* or the economic benefits from a large unified market with equal competitive chances throughout. This is not the same thing as *monetary integration,* which is the achievement of conditions such that national price levels move closely in line. Indeed, it is important to recognize that, in theory at any rate, all the economic benefits of integration could be obtained without ever achieving the conditions necessary for monetary integration—so long as exchange rates are flexible. This is presumably why Kasper seems relatively unconcerned about his view that it may take generations of common experience before monetary integration becomes possible.

Many in the European movement—one suspects they are a majority —would not share this lack of concern. To them the material benefits expected from economic integration are mainly a selling point; far more important is the role of economic integration as a vehicle for promoting political integration. They may not share Professor Mosconi's pessimistic view that without political integration we would go back to the crises and woes of pre-Keynesian capitalism. Like him, however, they want to see as rapid as possible progress toward monetary integration simply because it requires, indeed demands, significant progress toward political integration.

But it is no good putting the cart before the horse. The attempt to force the pace of monetary integration by fixing exchange rates with no provision for limited adjustment was a gamble that did not come off. It was probably well worth trying. Nobody could tell in advance how fast integrating forces would gather momentum and, as Mosconi says, the aims of the European movement will not be attained without challenge and struggle. But now it is time to consider carefully the lessons for the future. What is the likelihood that from now on price levels within the EEC will move sufficiently in line to obviate the need for futher exchange-rate changes? The events of the last two or three years may give an exaggerated idea of the difficulties. Lessons have been learned, and the growing interdependence between members is a powerful force making for more uniform attitudes and behavior. There are also proposals for new initiatives at the Community level: taking steps leading toward setting up what should eventually become a European Monetary Board, and elaborating Community guidelines for the conduct of fiscal policy.

These prospects and possibilities need to be examined thoroughly. Views may differ, but, even on the most optimistic assumptions, it is hard to believe that conditions such that exchange-rate changes will never be required can be achieved for a least ten or fifteen years.

If this is correct what implications should be drawn for the rules governing exchange-rate changes? What is wanted is a set of rules that exerts continuous pressure on member countries to make progress along the road to monetary integration, without demanding the impossible in terms of current economic and political realities. The proposals for a "crawling peg" now under consideration seem to meet these requirements rather well. In a first transitional period the prime aim would be to banish large exchange-rate changes of the 1969 variety. If member countries were prepared to accept a commitment not to alter their parities by more than, say, 1 or 2 per cent in any one year, and proved able to honor it, this would surely be more concrete evidence of progress toward monetary integration than a period of fixed parities followed five or ten years later by another major upheaval. As time went by, progress could be reviewed and the exchange-rate constraint could be progressively strengthened by reducing the permissible rate of parity change.[3]

Apart from putting the cart and horse in their proper relationship, as far as monetary integration is concerned, limited flexibility of exchange rates should also facilitate European integration in other ways. First, as discussed above in connection with the common agricultural policy, it should be easier at the technical level to push ahead with the laborious but essential task of promoting functional integration. Many examples could be drawn from the fields of tax harmonization, social policy, regional policy, transport policy, energy policy, etc. The basic point is that with limited flexibility it would be possible to concentrate on finding the best solution to the specific problem under consideration, without having to worry so much about the distorting effects of divergent national price levels or the possibility of abrupt and disruptive exchange-rate changes. As Kasper points out, this would also be true for the private sector; companies would be able to plan ahead in the knowledge that what really mattered would be their efficiency in real terms and not the vagaries of the present exchange-rate system.

Second, at the wider political level, member countries should be more willing to accept new commitments because, with limited flexibility of exchange rates, they would have a safety valve in the event of unforeseen consequences for their balance of payments. This concept of a safety valve is also valid in a more general way. If monetary integration

[3] There are many versions of the crawling peg. Whether in some form it would be workable in practice and give promise of better economic management is discussed at length elsewhere in this volume, and is now under study by the IMF. The point being made here is that if it passes the test on these other grounds, then it would seem particularly well suited to the EEC.

is to be achieved, some member countries will have to learn to live with more inflation than they have been used to, others with less. Although Kasper sounds somewhat unhappy about this, it seems a relatively small price to pay in relation to the prize at stake. But it will take time, and he is surely right when he warns that nationalistic sentiment still runs deep in Europe. By trying to force too fast a pace in this area we may use up reserves of political will and popular support that are badly needed to achieve other, more immediately important and realizable objectives.

The ultimate objective of the EEC should not be just fixed exchange rates, but the abolition of exchange rates. No one can say today how long this may take, although, if political momentum can be regained, many present estimates could turn out to be unduly pessimistic. But before adopting a negative attitude to the proposals for greater flexibility now under discussion, supporters of the EEC should re-examine their instinctive objections to see whether (1) they are applicable to a carefully designed system of limited flexibility to apply during a transitional period, (2) they are not based on a money illusion, and (3) that they take sufficient account of the lessons learned since 1958 about the economic and political facts of life.

· 49 ·

The Agricultural Regulations of the European Economic Community as an Obstacle to the Introduction of Greater Flexibility of Exchange Rates

FRIEDRICH A. LUTZ

IN THE Common Market support prices are fixed for certain agricultural products (the principal ones being grains, sugar, milk, and milk products) in units of account that have the same gold parity as the dollar. In this paper I shall, for simplicity, restrict the discussion exclusively to wheat.

A basic support price for wheat is set for Duisburg as the center of that area (Ruhr District) of the Common Market that is the largest "importer" of wheat. From this basic price are calculated regional support prices for altogether 610 different intervention points, of which 113 are in West Germany. The general rule (to which exceptions have been made [1]) is that the regional support prices in Germany should be equal to the basic support price *minus* transport costs from the respective regional intervention points to the base point (Duisburg).

If the parities of one or more, but not all, of the currencies of the member countries are altered, the EEC Council of Ministers must decide, by unanimous vote, within three days, with the advice of the EEC Commission, and after hearing the Currency Committee, whether and by how much the gold parity of the unit of account should be adjusted. And the Council may adjust the agricultural support prices. While it has the right to make such adjustments in theory, it would doubtless have difficulty in making them in practice.

I

Let us first proceed on the assumption that the German mark is revalued upward, but that there is no widening of the limits within which its foreign-exchange value may move. Let us also assume that after the revaluation, neither the gold parity of the unit of account, nor the agricultural prices are altered, as we have supposed would be the case in practice.

The appreciation of the German mark by a certain percentage means, under our assumptions, that the German producers of wheat receive a

---

[1] For example, in West Germany the government has aided the producers in some regions (especially Bavaria) by setting regional support prices which fell short of the basis support price by less than the relevant transport costs.

price in German marks that is reduced by nearly that same percentage, whereas the producers in the other five EEC countries continue to obtain the same price in terms of their domestic currencies as before. The German importers of wheat from France now buy it more cheaply in terms of marks than previously, but, since the mark price they obtain at a German delivery point is correspondingly lower, there is no incentive under our present assumptions for them to import more wheat than before from France (or other EEC countries). In other words, the appreciation of the German mark does not stimulate wheat imports into Germany.

The difficulty for Germany is that the German wheat producers will demand compensation for the reduction in their income due to the lower receipts from wheat farming. During the currency crisis of November 1968, it was repeatedly claimed in public discussion that, for the reason just given, every 1 per cent upward revaluation of the mark would entail an additional budget outlay for the German Federal Republic of some DM 250 million, account here being taken of the effect on farm incomes of the reduction in receipts, not only for wheat, but also for other products. I am unable to give any independent judgment as to how nearly correct this estimate was; but some agricultural experts have held that it was too high.

We may consider the claim for compensation by the German wheat producers as referring to two alternative aims. One is the maintenance of the relative income position as before vis-a-vis to that of the wheat producers in the other EEC countries. The other is the maintenance of the same relative position vis-a-vis those employed in German industry. Regarding "parity" with the producers in other EEC countries, the following considerations are relevant. The appreciation of the German mark has been made necessary, we may suppose, because the cost- and price-level in the Federal Republic has for some years been rising more slowly than the level in other countries, including those of the EEC, so that there has been a growing surplus in the balance of payments on current account, a surplus that the appreciation of the German mark is designed to remove. During these years, then, the position of the German farmers must have improved relative to that of the farmers in the other EEC countries because the general cost- and price-level has risen in relation to the fixed wheat price less in Germany than in those other countries. The appreciation of the German mark simply means that the German farmer now loses this former relative advantage through the fall in the price of wheat in marks. Supposing that we had exact figures for the rise in production and living costs in the various EEC countries, and given that the wheat support price is still at the same level as first fixed, we could *ceteris paribus* calculate just what percentage appreciation of the mark would be necessary to re-establish the initial relative positions.

It would doubtless be difficult to convince German farmers on the basis of the above argument that a comparison of their position with that of other EEC farmers gives them no grounds for claiming compensation. They will make their comparison, using as the base date not the time when the fixed support price for wheat was introduced, but the time when the German mark was revalued; they are, of course, then right in saying that their relative position has deteriorated. There is, however, another point to be considered. The purpose of the appreciation of the German mark is to stop the importation of inflation from countries with rates of inflation regarded by the German authorities as excessively high. Let us suppose that the Federal Republic now succeeds in keeping its own rate below the rates, which continue to be high, in the other EEC countries. In that case the German farmers will once more obtain a gradual improvement in their income position relative to that of other EEC farmers. Thus, even taking as the base date the time when the German mark is revalued upward, the farmers could at best justify a claim to compensation at a declining rate over a limited period. (Although, of course, the process might start all over again in response to the necessity of a new upward revaluation.) Only in one case could it be held, always assuming that we accept the argument for intra-country "parity" *with the time of revaluation as the base date,* that the German farmers had grounds for demanding permanent annual compensation on a scale equivalent to the initial annual loss at that time. This is the case where, following the revaluation, the rate of domestic inflation was henceforth at least equal to the rates in the other EEC countries.

An analysis of the implications of satisfying a possible claim on the part of German farmers to compensation in order to preserve "parity" with German industry would require a discussion of how an upward revaluation of the currency affects industrial incomes. Such a discussion cannot be undertaken here. Given, however, that the appreciation cannot be expected to lead to a fall in the German mark prices of industrial products, there seems to be a presumption that the income position of domestic farmers will worsen in relation to that of people employed in domestic industry. Thus, it appears that there would be more justification in a claim for compensation based on the concept of "parity" with domestic industrial workers than in one based on the concept of "parity" with farmers in the other EEC countries. This does not, of course, mean that I personally am a defender of either "parity" claim.

II

Now let us turn to the case where the limits within which the foreign-exchange rates may move are made very much wider than at present. We assume, not that the parity of the German mark is altered, but that it moves to its upper limit while the French franc is at its lower limit, so that the mark appears to have appreciated in terms of the French franc

403

by, let us say, 10 per cent. Here, since the parity rates of exchange of the two currencies have not changed, and since the domestic support price of wheat alters only when the parity rates change, no claim for compensation can be established by German farmers. For the support price for wheat is the same in marks for German producers, and the same in French francs for French producers, as before. On the other hand, German importers of French wheat who buy it from French exporters at the French support price now pay for it considerably less (approximately 10 per cent less in our example) in German marks than the German mark support price at which they can sell it at home. In these circumstances we should expect large quantities of French wheat to be delivered to the official German buyers. This is what actually happened during the currency crisis of May 1969. With the franc at a substantial discount on the forward market, German wheat importers bought forward francs to finance purchases in France, and did it to such an extent that the EEC Commission finally decided that the German official buyers should be under an obligation to purchase only domestic wheat.

It is doubtless possible to extend the limits of the exchange rate somewhat beyond the 0.75 per cent on either side of the parity that is now usual, without substantially distorting the channels of trade in wheat between the EEC countries, since small fluctuations in the exchange rates will not be sufficient to induce great shifts. However, the limits that would be admissible from this point of view are far narrower than those envisaged by current proposals for introducing greater exchange-rate flexibility. In other words, flexibility within fairly wide limits is incompatible with the present agricultural arrangements between the countries of the EEC. The same holds a fortiori for the case of unlimited flexibility; indeed, given that there would in this case be no exchange-rate parities at all, the present arrangements would be totally impossible. This conclusion is not so much an argument against flexibility of exchange rates as against the present agricultural setup in the EEC, a setup that is, for many other reasons also, to be regarded as misconceived.

Since an upward revaluation of a currency poses the problem of compensation for the wheat farmers in the country concerned, and since significantly greater flexibility of exchange rates poses the problem of the distortion of trade in wheat, the combination that is frequently proposed of periodic revaluations (or the "crawling peg") with greater flexibility round the parity raises both problems together. Hence, this proposal cannot be carried into effect by any country belonging to the EEC so long as the latter's present agricultural arrangements persist.

The "distortion" problem connected with flexible exchange rates could be solved provided the support price in each country were always adjusted in proportion to any change in the exchange rate. If, for example, the German mark rose in terms of the dollar and the French franc fell, it would be sufficient correspondingly to lower the German, and raise the French support price in order to remove the incentive for German importers to import more wheat from France. But the "compensation" problem would then reappear. The French farmer would receive a higher price for wheat in terms of his own currency, and the German farmer a lower one, than before. This is one reason why it seems unlikely that the agricultural arrangements of the EEC will be adjusted along these lines.

Postscript

When this paper was written, an upward revaluation of the German mark seemed the most likely prospect as regards currency adjustments in the near future, and I, therefore, used this eventuality to illustrate my argument. In the meantime the French franc has, somewhat unexpectedly, been devalued, while the German mark has been kept at the old parity. On August 10, 1969, the gold value of the franc was reduced by 11.11 per cent. The associated events have confirmed the conclusion of this paper that the present agricultural regulations of the Common Market are not compatible with exchange-rate adjustments by individual member countries.

Had the regulations been strictly observed, the wheat price expressed in units of account would have been kept constant for France, and the support price for French producers in terms of French francs would have been raised by 12.5 per cent. This would have implied that the other Common Market countries would have had no inducement to import more wheat than before from France, since the fall in the foreign currency value of the franc would have been counterbalanced by the rise in the franc price for wheat. However, in the meeting that was immediately called of the Council of Ministers, the French representatives opposed raising the franc price of wheat, and for obvious reasons. Not only would such a rise have aggravated the domestic overproduction of wheat, but it would also have raised the domestic cost of living, thus jeopardizing the success of the devaluation.

The Council of Ministers finally decided upon a compromise that leaves the franc wheat price for the agricultural year 1969–1970 unchanged, and implies a reduction for the time being in the price in terms of units of account by 11.11 per cent. In the agricultural year 1970–1971, the price in francs is to be raised sufficiently for the price in units of account for France to be no more than 5.6 per cent below that prevailing in the other Common Market countries; and in the agricultural year 1971–1972, the same price in units of account is again to apply to all the countries.

With franc prices for wheat in France unchanged (first year), or higher by a smaller amount than corresponds to the devaluation (second year), the wheat importers in the other Common Market countries have an inducement to import more wheat from France. It is true that the purpose of a currency devaluation is to increase the exports of the country concerned. But it is also understandable that, given the huge stocks of wheat already accumulated in the other five Common Market countries, the representatives of these countries sought to prevent further accumulation due to larger imports. Accordingly the Council decided that French exports of wheat (and of other agricultural products) to other Common Market countries should be taxed, and French imports from those countries subsidized, in order to keep the trade in wheat inside the Common Market more or less within the old bounds. The consequence is that the important French wheat market is for the time being "isolated" from the rest, or that the "common market" is suspended.

· 50 ·

The Concept of Optimum Currency Areas and the Choice Between Fixed and Flexible Exchange Rates

THOMAS D. WILLETT AND EDWARD TOWER

FROM the standpoint of maximizing the usefulness of money, there should be a single world currency. This would not require a full-fledged world government, and the high capital mobility that a genuine world currency would foster would greatly ease financing deficits. The institution of a world currency would not be without costs, however. At a minimum, constraints would have to be placed on individual countries' abilities to create money to suit their own desires and on their abilities to use external measures, such as exchange-rate adjustments, to escape domestic deflation in the face of payments deficits. High capital mobility is not sufficient to eliminate the need for adjustment policies under all circumstances, as is indicated, for instance, by the problems of depressed regions. For many countries, the costs of relying for international adjustment upon the mechanisms that now exist for interregional adjustment and financing within a country would be too great to be outweighed by the benefits of a greater currency domain.

If the world were being begun afresh, the optimum-currency-area approach would dictate the design of currency areas such that, at the margin, the costs and benefits of extending each currency area would just balance. Such an exercise would, of course, be purely academic. Nevertheless, the optimum-currency-area approach has considerable relevance to contemporary policy. Nation states are not likely to split down the middle because an optimum currency area would be so drawn. But many countries, both industrial and developing, face the decision of whether they should combine together in closer financial ties, or perhaps alternatively seek greater monetary independence from one another.

The decision to join in the formation of a currency area is, of course, ultimately a political one. The political costs of the limitations placed on the independent use of traditional instruments of national policy will depend both on the economic costs (or benefits) of giving up at least nominal sovereignty in these areas and the extent to which governments give weight to the welfare of their prospective partners in the currency area.

The authors are Senior Staff Economist at the Council of Economic Advisers, on leave from Harvard University, and Teaching Fellow at Harvard University, respectively. They wish to thank Paul Wonnacott and Ralph Wood for helpful comments on a longer version of this paper.

The willingness to think more in group rather than strictly national terms will be influenced by such factors as cultural heritage, language, and political and ideological similarities. The less are the likely economic costs (or the greater the likely benefits) and the greater the consideration given to the welfare of the other members of the group, the greater would be the willingness of the members to make the compromises necessary to successfully operate the jointly-determined macro and regional policies required for a smoothly functioning currency area.

Adjustment Under Fixed Exchange Rates

The economic importance of the reduction of control over some of its traditional instruments of economic policy, which would be brought about by a country's joining a currency area, will depend on how the severity of the country's balance-of-payments adjustment problems are affected. This, in turn, depends upon the size and nature of the balance-of-payments disturbances that the country will face (or would face if it were following its desired internal policies) and the ease with which adjustment takes place via the mechanisms that remain (the use of exchange-rate adjustments and controls having been ruled out).

These mechanisms are, or course, the same as those that operate in interregional balance-of-payments adjustment within a country. Writers such as Ingram and Scitovsky have placed emphasis on the cushioning role played by the high mobility of private financial capital between regions.[1] This mechanism serves primarily to finance rather than to correct or adjust an imbalance of payments. Nevertheless, such financing may ease the burden on actual adjustment by tiding an area over a period of temporary disequilibrium where long-term adjustment is not necessary, and by allowing adjustment to be spread out over a longer period of time.

The removal of a trade deficit through market forces under fixed exchange rates generally requires that the money income of the area in question decline relative to that abroad. Unemployment will be minimized if this fall in income takes place via a combination of relative wage and price reduction and outward migration stimulated by the decline in money incomes in the area. Allowing considerable time for full adjustment to take place may ease the cost of adjustment by increasing

[1] See, for instance, James C. Ingram, "State and Regional Payments Mechanisms," *Quarterly Journal of Economics* (November 1959), and "A Proposal for Financial Integration in the Atlantic Community," in *Factors Affecting the United States Balance of Payments,* Joint Economic Committee of the U.S. Congress, 87th Congress, 2nd Session (Washington: U.S. Government Printing Office, 1962); Tibor Scitovsky, "The Theory of Balance of Payments Adjustment," *Journal of Political Economy* (August 1967 Supplement), and *Money and the Balance of Payments* (Chicago: Rand McNally, 1969); Marina V. N. Whitman, *International and Interregional Payments Adjustment: A Synthetic View,* Princeton Essay in International Finance, No. 19, 1967.

the degree both of relative wage and price flexibility and of factor mobility. The downward inflexibility of money wages and prices is, of course, a major reason why exchange-rate flexibility may be needed to allow adjustment to take place without an unnecessary cost in terms of unemployment. But, as Haberler has stressed, in a world that displays some inflationary trend, an area's wages and prices can fall relative to those abroad without requiring an absolute decline. A country that keeps its rate of increase of money income 1 per cent below normal for four years may face less aggregate unemployment than if it were required to reduce its rate of growth of money income by 4 per cent in one year. The scope for adjusting relatively painlessly via differential growth of money income is small and, hence, adjustment might have to be stretched out over a long period of time. Where adequate financing was available, the cost of adjustment might be eased.

This possibility is reinforced by the consideration that labor mobility is considerably higher in the long run than in the short run. Hence, the longer the time period within which adjustment must take place, the greater would be the outward movement of factors. Both the greater relative wage-price flexibility and higher mobility of labor would tend to reduce the amount of unemployment felt in the deficit area at any given level of aggregate demand. Likewise, the inflationary pressures on surplus areas should also be reduced.[2]

Another important factor influencing the amount of the inflation or deflation necessary to correct a given imbalance of payments is the openness of the area in question. Open economies tend to be the smallest and exhibit the largest propensities to import. The higher is an area's marginal propensity to import, the less is the change in internal aggregate demand required to correct a given imbalance. On the other hand, a low marginal propensity to import means that considerable domestic deflation would be required to bring about a relatively small change in imports.

Furthermore, the degree of openness of an economy may influence the employment impact of any given degree of financial restraint. In a very open economy, excessive domestic inflationary pressure tends to spill

---

[2] Factor mobility was adopted by Mundell as the primary determinant of optimum currency areas; see Robert A. Mundell, "A Theory of Optimum Currency Areas," *American Economic Review* (September 1961), and *The International Monetary System: Conflict and Reform* (Montreal: Canadian Trade Committee, 1965). See also the critical discussions of the role of labor mobility in Peter B. Kenen, "The Theory of Optimum Currency Areas: An Eclectic View" in Robert A. Mundell and Alexander K. Swoboda (eds.), *Monetary Problems of the International Economy* (Chicago: University of Chicago Press, 1969); Anthony Lanyi, "The Case for Floating Exchange Rates Reconsidered," Princeton Essay in International Finance, No. 72, February 1969; and Delbert A. Snider, "Optimum Adjustment Processes and Currency Areas," Princeton Essays in International Finance, No. 62, October 1967.

over directly into increased imports rather than onto prices. This has an important implication for demand management in a world in which wages and prices are inflexible downwards, for it amounts to what Machlup has termed "the simple case" in which the maxim that balance-of-payments cures should be tailored to the cause of the disequilibrium is correct. This is the case in which excessive monetary or fiscal expansion at home has led to overspending on foreign goods, but has not yet led to an increase in wages or prices. In this case, tighter financial policy can reduce aggregate demand and remove the payments deficit without increasing unemployment. In other words, this is a genuine nondilemma case. As Machlup goes on to argue, "The 'simple case' stops being simple as soon as the increase in demand leads to an increase in wage rates." [3] Then demand can be deflated quickly only at the cost of unemployment. Thus, whether a given mistake in demand management becomes irreversibly incorporated into a country's wage-price structure will depend in large measure on the openness of the economy. Given the same mistakes in domestic demand management, the incidence of dilemma relative to nondilemma cases will be greater, the more closed is the economy in question.

The influence of openness on the efficacy of internal versus exchange-rate adjustment is symmetrical in that not only does the absolute efficiency of internal adjustments increase with openness, but the efficiency of exchange-rate adjustments declines.[4] Devaluation by a small, open economy will raise the price of tradable goods more and, since they comprise a larger proportion of the consumption bundle, cost-of-living clauses in wage contracts will cause a much more significant hike in money wages. Furthermore, in an open economy, the improvement in the trade balance resulting from the devaluation will put more inflationary pressure on domestic resources than would be the case in a more closed economy.

Balance-of-Payments Disturbances and the Choice Between Fixed and Flexible Exchange Rates

The preceding section dealt with the costs of adjustment to given payments imbalances, that is, the cost per unit of adjustment. But the total

---

[3] Fritz Machlup, "In Search of Guides for Policy," in William Fellner et al., *Maintaining and Restoring Balance in International Payments* (Princeton, N.J.: Princeton University Press, 1966), p. 41.

[4] See, for instance, Ronald I. McKinnon, "Optimum Currency Areas," *American Economic Review* (September 1963), and "Optimum World Monetary Arrangements and the Dual Currency System," *Banca Nazionale del Lavaro Quarterly Review* (December 1963); Guy H. Orcutt, "Exchange Rate Adjustment and the Relative Size of the Depreciating Bloc," *Review of Economics and Statistics* (February 1955).

costs of adjustment will depend as well upon the source and magnitudes of the payments imbalances that will occur. To the extent that countries have expectations concerning the source and magnitudes of payments imbalances they are likely to face, this may also influence their choice of exchange-rate systems.

Perhaps of primary importance for a successful currency area with a less than perfect internal-adjustment mechanism is that there be a reasonable degree of compatibility between the member countries' attitudes toward growth of inflation and unemployment and their abilities to "trade off" between these objectives. A nation with a low tolerance for unemployment, and strong wage push from labor unions and price pressures from concentrated industries, would make a poor partner for a country with a low tolerance of inflation and high productivity growth, making for a very favorable "Phillips Curve." Likewise, the pace of technological advance and the magnitude of income elasticities of demand for exports and imports may have important influences upon countries' balance-of-payments trends. Where there are significant differences in the resultants of all these factors, the formation of an effective currency area would prove extremely difficult.

Cyclical and microeconomic disturbances may also influence the relative desirability of fixed and flexible exchange rates. Kenen has recently argued that diversified economies make the best candidates for currency areas. Because of the law of large numbers, the independent microeconomic disturbances that influence each sector will tend to have cancelling effects on the aggregate trade balance. Fluctuations in the total trade balance would be much less than the sum of the fluctuations in its constituent parts. Thus "from the standpoint of external balance, taken by itself, economic diversification, reflected in export diversification, serves, *ex ante,* to forestall the need for frequent changes in the terms of trade and, therefore, for frequent changes in national exchange rates." In addition to his argument that "a well-diversified national economy will not have to undergo changes in its terms of trade as often as a single product national economy," Kenen also presents arguments that "when, in fact, it does confront a drop in the demand for its principal exports, unemployment will not rise as sharply as it would in a less-diversified national economy" and that "the links between external and domestic demand, especially the link between exports and investment, will be weaker in diversified national economies, so that variations in domestic employment 'imported' from abroad will not be greatly aggravated by corresponding variations in capital formation."[5]

While Kenen's diversification argument, which was also made by Orcutt, is theoretically valid, there is some question about its quantitative

---

[5] Kenen, op. cit., p. 49. See also the following commentary on his paper.

importance.[6] Furthermore, it could be interpreted alternatively as saying that a flexible rate would tend to fluctuate less for a more diversified economy than for a less diversified one. In a diversified economy, domestic goods generally will be better substitutes for foreign goods than in an undiversified economy. This would lead to higher elasticities of excess demand and supply in the foreign trade sector. This combined with the argument made by Orcutt and McKinnon, that openness in itself leads to lower elasticities of excess demand and supply, implies that exchange-rate adjustments will be most effective in relatively closed economics. Furthermore, as Kenen himself notes, a diversified economy would tend to have a rather low marginal propensity to import, that is, it would be relatively closed, and would, thus, find internal adjustments to be very costly.

Conceptually, one could balance off the reduced need for adjustment by a diversified economy against the greater effectiveness of exchange-rate adjustment and the higher cost of making internal adjustments because of a low marginal propensity to import. Unless the reduction in the need for adjustment were substantial, however, it seems unlikely to us that this consideration would dominate.

A second type of argument concerns the source of disturbances. It is rather widely accepted that a country has the strongest case for flexible rates when the disturbances to its balance of payments typically come from outside its borders and the weakest case when they come from inside. There are two main rationales for this view. One is that under fixed rates without controls, the effects of disturbances in one country tend to be spread out over other countries, while under flexible exchanges, they are, to a greater degree, bottled up within the country of origin. Hence, flexible rates tend to insulate a country from disturbances abroad, but make it bear more fully the effects of disturbances originating at home, while fixed rates make it more susceptible to disturbances abroad, but also gives it greater scope to pass along the effects of domestic disturbances onto others.

The case that a country has the strongest need for flexible exchange when disturbances originate abroad may also be made from another point of view—that of the requirements necessary for domestic financial or expenditure policy to attain both internal and external balance. The need for an additional policy instrument such as exchange-rate adjustment arises when there is a conflict between the two requirements, that is, when a dilemma case exists. In general, we find that when a disturbance originates abroad, or in the foreign-trade sector, the require-

---

[6] See, for instance, Alasdair I. MacBean, *Export Instability and Economic Development* (Cambridge: Harvard University Press, 1966), and references cited there.

ments for internal and external balance clash. Hence, again by this line of argument, we reach the conclusion that *ceteris paribus* the case for exchange-rate adjustments is greater, the greater the likelihood that most disturbances occur abroad or in the foreign-trade sector.[7]

Combined with the argument that the more open the economy, the more likely are the majority of disturbances to occur abroad or in the foreign-trade sector (see, for instance, Giersch's paper in this volume), the preceding proposition is also a valid counterargument to the generalization that less open economies are better candidates for flexible exchange rates. Again, however, the quantitative importance of this line of argument is open to question. The reliability of the postulated insulating properties of flexible exchange rates is diminished in a world of capital mobility [8] and openness in trade tends to diminish the effectiveness of exchange-rate adjustments so that the more open an economy, the less powerful would be flexible exchange rates in insulating it from disturbances originating abroad. Furthermore, it is possible that by joining a currency area a country may be able to secure greater control over its external environment.

Concluding Remarks

As has been indicated in the discussion above, there is no general agreement on the relative importance of the determinants of optimum currency areas. We do not have a unified theory of optimum currency areas; and while there remains a wide scope for fruitful research on this topic, the goal of such a unified theory is probably illusionary. Nor, if our knowledge attained such a state, could we expect that a pattern of currency areas that would be optimal from an economic point of view would prove politically feasible.

Nevertheless, the concept of optimum currency areas is of considerable importance. It provides useful information for the formation of "good," even though nonoptimum, currency areas, and it tends to raise the general level of discussion of fixed versus flexible exchange rates. It points to the illegitimacy of ascribing all of the benefits of a genuine currency area to the present system of adjustable pegs and various degrees of capital controls. It illustrates how disagreements concerning the relative desirability of fixed versus flexible exchange rates frequently may be traced to differences in the types of economies in the minds of the dispu-

---

[7] See, for instance, Richard E. Caves, "Flexible Exchange Rates," *American Economic Review* (May 1963); L. B. Yeager, *International Monetary Relations* (New York: Harper & Row, Publishers, 1966), Chapter 6.

[8] See, for instance, the excellent survey by Robert G. McTeer, "Economic Independence and Insulation Through Flexible Exchange Rates," in N. A. Beadles and L. A. Drewy (eds.), *Money, The Market and the State* (Athens: University of Georgia Press, 1968), and references cited there.

tants. The importance of the possible cost push effects of exchange-rate depreciation, for instance, will be strongly influenced by the openness of the economy in question.

The objective of an exchange-rate system is to secure the best possible combination of fixity and flexibility. The Bretton Woods adjustable-peg system was an attempt at such a combination. As it has operated in practice, however, many feel that it has tended to combine the worst rather than the best features of fixed and flexible rates. At least two other basic approaches are possible. The optimum-currency-area approach focuses on the advantages of providing greater fixity of exchange rates than Bretton Woods among groups of countries that combine to form a currency area, and greater flexibility in the exchange rates between such groups. A third approach to the question of the degree of fixity of exchange rates is that of limited flexibility of exchange rates, under which small, gradual changes in exchange rates are more frequent than under Bretton Woods, but large, discrete changes are less likely. These three approaches, while conceptually distinct, are not mutually exclusive. Indeed, it seems likely that an optimum system might display currency areas, sliding parities, and relatively free rates. Sliding parities, for instance, could provide a half-way house for countries that display many of the characteristics conducive to forming a currency area, but are not sufficiently attuned in balance-of-payments trends to form a true currency area.[9]

Consider the EEC. The economic ties between the member countries are such that they probably would not consider free rates desirable. But given their national attitudes, degrees of labor mobility, and likely balance-of-payment trends, France and Germany, for instance, do not appear to be good candidates to join together in a full-fledged currency area at the present time. A sliding parity might be the most efficient mechanism at this state of these countries' integration. One might conceive of a number of the European countries combining in full-fledged

---

[9] We should note that contrary to the popular dictum that flexible exchange rates would be a disintegrating force in the world economy, it is not at all clear that "fixed" rates maintained by frequent controls and subject to the possibility of occasional large discrete changes are more conducive to economic integration. See, for instance, James E. Meade, "The Balance of Payments Problems of a European Free-Trade Area," *Economic Journal* (September 1957); L. B. Yeager, "Exchange Rates within a Common Market," *Social Research*, Vol. XXV, No. 4 (Winter, 1958), and the paper by Harry G. Johnson and Paul Wonnacott in Johnson, *et al., Harmonization of National Economic Policies under Free Trade,* published for the Private Planning Association of Canada by the University of Toronto Press, 1968.

We should also warn against the identification of "fixed" rates with internationalism or a global point of view and "flexible" exchange rates with isolationism or an inward looking political philosophy. Nor is the concept of optimum currency areas properly identified with regionalism as opposed to multilateralism in trade and payments.

currency areas (Benelux, for instance) within a larger and looser European currency group connected by narrow-band parities. The whole group could establish a central stabilization fund that would maintain a much wider band around a sliding parity or smooth a relatively free rate, vis-a-vis the dollar.

Part VII. Miscellany

THE two papers in this section would not fit easily into any of the preceding sections, but as they are relevant to the general discussion, they deserve inclusion in this volume.

Gottfried Haberler's study, "Import Border Taxes and Export-Tax Refunds Versus Exchange-Rate Changes," is a comparison between open and disguised revaluation. The Germans called their border-tax arrangements a "substitute revaluation" of the mark. It would be most appropriate to have this paper followed by others discussing alternative forms of disguised changes in the external value of a currency. The interest-equalization taxes imposed (and taxes on foreign travel proposed) in the United States were concealed partial devaluations of the dollar, and several other countries have introduced similar devices to influence specific accounts in the balance of payments. Alas, no other participant of the Bürgenstock Conference has offered to write about these subjects.

Haberler admits that *specific* border taxes and export-tax refunds can be justified if they merely offset the effects of *indirect* taxes on costs of production. A tax-subsidy scheme as substitute for exchange-rate variations, however, must be *general*. Moreover, the scheme could never be entirely uniform, and would lead to distortions in international trade, even if the participating countries avoided conscious discrimination. The proposal to substitute a tax-subsidy scheme for variations of exchange rates "is part and parcel of the general tendency to substitute controls for policies that rely on market forces."

Harry G. Johnson's note, "Government and the Corporation: A Fallacious Analogy," grew out of a discussion at Bürgenstock in which Robert V. Roosa compared investment-decision-making by the private corporation with the government's unwillingness to give up control over the exchange rates. Johnson rejects Roosa's comparison on several counts.

· 51 ·

Import Border Taxes and Export-Tax Refunds Versus Exchange-Rate Changes

GOTTFRIED HABERLER

IT IS well known that a uniform ad valorem tax of X per cent on all imports plus a uniform ad valorem subsidy of X per cent on all exports is equivalent, as far as commodity trade is concerned, to an X per cent devaluation of the currency. Similarly, an equal and uniform reduction of the rate of tax and subsidy is equivalent to an appreciation of the currency.

The reader may recall that prior to the devaluation of sterling in 1931, Keynes had recommended a system of import tariffs and export bounties. He claimed that such a scheme would be much superior to devaluation because it would avoid the depreciation, in terms of gold, of British foreign assets denominated in sterling. "This proposal would avoid the injury to the national credit and to our receipts from foreign loans fixed in terms of Sterling which would ensue on devaluation." "A plan of this kind would be immeasurably preferable to devaluation." [1] At first he recommended a uniform ad valorem duty on all imports and an equal uniform ad valorem bounty for all exports. But he later dropped the uniformity principle and recommended different percentage taxes and subsidies for different commodities. Keynes must, thus, be regarded as the inventor of what later became known as the "Schachtian" system of international trading. This system was admired and advocated for adoption elsewhere in different variations and guises by Keynes's more radical disciples. But Keynes himself later returned to more orthodox trading methods, and, in his famous posthumously published article on the American balance of payments,[2] sharply rejected the modern stuff "gone silly and sour" of his radical erstwhile followers, who in the meantime had become his critics.

Later on, the proposal to substitute import taxes and export subsidies for a change in the exchange rate was occasionally mentioned in the literature, but it was only in the postwar period that the idea gained popularity and was put into practice.

During the crisis of the French franc in November 1968, when France was urged to devalue her currency and Germany to appreciate

---

[1] See Addendum I, which Keynes, together with six others, submitted to the "Macmillan Committee" report. Committee on Finance and Industry, *Report* (London, 1931), pp. 199 and 200.
[2] *Economic Journal* (June 1946).

hers, a stop-gap "solution" was adopted. Germany offered what the Germans now call an *"Ersatz* upvaluation" of the German mark in the form of a 4 per cent reduction of the border tax and a 4 per cent reduction of tax refunds on exports, and France agreed to an *"Ersatz* devaluation" of the franc of the same nature. When the German mark was at last upvalued in October 1969, the change in the border tax was rescinded. (In this connection the German word *Ersatz* is preferable to the English "substitute," because the German word carries the connotation of an inferior, unsound, makeshift replacement for the real thing.)

In the current discussion, the idea of a tax-subsidy scheme as a substitute for exchange-rate changes is linked with the theory that, quite apart from balance-of-payments and exchange-rate problems, *general* internal taxes, such as turnover, value-added or income taxes, should be levied on imports and refunded on exports, presumably in order to avoid distortions and unfair burdens on domestic producers of importable and exportable commodities. In addition there is the questionable theory that only indirect taxes, such as the turnover or value-added tax, justify adjustment at the border, not, however, direct taxes such as the income tax. This principle has been enshrined in the GATT regulations, which permit border taxes and tax refunds on exports to offset the effect on cost of production of indirect taxes, but not of direct taxes.

It is unfortunate that the two issues—the macroeconomic tax-subsidy schemes for balance-of-payments purposes, on the one hand, and the microeconomic border-tax adjustments to avoid distortions and inequities on the other—are being linked, because the two issues are in fact entirely independent problems and should be dealt with each on its own merits. I will take up the second problem first.

MICROECONOMIC ASPECTS OF BORDER-TAX PROBLEMS

Contrary to what is often assumed, there is no justification, on grounds of allocative efficiency or avoidance of distortions and inequities, for protecting domestic production from foreign competition, on account of *general* taxation, by border taxes and refunds on exports. The confusion results from not distinguishing between *specific* taxes and *general* taxes. It would indeed be absurd for a country that has a high specific tax on whiskey, Great Britain for example, *not* to tax imports or to forego export possibilities by *not* refunding the tax on exports of whiskey. The reason is that a specific tax does distort the comparative cost situation; in other words, it creates a difference between private and social cost and, therefore, requires adjustment at the border. A perfectly general tax does *not* distort the comparative cost situation and, therefore, does *not* require adjustment at the border.

The difference was lucidly demonstrated by David Ricardo more than 100 years ago:

For the same reasons that protecting duties are not justifiable on account of the rise of wages generally, from whatever cause it may proceed, it is evident that they are not to be defended when taxation is general, and equally affects all classes of producers. An income tax is of this description . . .

. . . The rise of wages, a tax on income, or a proportional tax on all commodities, all operate in the same way; they do not alter the relative value of goods, and therefore they do not subject us to any disadvantage in our commerce with foreign countries . . .

A tax, however, which falls exclusively on the producers of a particular commodity tends to raise the price of that commodity . . .

. . . If no protecting duty is imposed on the importation of a similar commodity from other countries, injustice is done to the producer at home, and not only to the producer but to the country to which he belongs. It is for the interest of the public that he should not be driven from a trade which, under a system of free competition, he would have chosen, and to which he would adhere if every other commodity were taxed equally with that which he produces . . .[3]

As can be seen, Ricardo also knew that it makes no difference whether the tax is direct or indirect so long as it is a general tax. The often repeated proposition that a general indirect tax, say a value-added tax, can be "shifted" while the income tax cannot be shifted, is entirely irrelevant. In fact, it is not at all clear who shifts the tax on whom. Everybody on everybody else? [4]

[3] See "On the Protection of Agriculture" (1822), *The Works and Correspondence of David Ricardo,* edited by P. Sraffa, Vol. IV (London, 1951), pp. 216–217.

[4] A theoretical qualification may be in order. The incidence of a "general" tax on different products and industries may after all be uneven. If this could be clearly demonstrated, an offsetting tax on imports or subsidy on exports would be in order—in theory at least; in practice, it is clearly impossible to cut things that fine. We simply do not know enough about the incidence of general taxes on different commodities to make possible tolerably accurate offsets by export subsidies and border taxes. But if a country thinks it can establish a distorting effect of a general tax, it clearly would be better to change the tax law in order to make the tax more nearly neutral or truly general than to attempt a complicated offsetting operation at the border. This is precisely the reason why Germany a year ago changed from a turnover to the value-added tax. The former, it was held, had certain distorting effects. In this switch, the Germans changed the rate of border taxes and export tax refunds. They claimed that no increase in the average rate of border tax or tax refund on exports was implied. American officials, on the other hand, asserted that the adjustments made in taxes and refunds have raised the average rate and thus constitute a "protectionist" measure. (It is more correct to say "constitute a depreciation of the mark.") It need not be decided here who was right in this dispute.

MACROECONOMIC (BALANCE-OF-PAYMENTS) ASPECTS OF BORDER-TAX PROBLEMS

I come now to the macroeconomic balance-of-payments aspect of the problem. The question is this: what are the advantages and disadvantages of substituting a tax-subsidy system for a change in the exchange rate? That this problem is entirely independent of the existence and height of domestic taxes becomes clear if one reflects that the rate of import tax and export subsidy that is required in any given case depends on the magnitude of the balance-of-payments disequilibrium in conjunction with the elasticities of demand and supply of exports and imports, but has nothing whatsoever to do with internal tax rates, for example the rate of value-added tax or turnover tax or income tax, that a country happens to have. Moreover, there is no reason to assume that a switch from a general income tax to a general value-added tax would influence the balance of payments in any systematic fashion.[5] Suppose it is desirable to use the tax-subsidy method rather than appreciation or depreciation of the currency: why should a country not use the tax-subsidy method if it would require an import tax and export subsidy much in excess of the internal tax rate? Or even if, in case of an extreme surplus country, restoration of equilibrium in the balance of payments would require a negative border tax, in other words, an import subsidy and a negative export subsidy, in other words, an export tax?

But now I come to the basic point: I maintain that the case *against* using the tax-subsidy system for balance-of-payments adjustment is overwhelming.

The fundamental objection to the tax-subsidy system is that, in actual practice, the rate of tax and subsidy will never be uniform. Even if it were uniform for merchandise, it would not apply to services. Thus, it does not apply to tourism, a very important item in the balance of payments of many countries.[6] But even in the commodity sphere there are always exceptions and exemptions, and the temptation is practically irresistible to discriminate and differentiate between commodities and, implicitly, between countries. (Remember that Keynes quickly pushed on from recommending a uniform tax-subsidy to recommending outright discrimination.)

An additional very weighty objection, which applies especially to the

---

[5] It is true, however, that under the existing GATT rules such a switch enables a country to impose a border tax on imports and to grant tax refunds on exports. This is precisely what the French did in November 1968.

[6] For example, if, in November 1968, the French franc had been devalued and the German mark upvalued, German tourists would have spent more in France and French tourists less in Germany, thus contributing to the restoration of balance-of-payments equilibrium. Tourist expenditures have been shown to be quite sensitive to relative price changes.

United States, is that for countries that do not practice general export subsidization the introduction of the tax-subsidy system would imply adding an entirely new dimension to commercial policy, and would necessitate setting up new administrative machinery. It is easy to see that there would be a standing invitation and temptation to use this new instrument for *other* purposes and there would be constant pressure from certain industries to obtain special treatment.

In the United States it has been proposed by influential economists, Henry Wallich for example, that the tax part of the full tax-subsidy scheme should be in the form of a uniform import surcharge. The author of the proposal correctly described the import surcharge as equivalent to "one half of a depreciation of the currency." He went on to say that if after a year or two it turned out that the surcharge were not enough to restore equilibrium, the other half could be added by dropping the surcharge and depreciating the dollar outright.

The import surcharge would be administratively much easier to apply than the full tax-subsidy scheme because it would require no, or little, additional bureaucratic machinery. But it would be a protectionist device because it leaves out exports. And to refer to it as "the first half of a depreciation of the dollar," which may or may not be followed later on by the other half, i.e., by full devaluation, could easily bring about massive speculation against the dollar. Suppose after six months or a year it appeared that the surcharge was not sufficient to restore equilibrium, the possibility of an outright devaluation of the dollar would become very strong—everybody would know it and many would act accordingly.

Another danger is that an import surcharge, once it has been in force for some time, would be difficult to remove, even if the balance of payments improved, because domestic industries would have become used to the added protection. Proponents of the surcharge answer this criticism by referring to the Canadian and British examples. Canada, in 1962, and Great Britain, in 1964, imposed surcharges on imports, and both countries abolished them within a reasonable period. The argument is, however, not convincing. Canada devalued her dollar drastically at the same time when she imposed the surcharge and, therefore, quite naturally, soon found she could get along without the surcharge. Great Britain eliminated her surcharge under fire and bitter criticism, especially from her partners in EFTA, who pointed out that the surcharge violated both the spirit and the letter of the EFTA agreement, and a year after she abolished the surcharge she was forced to devalue anyway. Thus, in both cases, the import surcharge was an unnecessary interlude that produced international ill will and frictions, and nothing else.[7]

[7] To bolster their case, the British Government argued that the GATT rules that permit the use of import quotas but forbid import duties (including surcharges) in

I conclude that the border tax on imports and tax refund on exports is an inferior, messy, wasteful, and inefficient substitute for exchange-rate adjustments. The United States is, for the reasons given, in an especially poor position to use this instrument. But the United States is, as far as economic logic and sound principles are concerned, in a strong position to urge the surplus countries to reduce the rate of their border tax and export-tax refund. The ideal solution would be for the surplus countries to drop the system altogether and, thus, get rid of the distortions the border taxes and export subsidies entail, because they are not truly general or neutral. This would be in the true interest of the surplus countries themselves.

The question arises why the method of the border tax and export-tax refund has become so popular. There are two main reasons. The first is the mistaken but widely held view, which was criticized above, that there is a case, apart from balance-of-payments considerations on microeconomic grounds, for border adjustment of general internal taxes. The second reason is, of course, the general aversion to exchange-rate changes. The reason for this aversion will not be discussed in the present paper. Let me say only that border taxes, surcharges, and the like are part and parcel of the general tendency to substitute controls for policies that rely on market forces. General border taxes and export-tax refunds are a part of generalized exchange control; they are better, no doubt, than other measures of control (such as quotas and other quantitative restrictions) but objectionable and inefficient nonetheless because they never are truly general.

An advantage claimed for rebates of border taxes and export taxes over exchange rate changes is that rebates do not apply to capital transactions and leave the value of outstanding assets and liabilities unchanged; as a consequence, they do not induce, it is asserted, anticipatory capital flows in the same manner exchange-rate changes do. However, the validity of this argument is open to serious doubt. As soon as it is generally realized that border tax adjustments (with or without rebates of export tax) are nothing but a substitute for exchange-rate adjustment, the possibility of the latter will always loom in the background. It then becomes very doubtful whether the tax-subsidy method is in fact superior to the adjustable-peg system, from the point of view of avoiding speculative capital movements, and the tax-subsidy method is certainly inferior to a regime of flexible rates that does not offer the same easy target to the speculator as the adjustable-peg system does.

It is often said that the border-tax adjustment has the advantage, over

---

case of balance-of-payments difficulties are inconsistent and ill-advised. I would go along with that criticism of the GATT provisions; if import restrictions are to be used at all, duties are a lesser evil than quotas. But the point is irrelevant, for my argument because the question is whether *any* import restrictions are necessary.

exchange-rate adjustment, that it can be more easily removed when the situation demands a change in policy. This may not be so easy, as was pointed out above, and, in any event, easy reversibility would be an advantage of the tax-subsidy method only in comparison with the current practice of a rigid, quasi-immutable exchange rate; but this alleged advantage of the tax-subsidy method disappears when compared with any system of exchange-rate flexibility.

It should also be observed that many objections to exchange-rate changes, whether valid or not, equally apply to the border tax. For example, if it is said that, for the members of the European Common Market, exchange-rate changes are unacceptable because they "counteract the process of economic integration," it should be clear that border taxes (or any other substitute for exchange-rate changes) are just as disruptive and retrogressive on integration.[8]

[8] I would deny that exchange-rate changes interfere with economic integration. If the countries of the EEC are unable (as they undoubtedly are at this time), to "harmonize" their financial and monetary policies sufficiently to forestall the emergence of serious balance-of-payments disequilibria, exchange-rate changes are the most efficient and integrative (or least disintegrative, if you wish) method of correcting imbalances.

· 52 ·

Government and the Corporation: A Fallacious Analogy

HARRY G. JOHNSON

In the course of the discussion of the definition of the balance of payments and the determination of balance-of-payments policy, Robert Roosa developed an analogy between the problems of the government as policy-maker and the problems of the corporation in making foreign-investment decisions. Out of the analogy he concluded that governments would, justifiably, not be willing to give up control over the determination of the exchange rates. Both the analogy and the conclusion drawn from it are fallacious for the reasons given here.

First, the corporation has to make a profit satisfactory to its shareholders. A government is subject to no such profits test of efficiency.

Second, a shareholder who is dissatisfied with the way a company is being managed can simply sell his shares in the market. He does not have to try to get a majority of the stockholders to agree with him, vote out the management, and take over control. For a nation, the latter course is the only alternative open.

Third, in most nations the electorate has a choice between two rival political parties, and, for reasons familiar from duopoly theory, the programs of these parties become very similar. Hence, the electorate cannot in fact radically alter the nature of economic management by the normal democratic processes.

Fourth, under the pressure of the profits test, the corporation has to integrate its decision-making across its various departments. In a government, however, decision-making with respect to key policy variables is largely delegated to particular institutions of government, each of which reacts to its own environment, according to its own traditions and organization. Thus, the central bank is typically responsible for monetary policy and the Treasury for fiscal policy. There is no guarantee that the selection of policy variables will be optimally made by this system of decision-making, even where the bank is formally subordinate to the Treasury. (This is a generalization of Mundell's "assignment problem.")

Finally, with regard to the question of limited versus unrestricted flexibility of exchange rates, the prices of corporate shares in the market are determined by the buying and selling decisions of investors, who, for this purpose, have to consider carefully the efficiency of the managements and the long-run prospects of the companies issuing the shares. This system is generally held to encourage efforts by company managements to maintain and increase efficiency and make wise decisions concerning the future. The analogy with government, to the extent that it is valid, would suggest that allowing exchange rates to be freely determined in the market would enable the same private capacities for judging efficiency and evaluating long-term prospects to be brought to bear on exchange rates, thereby relieving governments of the incredibly complex task of deciding on the appropriate exchange rate, and possibly bringing pressure to bear on them to improve their performance in economic management. Why should it be assumed that governments will be better at choosing appropriate exchange rates than private traders in the market, who, as Friedman has frequently pointed out, are after all risking their own money?

Contributors

W. F. J. BATT, Foreign Exchange Department, Westminster Bank Limited

C. FRED BERGSTEN, Senior Staff, National Security Council (formerly Visiting Fellow, Council on Foreign Relations)

GEORGE H. CHITTENDEN, Senior Vice President, Morgan Guaranty Trust Company

HAROLD VAN B. CLEVELAND, First National City Bank of New York

RICHARD N. COOPER, Professor of Economics, Yale University

WILLIAM FELLNER, Professor of Economics, Yale University

MILTON FRIEDMAN, Professor of Economics, University of Chicago

HERBERT GIERSCH, Direktor des Instituts für Weltwirtschaft, University of Kiel

DAVID L. GROVE, Chief Economist, IBM Corporation

GOTTFRIED HABERLER, Professor of International Trade, Harvard University

GEORGE N. HALM, Professor of Economics, Fletcher School, Tufts University

MARIUS W. HOLTROP, former President, De Nederlandsche Bank

TADASHI IINO, Deputy President, The Mitsui Bank Limited

MAX IKLÉ, Eidgenössische Bank (former General Director, Schweizerische Nationalbank)

HARRY G. JOHNSON, Professor of Economics, London School of Economics

WOLFGANG KASPER, Assistant Professor of Economics, University of Kiel

LAWRENCE B. KRAUSE, Senior Fellow, Brookings Institution

EMIL KUSTER, Senior Vice President, J. Henry Schroder Banking Corporation

ERIK LUNDBERG, Professor of Economics, Stockholm School of Economics

ÅKE LUNGREN, Senior Vice President, Skandinaviska Banken

FRIEDRICH A. LUTZ, Professor of Economics, University of Zurich

FRITZ MACHLUP, Professor of Economics and International Finance, Princeton University

STEPHEN N. MARRIS, Visiting Professor of International Economics, Brookings Institution

DONALD B. MARSH, Assistant General Manager, Royal Bank of Canada

ANTONIO MOSCONI, Collaborator, Istituto di Economia, University of Turin; Economic Adviser, Fiat Company

PETER M. OPPENHEIMER, Lecturer in Economics, Oxford University

GIULIANO PELLI, Senior Vice President, Swiss Bank Corporation

EDWIN A. REICHERS, Senior Vice President, First National City Bank of New York
ROBERT V. ROOSA, Partner, Brown Brothers Harriman and Company
EGON SOHMEN, Professor of Economics, University of Heidelberg
EDWARD TOWER, Teaching Fellow, Harvard University
CONSTANT M. VAN VLIERDEN, Executive Vice President, Bank of America
JOHN H. WATTS III, Banking Executive, Brown Brothers Harriman and Company
THOMAS D. WILLETT, Assistant Professor of Economics, Harvard University

Index

Ablin, Richard, 286
adjustable-peg system, 7, 77, 91, 262; enhances inflation and deflation, 105; leads to restrictions, 105; offers one-way options for speculators, 104, 160, 225-226, 324; as poor compromise, 4-5
adjustment formula for parity changes, 20, 37-39, 272-273
adjustment inflation, 38
adjustment mechanism, asymmetry of, 126; causes for inadequacy of, 138-140; and international liquidity reserves, 10, 15, 261-262; via absolute deflation of effective demand, 133-140
adjustment of parity, *see* parity adjustment
Agricultural Common Market, *see* common agricultural policies
Aliber, Robert Z., 186, 334
arbitrage funds, 313-314
Articles of Agreement (IMF), *see* International Monetary Fund
asymmetry, of adjustment mechanism, 126; of band, 34-35, 234, 240, 245-249; between dollar and other currencies, 22-23, 255; of crawl, 35, 87, 234, 240; of devaluation, and revaluation, 61, 68, 70, 87, 234

Baffi, Paolo, 120
Bagehot, Walter, 51
balance of payments, on basic account, 130; causes of surpluses and deficits, 131-132; disequilibrium, 130, *see also* fundamental disequilibrium; equilibrium balance, 145; on liquidity basis, 130-131; national liquidity surplus and deficit, 131; on official account, 130-131
bancor, 17-18
band for variations of exchange rates, *see* widened band
Batt, W. F. J., 295, 317, 320, 427
Beadles, N. A., 413
beggar-my-neighbor policies, 9, 273
Bergsten, C. Fred, 1, 27, 61, 427
Bernstein, Edward, 119-121
Black, J., 283, 284
blocs, *see* currency blocs
Bodner, David, 283
Bonn meeting of November 1968, 92, 106
border taxes, 100, 123, 252, 418, 422-423

Bryant, Ralph, 283
Bürgenstock communiqué, vii-viii
Bürgenstock conference, v-viii

Canada, 194, 261-269, 278, 325; austerity program, 341; beggar-my-neighbor policy, 341; devaluation of 1949, 338; devaluation of 1961-1962, 341; and dollar area, 66, 330; experience with floating exchange rate, 337-344; under "true" floating rate, 261, 338-339; war-time exchange controls, 337-338
Cannan, Edwin, 337
Canterbery, E. Ray, 16, 20
CAP, *see* common agricultural policy
capital goods trade and wider bands, 211-212
capital movements, private, and crawling peg, 17, 253, 292-293; disequilibrating, 14-15; equilibrating, 12-13; and flexible exchange rates, 18, 279; and widened band, 12-13, 171-172, 292-293
Carli, Guido, 391
Caves, Richard E., 91, 413
center currency, 49
central banks, and flexible exchange rates, 6, 92; and foreign exchange market, 210, 236; intervention inside widened band, 196, 227, 229, 280-281, 323-324; regulation of foreign operations, 236; as residual buyers and sellers, 161; smoothing operations, 323, 325; swap arrangements, 264
Chittenden, George H., 219, 245, 427
Cleveland, Harold van B., 295, 323, 427
Cohen, Benjamin, 287
commercial loan theory, 57
common agricultural policy (CAP), 386-387, 390-391, 393-397, 401-406
common market countries, *see* European Economic Community
comparative advantage, 223
compartmentalization of credit market, 14
competition and forward market, 299, 301
competitive devaluation, 10
competitive exchange depreciation, 8, 9, 12, 39, 199, 262, 271, 276
controls, *see* exchange controls, quantitative restrictions
Coombis, Charles, 236

429

Cooper, Richard N., 39, 178, 216, 220, 251, 273, 294, 427
coordination of policies, *see* integration
Council of Economic Experts (Germany), 37-38, 345, 347
covered interest arbitrage, 82, 253, 277-278, 288-289, 293, 302, 313-314, 326-327
crawl equalization tav, 286
crawling peg (or parity) system, adjustment formula, 20, 37-39, 272-273; advantages of, 16-17; asymmetrical crawl, 85, 87, 234, 240; automatic crawl, 17; and capital movements, 17, 253, 292-293; as compromise, 107-108; disadvantages, 182-183; discretionary crawl, 17, 37-38; and fixed reserve standard, 266-267; formula-determined crawl, 20, 37-39, 272-273; and interest rates, 72, 283-294; and movable band, 20-24; and moving averages, 19; neutralized through wage and price increases, 182; neutralizes disturbances from abroad, 347; one-way crawl, 234, 240; as policy instrument, 288; presumptive crawl, 37-39, 251-259; prophylactic crawl, 37-39; rate of crawl, 33-35, 294; and stock adjustment, 289-291; therapeutic crawl, 37-38; upward crawl, 234, 240; and widened band, 36, 81, 108, 112-113, 280-281
credit market, compartmentalization of, 14
currency, alignment of, 180, 242, 246, 275, 276; center currency, 49; intervention currency, 10, 21-22, 35, 41, 61, 74, 143; key currency, 61-75, 277; pivot currency, 62, 65, 255, 271; transaction currency, 22, 61, 122
currency blocs, 8, 98, 101, 140, 241, 330; antagonistic blocs, 140
currency speculation, *see* speculation
currency unions and crawling parity, 258

Dale, William, 283
decision making on exchange rates, 77-88
deflation, 73, 119-120; "bottling up" of, 120; "spilling over" of, 119-120
demonetization of gold, 181, 185
Denmark, 378-380; fixed rates restrict employment and growth, 378-379; fundamental disequilibrium, 378; perference for fixed exchange rates, 379-380; trade-off between inflation and unemployment, 379
depreciation, self aggravating, 324; and U.S. dollar, 21, 72, 122, 243; as warning signal, 6, 40, 86, 121, 164, 241
depressed areas, 94-95, 121
devaluation, asymmetry of devaluation and revaluation, 61, 68, 70, 234; competitive devaluation, 10; concealed partial devaluation, 44; and income distribution, 78; and national prestige, 78, 86; as symbol of defeat, 107
Diamond, Marcus, 157
dilemma cases, 12-15, 18, 63, 118, 138
direct investments, *see* foreign direct investments
disaligned exchange rates, 4, 37, 41-45
discrete parity adjustments, 5, 6, 11, 34, 83, 127, 285
discretionary basis for crawling peg, 17, 37-38, 82, 142, 256, 267
disinflation, 118
D-mark, *see* German mark
dollar (U.S.), accumulation of dollar balances, 239; appreciation, 62, 71; asymmetry between dollar and other currencies, 21-23, 255; as center currency, 49; as common denominator, 21-22; depreciation, 21, 72, 122, 243; as financial asset, 62; and flexibility of exchange rates, 66-68; a floating dollar, 122-123; and gold, 4, 21-24, 62, 72-73, 122, 181, 242; inconvertibility of, 242, 244; as intervention currency, 10, 21-22, 35, 41, 61, 74, 143; as key currency, 61-75; and movable band, 21-23; in official settlements deficit, 73; overvaluation, 156, 246; as pivot currency, 62, 65, 255, 271; quadruple bias against, 68-70, 74; as reserve currency, 61, 122; as transaction currency, 22, 61, 122
dollar balances, 70-72
dollar bloc, 66, 369-370
dollar standard, 180
Drewy, L. A., 413
Dutch guilder, revaluation 1961, 34, 187
dynamic peg, 54

EEC, *see* European Economic Community
EFTA, 369
Emminger, Otmar, 234
England, *see* Great Britain
entrepreneurial risk and flexible exchange rates, 145-149

ersatz devaluation (substitute devaluation), 44, 418
ersatz upvaluation (substitute upvaluation), 44, 418
Eurobond market, 188, 192
Eurocurrency market, 179, 204, 207-208, 209, 367
Eurodollar market, 63, 179, 196, 209, 213, 319, 367, 388-389
European Commission, 200
European Economic Community, 1, 66, 135, 200, 277, 330; agricultural policy, 386-387, 390-391, 393-397, 401-406; British entry, 66-67, 71, 387, 391; a common currency?, 200; common monetary policy, 200; and flexible exchange rates, 385-399; and optimum currency area, 414-415
European Green Plan, 390
European integration, 385-399
European monetary policy, 388, 397
European Payments Union, 66
exchange controls, 6, 44, 122-123, 311-315, 317-319, 321
exchange equalization duties, 251, 257
exchange-rate changes and interest rates, 148-149, 289
exchange rates, criteria for setting exchange rates, 50; cross rates, 35, 275; decision making on, 77-88; depoliticized, 271; fixed, *see* fixed exchange rates; flexible, *see* flexible exchange rates; freely flexible or floating exchange rates, 7-9, 91-111; overvalued rates, 41-45, 126, 152-155, 161-165; undervalued rates, 9, 38, 41-45, 126, 155-158, 165, 350
exchange restrictions, *see* exchange controls, quantitative restrictions
export-tax refunds, 417-423

Fellner, William, 7, 16, 35, 181, 219, 237, 239, 240, 245, 286, 410, 427
Ferrero, Romulo, 344
Finland, 380-382; devaluation of 1969, 380-381; inflationary policies, 380; stable exchange rate as disciplinarian, 382
fiscal policies versus monetary policies, 14-15
fixed exchange rates, and automatic adjustment, 133-140; case against, 7-9, 98-102, 117-121; case for, 5-7, 93-98, 117-121; diffuse inflation and deflation, 100, 119-120; and discipline, 96; and exchange control, 5, 86, 100-101, 123; and foreign direct investment, 152-158; and integration of national policies, 6, 94; and market mechanism, 125-128; and one-sided speculation, 104, 160, 225-226, 324; and "socialization of risk," 300; as subsidy to international sector, 167, 175, 216
fixed reserve standard, 261-269; and crawling peg, 266-267; and widened band, 265-266
flexible exchange rates, "bottle up" inflation and deflation, 73, 119-120; case against, 5-7, 102-106, 117-121, 216-217; case for, 7-9, 91-111, 117-121; and central banks, 6, 92; and common agricultural policy, 383-387, 390-391, 393-397, 401-406; and confidence, 146, 195; and discipline, 6, 9, 40, 86, 121, 164, 241; and the dollar, 66-68; and entrepreneurial risk, 145-149; and European integration, 385-399; and exchange crises, 324; facilitate British entry into EEC, 387, 391; and foreign direct investment, 158-166; and forward market, 12, 101, 295-331; fully flexible rates, 7-9, 91-111; geographical limitations, 121; and inflation, 103, 105, 119-120, 176; and interest rates, 13, 19, 72, 148-149, 239, 283-294; neutralize impact of cyclical fluctuations, 147; and optimum currency areas, 407-415; and portfolio investment, 278; and private capital movements, 18, 279; and small countries, 97, 121, 129, 149; and speculation, 11, 18, 47, 160; and uncertainty, 103, 141, 168, 198, 204, 212, 227; and United States, 61-75; as warning signals, 6, 40, 86, 121, 164, 241
floating exchange rates, 7-9, 18, 98-111; Canadian experience, 337-344; a floating German mark, 345-355; a floating pound sterling, 109-111
foreign direct investments, and fixed exchange rates, 152-158; and flexible exchange rates, 158-166
Forte, Francesco, 286
forward cover, availabiilty of, 204-205; cost of, 103-104, 151, 206-207, 213, 217, 235, 278, 299-301, 307-309, 317, 319, 320, 326-329; demand for, 278, 297-298, 319, 325-326; and exchange risks, 311-315; imperilled by exchange restrictions, 311-315; and inflation, 207; insurance theory of, 313; and interest-rate arbitrage, 82, 253, 277-278, 288-289, 293, 302, 313-314, 326-327; supply of, 297-298, 326; and widened band, 158, 277-278, 325-326

431

forward exchange market, *see also* forward cover, alleged limitation of capacity, 299, 303; and allocation of productive resources, 300-301, 309; and brokerage business, 304; development of new market institutions, 217, 303-304, 318; imperfect competition, 299, 301; misunderstandings between practitioners and economists, 297-306; oligopolistic arrangements, 29, 301; and widened band, 12, 158, 277-278

France, devaluation of, 1949, 34; *erstaz* devaluation, 115, 117; student and worker rebellion, 1968, 115, 187, 194, 417

freely flexible exchange rates, 7'), 18, 98-106

Friedman, Milton, 1, 10, 27, 91, 334, 350, 426, 427

fundamental disequilibrium, 5-7, 19, 37, 46, 80, 91, 117, 126, 199, 226, 262, 275

German mark (D-mark), a floating mark, 345-355; floating in 1969, 269, 337; key currency status of, 71; revaluation of 1961, 34, 187, 312, 351, 365; revaluation of 1969, 38, 118, 235; undervaluation of, 38, 345, 350

Germany, balance of payments surplus, 188-191; *erstaz* revaluation, 44, 115, 418; floats D-mark, 269, 337; policy of undervaluation, 38, 53, 117-118, 234, 346; revaluation of 1961, 34, 187, 312, 351, 365; revaluation of 1969, 38, 118, 235

Giersch, Herbert, 35, 89, 145, 332, 345, 413, 427

Gilbert, Milton, 184

gliding pegs or parities, *see* crawling pegs or parities gold, crisis of March 1968, 92; demonetization of, 181, 185; differential gold revaluation, 242; and dollar, 4, 21-24, 62, 72-73, 122, 181, 242; increased price of, 181, 184, 268; as numeraire, 65; revaluation of, 181, 184, 243-244, 268; two-tier gold system, 23, 63, 115, 180, 201, 234

gold bloc, 370

gold bullion standard, 33

gold coin standard, 33

gold crisis of March 1968, 92

gold flow and commercial loan theory, 57

gold points, 13

gold pool, discontinuation of, 115

gold revaluation, 181, 184, 243-244, 268

Goldstein, Henry N., 186, 293

gold standard system, 95, 261-262

gold value guarantees, 24

Goodwin, R. M., 273

Gray, H. P., 291

Great Britain, devaluation of 1967, 52, 92, 110, 115, 187, 193, 214, 317; entry into EEC, 66-67, 71, 387, 391; and a floating pound sterling, 93, 109-111; incomes policy, 93, 109; inflation, 192-193; insufficiency on international liquidity reserves, 192-193; "stop-go" policy, 93, 109

Green Plan, *see* common agricultural policy

Gresham's law, 186, 202

Group of Ten, 3-4, 66, 318, 367

Grove, David, L., 89, 151, 427

Grubel, Herbert G., 291

Haberler, Gottfried, 89, 115, 120, 416, 417, 427

Halm, George N., 1, 57, 89, 112, 125, 427

harmonization of national policies, *see* integration

Harrod, Roy, 7, 127

Hawkins, Robert G., 334

Heckerman, D. G., 291

hedging, 172, 211, 213, 217, 235, 308, 313; cost of, 103-104, 151, 206-207, 213, 235; and multinational corporations, 169, 173; and trading firms, 170

Heimlich, Norman, 337

Hendershott, P. H., 291

Hinshaw, Randall, 120

Holtrop, Marius W., 89, 129, 280-281, 427

Houthakker, Hendrik S., 238, 272

Iino, Tadashi, 178, 187, 332, 357, 427

Iklé, Max, 177, 187, 296, 332, 365, 427

IMF, *see* International Monetary Fund

imported inflation, 35, 120, 234

incomes policy, 7, 93, 100, 106, 109, 127

inflation, adjustment inflation, 38; "bottling up" of, 73, 119-120; demand inflation, 34-35; differential rates of, 46, 116, 132, 147, 259, 286; disinflation, 118; endemic inflation, 8; "export" of, 119-120; and flexible exchange rates, 103, 105, 119-120, 176; and forward cover, 207; "imported" inflation, 35, 120, 234; open

INDEX

inflation, 32, 118; repressed inflation, 118; and resistance to revaluation, 84; "spilling over" of, 119-120; "turned inward," 120
Ingram, James C., 408
inner band, 36, 228
integration, international, definition, 385; in EEC, 385-399; and fixed exchange rates, 6, 94
interest arbitrage, see covered interest arbitrage
interest equalization tax, 183, 246
interest-rate constraint, 72, 283-294
interest-rate differentials, 13, 19, 33, 288, 289
interest rates and crawling peg, 72, 283-294; differentials of, 13, 19, 33, 288, 289; effective interest rates, 289; and flexible exchange rates, 13, 19, 72, 148-149, 239, 283-284; real rates, 239
International Clearing Union, 17-18, 21
international cooperation, see integration, international
international coordination, see integration, international
international integration, see integration, international
international liquidity, see liquidity
International Monetary Fund (IMF), revision of Articles to accommodate greater flexibility of exchange rates, 55-56, 73, 233-236, 245, 247, 271, 276, 330
international monetary system, 223-231; as means to an end, 223; objectives and rules, 223-224; operating constraints, 224-225; rules of the game, 225-226
international reserve pool, 39
international reserves, 261-274; defined, 257, 263; and fixed reserve standard, 261-269; manipulation of, 257
intervention currency, 10, 21-22, 35, 41, 61, 74, 143
intervention within bands, 227, 229, 271
Italy, 184, 191-192, 246

Japan, 246, 357-363; deflation maintains parity, 359; and dollar area, 66, 330; experience with a fixed parity, 357-363; monetary and fiscal policies, 360-361; price and trade controls, 357, 360; price stability, 362; saving and investment, 361-362
Johnson, Harry G., 89, 91, 112-113, 157, 159, 184, 220, 245, 280, 287, 414, 416, 425, 427

Joint Economic Committee, 3-4
Josling, Timothy, 387
Jumping parity or peg, 32

Kasper, Wolfgang, 177, 332, 333, 345, 385, 388-391, 392-399, 427
Katz, Samuel I., 283, 288, 293
Kenen, Peter B., 184, 186, 409, 411
Kennedy round of tariff negotiations, 116, 179
key currency, 61-75, 269, 277
Keynes, John Maynard, 12-13, 14, 17-18, 57, 92, 128, 181, 397, 417, 420
Keynes Plan, see International Clearing Union
Krause, Lawrence B., 219, 223, 427
Kuster, Emil, 178, 209, 216-217, 296, 427

Laffer, A. B., 291
Lanyi, Anthony, 167, 409
limited flexibility of exchange rates, see flexible exchange rates
liquidity, international, and adjustment process, 15; demand for, 252; overemphasized in Bretton Woods, 5, 128, 261-262; as source of flexibility, 126, 195, 252
Lundberg, Erik, 11, 333, 371, 427
Lundgren, Åke, 333, 371, 427
Lutz, Friedrich, 239, 286, 287, 334, 345, 401, 427

MacBean, Alasdair I., 412
Machlup, Fritz, 1, 7, 16, 31, 39, 217, 239, 240, 295, 297, 307, 309, 320, 410, 427
Magee, Stephen P., 238
managed flexibility, 36
managed money, 51, 58
mandatory versus presumptive rules, 37-39, 251-259
market economy and fixed exchange rates, 125-128
Marris, Stephen, 1, 77, 265, 333-334, 392, 427
Marshall Plan, 129, 190
Marsh, Donald B., 37, 219, 220, 261, 272, 296, 332, 337, 427
Marsh Plan, 261-269
McClam, W. D., 288
McKinnon, Ronald I., 410
McTeer, Robert G., 413
Meade, James E., 11, 16, 17, 18, 19, 31, 276, 283, 414
Mellish, G. Hartley, 334
Modigliano, Franco, 287
monetary blocs, see currency blocs
monetary discipline, 6-7, 9, 10

433

monetary illusion, 125
monetary reserve-base coefficient, 20
monetary versus fiscal policies, 14-15
money, needs of trade theory of, 50-52
monopoly and foreign exchange market, 299, 301
Mosconi, Antonio, 177, 178, 199, 333, 388, 392-399, 427
movable band, 16, 20-24, 47, 141, see also widened band and crawling peg
Mundell, Robert A., 264, 266, 337, 409, 425
multilateral surveillance, 9, 97
multinational corporation and greater flexibility of exchange rates, 169, 173
Murphy, J. Carter, 16, 19, 276

Nash, John E., 91
needs of trade doctrine and money supply, 50, 57-59
Netherlands, 129, 139; revaluation of 1961, 34, 187
Niehans, Jürg, 294
Nixon, Richard M., 201
numeraire, dollar as, 65; gold as, 65; SDRs as, 65
nondilemma cases, 12-15, 188

objectives of international monetary system, 223-224
Officer, Lawrence H., 186
open economies, 46, 410
"operation mix," 118
"operation twist," 118, 287
optimum currency area, 407-415; compatibility of members, 411; and diversification, 411-412; and EEC, 414-415; and factor mobility, 409; and fixed exchange rates, 408-410; and openess of economy, 410; and Phillips curves, 411; and wage-price flexibility, 409
Orcutt, Guy H., 410
overvaluation, chronic overvaluation, 163; and controls, 43; criteria of, 42; and foreign direct investment, 152-155, 161-165; and loss of export markets, 163; of U.S. dollar, 156, 246
Oyster Bay conference, v-vi

paper gold, 243
parity, adjustable, 33; crawling, see crawling peg or parity system; formula for change of, 20, 37-39, 272-273; gliding, 32-33, 37-39; jumping, 33; and peg, 31-33; sliding, 31; unchangeable, 33
parity (or peg) adjustments, automatic, 142-143, 256, 274; discrete, 5, 6, 11, 34, 83, 127, 285; discretionary, 17, 37-38, 82, 142, 256, 267; disequilibrating, 37-38; equilibrating, 37-38; formula determined, 20, 37-39, 272-273; involuntary, 39; mandatory, 37-39, 274; presumptive, 37-39, 251-259; prophylactic, 37-39; and sanctions, 251; small and undramatic, 83; spontaneous, 37-39; therapeutic, 37-39; upward only, 234, 240; and width of band, 280-281
peg, adjustable, 7, 33, 77, 91, 262; crawling, see crawling peg or parity system; dynamic, 54; gliding, 32; as intervention rate, 32; jumping, 32; moving, 54; pairs of pegs, 32; and parity, 31-33; sliding, 31; trotting, 32
peg adjustments, see parity adjustments
Pelli, Giuliano, 177, 203, 296, 427
Phillips curve, 125, 139, 390, 411
pivot currency, 62, 65, 255, 271
Polk, Judd, 174
Poole, William, 335
pound sterling, 192-193; devaluation of 1949, 245; devaluation of 1967, 92, 115, 214, 317; dollar guarantee, 110; a floating pound, 93, 109-111
presumptive parity changes, 37-39, 251-259
prophylactic parity changes, 37-39
purchasing power parity, 42, 50, 393

quantitative restriction, 4, 5, 8, 122-123

realignment of parities, 180, 242, 258, 266, 275; as condition for widened band, 11; and gold revaluation, 242
real rate of interest, 239
Reichers, Edwin A., 295, 323, 428
reserve band, 263
reserve currency, 61, 122
reserves, international, and fixed reserve standard, 261-269; and formula for parity changes, 272; and monetary discipline, 317; permissible accumulation and depletion, 37
Reserve Settlement Account, 65, 74
revaluation, as anti-inflation policy, 85; asymmetry between revaluation and devaluation, 61, 68, 70, 87, 234; of Dutch guilder 1961, 68, 187; of German mark 1961, 34, 68, 187, 312, 351, 365; of German mark 1969, 38, 44, 118, 235; of gold, 181, 184, 243-244, 268; substitute revaluation, 44, 418; as symbol of surrender, 107
Ricardo, David, 9, 418-419
Roosa, Robert V., 1, 9-10, 27, 49, 57-

434

59, 219, 233, 264, 265, 266, 334, 416, 425, 428
Roosa bonds, 196

Scandinavia, 371-383
Schweitzer, Pierre Paul, 201
Scitovsky, Tibor, 408
Scott, Ira O., 286
semantics, 31-47
Sherman, Roger, 287
sliding peg, *see* crawling peg
small countries and flexible exchange rates, 97, 121, 129, 149
smoothing operations in foreign exchange markets, 323, 325
Snider, Delbert, 409
socialization of risk in the foreign exchange market, 149
Sohmen, Egon, 148, 295, 315, 334, 345, 428
Special Drawing Rights (SDRs), 4, 21, 44, 55, 65-66, 180-181, 182, 183, 198, 201-202, 244, 257, 262, 268, 272, 276, 277
speculation, and adjustable-peg system, 104, 160, 225-226, 324; and flexible exchange rates, 11, 18, 47, 160; one-way speculation, 104, 160, 225-226, 324; as operating constraint, 225
Sraffa, P., 419
Stein, Jerome L., 291
sterling, *see* pound sterling
stock adjustment and crawling peg, 289-291
"stop-go" policies, 93, 109
Strong, Benjamin, 57
subsidies as alternatives to flexible exchange rates, 417-426
substitute upvaluation, 44, 418
surplus in balance of payments, causes of, 131-132; in Germany, 188-191; and "imported" inflation, 35, 120, 234; and wage-price inflation, 134
swap arrangements, 43, 44, 180
Sweden, 372-378; potential impact of flexible exchange rates, 376-379
Switzerland, 196, 365-370
Swoboda, Alexander, 337, 409

tax-subsidy schemes versus flexibility of exchange rates, 417-423
therapeutic parity changes, 37-38
threefold exchange-rate flexibility, 237-244
Tobin, James, 184
Torrens, Robert, 9
Tower, Edward, 283, 334, 407, 428
trading band, *see* widened band
transaction currency, 22, 61, 122

transition problems, 4, 11, 258, 275
Treaty of Rome, 200, 388, 390
Triffin, Robert, 7, 8, 16, 37, 184, 186, 199, 239, 240, 273
trotting peg, 32
two-tier gold market, 23, 63, 115, 180, 201, 234

undervaluation, 9, 41-45, 126; and foreign direct investment, 155-158, 165; of German mark, 38, 345, 350
United Kingdom, *see* Great Britain
United States dollar, *see* dollar
United States of America, 61-75; and adjustment mechanism, 138; advantages of key-country position, 23; asymmetrical position, 22-23, 255; balance of payments deficit, 188-189; capital flows, 64, 69, 239; competitive position, 69, 201; and flexible exchange rates, 61-75; and foreign direct investment, 152-166; and gold, 4, 21-24, 62, 72-73, 122, 181, 242; as key-currency country, 21-24, 49, 61-75; labor costs, 69, 238; official settlements deficit, 73; and selective controls, 63, 64, 115, 123, 179, 180
upside bands, 234, 240, 245-247
upvaluation, *see* revaluation
upward crawl, 234, 240
upward revaluation, *see* revaluation

van Vlierden, Constant M., 220, 275, 428
Viner, Jacob, 9

Wallich, Henry, 421
Watts, John H., 89, 167, 295, 307, 309, 428
West Germany, *see* Germany
Whitman, Marina V. N., 408
widened band for exchange-rate variations, asymmetrical band, 34-35, 54, 87, 234, 240, 245-249; border bands, 36; and capital goods trade, 211-212; choice of width, 33-35, 226; as compromise, 9, 107-108; and confidence, 195; and crawling peg, 26, 81, 108, 112-113, 280-281; and cross rates, 35, 203; and fixed reserve standard, 265-266; and forward market, 12, 158, 277-278; gradual widening of band, 11; inner band, 36, 228; intervention within band, 227, 229, 271; movable band, 16, 20-24, 47, 141; and multination corporations, 169; and private speculation, 11, 127; and uncertainty, 141, 168, 198,

435

widened band (*cont.*)
204, 212, 227; upside bands, 234, 240, 245-249
Willett Plan, 267-268, 271-274
Willett, Thomas D., 72, 120, 177, 182, 186, 220, 221, 265, 267-268, 271, 283, 287, 291, 293, 334, 407, 428
Williamson, John H., 16, 17, 19, 31, 276, 283

Wonnacott, Paul, 273, 283, 339, 407, 414
Wood, Ralph, 283, 407

Yeager, Leland B., 334, 337, 413, **414**
yen, 71, 357-363
yen area, 67